The Other Fifties

The Other Fifties

Interrogating Midcentury American Icons

Edited by Joel Foreman

University of Illinois Press

Urbana and Chicago

© 1997 by the Board of Trustees of the University of Illinois
Manufactured in the United States of America
1 2 3 4 5 C P 5 4 3 2 1

This book is printed on acid-free paper.

Library of Congress Cataloging-in-Publication Data
Foreman, Joel.
   The other fifties : interrogating midcentury American icons / edited by
Joel Foreman.
      p.   cm.
   Includes bibliographical references and index.
   ISBN 0-252-02271-8 (cloth : alk. paper). — ISBN 0-252-06574-3 (pbk. :
alk. paper)
      1. United States—Civilization—1945– 2. Popular culture—United
States. 3. United States—Social life and customs—1945–1970.   I. Foreman,
Joel.   II. Title.
E169.12.F67   1997
973.92—dc20   96-10004
                                                                        CIP
Digitally reprinted from the first paperback printing

CONTENTS ◢

Part 3 FILM AND GENDER

Part 4 LITERARY AND SOCIAL TEXTS

INTRODUCTION ━

Joel Foreman

F *The Other Fifties* were to realize its intent, few Americans would be able to think of the 1950s as either simple, innocent, happy, unanimously supportive of a broad spectrum of beliefs, or radically separated from the 1960s by a culture of complacence. I do not mean to claim, however, that this anthology is unique in its opposition to these clichés; rather, the essays contained herein contribute to a critical effort that appeared in the 1950s, has manifested itself quite regularly ever since, and (as I will argue) needs to be sustained into the indefinite future. Peter Biskind, writing in the early 1980s, is representative of those scholars who, in his words, have felt the need to provide "another picture of the fifties . . . a picture of an era of conflict and contradiction, an era in which a complex set of ideologies contended for public allegiance" (4). Other notable participants in the intellectual movement that would deny simplification are Lary May and Joanne Meyerowitz—both editors of collections on the 1950s. Their aim: to combat the theories of consensus placidity governing far too many treatments of the decade. May's subtle account of consensus theorizing and the conditions of its demise complements Meyerowitz's eloquent critique of stereotypes still in need of interrogation and helps to ground her contention that "the postwar era now seems a time of notable social change and cultural complexity" (5).

As an editor who has managed to assemble a collection of essays that particularize the turbulence of midcentury American culture and the subversive assaults upon its norms and ideals, I second (though with reservation) Meyerowitz's assertion. It may well be that most scholars now see the fifties as an age of complexity. Moreover, David Halberstam's widely distributed popular treatment, The Fifties, which defines "social ferment" (ix) as the decade's most notable characteristic, seems to signify that a more complicated view of the fifties is slowly creeping into the mass media. What worries me is that so many writers have been making similar points for quite some time without having an appreciable impact upon public understanding of the age.

In brief, I am convinced by ten years of discussions with students and with various survivors of the fifties that any changes in scholars' accounts of the midcentury decade have yet to bring about more than minimal changes in the thinking of large audiences outside of academe and that conditions are in place which mitigate against any easy transfer of scholarly knowledge. Although many of those who were active in the fifties remember the decade as one of wrenching problems—the Korean call up, the fear of pregnancy, McCarthyism, polio, recession, and desegregation—others are just as likely to construct their past lives as a nostalgic montage of sock hops, barbecues, suburban ranch houses, and a smiling Ike presiding over a contented electorate. It is, however, the historical consciousness of Americans who do not remember the fifties that is particularly at risk. They typically depend for their sense of the era upon television artifacts such as I Love Lucy and Happy Days, the stage play/film of Grease, and a limited assortment of figures— most notably Marilyn Monroe, Elvis Presley, and James Dean—whose lives and careers have been romanticized and cut loose from any meaningful historical context.

Those without an appreciation of the historical embeddedness of interpretation may conclude that an exposure to more midcentury texts will serve as an antidote to the entropic force of nostalgia and historical forgetfulness. But I think this is hardly the case. Transformations in our attitudes toward sexuality, gender, race, and class (to mention but a few) have so removed us— and the younger generations in particular—from the sensibility of the fifties that what was perceived then as shocking and troubling seems either difficult to grasp or quite tame and inoffensive now. From the perspective of this assessment, public understanding of the fifties is like the space behind a heavy door that the collective force of many scholars has only managed to set ajar. The writers in this collection have added their weight to that expansive effort—by specifying, amplifying, and further complicating the view of the fifties—in the hope that they can make some headway against the resistance of uninformed and nostalgic opinion. But there is every reason to believe that the door might slam shut again, leaving intact and dominant a narrative of bland homogeneity and successful repression.

Part of the blame for this condition must be laid at the feet of those who have tried to generalize about the fifties. First and foremost among these are the midcentury polemicists—I am thinking of such writers as Erich Fromm, C. Wright Mills, Gilbert Seldes, and William Whyte—who persuasively argued that economic prosperity, automation, white-collar culture, and the media had transformed Americans into a contented nation of mass-produced and uncritical conformists. Seymour Krim provides but one example of this point. Writing a brief introduction to *The Beats,* he offers "Madison Avenue's manicured robot hand" (10) as an image of the seductive but stultifying forms imposed by a postindustrial information age commercialism. Outside the temporal confines of the fifties the complaint of conformism has been augmented by the widespread nostalgia for the anti-authoritarian protests of the sixties and seventies, decades that are frequently cast as America's emergence from a quiet and morally debilitating complacence. Thus we find Marty Jezer (who writes from the perspective of the Vietnam War years) painting the fifties as a postwar "dark ages" preceding a temporary lightening in the sixties. In more recent years, Elaine Tyler May's ambivalent tale of domestic containment, Thomas Hill Schaub's study of the ideological appropriation of postwar liberal narratives, and Robert J. Corber's examination of Alfred Hitchcock's homophobic anticommunism exemplify the studies that depict the early years of the cold war in terms of massively invasive systems of repression operating most powerfully at the level of ideology.

While these accounts have enriched our understanding of the time, they have also contributed to an imbalanced view that so amplifies the effect of sociopolitical coercions that the substantial manifestations of dissent and resistance disappear into an easily overlooked background. To one degree or another, most studies of the fifties are affected by this disposition and thus appear as histories of victimization rather than as histories of nascent rebellion and liberation. A survey of these efforts identifies one representative group of writers who acknowledge the conservative forces constraining postwar American behavior but who are also at pains to emphasize the progressive resistances that anticipate the succeeding decades. Eric Goldman's treatment of the "crucial" years 1945 to 1955 highlights the making of "fundamental decisions" that would continue to affect America into "the foreseeable future" (vi). This "continuity" thesis reappears in any number of variants that followed. In his treatment of liberalism in the forties and fifties, Richard Pells counters the view of a rupture between decades and argues that in the sixties the "rise of a generation of dissidents based in the universities had its own antecedents in the youth culture of the 1950s" (402). Others have described the fifties as "the spawning ground of the remarkable decade that followed" (Gilbert 6); the location of a shift in values and culture (May); and the initiator of a new "cultural cycle" (Lhamon). Lastly, the feminist cultural historians Wini Breines, Jackie Byars, Brandon French, Brett Harvey, and Eugenia Kaledin see the fifties as an incubator for the activities of the women's movement to come in the sixties.

A second set of works tries to straddle the divide between the stasis of consensus and the dynamism of cultural transformation and to maintain a sense of their mutual interactions. Thus John Diggins notes that too sharp a focus on consensus neglects the "creative activities throbbing with restlessness and dissonance during the period" (xiv). For William O'Neill, the fifties was an "age of reconstruction" during which the development of the infrastructure took precedence over social reform. Yet "in meeting these needs the preconditions for social reform were being established too, even though no one knew it" (xi). Lastly, Wendy Kozol's study of postwar photojournalism finds that "great instabilities and contestations in race relations and class antagonisms" coexisted with the "many cultural representations promot[ing] a vision of unity and homogeneity" (15).

These works are marked by a duality due, I suggest, to our preoccupation with what Bakhtin calls the "process of historical becoming" (288). Participating in this process, language in general (and more specifically, the language of midcentury texts) always displays "the coexistence of socio-ideological contradictions between the present and the past" (291). Thus any text is a field within which the competing forces of tradition and cultural innovation may be exposed "as a contradiction-ridden, tension-filled unity of two embattled tendencies in the life of" a culture (272).

Although the essays in *The Other Fifties* also treat texts in just this light, they do so within a framework that privileges the emergence of oppositional forces that, in subsequent decades, achieve either general acceptance or dominance. It is my contention that to so privilege disruption and struggle is to resurrect and reaffirm what was abundantly apparent to the people of the postwar era, namely, that they were living during a time of "social change and cultural complexity." Martin Luther King knew it. As did Paul Robeson, Eleanor Roosevelt, Whittaker Chambers, Frantz Fanon, Hugh Hefner, Alfred Kinsey, John Kenneth Galbraith, Christine Jorgenson, and Alan Freed—just to name a diverse few. Even the notable conservatives of the time—the J. Edgar Hoovers and the Marynia Farnhams and the Ferdinand Lundbergs—knew it. Why else were they struggling so determinedly to withstand change and cultural innovation?

Margaret Mead, writing about the condition of women, regarded the time as a "period of discrepancy" (300). Robert Penn Warren, assigned by *Life* to examine segregation, documented the "self-division" (59) afflicting the people of the South. David Riesman coined the phrase "characterological struggle" (31) to describe the internal process activated by massive social and technological change. Writing with reference to the transformation of sexual mores and practices, the sociologist Ira Reiss resuscitated the body politic trope to represent an America torn between alternatives: "Our society is like a man whose past way of life has been challenged. He cannot ignore the challenge, for the challenge originates within himself. Yet he is so strongly tied to the past that he is not certain that he wants to or is able to change. This is a portrait of internal conflict . . . in America today" (69). And the social psychologists Alfred R. Lindesmith and Anselm L. Strauss, reflecting on the American problems of class and race, wrote of a "polarized personality" produced by a "polarized culture" (596).

Informed by the culturalist tenets of postwar anthropology, sociology, and psychology, these commentators were sufficiently free of individualist dogma to see identity as a collective production. Thus, for them, the psyche of any given American subject was the site of an intellectual and moral competition between value systems associated respectively with the past and a future that was trying to come into being. At stake was the identity and the behavior of American citizens. How would they conceive of themselves? And, as a consequence, to what causes and practices would they lend their support: as voters, as actors within diverse institutions, and as consumers?

The general goal of *The Other Fifties* is to resist simplification by drawing attention to these ideological and identitarian competitions and by examining the discords that charged the lives of midcentury Americans and deflected them from the trajectories of habit, custom, received belief, and tradition. *The Other Fifties* has its own special niche in this endeavor. The essays herein locate struggle, resistance, instability, and transformation in what is for many the least likely place: mass media popular culture. In the figures of Molly Goldberg, Doris Day, Elvis, Ayn Rand, Holden Caulfield, and Nikita Khrushchev we detect the gradual "unmaking" and dismantling of obsolete systems of normative control as a culture in transition cultivated radical changes in desegregation, the economic enfranchisement of young people, the emancipation of both men and women from the confines of normative gender categories, and a near breakthrough in the superpower conflict.

The justification for this volume's focus on popular culture artifacts drawn from diverse mass media stems from the demonstrably representative character of mass media representations. Although every artifact is of necessity a representation of its culture, those which receive wide distribution (e.g., such products as the midcentury images of Lana Turner and Kirk Douglas, Art Carney's "Norton," *Mad* magazine's "what me worry" Alfred E. Neuman, and *Peyton Place*'s struggling women) achieve their commercial successes because they issue from and appeal to a massive demographic and economic formation. As highly successful commodifications whose American consumers numbered in the millions, the mass media representations of the fifties are quintessential representatives of their time, and we can say about them (with little doubt or hesitation) that they captured the needs, desires, and expectations of so many people as to provide significant indexes of the changing behavior and the internal tensions of that cultural body we call America.

Furthermore, *The Other Fifties* stands apart from works with similar revisionist goals and a similar regard for popular culture because of the intent, embodied in this introductory essay, to question the prevailing view of mass media markets in the consumer culture at midcentury. Many of the scholarly works noted above focus on the relationship between cultural representations and cultural change but none explicitly acknowledge that progressive changes (e.g., the civil rights movement, the emancipation of teenagers from excessive adult control, and the women's movement) may be credited—at least in part—to the actions of cultural entrepreneurs looking for profits in capitalist markets. Such a contention is contrary to the widely held scholarly opinion that capitalism is usually a socially conservative force. There is no question that capitalism and capitalist markets have enforced conservative codes of behavior. But it is equally true, as the following essays demonstrate, that markets have aided and abetted the production and dissemination of subversive ideologies.

To make such an argument, I will need to develop a line of reasoning that leads from point A (the desire to generalize about culture) to point B (the contention that midcentury markets contributed to socially progressive cultural transformation).

THOUGH their conclusions may differ, the works that attempt to comprehend the fifties are linked by a desire to generalize about culture. Max Lerner described this desire in 1957 when he set out "to grasp . . . the pattern and inner meaning of contemporary American civilization" (xi). Today we might prefer "discursive structure" to "inner meaning" and substitute "culture" for "civilization," but otherwise Lerner's formulation is compatible with the collective interpretive enterprise of May, Meyerowitz, and the others cited above. Although *The Other Fifties* (and this introduction) is an enthusiastic participant in this enterprise, the implicit promise to "grasp" the culture of an entire decade is quite problematic and compels me to pause (if not for long) to consider the economic grounds upon which such a promise may be founded and fulfilled.

At the root of the problem is the sheer magnitude of fifties culture. When Lerner was writing, the culture was the living experience of all of his contemporaries and thus included a set of events as diverse as a young girl's purchase of an "orlon" sweater and a pair of saddle shoes; Miles Davis punching John Coltrane because the saxophonist was too drug-wasted to perform; Emmett Till's fatal encounter with Carolyn Bryant in her Mississippi backcountry grocery store; the publisher Kitty Messner's decision to buy the rights to Grace Metalious's *Peyton Place;* and the moment when, at the age of ten, in 1953, I semi-seriously accused my cousin of being a "commie" because he wanted to have dinner at a Russian restaurant in Greenwich Village. I conclude this series with a prosaic example drawn from personal experience to amplify what so far has only been implied: that the anthropological notion of culture I am employing extends well beyond the production of such elite artifacts as, for example, the poems of Marianne Moore or the abstract paintings of Robert Motherwell; it includes not only mass media popular culture but also the nearly infinite set of microevents that constitute everyday life.

Despite such an expansive notion of culture, grasping the American fifties has been eased somewhat for contemporary and future scholars (at least from a quantitative perspective) because the living culture is now available only in the memory of its participants or in the textual traces of the time. Already significantly reduced, the former is rapidly disappearing and will be extinguished in perhaps forty years. The latter is still enormous. The paper record alone (which excludes the massive amount of film, video, and audio records) includes whatever remains of the "1,500 daily newspapers, over 8,000 weeklies, and about 6,000 magazines" which the *World Book Encyclopedia* cites as the output of "private publishers" (69) during the period. Given the magnitude of this textual record, how can we make valid generalizations about an entire decade when those generalizations are derived from what must always be a relatively small sampling of texts?

The Socratic dialogue is an early example of the Western struggle to systematize the ways in which knowledge may be derived from data. More recent efforts to deal with data networks have compelled us to contemplate Derridean deferrals of meaning and Lacanian chains of endless signifiers. A fifties version of the problem appears in the early pages of John Barth's *The Floating Opera:* attempting to grasp the meaning of his own behavior, the existential protagonist—Todd Andrews—concludes that "to understand any one thing entirely, no matter how minute, requires the understanding of every other thing in the world" (6). Acting out this dictum, Barth devotes the entire novel to the explanation of one moment, one decision, in the life of his anti-hero.

Todd Andrews's existential angst over the meaning of a lifeworld no longer bounded by the mind of the Judeo-Christian God converges with midcentury speculations that appear in the field of information science. Norbert Wiener provides a model. Writing in *The Human Use of Human Beings: Cybernetics and Society,* he invokes an artificial intelligence—a "machine gouverner"—that could gather and store the total sum of all human knowledge and generate interpretations based on "the average psychology of human beings" (244). Isaac Asimov, unconstrained by the requirements of scientific exposition, takes a similar conception and reaches much more grand conclusions at the end of *I, Robot,* in which a supercomputer with the capacities of the one envisioned by Wiener assumes the power and position of a benign god and imposes utopia upon the human race. As such, Barth, Wiener, and Asimov are all concerned with the kind of knowledge problem faced by this collection of essays: how to render a good explanation, judgment, or decision when huge amounts of information are available for processing. The assumption for each writer is that the task requires comprehension of much or all of human knowledge, a seemingly impossible task.

There is, however, another way to think about the knowledge problem: namely, to conceive of a given culture (e.g., midcentury America) as organic—because it is made of living people—and superintelligent—because its collective cognitive power synergizes the local knowledge held by its individual constituents and is thereby able to render socially useful decisions. Friedrich Hayek develops such a conception (the "market") in what amounts to an economic analysis of culture. A market process economist widely known for his critique of centralized planning, Hayek writes that a market "constitutes an information-gathering process, able to call up, and to use, widely dispersed information that no . . . individual could know as a whole, possess or control" (14). I would like to elucidate this passage with respect to midcentury America (which I invite you to regard as a market) and with specific reference to a particular kind of marketable product—what Wendy Kozol refers to as "cultural representations" (e.g., photographic images in *Life* magazine, television shows, films, novels). The point is that the 165 million people massed within the territorial boundaries of the United States at midcentury constituted a living information system (and thus an intelligent Hayekian superorganism) that through the medium of exchange relations, pricing mechanisms, resource allocation, and productive activities organized and maintained itself as a distinct entity.

In basic market terms, this sustained organization resulted from a steady stream of signals generated when Americans accepted or rejected the various representations offered for their consumption. Such an organization implies a feedback loop that collects the knowledge dispersed throughout the 165 million units in the system and uses it to direct the productive activity of novelists, ad agencies, film producers, magazine editors, book publishers, cartoonists, even politicians—in short, any and all producers of cultural representations. Best-selling books and prime-time network television programs are good examples. Guided by the signals generated by the sales of previous successes, numerous producers competed for market share in these commercial domains, but only a very few succeeded. Those who did—the Sid Caesars and Imogene Cocas, the James Micheners and Sloan Wilsons—effectively (though intuitively) responded to consumer desires with commodified representations designed to facilitate mass consumption. These products made the most efficient use of scarce creative resources by collecting and encoding significant cultural knowledges in representations that were distributed at low per capita cost via a national information infrastructure (i.e., television transmission and the book publishing apparatus).

Americans at the time conceived of themselves as Americans precisely because the nearly infinite number of decisions they made every day were aggregated by media markets, commodified and re-presented for consumption by the large demographic blocs from which the signals had initially issued. Thus decisions of individual Americans (e.g., to buy a Desoto rather than a Studebaker or to move out of a neighborhood because a "colored" family "broke the block" or to save time to watch *The Goldbergs* rather than *Arthur Godfrey's Talent Scouts* or to vote for Eisenhower rather than Stevenson or to have a conversation about the adverse effects of comic books) were mediated by the actions of millions of other individuals whose behavior had been shaped by previously established patterns of consumption. From this perspective, American culture of the fifties is the cyclical relationship between supply and demand in a market of representations.

To ask which is most important—supply or demand—is to ask the chicken or the egg question. More pertinent are issues of cultural stability and cultural innovation. On the one hand, the looped feedback relationship between production and consumption assures a large measure of unity, continuity, and predictability in the life of a culture. It reinforces prescribed behaviors and sanctions various proscriptions. On the other hand, the market rewards cultural slippage, free play, and invention. In fact, Hayek's celebration of and fascination with markets focuses on the spontaneous emergence of desires and demands that cannot be predicted with certainty. The magnitude of the American market and the incalculably complex decisions of its millions of constituents preclude central control and provide the enabling conditions for cultural change. As the case of the Edsel shows (or the inability of regulatory actions to avoid the recessions of the fifties), the market quite regularly defied the well-funded plans of producers (and would-be controllers) even as it unexpectedly selected and rewarded others—such as Edward R. Murrow, Sidney Poitier, and Little Richard—whose intuitive combinations of local knowledges supplied previously inchoate national demands.

Although formal and informal modes of cultural conservation were very much in place, they could be challenged, and for the cultural entrepreneur who was able to interpret the market's signals, to commodify and represent this knowledge, and then manage to bypass the censors, there were significant rewards. The knowledge that was commodified for the popular infomedia could come from any locality (Fats Domino out of New Orleans or the Coasters out of California) or from any "minority" group (the Jewish Gertrude Berg, the African American Nat King Cole, the Italian Perry Como). These examples demonstrate a most important point: the market, in its pursuit of profits, produced and distributed commodities (i.e., cultural representations) whose vitality was often due to their difference from the dominant norms. As such, the mass media market was an agent of cultural subversion, an institutionalized structure of supply and demand that frequently commodified and distributed deviations from conservative norms. Most of the essays in this collection show that a subversive component built into products that were otherwise consistent with these norms acted as an ideological virus transmitted by national media whose commitment was more to profit (read this to mean the distributed and inarticulate desire of millions of American consumers) than the dominant morals of the moment.

An example: despite the early opposition of radio stations, the majors in the recording industry, the television censors, and the conservative parents who associated rock 'n' roll with negro sexuality and juvenile delinquency, Elvis Presley could sneer, pelvic jolt, and hillbilly twang his way to national exposure. As David R. Shumway's essay shows, Elvis's efforts to achieve success as a recording artist were in fact a product of the system responding to the demand of its individual members. None of those consumers could have articulated the exact form of her or his desires before Elvis appeared; nor could Elvis have known consciously that the particulars of his performance would so precisely fulfill those desires and on such a grand scale. Nevertheless an exchange of information between consumers and producers shaped the pre–rock 'n' roll traditions within which Elvis labored, and a collective demand (an information-based decision issued by the culture) selected him from the ranks of his many competitors and thereby changed the system despite the unpredictability of the change and the opposition of those who were offended by it.

Which brings us to the following essays. All of them deal with the kind of cultural conflicts generated by the interaction of conventional and emergent norms manifesting themselves in the production and consumption of diverse mass media representations. The market for these representations served as an accelerator of emancipatory change and progressive cultural transformation and thus created the trends that now direct us to look for their origins in an era—the fifties—generally regarded as one of repressive excess.

IN the editor's preface to an early collection of materials from the fifties, Joseph Satin writes that the "selections" and "statistical tables" provide "pictures . . . in narrow focus rather than in panoramic view," pictures that may "be used as evidence that the decade was fundamentally placid—or that it was deeply disturbed" (x). With some modifications, these statements may serve as an appropriate introduction to the selections in this book. Since most of the following essays are close readings of one text or a single figure, they provide a "narrow focus." Since they are historically informed readings of representative representations, they aspire to the level of the valid generalization and thus also provide a "panoramic view" of culturally significant formations. The argument for validity and significance is based not so much on an exhaustive survey of documentary evidence as it is upon the common knowledge of our own historical moment.

In this we have an advantage over Satin. Writing in the late fifties, he could not possibly interpret as we do the emergent trends (civil rights, cultural diversity, feminism, the collapse of the communist bloc) which are now so visible and so unavoidably shape our thinking about the past. With the knowledge of these trends as an interpretive foundation, the writers of the essays in this book tease out the contradictions built into the representations of a culture in transition. Rather than come down on either side of Satin's distinction between "placidity" or "deep disturbance," they usually find evidence of both.

The first set of essays consider what it took to change minds in the fifties. James Baughman's essay is about a notable failure in this respect, whereas

Wini Breines's and my own explore the complex ways in which the changes in racial relations corresponded to the fantasies produced in the minds of readers and writers. It is hoped that the juxtaposition of an essay on advertising with two essays about fiction and fantasy will provoke some speculation about the similarity between these processes. Deliberately or otherwise, the producers of fiction (whether in the form of a film, a television program, a stage play, or a novel) are as likely as advertisers to change minds. This is actually one of this anthology's major concerns. We all know that a text is fabricated from the material conditions extant during its time of production. Once fabricated, how does the text then contribute to changes in the behavior of its consumer? The failure of the Edsel campaign is as informative in this matter as the successes (relative though they may still be) of desegregation and integration.

As is well known, the Edsel texts were part of a conscious and carefully orchestrated postindustrial effort to influence the purchasing decisions of American consumers. Baughman provides us with a detailed, behind-the-scenes account of this effort and the consumer resistance it encountered. As he notes, the unsuccessful marketing campaign offsets the contention that a manipulative "Madison Avenue" is uncontested in its ability to govern the behavior of American consumers. This argument maintains its influence in part because it is so easy to forget the numerous promotions that fail. The Edsel campaign is the notable exception. The multimillion-dollar media event crafted by the best technicians available did manage to get potential consumers into Ford dealerships, but the campaign could not make them buy. What does this reveal about the intelligence of the marketplace? People simply do not part with their money as easily or as capriciously as consumer phobes imagine. The conclusions to be drawn: a media campaign can tap into the deepest desires and fears of the people to which it is directed, but the product (particularly one that costs as much as an automobile) is going to have to deliver a value that exceeds the associations created by the product's image. A case in point is the Maidenform "Dream" campaign. It produced over forty different ads (e.g., "I dreamed I was a knockout in my Maidenform bra") and helped to keep the company at the top of its market by maintaining the "bullet bra" in the consciousness of the American public for the entire decade. But the fantasy of erotic abandonment that the ads cultivated was not sufficient in and of itself to compel millions of American women to buy the bra. Quite simply put, the Maidenform bra was a better product than the Edsel. That is, ad campaigns do not create desires from scratch; they identify, articulate, and focus them within an extremely complex set of social and material circumstances that include the performance requirements of the product. A campaign is no less dependent upon those circumstances than are the buying decisions of the consumer.

The two essays on race (Breines's and my own) make a similar point. The form and organization of mass media products cannot exceed the audience's horizon of expectations. Both essays ask, How did the deep transformations in race relations that were taking place at the time affect the fantasies and other creative activities of people in the fifties?

Wini Breines's essay develops her previous work in exhuming the experience and responses of white girls. In this case she is concerned with white girls' attraction to and use of African American culture. The thesis, which I think is both provocative and quite reasonable, aligns Breines's essay with David Van Leer's in that both are concerned with taboo-defying behavior of the most serious sort. That is, in the fifties, homosexuality and interracial heterosexual activity were equally unacceptable and proscripted behaviors. Breines's argument is, however, not so much about interracial dating itself as it is about a historical moment during which fantasy (rather than action) predominated. As such, Breines attempts to get at cognitive activity that, though a precondition to action, is still unaware of itself and its motivations. As she notes, finding unconditionally supportive evidence that such fantasy work existed in the fifties is difficult. The notion that white girls of a certain sort were attracted to blackness emerges from Breines's own experience of the fifties and sixties. My sense is that this is an important exploratory essay whose strong assertions will encourage others to seek out corroborating materials.

I regard my essay as a new historicist attempt to describe and trace the social energies that became attached to a totally new signifier, Mau Mau. I attempt to conceive of these words as a kind of public property that could be appropriated and packaged for sale in various mass media markets after being imported to the United States as a result of the Kikuyu uprising in British East Africa. Since the essay considers the commercial success of Mau Mau both as a conservative racist signifier and as a more socially progressive one, I demonstrate the degree to which the marketplace is an ideological arena that will support both repression (the implicit ideological goal of Robert Ruark's novelistic treatment of Mau Mau) and liberation (the explicit ideological goal of Richard Brooks's film version of the same story). The coexistence of these functionally opposed texts merely reinforces the fractured and contradictory state of national race relations after *Brown vs. Board of Education*. The essay also draws attention, as do most of those in the book, to the contradictions within specific texts and to the limits of a progressive vision at the time. On the one hand, Robert Ruark writes a racist treatise that believes itself to be enlightened. On the other hand, Richard Brooks treats Mau Mau as a politically legitimate and rational endeavor. Yet his film concludes with actions and images that recuperate white supremacism.

Like the notion of a placidly conformist fifties, the view of network television as a wasteland, as a panderer to the base taste of the masses, as a bland homogenizer and perpetrator of capitalist hegemony has been challenged but nonetheless maintains its sway over many of those who think about the medium. Horace Newcomb's essay is for those who still need to be convinced that early television was something other than a monolithic agent of social control. From Newcomb's perspective, the medium was a cultural forum within which competing ideologies were represented. The medium regularly transgressed boundaries, provided a rich and diverse text composed of wide-ranging formats, genres, and venues. Alternative perspectives appeared often and presented a wide, though not completely open, range of social alternatives.

Stimulated by Newcomb's view, the reader may begin to cite other programs in support of his thesis. My own additions include Edward R. Murrow's *See It Now,* which is notable for its independence of its sponsor's opinions and its inclination to challenge the idealized versions of American life. Even *Queen for a Day,* which rewarded its most pathetic women contestants with a load of consumer delights, produced ironic juxtapositions of those gewgaws with the plight of the women. The spectacle of often poor and disadvantaged women provided a stark contrast with the affluence of Harriet Nelson, Donna Reed, and June Cleaver. Moreover, a contrarian reading of *I Love Lucy* and *The Honeymooners,* perhaps the most mainstream of all mid-century sitcoms, foregrounds Lucy and Alice's comic contestations of Ricky and Ralph's paternal powers and situates those programs within the structure of emergent feelings discussed by Jackie Byars.

This instability suggests that a relaxation of social constraints in the fifties opened a space within which the media could manufacture and distribute profitable alternatives to conventional gender roles. David Shumway's examination of Elvis Presley shows that the singer's spectacular performance joined previously segregated elements and the resulting perfectly calibrated combination managed to unlock a huge reservoir of consumer energy. In the age of television, singing ability alone was not sufficient to generate a sustained national demand for a product. As Shumway argues, it was Elvis's unique orchestration of the full panoply of available audio-visual effects that assured his success. The most familiar of these Elvis borrowed from the performance style of his African American blues predecessors. But others made similar borrowings without similar impact. What in particular set Elvis apart was his appropriation of the gaze: his controlled and customized presentation of a self that transgressed the line between male and female visual identity. Though relatively subtle, the transgression projected enough of a difference to stimulate the developing female ability to acknowledge sexual desire but not one so great as to aggravate male homophobia. Such a positively perceived difference attracts attention in part merely because it is novel, in part because it aggregates, articulates, and amplifies the consumers' latent desire.

Donald Weber's essay focuses his attention on the production and consumption of *The Goldbergs,* its radio prehistory, its divergence from earlier traditions of Yiddish humor, and its simultaneous affirmation and critique of postwar commodity capitalism. The essay is rewarding on many levels, though none so much, I think, as in its consideration of the series as a response to the influence of ethnic stereotyping. In an age when American anti-Semitism was still quite pervasive and powerful, Gertrude Berg diluted the "Jewish" content of the program, thereby making Jews assimilable to American ideals. How should we view this response to the dictates of the market? Was this a co-optation or a necessary and ultimately successful strategy? Weber provides us with examples that can support either position. My own sense is that Berg found the level required to attract a national audience. The show found its niche with a pragmatic balance of subversion and accommodation. Otherwise it would have never made the national scene. Yes, Berg systematically (though not completely) repressed the political, ethnic, and labor issues associated with Jews, and she did so while celebrating the new consumer culture. Like the careful calibration of Elvis's performance, the shape of the resulting product—*The Goldbergs*—fit the needs of the time.

As representative representations, the Broadway and Hollywood versions of the musical *Damn Yankees*, the star image Kim Novak, and the Doris Day–Rock Hudson film vehicle *Pillow Talk* are the results of an intensely selective cultural process. Given the enormous profits to be derived from the production and distribution of such products, the competition singled out those that were likely to address and organize the largest possible national audiences. The implicit questions that David Van Leer, Jackie Byars, and Cynthia J. Fuchs raise are, Why these products? What did they have that set them apart from the competition? In all cases the answer is that a transformation in identity (David Riesman's "characterological structure") was in process and was generating a considerable amount of instability that, in diverse ways, energized these products. Each of the writers takes as a given the notion that identity is a social construction which reveals itself in everyday life as performance. Here the particular facet or subcomponent of identity is gender, alterations to which were being produced first and foremost through the changing relations of men and women.

At first pass it appears that these alterations did not affect the homophobic system of repression in place during the fifties. That is, few, if any, positive representations of homosexuality were widely distributed by the mass media. James Baldwin's *Giovanni's Room* is sympathetic, but presents a portrait of an anguished existence of self-denial. Robert Anderson's *Tea and Sympathy* shows how the fear of homosexuality could prey upon the mind of a young man. *My Son John, Strangers on a Train,* and *The Manchurian Candidate* go so far as to forge links between momism, homosexuality, and communism (Rogin). Yet Van Leer argues that in *Damn Yankees* one can detect a subtle assault on the prevailing heterosexual norms.

His thesis is a familiar one to the readers of new historicist commentaries on power and culture: the cultural dominance of heterosexual norms at mid-century was so powerful that it created the conditions for its own subversion. In other words, the "success" of homophobia engendered a carelessness and a resulting space for subversive performances. Like Fuchs, Van Leer argues that a text such as *Damn Yankees* could and did subvert for two reasons: first, because it revealed the constructedness of gender, and second, because it criticized and thus challenged the heterosexual norm. My own reflections upon Van Leer's essay lead me to think of Milton Berle's prime-time drag performances and to conclude, along the lines laid down by Van Leer, that the outrageous excess of the Berle performance issued from a cultural certainty so great as to allow the distribution of a potentially subversive representation. Thus in the moment of maximum control, resistance appears in the products a culture uses to entertain itself.

That such a case could be made for the star image Kim Novak is ironic given the contributions that image appears to have made to a socially regressive view of female sexuality. Like a number of other film icons of the period—Brigitte Bardot, Jayne Mansfield, and Terry Moore are a few that come to mind—much of Kim Novak's box office appeal had to do with her conformity to a Hugh Hefnerian conception of woman as sex toy. Yet as Jackie Byars contends, an analysis of Novak's midcentury oeuvre discloses a structure of feeling (a detectable but inarticulate resistance) that anticipates the conscious and calculated oppositions to patriarchy that would develop in the sixties. The assumption, as is the case with so many of the essays in this collection, is that the overt political disruptions of the sixties and later decades were indeed precedented in the fifties, but not by cultural work that could acknowledge itself as such. Rather, the cultural work performed by the Novak image—its modest interrogation of rigid gender roles—was the result of that general sense of discomfort that Betty Friedan called the "problem that had no name." Supporting and working within the edifice of patriarchal domination, the Novak image also had its moments of deconstructive rebellion. As such, its dismantlings of an old mind-set helped to make way for something new.

Cynthia Fuchs's close textual analysis of *Pillow Talk* discloses a complex of gender problems in what otherwise appears to be an insubstantial comedic work. On the one hand, Rock Hudson and Doris Day, the male and female epitomes at the center of the film, offer seemingly stable and ideal performances of conventional gender categories. On the other hand, the filmwork pathologizes Doris Day's stubborn virginity and suggests that beneath Rock Hudson's prototypical masculinity lies the specter of homosexuality. In its representation of women, the film thus captures the conflict between the still-powerful notion of female sexual purity and the emerging desire documented by Kinsey and many others. With respect to men, it displays that crucial subsurface constituent of maleness in the fifties: for a man to be a man, he had to define himself in opposition to the homosexual stereotype. As such the film simultaneously offers a dominant, conservative, and comforting reading of proper heterosexual ideals even as it subverts them with emerging alternatives.

Part 4, "Literary and Social Texts," features two of the most widely read novelists of the decade, Ayn Rand and J. D. Salinger, and exposes their work to an analysis of the ideological contradictions incorporated in their texts. There is a marked contrast between the two in that they address and/or appeal to readers at opposite poles of the ideological spectrum.

Readers familiar with Thomas Hill Schaub's explications of the displacements, inversions, and repressions that the cold war experience introduces to liberal discourse will recognize a similar interest in Lee Medovoi's essay. Given the disillusion wrought by the revelations about Stalinism and the dictatorial intimidations of a communist Soviet Union, liberals were compelled to reconsider their approach to intellectual issues and to forge what they regarded as a more pragmatic, more realistic view of politics and culture. Medovoi's discussion of *Catcher in the Rye* details the particulars of its liberal reception and the maneuvers required of the critics in their attempts to account for and legitimate its success among young readers.

The three parts of Medovoi's essay consider the ways in which the liberal critics read Holden Caulfield's adolescent narrative as a metaphor for their own political experience from the thirties to the fifties; the complications introduced in this reading by liberal anxieties about a massified youth paperback book market; and the constraints that prevented a progressive reading which might have linked commodification, capitalism, and Caulfield's obsession with phoniness.

Olster takes us to a different register in the political spectrum as embodied in Ayn Rand's remarkably popular brand of free market capitalism. The reading is welcome because the political cast of the novel as well as its length have been deterrents to critical analysis of the book. *Atlas Shrugged* is either too easy to attack or too politically offensive to have found a place in any new pantheon of noteworthy works. Within the context of Rand's own well-documented ideological position, Olster asks to what degree various elements in the novel are consistent with the author's public pronouncements or even with other elements in the book. Like the liberal discourse generated by *Catcher in the Rye*, *Atlas Shrugged* is a response to the failure of Left politics and policies. The book sets out to describe a platform for a peaceful and productive laissez-faire political economics but winds up asserting a kind of totalitarianism that looks remarkably like the Stalinism which Ayn Rand rejects. So, too, the politics of personal freedom inevitably devolve into power and domination, particularly in the realm of male-female relationships that are brutal and structured by property economics rather than some putatively more human alternative.

These contradictions remind us once again of the highly unstable ideological terrain of the fifties. Efforts to make sharp divisions—in this case between a welfare state and free market economics or between a generalized notion of personal emancipation and the belief in the natural subordination of woman to man—are destined to fail. The oppositions inevitably interpenetrate, influence, and "infect" one another to produce curious ideological hybrids.

This is also the case with the conflicts Stephen J. Whitfield displays in his essay on Nikita Khrushchev's momentous 1959 visit to America. The competitive context for Khrushchev's visit was a conflict serious enough to be dubbed a war—albeit a "cold" one. This particular round in the U.S.-Soviet contest was played out on American turf, while mediated by images and representations, and the stakes at risk were the minds and sympathies of the American public.

Although Khrushchev was a real person, the overwhelming majority of Americans experienced him as a text—either in a magazine, in a newspaper, on television, or in a newsreel for theatrical display. Thus Whitfield's essay, as much as any of those above, is a textual study of the power of representation to shape American attitudes, in this case toward foreign policy. Whitfield is quite clear about the fears of those who saw Khrushchev's visit as a manipulative public relations strategy designed to soften the American response to communism. Moreover, he shows that those fears were warranted. In the years after Stalin's death, as Khrushchev rose to unitary power, the American news media constructed a simplistic Khrushchev-as-thug image that, during the 1959 visit, was reconstructed. A multidimensional Khrushchev image—a picture of a witty, resourceful, and very human "person"—took its place and made it possible for Eisenhower to move from confrontation to talk of détente.

The news agencies generating and disseminating the words and pictures that reconstructed the Khrushchev image were, of course, all agents of profit-making organizations. To the degree that they helped form a foundation for diminished cold war anxieties and for the proposed summit meeting, they subverted (if only temporarily) restrictive and reflexive attitudes toward communism and its political intents. This subversion is, I believe, typical of the way mass media markets represented and thus contributed to the cultural transformations that most scholars now agree were in process at midcentury.

These changes were not easily effected, nor did they occur without accommodation to vestigial systems of social discipline. The fact remains, however, that the market commodified the emancipatory knowledge of such dissenters and anticipators as Simone de Beauvoir and Jerry Lee Lewis, Tennessee Williams and Grace Metalious, Richard Wright and Allen Ginsberg, James Baldwin and Mort Sahl. Well before Bob Dylan had anything to sing about, the times they were a changin', and any number of people understood that those changes could be packaged, marketed to national audiences, and reaped for unprecedented profits. We must distinguish, however, between the financial profits earned by successful cultural entrepreneurs (individuals such as J. D. Salinger and corporations such as Twentieth Century-Fox) and the social profits earned by the culture at large as it used that knowledge to leverage progressive change.

This is to say no more or less than what I have already said, namely, that the mass media representations of the time played a significant role in the dismantling of very powerful and regressive mores and systems of belief. The details of this dismantling are particularized in the essays that follow.

WORKS CONSULTED

Anderson, Robert. *Tea and Sympathy.* New York: Random House, 1953.

Asimov, Isaac. *I, Robot.* 1950. Greenwich: Fawcett Crest, 1970.

Bakhtin, M. M. *The Dialogical Imagination.* Ed. Michael Holquist. Trans. Caryl Emerson and Michael Holquist. Austin: University of Texas Press, 1981.

Baldwin, James. *Giovanni's Room.* 1956. New York: Laurel-Dell, 1988.

Barth, John. *The Floating Opera.* New York: Bantam Books, 1956.

Biskind, Peter. *Seeing Is Believing: How Hollywood Taught Us to Stop Worrying and Love the Fifties.* New York: Pantheon, 1983.

Breines, Wini. *Young, White, and Miserable: Growing Up Female in the Fifties.* Boston: Beacon, 1992.

Byars, Jackie. *All That Hollywood Allows: Re-Reading Gender in 1950s Melodrama.* Chapel Hill: University of North Carolina Press, 1991.

Chambers, Whittaker. *Witness.* New York: Random House, 1952.

Corber, Robert J. *In the Name of National Security: Hitchcock, Homophobia, and the Political Construction of Gender in Postwar America.* Durham, N.C.: Duke University Press, 1993.

Diggins, John. *The Proud Decade: America in War and Peace, 1941–1960.* New York: W. W. Norton, 1988.

Doherty, Thomas. *Teenagers and Teenpics: The Juvenilization of American Movies in the 1950s.* Boston: Unwin Hyman, 1988.

Eisler, Benita. *Private Lives: Men and Women of the Fifties.* New York: Franklin and Watts, 1986.

Fanon, Frantz. *Black Skin White Masks.* 1952. Trans. Charles Lam Markmann. New York: Grove Press, 1967.

French, Brandon. *On the Verge of Revolt: Women in American Films of the Fifties.* New York: Ungar, 1978.

Gilbert, James. *A Cycle of Outrage: America's Reaction to the Juvenile Delinquent in the 1950s.* New York: Oxford University Press, 1986.

Goldman, Eric F. *The Crucial Decade—and After: America, 1945–1960.* New York: Vintage, 1960.

Graebner, William. *Coming of Age in Buffalo: Youth and Authority in the Postwar Era.* Philadelphia: Temple University Press, 1989.

Halberstam, David. *The Fifties.* New York: Villard, 1993.

Harvey, Brett. *The Fifties: A Woman's Oral History.* New York: HarperCollins, 1993.

Hayek, Friedrich A. *The Fatal Conceit: The Errors of Socialism.* London: Routledge, 1988.

Hoover, J. Edgar. *Masters of Deceit: The Story of Communism in America and How to Fight It.* New York: Holt, Rinehart, and Winston, 1958.

Jezer, Marty. *Dark Ages: Life in the United States, 1945–1960.* Boston: South End Press, 1982.

Kaledin, Eugenia. *Mothers and More: American Women in the 1950s.* Boston: Twayne, 1984.

Kozol, Wendy. *Life's America: Family and Nation in Postwar Journalism.* Philadelphia: Temple University Press, 1994.

Krim, Seymour, ed. *The Beats.* Greenwich: Gold Medal–Fawcett, 1960.

Lerner, Max. *America as a Civilization: Life and Thought in the United States Today.* New York: Simon and Schuster, 1957.

Lhamon, W. T., Jr. *Deliberate Speed: The Origins of a Cultural Style in the American 1950s*. Washington, D.C.: Smithsonian Institution Press, 1990.

Lindesmith, Alfred R., and Anselm L. Strauss. *Social Psychology*. Rev. ed. New York: Holt, Rinehart, and Winston, 1956.

Lundberg, Ferdinand, and Marynia F. Farnham. *Modern Woman: The Lost Sex*. New York: Grosset and Dunlap, 1947.

Marling, Karal Ann. *As Seen on TV: The Visual Culture of Everyday Life in the 1950s*. Cambridge, Mass.: Harvard University Press, 1994.

May, Elaine Tyler. *Homeward Bound: American Families in the Cold War Era*. New York: Basic Books, 1988.

May, Lary, ed. *Recasting America: Culture and Politics in the Age of Cold War*. Chicago: University of Chicago Press, 1989.

Mead, Margaret. *Male and Female: A Study of the Sexes in a Changing World*. New York: William Morrow, 1949.

Meyerowitz, Joanne, ed. *Not June Cleaver: Women and Gender in Postwar America, 1945–1960*. Philadelphia: Temple University Press, 1994.

O'Neill, William. *American High: The Years of Confidence, 1945–1960*. New York: Free Press, 1986.

Pells, Richard H. *The Liberal Mind in a Conservative Age: American Intellectuals in the 1940s and 1950s*. New York: Harper and Row, 1985.

Reiss, Ira L. *Premarital Sexual Standards in America*. New York: Free Press, 1960.

Riesman, David. *The Lonely Crowd: A Study of the Changing American Character*. New Haven: Yale University Press, 1950.

Robeson, Paul. *Here I Stand*. Boston: Beacon Press, 1958.

Rogin, Michael. "Kiss Me Deadly: Communism, Motherhood, and Cold War Movies." *Representations* 6 (Spring 1984): 1–36.

Satin, Joseph, ed. *The 1950s: America's Placid Decade*. Boston: Houghton Mifflin, 1960.

Schaub, Thomas Hill. *American Fiction in the Cold War*. Madison: University of Wisconsin Press, 1991.

Warren, Robert Penn. *Segregation: The Inner Conflict in the South*. New York: Random House, 1956.

Whitfield, Stephen J. *A Death in the Delta: The Story of Emmett Till*. New York: Free Press, 1988.

Wiener, Norbert. *The Human Use of Human Beings: Cybernetics and Society*. 1950. New York: Avon, 1967.

Part One   Changing Minds

James L. Baughman

 THE FRUSTRATED PERSUADER
One
Fairfax M. Cone and the Edsel Advertising Campaign, 1957–59

I N the late 1950s, the prophets of abundance were being stoned. Critics dismayed over the emergence of a culture of consumption began casting advertising agents as the villains of post-war society. Americans spent

Ford Edsel, 1957.
(Courtesy of the Library of Congress)

too much money on marginal if not worthless goods. Such spendthrift ways, these observers insisted, could not be explained by the rising incomes most Americans enjoyed during the period. Demand had been manipulated by Madison Avenue. In the best-selling *The Hidden Persuaders* (1957), Vance Packard listed as proof every assertion of mass persuasion's effects made by advertisers and their consultants (see also Goodman; Fox 199–200; Horowitz 104–9).

The English writer Aldous Huxley went further. Huxley, living in consumer-driven southern California, likened advertising agents to Hitler in their skill at molding the mass mind. "It is by manipulating 'hidden forces' that the advertising experts induce us to buy their wares—a toothpaste, a brand of cigarettes, a political candidate. And it is by appealing to the same hid-

den forces—and others too dangerous to Madison Avenue to meddle with—
that Hitler induced the German masses to buy themselves a Fuehrer, an in-
sane philosophy and the Second World War" (43).

The Harvard economist John Kenneth Galbraith gave such diatribes an
academic gloss. In *The Affluent Society* (1958), Galbraith stressed the role of
advertising in "want creation." Much as Walter Lippmann a generation earlier had challenged the notion of the omnicompetent citizen, Galbraith questioned economists' idealization of the omnicompetent consumer. "Producers,"
he wrote, "may proceed actively to create wants through advertising and
salesmanship" (158).

To such assertions of advertiser power in the fifties came a very expensive exception. In September 1957, the Ford Motor Company, the nation's
second largest automaker and fourth largest corporation, unveiled eighteen
different car models to form the new Edsel Division. Just over two years later, in November 1959, Ford announced the end of the Edsel; the company
had lost $100 million dollars on the project (L. White 3, 74). And a carefully
planned product promotion campaign had failed. "If ever advertising should
have worked," remarked Fairfax M. Cone, who had handled the car's advertising campaign, "the Edsel advertising should have." Instead, Cone wrote
in his memoirs, the Edsel proved to be "the greatest tragedy in American
manufacturing history" (*With All Its Faults* 251; see also "A Talk with Fax
Cone" 26).

THE CLIENT

The Edsel symbolized everything that appeared to be wrong with the U.S.
automobile industry in the fifties. Except for its controversial exterior design,
the car scarcely differed from any other large American car. The Edsel was
big, laden with chrome and horsepower. Its technical innovations were few
and forgettable. Moreover, many of the 1958 models were poorly assembled.
How could Ford not have anticipated what proved (and remains) the greatest challenge to the American automobile industry: mechanically reliable,
fuel-efficient exports, first from Germany, then Japan (Tedlow 175–76)?

Still, the decision to create the Edsel Division came well before the energy crises of the seventies and the magnitude of the import threat had become
manifest. Ford acted in 1955 when the automaker's commitment to a new
division of full-sized, medium-priced cars possessed much logic. The failure

of the Kaiser-Frazier autos, which had stressed fuel efficiency, and the unpopularity of several imports that similarly emphasized economy indicated little enthusiasm among consumers for inexpensive, economical transportation.[1] Moreover, the Big Three carmakers (GM, Ford, and Chrysler) assumed they had a captive market. In 1955, they controlled 94 percent of the U.S. domestic market. Two smaller manufacturers, American Motors (AMC) and Studebaker-Packard, together held a 4 percent share. Imports accounted for 2 percent (Flink 278).

Consumer behavior appeared to favor certain domestic makes. Despite predictions that demand had been satiated in the midfifties, new car sales continued to grow. And more and more had expensive options. The percentage of automobiles sold with power steering rose from 5 percent in 1952 to 38 percent five years later. The percentage with automatic transmission increased from 25 percent in 1949 to 80 percent eight years later (Flint 150, 158). More and more cars had huge V-8 engines.

The fifties car came ornately styled, with large amounts of decorative chrome. The grille on the front of Groucho Marx's 1952 DeSoto, the comedian cracked, looked "like a set of bad teeth" (Marx and Arce 116). More autos mimicked the 1949 Cadillac by including plane-like tail fins. In the postwar years, the Chrysler Corporation had stressed its tradition of engineering expertise and saw its market share fall. But in 1955, when the cars of Chrysler's four divisions—Dodge, DeSoto, Plymouth, and Chrysler—packed bigger engines and a major "Forward Look" redesign, which included fins, sales almost doubled. After years of dour solidity, the 1955 Chevy had a sporty appearance—and a V-8. "If we build automobiles for a thousand years," auto writer Jerry Flint recalled, "we will still remember 1955 as Chevrolet's finest hour" (150, 158).

In its attention to style and power, the auto industry celebrated what Thomas Hine has termed the "Populuxe" style, an ornateness found in much fifties culture. Americans had emerged from the depression and war not only wanting it all, but wanting it all with chrome. "During the Populuxe decade," Hine writes, "the objects people could buy took on a special, exaggerated quality. They celebrated confidence in the future, the excitement of the present, the sheer joy of having so much" (4).

Cars grew in size, though not in efficiency of operation. Gasoline remained relatively cheap, with the real cost of energy between 1950 and 1973 declining by 5 percent (Jackson 293, 297). Cars gradually obtained fewer miles to the gallon. Asked in 1958 what Buick was doing to promote fuel efficiency, division general manager Edward T. Ragsdale replied, "We're helping the gas companies, the same as our competitors" (Keats 14).

Although the Ford Motor Company shared such attitudes and had prospered overall, the automaker had one, seemingly severe, disadvantage. More buyers "traded up," that is, they exchanged an inexpensive Ford for a medium-priced vehicle, but usually this was not a member of "the Ford family of fine cars." Ford Motor Company had only one medium-priced car division, Mercury, compared to GM's three and Chrysler's two. And Mercury, consumer surveys suggested, had the wrong image: the choice of a "racing driver" or "dance-band leader" (Larrabee, "The Edsel" 72; Wallace). With Mercury so ill-regarded, Ford had to do something to expand its market share. A Lehman Brothers study indicated that much of the expansion in new car sales had been in the medium-price field: at GM, 45 percent, at Chrysler, 47 percent. The absence of a second medium-priced car, *Business Week* reported in 1956, "has been a terrific handicap to Ford's growth" ("Ford vs. GM" 30–31; see also "The Role of the Edsel Line"; Krafve, "Investment in Tomorrow"; Reynolds 39–41).

The trading-up phenomenon offered new support for Alfred Sloan's strategy, developed for GM in the twenties, of autonomous divisions manufacturing distinct lines of cars, each priced for a different income group. The Sloan model envisioned an American autobuyer lifeline. Adulthood began in a Chevrolet and ended in a Buick Roadmaster or, if unusually prosperous, a Cadillac (65, 67–69, 158, 160). This approach appeared to explain GM's dominance of the domestic automobile market; in 1955 General Motors had a 51 percent share compared with Ford's 28 percent; Chrysler trailed at 17 percent (L. White 292).

To cut into GM's share, analysts at the time assumed, Ford had to be more like the industry leader. GM had already been acting as a model for the number two carmaker ever since Henry Ford II named Ernest Breech Jr. executive vice president and his second-in-command in 1946. A GM veteran, Breech immediately began reorganizing Ford along the lines of his former employer. He recruited young efficiency experts, dubbed "The Whiz Kids," and whose ranks included Robert S. McNamara. This new team stabilized the company's wobbly financial condition and instituted long overdue inventory controls (Chandler 46, 463; "The Rebirth of Ford" 88; Nevins and Hill 315,

325–26, 329–32, 357–58; Shapley 43, 45). Ford also enjoyed some spectacular marketing successes, notably with the 1949 Ford and the 1955 Thunderbird, that led some within the company hierarchy to believe Ford could overcome General Motors to become the world's number one automaker. To this faction of Ford executives that meant adding a new line of medium-priced cars. Despite Breech's misgivings, Ford's executive committee in April 1955 voted to create a separate division modeled after GM's Buick (Warnock 3–6; Hughes 28–29).

Ford did not plan a distinctive automobile. The new car would be distinguished mainly by its exterior design and a few unusual features, including push-button, "teletouch" automatic transmission centered in the steering wheel.[2] Otherwise it would be a Ford or Mercury in costume. Of the four main models, two would have the full-size Ford Fairlane's shell, two would use a Mercury shell.[3]

In retrospect, Ford's strategy had several fundamental flaws.[4] Company planners assumed that the midfifties sales trends would continue unabated. In that regard, the company conveyed a widely shared faith in the strength of the American economy. Although later mocked by John Brooks of the *New Yorker*, Ford's estimates of growth in the Gross National Product and automobile registrations were, if anything, insufficiently expansive.[5] Richard E. Krafve, the division's new chief, assured a 1956 audience, "We are not merely trying to cut ourselves a slice of the same size pie, but rather we will be going after a slice of a much larger pie" (7). Yet Ford did not allow for bumps along the way, like the recession of 1957–58 that temporarily shrank the market for bigger cars.

Relatedly, Ford expected the *shape* of demand to remain constant. That is, buyers would continue to seek large cars with massive engines and an ever-burgeoning array of options. When the Edsel was finally unveiled, however, recession and other factors had altered many consumers' auto-buying habits. Money that might have been spent on a car went for other things. Or, as *Fortune* had predicted, many Americans were looking for a second vehicle, something cheap and convenient for short commutes ("A New Kind of Car Market" 220, 222, 224, 227–28; see also Larrabee, "Detroit's Great Debate" 20; Levitt 48). New cars of this period from other manufacturers had fewer costly options. For example, the percentage of automobiles with automatic transmission actually fell between 1957 and 1959, from 80 to 72 percent (Flint 106).

A third flaw to Ford's strategy related to the first two. The sales boom of 1953–56 had convinced the automaker that most buyers based their decisions on the image of a car—and their own rising status or class aspirations. There was, after all, little logic to purchasing a more costly Buick when a Chevrolet or Ford provided transportation as cheaply. But trading up signaled ascending the class ladder, a move that could be *bought*. And one of the marketing conceits of fifties advertising was that everyone aspired to a middle-class standard. "You can't sell [a car] just to the smart young executive," a Ford publicist remarked. "What you want to do is sell everyone the idea that he is a smart young executive" (Mayer, Warnock interview; Mayer, *Madison Avenue, U.S.A.* 7, 69). Ford planners had not recognized that, as in the twenties, a sales pitch predicated on concerns over status might only work during a boom; an economic downturn would likely restore common sense (Curti 353–54; Marchand 288–89). Other consumers might simply cease worrying about the image of the car they drove. This indeed began to happen in the late fifties. "Formerly you wouldn't drive a Chevy up to a country club," observed one Ford planner in 1958, "now you would" (Larrabee, "Detroit's Great Debate" 20).

Nevertheless, earlier in the decade in-house marketing research confirmed Ford's emphasis on a car as a symbol of self-image. Planning for the new division relied heavily on motivational research (MR), whose advocates loosely mixed sociology and psychology in seeking to understand and control demand.[6] Disregarding a product's rational attributes, such as its quality or price, MR stressed instead its image and whether it met a psychological need. Ford commissioned an elaborate survey, conducted by Columbia University's Bureau of Applied Social Research, which polled 1,600 automobile owners in Peoria, Illinois, and San Bernardino, California. They were not asked about price or product quality or, indeed, what type of car they wanted. Instead, the survey, coordinated by David Wallace of Ford, identified the "personality" of, say, a Buick owner ("a strong image of upper class solidarity") or a Plymouth owner ("a weak image of plain respectability") as well as the gratifications achieved through car ownership. Wallace himself had concluded that an automobile "is a very powerful status symbol" (Mayer, Wallace interview; see also Brooks 27–28; "History of the BASR Edsel Study; "A Case History").

From Wallace's surveys, Ford selected an image for the Edsel around which its advertising would be organized. The car, Wallace commented, had to "avoid the image of [the] hot-rod," which, polling had indicated, lessened the Mercury's acceptance within the middle class. The marketing "theme is going to be elegance—we're classy" (Mayer, Wallace interview; see also Larrabee, "The Edsel" 72). Yet it would be affordable elegance, at least to the upwardly mobile middle class. The Edsel, remarked a Ford executive, would be "the smart car for the young American family on its way up" ("A Case History" 410).

THE AGENCY

To sell the car, Ford selected the Foote, Cone, and Belding agency (FCB), based in Chicago. Ford had deliberately chosen a firm that had not heretofore handled an automobile account and had a reputation for creativity. The successor to Lord and Thomas, FCB had produced some of the decade's most effective—and memorable—advertising. The agency combined the latest photographic techniques with the best tradition of sloganeering for such products as Hallmark cards ("When you care enough to send the very best"), Toni home permanent ("Which twin has the Toni?"), Clairol hair coloring ("Does she or doesn't she?"), Dial soap ("Aren't you glad you use Dial? Don't you wish everyone did?"), and Pepsodent toothpaste ("You'll wonder where the yellow went when you brush your teeth with Pepsodent"). FCB had put the smiling face on Kool-Aid pitchers and had given America Smokey bear. All in all, FCB was a rising force in fifties advertising. Between 1943 and 1956, the agency's billings had increased from $29 million to $100 million ("Fairfax Cone Gives Inside" 18, 26; Cone, *With All Its Faults* 169, 206, 210, 217–18, 238–39, 240). Fairfax Cone, FCB's managing partner, declared one trade journal, was "converting FC&B into a truly national agency, with ambitious programs of growth both here and overseas" ("Intense Fairfax Cone" 63).

From his earliest days at Lord and Thomas, Cone had been part of the agency's creative team despite his role in management. Although staff members had developed most of FCB's greatest successes, Cone himself had come up—or so everyone said at the office—with the Dial slogan while using the soap in his shower (Cone oral history transcript, tape 6, p. 1; "It's Cone Two to One"; "Intense Fairfax Cone"). A rival called Cone "among the most 'creative' men in the advertising business" (Ogilvy 91).

In his presentations to Ford, Cone made no secret of his affinity for the status orientation of Ford's marketing studies. Cone admired Pierre Martineau, director of research for the *Chicago Tribune,* an FCB client. Dubbed "the most tireless publicist" of motivational research (Fox 183), Martineau had provided a model for the "depth interviews" Wallace and others had conducted for Ford (Larrabee, "The Edsel" 72). Martineau argued that the similarity of mass-produced goods necessitated appeals to image. "Leading" advertising agencies, he declared in a 1957 paper, had concluded that "even when competitive brands are functionally indistinguishable, their images may be very different; that it is extremely important to create these psychological distinctions for a brand because the consumer is not happy when his choice has no character" (Martineau, "The Public Image" 15; see also Martineau, *Motivation in Advertising* 7, 76, 80). Praising Martineau's 1957 book, *Motivation in Advertising,* Cone wrote, "All advertising, whether it be for a department store or a cake mix or whatnot, utilizes two sets of motivation: the basic wish for ownership of the product involved and the personality, or image, of the particular brand" (Cone review; see also Cone address to General Foods).

Seeking the Edsel account in a December 1955 presentation, Cone emphasized the primacy of image. Ford's new line would have no unusual features, he realized. Indeed, the new car would not differ significantly from a Mercury or Buick. "Everyone knows that all standard American automobiles run easily and well," Cone said. That uniformity rendered two images—the vehicle's and the buyer's—all important. "Selection is a matter of personal, emotional appeal; How do I look in this car, how do I feel in this car, how do my friends look at me in this car? How do I fit with my friends in this car. . . . We are not, almost never buying transportation. *We are buying satisfaction* of an urge that is in all of us to reach an ideal" (Cone, typed notes). In another talk to Ford executives, Cone stressed the theme of the car as status symbol. "If you own a good automobile, you are a person of substance—and the proof is obvious," he remarked. "Your car indicates your status in the world" ("What We Believe").

Soon after winning the account in February 1956, FCB established a Detroit office with seventy employees and Charles S. Winston Jr., a ten-year FCB veteran, as head. Things generally went smoothly, though Ford ignored exhaustive research on the car's name. Company officials rejected FCB's recommendations (Corsair, Citation, Pacer, or Ranger)—and several from the poet Marianne Moore—in favor of Edsel, for young Henry's late father. Experienced copywriters winced, largely because of the name's rhythmic problems ("pretzel," "diesel," "hard sell") (Brooks 33–36; Larrabee, "The Edsel" 71, 73; Cone, *With All Its Faults* 249–50). In other matters, FCB and Ford were in harmony. Cone praised Wallace's surveys as the best research he had ever seen (Mayer, Cone interview).

THE CAMPAIGN

Cone prepared a two-stage campaign. The first involved product promotion, preparing the public for the car's introduction on "E Day," September 4, 1957. The second, more sustained effort would be a one-year series of advertisements—with two-page layouts in *Life* the major buy—promoting the car to an upper middle-class market most likely to subscribe to the periodical.[7] For that same audience, FCB would produce elaborate television specials.

Cone labored with the help of Edsel's chief publicist, Gayle Warnock, on the introductory phase. In *Life* beginning in July 1957, FCB ran two-page, black-and-white ads of veiled cars being tested or transported to new Edsel dealers across the country. They reflected Cone's preference, he told Martin Mayer, for "restrained" copy (Mayer, Cone interview). Over a white background, black headlines declared, "Lately, some mysterious automobiles have been seen on the road," "These carriers with covered cars are headed in your direction," and "A man in your town recently made a decision [to become an Edsel dealer] that will change his life." Most of these "covered" ads commanded attention, according to the Daniel Starch survey of *Life* readers, and won Cone the praise of fellow members of the University of Chicago's board of trustees.[8]

FCB and Ford took elaborate precautions to prevent anyone from seeing an Edsel before E Day. Models transported to dealers were carefully wrapped. Because some Edsels had to appear in a TV commercial filmed before E Day, armed guards surrounded the Hollywood studio that FCB had rented and closely screened those seeking admittance. When not being filmed, the cars were kept in a drive-in vault ("Not To Be Opened"; "Edsel's Strip-Tease").

Meanwhile, Warnock very successfully courted the reporters and columnists who covered the automobile industry. In late August, he organized a massive press party at Ford's Dearborn headquarters. Ford lent Edsels to journalists to return home. Back in the office, they filed stories praising the newest member of the Ford family of fine cars. *Time* compared the Edsel's grill to "the elegant Cord of the '30s" ("The Newest Car"; see also Warnock 145, 148–77,

251). "It remains for one to drive an Edsel," wrote a *Cleveland Plain Dealer* columnist, "to appreciate the engineering features and innovations which help make this newcomer outstanding" (Edsel ad, "factory newspapers"). "The publicity job done for the Edsel," commented a Warnock colleague, "is the largest sustained p.r. job ever done for a product" (Mayer, Rapp interview). "Your job in publicizing the Edsel," Cone wrote Warnock on August 27, "has no equal that I have ever seen or heard of." "We have a very hot property," Warnock exclaimed. "It's like having Kim Novak" (Mayer, Warnock interview; Cone to Warnock).

The effectiveness of Warnock's efforts and FCB's magazine ads became clear the following week. On E Day, some 2.5 million Americans poured into Edsel dealerships. "The introduction of the Edsel has filled dealers' showrooms from Coast to Coast," Cone wrote a Los Angeles FCB agent. "Individual suburban dealers in the Chicago area, for example, have been overwhelmed with three to four thousand 'lookers' per day" (Cone to Braun). An Inglewood, California, dealer reported serving forty-six gallons of coffee and twenty-six dozen donuts (Edsel ad, *Automotive News*).

After E Day came the campaign's second phase and a very different tone, what Cone termed "distinctive understatement." Neither he nor Edsel's sales staff wanted the advertising to be *too arresting*, that is, to shift attention from the car itself. "We hope no one will talk about our advertising," remarked one Edsel executive, "but that everybody will talk about the Edsel" ("Ford's Edsel" 16).

With this approach in mind, Cone broke with industry habit. In the midfifties auto advertising took two forms. During the first weeks of a new model's appearance, ads had a flashy, showroom look. The cars appeared in elaborate sets, suggesting a big-city showroom or even a network TV studio, with exceedingly well-dressed consumers admiring the vehicles. After this two-to-four-week introductory phase, ads showed cars in conventional settings and with drivers usually attired more casually. Because Warnock's efforts had been so successful thus far in the campaign, Cone eschewed the traditional showroom look for the new ads in favor of a quiet, almost "conversational" pitch to potential buyers. He specified two-page magazine layouts of three horizontal bars, with the top for the "This Is the Edsel" headline, the middle for an illustration of the car, and the bottom for copy. To escape the busy appearance of the showroom ads, FCB artists left ample white space and

used simple black print.[9] Above all, Cone sought to avoid—and Edsel executives had given him every reason to believe he was not to adopt—what he
regarded as the exaggerated visual displays and verbal claims in most American automobile advertising. FCB had been hired, he reminded Winston, "to
make advertising that was free from traditional automobile advertising rules
and regulations."[10]

Cone planned to run such understated ads during the Edsel's entire first
year. Slowly, Edsel would nurture a relationship with potential buyers, and
the product, as Cone had told Ford in 1955, would acquire a "halo" that would
make it more coveted than, say, a DeSoto or a Buick. "Keep in mind the long-
range view," he had told Ford executives. "Over the years, your new car
should seek to establish itself as something special, worthy of great admiration. It must grow to be, in people's minds, a part of the good life, a symbol
to mark advancement and achievement."[11]

There were early signs that Cone's approach was effective. His Chicago-
based rival, Leo Burnett, praised the ads, as did others (Burnett to Cone;
Chaffin to Cone). More importantly, readers remained unusually interested
in the Edsel ads. The Starch studies indicated continued high levels of attention to the two-page layouts. The Edsel *Life* ad of September 9, he told a Ford
executive, "recorded the highest Starch ratings I had ever seen" (Cone to
Winston, Oct. 29, 1957; see also Cone to Copeland).

THE PANIC

Demand for—as opposed to curiosity about—the Edsel failed to materialize,
however. Part of the problem related to the timing of the car's introduction.
The Edsel's debut came some six weeks before those of the other 1958 cars.
But rival dealers, including ones for Ford and Lincoln-Mercury, undercut this
new competitor by sharply discounting their remaining 1957 models ("Edsel Gets a Frantic Push" 36). Then, too, some Edsel dealers had passively assumed that the Warnock-Cone promotional campaign would sell cars all by
itself. But Warnock had succeeded too well. Millions had been drawn into
showrooms dying to see, after several months of public relations teasing, what
was under the sheet. Most were "lookers." Only a minority planned to purchase a car and what they saw—a 1958 Ford or Mercury with a funny front—
failed to move them. "The Edsel," the Consumer Union concluded, "has no

important basic advantages over other brands" ("The New Edsel"). A Sind-linger and Company survey indicated that public enthusiasm for the car, initially high, began to drop sharply in September after E Day. Sales fell 45 percent in October. Ford had hoped to sell 600 cars a day; in November, an average of only 222 Edsels were sold daily (Warnock 199–201, 212). Worse, Edsel buyers were not singing the car's praises. A survey of purchasers of seven different 1958 models found Edsel owners the least likely to rank their cars "excellent."[12]

Not even the newest advertising medium, television, could stop the bleed-ing. On October 13, 1957, Edsel sponsored a one-hour special hosted by Bing Crosby and featuring Frank Sinatra, Louis Armstrong, and Rosemary Clooney. Aired on CBS, *The Edsel Show* preempted Ed Sullivan's popular Sunday night variety hour and achieved enormous ratings, a reported 50 million viewers (Warnock 204). The program carried three commercials, each of which ran about two and half minutes. A few cheery references to the car came during the show itself. "It's a great car," Sinatra told Crosby early in the program (*The Edsel Show*). But not everyone would take Sinatra's word for it. An FCB-commissioned study indicated that *The Edsel Show* had created some good-will for the car—the percentage of viewers rating it "very good" doubled but more than half remained uncommitted when asked if the Edsel was "very good" or "very bad" ("Before-and-After Test"; see also "Measuring Edsel's TV Impact"; Warnock 203). The TV special brought more people to show-rooms, Brooks reported, but no spurt in purchases.[13]

What had happened? The Edsel's appearance, many maintained, crippled the car's prospects. Ironically, given all the funds poured into surveys, Ford had not market-tested the design (Springer). One weakness might have been the absence of a stylistic feature that annoyed the industry's detractors: the Edsel, like other Fords, did not have fins. Compared to virtually all GM and Chrysler models, the Edsel was also unusually rectangular ("Coming Out"). In other ways, the car stuck out. The grille seemed simply ugly—if not ob-scene.[14] To some, the car resembled an Oldsmobile sucking a lemon. Picking up his Edsel, Cone shared his enthusiasm for the car with his South Chicago dealer. "I wanted to be pleasant," Cone recalled, "and I said, 'pretty nice, huh?' And he said, 'yeah, all but that Goddam front end'" (Cone oral histo-ry, tape 5, p. 14; see also "The $250 Million Flop"). Still, FCB only reinforced this perception of the car as a stylistic oddity when an "Edsel Show" com-mercial announced, "This is the Edsel. Unlike any other car you've ever seen!"

Worse were repeated reports of mechanical problems. Wanting people to see the car, the division rushed models to dealers; many should have been tested at the factory for defects first. As a result, the car was haunted by mechanical failures: heaters kept blowing hot air after being switched off, hoods did not open or would not shut. Some Teletouch automatic transmission buttons required very strong fingers. Gremlins inhabited the Edsel driven by Ken Thurston of FCB's Los Angeles office. The air-conditioning, the heater, and the compass all failed to function. The accelerator only worked if Thurston floored it. Pinging noises caused him to use the radio at all times. And repeated visits to Edsel dealerships failed to remove all of the bugs. The car, Thurston complained, was "a booby trap" (Thurston to Cone, Nov. 8, 14, 1957; see also B. S. White to Cone). *Consumer Reports* proved unforgiving: Its test vehicle "had, among other troubles, the wrong axle ratio, loss of water when an expansion plug blew out, a noisy and leaking power-steering pump, [and] noisy rear-axle gears" ("The New Edsel"; see also Keats 102–3). One Edsel executive later confessed to John Brooks that only half of the first year's models performed properly.[15]

Moreover, a recession that began in 1957 had weakened demand for medium-priced vehicles. Their share of the market, *Time* reported, had slipped from 37 percent in 1955 to 29 percent in 1957. The January 1958 sales of medium-priced cars dropped 33 percent compared to those of the previous January. "Conspicuous consumption is waning," *Time* proclaimed. "The stepping stone is no longer attractive—or necessary—to most Americans" ("Conspicuous Consumption"; see also Larrabee, "Detroit's Great Debate" 19–20). To the surprise of the Big Three, potential buyers started going to American Motors dealers showcasing inexpensive compacts. The sudden appeal of the practical if plain AMC Rambler all but mocked the theories of Martineau and others. The attraction of the Rambler, Cone recalled, "was its unobtrusive, uncluttered *lack* of personality" (*With All Its Faults* 253). At the same time, sales of small, inexpensive foreign cars boomed, with *Time* reporting a one-year increase of 110 percent in 1957 ("Conspicuous Consumption"). The leader was Volkswagen's Beetle, which, in contrast to Detroit's models, barely changed in design from year to year.

The Edsel's disappointing sales left Cone, once described as "a guy who doesn't panic easily," dealing with terror-stricken clients. Dealers, pleased with the initial publicity effort, had begun demanding that the second phase of the campaign be drastically revised. Division executives in turn ordered

FCB to abandon Cone's understated pitch, an approach they had embraced only a month earlier. At a mid-October meeting, Winston wrote, Edsel's top managers admitted "freely that they are running away from everything that they told us about why the car was planned the way it is." They called for "more action, that's more glamorous, more impelling and has more impact." The illustrations did not do the car justice, they argued. The advertising must, after all, be more striking. One Edsel executive admitted, "originally we said we wanted people to only talk about the Edsel and not its advertising. Now I think we want them to also talk about our ads."[16] Everyone was harried by Robert McNamara, who had become Ford's vice president for all cars and trucks a month before E Day. McNamara had never supported the car's introduction and its limp sales and production problems only hardened his position. He started behaving like a corner butcher whose largest refrigeration unit had just blown a fuse. One rainy morning, McNamara met with FCB representatives and Warnock. Forgetting to remove his muddy galoshes, McNamara jumped on leather chairs, tearing down ads mounted on the walls. They were all wrong, he cried. The room soon looked as if it had been sacked (Warnock 209–10; Shapley 53–56).

Cone lost control of the account. Copy became confusing. "A car for the man whose taste is sure" in September became "THE ONE THAT'S REALLY NEW IS THE LOWEST PRICED, TOO" three months later.[17] TV commercials started stressing value and applying a reverse psychology that was probably too obvious to all but the dimmest potential customer. Several ads asserted that the Edsel would soon be imitated by other automakers; Edsel buyers would therefore be ahead of the pack. "Edsel gives you next year's features, next year's styling—Now!" one TV spot declared. Another claimed, "It's an open secret in Detroit. The Edsel is going to be copied" ("Commercials.Automobiles").

Ford demanded that Edsel sponsor the new TV western *Wagon Train*. FCB objected, saying that the program had the wrong viewership. The audience for *Wagon Train,* the agency contended, was at once too young, too old, and too rural. Not enough younger, upwardly mobile adults took in the series. FCB had instead sought more specials along the lines of *The Edsel Show*. The *Wagon Train* sponsorship failed to increase interest in the car. Undaunted, Edsel executives, using the show as a tie-in, had each dealer run a contest offering a free pony. Children were to register at the local Edsel dealer and have their parents test-drive the car. The pony promotion proved an unmitigated disaster for parents as well as the division.[18]

Cone and others still believed the Edsel could be saved. Perhaps FCB, especially Warnock, had erred. The initial campaign had created excessive expectations. "Almost everyone was disappointed," Cone wrote in September 1958, "when the Edsel turned out to be an automobile with the same four wheels and with [an] engine in the front that every other car had" (Cone to Nance, 3 Sept. 1958). The 1957 campaign had been "confused," he admitted. Warnock had attracted a mass audience while FCB had courted a class audience. Cone argued that the "Edsel is going to have to start all over; it's going to have to run a new race. But I think it can do this and I think it can win." For the 1959 model, FCB finally came up with a slogan: "Making history by making sense" (Cone to Nance, 30 Jan. 1958; Cone, Edsel presentation 4).

However, the Edsel account was not making sense or money for Ford. One glimpse of the future came in January 1958, when McNamara merged Edsel into a new Mercury-Edsel-Lincoln division. The separate division strategy associated with Sloan had been discarded. In December, Ford reassigned the Edsel account to Kenyon and Eckhardt and gave FCB the Lincoln (Cone to Remington). Eleven months later, Ford announced that the Edsel would be discontinued.[19]

Cone's reputation managed to survive the Edsel debacle. In 1962, he made the cover of *Time,* along with other prominent advertising agents, and shortly before his death in 1977, earned admission to the Advertising Hall of Fame ("The Mammoth Mirror"; "Fairfax M. Cone"). Yet Cone could not forget the Edsel. Late in his life he listed the Edsel campaign as one of his "greatest disappointments" (Cone oral history transcript, tape 7, p. 13).

Rather than one of Packard's "hidden persuaders," Cone had been a thoroughly frustrated pitchman. But the Edsel's fate had served one purpose for Cone. Ever sensitive to the attacks of Packard and others, Cone in a 1961 speech pointed to his agency's greatest failure as proof that advertising could not create demand. "So much for the charge that advertising manipulates the public" (Cone address, 11 Oct. 1961). Referring to the Edsel two years later, Cone remarked, "Advertising can't control the public taste." The Edsel campaign "worked to get people in, but it couldn't sell them" ("A Talk with Fax Cone" 26).

Cone had a point. Critics had clearly overstated the power of mass per-suaders. With tens of millions of dollars at stake, one of the nation's largest corporations and a major advertising agency could not engage in what Galbraith had dubbed "want creation." Cone and the Edsel's publicists had engendered interest in the car, and in that regard, their campaign succeeded. Millions visited Edsel showrooms on E Day. Some quietly shook their heads, baffled by the car's look; others laughed at it. Their curiosity satisfied, most walked out without making a purchase. Even if they had liked the car's appearance, with rival dealers discounting their models and a recession underway, the Edsel was no bargain. And the would-be buyer honored Freud's "reality principle." The vast majority of consumers, S. I. Hayakawa wrote, "are reasonably well oriented to reality. We do not indulge our fantasies unless it is socially and psychologically safe to do so . . . and within our financial means."[20]

THE MEANING OF FAILURE

Perhaps the easiest inference to be drawn from the Edsel's failure is that the mass persuaders' powers were limited. Helpful here is a comparison between the Edsel and attempts to commercialize (and sometimes in the process create) certain holidays between 1870 and 1920. As Eric Leigh Schmidt found, coalitions of merchants and manufacturers did transform Christmas, Valentine's Day, and Mother's Day into gift-giving occasions. But confectioners could not establish a national Candy Day, and Americans resisted similar initiatives, including Baby Week, all to encourage more consumption. As Schmidt observed, "Commercial power to manipulate the calendar was not hegemonic" (913–15).

Nevertheless, dismissing the Edsel as nothing more than a marketing anomaly lets the critics of advertising in the fifties off too easily. They did not acknowledge the extent to which incessant product promotion after 1945 reflected rather than fashioned the new consumer culture. The postwar demand for goods and services had not been the contrivance of producers and their publicists, but the result of real increases in income and discretionary dollars. Between 1946 and 1961, national income rose 60 percent; the number of Americans with discretionary income, that is, money that did not have to go to necessities, doubled; the total amount of discretionary income rose from $160 million to $350 million (May 165; Department of Commerce 1:224; Vatter 223–24). Despite huge increases in advertising expenditures in the thirty years following World War II, Daniel Pope has noted, the ratio of advertising spending to national income remained relatively constant (39).

Yet the national shopping spree conveyed more than an expansion in spending money. A majority of Americans had become home owners in the years following World War II as record numbers of families bought their first homes. Between 1946 and 1961, 15 million American families became first-time home owners; by 1961, just over 60 percent of nonfarm families lived in owner-occupied dwellings (May 165). In the sixties the economist Harold Vatter estimated that one-fourth of the nation's housing stock had been constructed in the fifties (224; see also Tobey, Wetherell, and Brigham 1401–2). Home ownership in turn entailed still more purchases, such as appliances and furniture. Much of the new spending of the fifties, Vatter found, had been on home-related consumer durables (58, 101, 224). Vance Packard himself lived in suburban comfort in New Caanan, Connecticut. Unlike many contemporary critics of the consumer culture, who were renters in Manhattan, Packard refused to blame consumers who fell prey to the hidden persuaders. He knew too well the temptations to spend money. If he earned more income, he later confessed to a friend, he and his family "probably wouldn't invest it anyway. . . . We are always close to broke" (Horowitz 197, 212–13).

Other factors promoted the consumer culture. The postwar baby boom required parents to purchase products to help them raise their children. With or without children, many Americans began shopping for food in new "supermarkets." These expanded retail units, advertising agent Rosser Reeves explained, had more shelf space for more product lines; brand competition became all the more fierce, fostering even more advertising (Whiteside 57). Not surprisingly, given all the dollars spent, some promotions failed. Products such as the Edsel automobile and Stripe toothpaste quickly entered and left the national marketplace.

Critics bewailing advertising remained. They had self-consciously avoided being anywhere near an Edsel dealership on September 4, 1957. They stayed home, read Vance Packard, and fretted about "hidden forces" molding the masses. John Kenneth Galbraith tried to have it both ways. Rather than grant that the Edsel had qualified his assertions about "want creation," he used Ford's fiasco as an example of the American economy's gross misallocation

of resources. The Edsel's introduction, he noted, had coincided with the Soviet Union's launching of the first space satellite (352). Fax Cone could not
win.

NOTES

The author thanks David R. Babb, Robert Chetov, Jacqueline Hitchon, Scott Latus,
Karen Miller, Paul Pass, Matthew Pass, Philip Ranlet, and Inger Stole for their assis-
tance. Part of the research for this study was supported by the Irwin Maier Faculty
Development Award of the School of Journalism and Mass Communication of the
University of Wisconsin at Madison.

1   See Kaiser-Frazier ad; L. White 178–82; Adams. Both Ford and GM had planned
    to introduce small, inexpensive vehicles in the late forties, but surveys found
    that although many people said they wanted a cheap car, their actual buying
    patterns suggested an unwillingness to sacrifice interior room and certain amen-
    ities that drove up costs. See Nevins and Hill 333, 369, 379; L. White 178–79.

2   The 1956 Packard had push-button automatic transmission placed on the right
    side, and the 1956 Chrysler to the left, of the steering column. See Packard ad;
    Chrysler ad.

3   The sides of the 1958 Edsel closely resembled the Mercury Turnpike Cruiser,
    an unproduced "future styled" model displayed at 1956 auto shows. See Edsel
    ad, *Cleveland Press.*

4   Not discussed here is perhaps Ford's greatest miscalculation, which was in try-
    ing to mimic GM. As Tedlow has argued in his case studies of major corporate
    rivalries, the number two competitor is better served by establishing new mar-
    keting strategies rather than in seeking to imitate the industry leader. See esp.
    368–75.

5   The Forward Product Planning estimate for GNP in 1965 had been $535 billion.
    It proved to be be $684.9 billion. The panel had predicted 70 million cars on
    the American road in 1965, an underestimate of 20.3 million. See Brooks 21;
    Krafve; *Statistical Abstract* 373, 556.

6   For discussions of MR, see Mayer, *Madison Avenue, U.S.A.* chap. 7; Bartlett to
    Mayer; Hayakawa, "Sexual Fantasy" 163; Hayakawa, "Why the Edsel Laid an
    Egg." See also Williams; Wiebe; Lazarsfeld, "Reflections on Business" 11–13; Fox
    183–87; Curti 354–56. Some agents failed to take MR seriously and used it only,
    if at all, to impress clients. See Seligman 233.

7   On the class bias to *Life's* subscription list in the fifties, see Baughman 170.

8 St. Clair to Cone. The Starch staff asked readers if they had read different magazine ads and to what extent. Although hardly infallible, this type of survey was one of the few means by which advertising agents could determine whether an ad was examined by readers. The first "covered" ad, which appeared in *Life* on July 22, 1957, 12–13, had the lowest Starch ratings: 48 percent of the men surveyed indicated they had "noted" it while only 32 percent claimed to have "read most" of the ad. The covered cars-on-the-carrier ad, in *Life* on August 19, 1957, 46–47, was noted by 61 percent of those surveyed compared with 36 percent who read most of it. Copy for some other cars enjoyed Starch ratings comparable to most of the covered ads. Starch studies.

9 All automobile ads run in *Life* in November 1956 and August, September, October, and November 1957, as well as Edsel copy in the FCB scrapbooks, were reviewed. Also useful is Ikuta. FCB's first Edsel TV commercials had a similarly quiet tone, introducing viewers to the car and its features. See *The Edsel Show*.

10 For more on this strategy see Cone to Winston, Aug. 30, 1957; Mayer, *Madison Avenue, U.S.A.* 114–15. Cone's contempt for most auto advertising frequently came up. See Cone to Krafve.

11 Cone, "What We Believe." Cone's notion of slowly nurturing an image was strongly supported by other advertising executives and scholars. See Burnett to Cone; Reeves 29–33, 42; Eldridge, esp. 250–51; Doyle 574.

12 The figures were Chevy owners (74 percent), Buick owners (72), Olds owners (69), Ford owners (66), Plymouth owners (65), DeSoto owners (65), and Edsel owners (49). The interviews were conducted in January, February, and April 1958. See National Broadcasting Company; see also Shapley 55.

13 Brooks 61. A Sindlinger survey suggested that TV advertisements, telecast in black and white on a small screen, may have diminished the car's appeal when compared to color layouts in periodicals. See Smith 79–80.

14 "Madison Avenue," John Keats wrote, "was quick to applaud the Edsel for its vaginal look" (71).

15 Brooks 59. Too much can be made of the poor workmanship factor. The popular 1949 Ford had more than its share of problems. A friend of Breech called it a "piece of junk" while another Ford executive counted eight thousand defects. See Nevins and Hill 343, 351.

16 On Cone's calm, see *New York World Telegram and Sun*, Feb. 20, 1956, clipping in Cone Papers, box 38. On attempts to abandon Cone's campaign see Winston to Cone; Cone, *With All Its Faults* 258–59; "Edsel Gets a Frantic Push."

17 Compare ads in *New Yorker*, Sept. 21, 1957, with ones in Los Angeles and San Francisco newspapers, Dec. 5, 1957, and Dec. 3, 1957, respectively, FCB scrapbook no. 658.

18   Warnock 222, 226–30; Cone, *With All Its Faults* 260; "Edsel—'Wagon Train'";
      Winston to Cone. For a *Wagon Train* promotion of the pony contest, with the
      program's star, Ward Bond, see "Commercials.Automobiles." Despite trying to
      suggest otherwise, NBC's own analysis shows only the most marginal difference
      between viewers and nonviewers in attitudes toward the vehicle.

19   For a discussion of the decision, see "The $250 Million Flop"; "The Edsel Dies
      and Ford Regroups." Within a few years, the large car market returned. Ameri-
      can Motors, the darling of industry critics in 1958, struggled to survive; AMC's
      market share fell from 6.4 percent in 1960 to 2.8 percent in 1966. Although
      imports improved their position, in 1967 they accounted for less than 10 per-
      cent of all U.S. automobile registrations. L. White, 6, 7, 74.

20   Hayakawa, "Why the Edsel Laid an Egg" 220, 221. A historical demonstration
      of the reality principle is Seidl's study of turn-of-the-century consumer prac-
      tices in Minnesota.

WORKS CONSULTED

Adams, Steve. "When Production Wasn't Enough: Kaiser-Frazier and the Culture of
    Consumption." *Business and Economic History* 2d ser., 19 (1990): 255–61.

Bartlett, Helen. Letter to Martin Mayer. May 29, 1958. Box 46. Fairfax M. Cone Pa-
    pers. Joseph Regenstein Library. Department of Special Collections. University
    of Chicago Library. University of Chicago. Chicago.

Baughman, James L. *Henry R. Luce and the Rise of the American News Media*. Bos-
    ton: Twayne, 1987.

"Before-and-After Test on Edsel TV." *Printers' Ink*, Nov. 22, 1957, 4.

Brooks, John. *The Fate of the Edsel and Other Business Misadventures*. New York:
    Harper and Row, 1963.

Burnett, Leo. Letter to Fairfax M. Cone. Sept. 9, 1957. Box 44. Fairfax M. Cone Pa-
    pers. Joseph Regenstein Library. Department of Special Collections. University
    of Chicago Library. University of Chicago. Chicago.

"A Case History in the Communication of Research Findings—From University Lab-
    oratory to Company Board Room." *Public Opinion Quarterly* 21.3 (1957): 409–10.

Chaffin, Edward J. Letter to Fairfax M. Cone. Sept. 11, 1957. Box 44. Fairfax M. Cone
    Papers. Joseph Regenstein Library. Department of Special Collections. Universi-
    ty of Chicago Library. University of Chicago. Chicago.

Chandler, Alfred P., Jr. *Strategy and Structure: Chapters in the History of American
    Industrial Enterprise*. Garden City, N.Y.: Anchor, 1966.

Chrysler. Advertisement. *Cleveland Press*, Jan. 24, 1956, 34.

"The Coming Out of the 1958 Cars." *Life*, Nov. 4, 1957, 99+.

"Commercials.Automobiles. 1957–1958." Videotape. Film and Television Archive. University of California at Los Angeles.

Cone, Fairfax M. Address. Oct. 11, 1961. Box 134. Fairfax M. Cone Papers. Joseph Regenstein Library. Department of Special Collections. University of Chicago Library. University of Chicago. Chicago.

———. Address to Perkins Food Division, General Foods. Dec. 5, 1957. Box 136. Fairfax M. Cone Papers. Joseph Regenstein Library. Department of Special Collections. University of Chicago Library. University of Chicago. Chicago.

———. Edsel presentation. July 25, 1958. Box 136. Fairfax M. Cone Papers. Joseph Regenstein Library. Department of Special Collections. University of Chicago Library. University of Chicago. Chicago.

———. "Good Advertising—And How It Sells Cars." Address. n.d. Box 38. Fairfax M. Cone Papers. Joseph Regenstein Library. Department of Special Collections. University of Chicago Library. University of Chicago. Chicago.

———. Letter to T. W. Braun. Sept. 16, 1957. Box 44. Fairfax M. Cone Papers. Joseph Regenstein Library. Department of Special Collections. University of Chicago Library. University of Chicago. Chicago.

———. Letter to R. F. G. Copeland. Nov. 13, 1957. Box 44. Fairfax M. Cone Papers. Joseph Regenstein Library. Department of Special Collections. University of Chicago Library. University of Chicago. Chicago.

———. Letter to Richard E. Krafve. Oct. 31, 1957. Box 44. Fairfax M. Cone Papers. Joseph Regenstein Library. Department of Special Collections. University of Chicago Library. University of Chicago. Chicago.

———. Letter to James J. Nance. Jan. 30, 1958. Box 51. Fairfax M. Cone Papers. Joseph Regenstein Library. Department of Special Collections. University of Chicago Library. University of Chicago. Chicago.

———. Letter to James J. Nance. Sept. 3, 1958. Box 51. Fairfax M. Cone Papers. Joseph Regenstein Library. Department of Special Collections. University of Chicago Library. University of Chicago. Chicago.

———. Letter to Al Remington. Dec. 3, 1958. Box 44. Fairfax M. Cone Papers. Joseph Regenstein Library. Department of Special Collections. University of Chicago Library. University of Chicago. Chicago.

———. Letter to Gayle Warnock. Aug. 27, 1957. Box 44. Fairfax M. Cone Papers. Joseph Regenstein Library. Department of Special Collections. University of Chicago Library. University of Chicago. Chicago.

———. Letter to C. S. Winston Jr. Oct. 29, 1957. Box 44. Fairfax M. Cone Papers. Joseph Regenstein Library. Department of Special Collections. University of Chicago Library. University of Chicago. Chicago.

———. Memorandum to Charles S. Winston Jr. Aug. 30, 1957. Box 44. Fairfax M.

Cone Papers. Joseph Regenstein Library. Department of Special Collections. University of Chicago Library. University of Chicago. Chicago.

———. Oral history. 1962. Transcripts. Box 140. Fairfax M. Cone Papers. Joseph Regenstein Library. Department of Special Collections. University of Chicago Library. University of Chicago. Chicago.

———. Papers. Joseph Regenstein Library. Department of Special Collections. University of Chicago Library. University of Chicago. Chicago.

———. Review of Martineau, *Motivation in Advertising*. Sept. 9, 1957. Typescript. Box 43. Fairfax M. Cone Papers. Joseph Regenstein Library. Department of Special Collections. University of Chicago Library. University of Chicago. Chicago.

———. Typed notes for Ford Motor Company presentation. Dec. 22, 1955. Box 38. Fairfax M. Cone Papers. Joseph Regenstein Library. Department of Special Collections. University of Chicago Library. University of Chicago. Chicago.

———. "What We Believe about Automobile Advertising." Address. n.d. Box 38. Fairfax M. Cone Papers. Joseph Regenstein Library. Department of Special Collections. University of Chicago Library. University of Chicago. Chicago.

———. *With All Its Faults: A Candid Account of Forty Years in Advertising*. Boston: Little, Brown, 1969.

"Conspicuous Consumption Is Waning." *Time*, Mar. 31, 1958, 76.

Curti, Merle. "The Changing Concept of 'Human Nature' in the Literature of Advertising." *Business History Review* 41.4 (1967): 335–57.

Department of Commerce. *Historical Statistics of the United States: Colonial Times to 1970*. 2 vols. Washington, D.C.: GPO, 1975.

Doyle, Peter. "Economic Aspects of Advertising." *Economic Journal* 78.311 (1968): 570–602.

Edsel. Advertisement. *Automotive News*, Sept. 23, 1957. FCB scrapbook no. 658. Foote, Cone, and Belding. Scrapbooks. State Historical Society of Wisconsin. Madison.

———. Advertisement. *Cleveland Press*, Jan. 20, 1956, 46.

———. Advertisement. "Factory Newspapers." Oct. 6, 1957. FCB scrapbook no. 658. Foote, Cone, and Belding. Scrapbooks. State Historical Society of Wisconsin. Madison.

"Edsel Dies and Ford Regroups." *Business Week*, Nov. 28, 1959, 27–28.

"Edsel Gets a Frantic Push." *Business Week*, Dec. 7, 1957, 34+.

The Edsel Show. CBS. Oct. 13, 1957. Videotape. Film and Television Archive. University of California at Los Angeles.

"Edsel's Strip-Tease." *Printers' Ink*, Aug. 10, 1957, 39.

"Edsel—'Wagon Train.'" Unpublished analysis. Foote, Cone, and Belding. Sept. 19, 1957. Box 44. Fairfax M. Cone Papers. Joseph Regenstein Library. Department of Special Collections. University of Chicago Library. University of Chicago. Chicago.

Eldridge, Clarence E. "Advertising Effectiveness." *Journal of Marketing* 22.3 (1958): 241–51.

"Fairfax Cone Gives Inside [sic] on His Ad Agency Success." *Editor and Publisher,* July 27, 1957, 18+.

Flink, James J. *The Automobile Age.* Cambridge, Mass.: MIT Press, 1988.

Flint, Jerry. *The Dream Machine: The Golden Age of American Automobiles, 1946–1965.* New York: Quadrangle Books, 1976.

Foote, Cone, and Belding. Scrapbooks. State Historical Society of Wisconsin. Madison.

"Ford's Edsel Hogs the Headlines." *Printers' Ink,* Aug. 30, 1957, 16.

"Ford vs. GM: New Line Makes It a Car-for-Car Battle." *Business Week,* Nov. 24, 1956, 30–31.

Fox, Stephen. *The Mirror Makers: A History of American Advertising and Its Creators.* New York: William Morrow, 1984.

Galbraith, John Kenneth. *The Affluent Society.* Boston: Houghton Mifflin, 1958.

Goodman, Ralph. "Freud and the Hucksters." *The Nation,* Feb. 14, 1953, 143–45.

Halberstam, David. *The Reckoning.* New York: William Morrow, 1986.

Hayakawa, S. I. "Sexual Fantasy and the 1957 Car." *ETC* 14.3 (1957): 163–68.

———. "Why the Edsel Laid an Egg: Motivational Research vs. the Reality Principle." *ETC* 15.3 (1958): 217–21.

Hine, Thomas. *Populuxe.* New York: Knopf, 1987.

"History of the BASR Edsel Study: 'Project Y' Only." n.d. Box 6. Paul F. Lazarsfeld Papers. Rare Book and Manuscript Library. Columbia University Libraries. Columbia University. New York.

Horowitz, Daniel. *Vance Packard and American Social Criticism.* Chapel Hill: University of North Carolina Press, 1994.

Hughes, Lawrence M. "Ford Bets Quarter-Billion on New Middle-Price Car." *Sales Management* 77 (July–Aug. 1956): 28–33.

Huxley, Aldous. *Brave New World Revisited.* New York: Perennial Library, 1958.

Ikuta, Yasutoshi. *Cruise O Matic: Automobile Advertising of the 1950s.* San Francisco: Chronicle Books, 1988.

"Intense Fairfax Cone of FC&B." *Printers' Ink,* July 10, 1959, 62–68.

"It's Cone Two to One." *Newsweek,* Aug. 16, 1965, 68–70.

Jackson, Kenneth T. *Crabgrass Frontier: The Suburbanization of the United States.* New York: Oxford University Press, 1985.

Kaiser-Frazier. Advertisement. *Washington Post,* Apr. 14, 1948, 11.

Keats, John. *The Insolent Chariots.* Philadelphia: Lippincott, 1958.

Krafve, Richard E. "Investment in Tomorrow." Address. Portland, Oregon, Chamber of Commerce. Apr. 9, 1956. Copy in Box 38. Fairfax M. Cone Papers. Joseph Regenstein Library. Department of Special Collections. University of Chicago Library. University of Chicago. Chicago.

Larrabee, Eric. "Detroit's Great Debate: 'Where Did We Go Wrong?'" *Reporter*, Apr. 17, 1958, 16–21.

———. "The Edsel and How It Got That Way." *Harper's*, Sept. 1957, 67–73.

Lazarsfeld, Paul F. Papers. Rare Book and Manuscript Library. Columbia University Libraries. Columbia University. New York.

———. "Reflections on Business." *American Journal of Sociology* 65.1 (1959): 1–31.

Levitt, Theodore. "Marketing Myopia." *Harvard Business Review* 38 (July–Aug. 1960): 45–56.

"The Mammoth Mirror." *Time*, Oct. 12, 1962, 85+.

Marchand, Roland. *Advertising the American Dream: Making Way for Modernity, 1920–1940*. Berkeley: University of California Press, 1985.

Martineau, Pierre. *Motivation in Advertising*. New York: McGraw-Hill, 1957.

———. "The Public Image—Motivational Analysis for Long-Range Merchandising Strategy." In *The Frontiers of Marketing Thought and Science*. Ed. Frank M. Bass. Columbus: Modern Art, 1958. 11–21.

Marx, Groucho, and Hector Arce. *The Secret Word Is Groucho*. New York: G. P. Putnam's Sons, 1976.

May, Elaine Tyler. *Homeward Bound: American Families in the Cold War Era*. New York: Basic Books, 1988.

Mayer, Martin. Interview with Fairfax M. Cone. n.d. Box 19. Martin Mayer Papers. Rare Book and Manuscript Library. Columbia University Libraries. Columbia University. New York.

———. Interview with Clyde E. Rapp. n.d. Box 19. Martin Mayer Papers. Rare Book and Manuscript Library. Columbia University Libraries. Columbia University. New York.

———. Interview with Gayle Warnock. n.d. Box 19. Martin Mayer Papers. Rare Book and Manuscript Library. Columbia University Libraries. Columbia University. New York.

———. *Madison Avenue, U.S.A.* New York: Pocket Books, 1958.

———. Papers. Rare Book and Manuscript Library. Columbia University Libraries. Columbia University. New York.

"Measuring Edsel's TV Impact." *Broadcasting*, Nov. 18, 1957, 41+.

National Broadcasting Company. Papers. State Historical Society of Wisconsin. Madison.

————. "Television's 43,000,000 Showrooms: Special Report on the Edsel." June 1958. Copy in Box 194. National Broadcasting Company Papers. State Historical Society of Wisconsin. Madison.

Nevins, Allen, and Frank Ernest Hill. *Ford: Decline and Rebirth, 1933–62.* New York: Charles Scribner's Sons, 1963.

"The New Edsel." *Consumer Reports,* Jan. 1958, 30–33.

"The Newest Car." *Time,* Sept. 2, 1957, 64.

"A New Kind of Car Market." *Fortune,* Sept. 1953, 98–102+.

"Not to Be Opened until October '57." *Broadcasting,* Aug. 5, 1957, 31.

Ogilvy, David. *Confessions of an Advertising Man.* New York: Macmillan, 1963.

Packard, Vance. *The Hidden Persuaders.* New York: David McKay, 1957.

Packard. Advertisement. *Cleveland Press,* Jan. 20, 1956, 47.

Pope, Daniel. *The Making of Modern Advertising.* New York: Basic Books, 1983.

"The Rebirth of Ford." *Fortune,* May 1947, 82–88.

Reeves, Rosser. *Reality in Advertising.* New York: Knopf, 1962.

Reynolds, William H. "The Edsel Ten Years Later." *Business Horizons* 10 (Fall 1967): 39–46.

"The Role of the Edsel Line in Loyalty to Ford Products." *Business Week,* June 8, 1957, 61.

Schmidt, Leigh Eric. "The Commercialization of the Calendar: American Holidays and the Culture of Consumption, 1870–1920." *Journal of American History* 78.3 (1991): 887–916.

Seidl, Joan M. "Consumers' Choices: A Study of Household Furnishing, 1880–1920." *Minnesota History* 48.5 (1983): 183–97.

Seligman, Daniel. "The Amazing Advertising Business." *Fortune,* Sept. 1956, 107–10+.

Shapley, Deborah. *Promise and Power: The Life and Times of Robert McNamara.* Boston: Little, Brown, 1993.

Sloan, Alfred P., Jr. *My Years with General Motors.* New York: Macfadden, 1963.

Smith, Richard Austin. "TV: The Light That Failed." *Fortune,* Dec. 1958, 138–39+.

Springer, P. Untitled report on Edsel project. Aug. 1962. Box 18. Paul F. Lazarsfeld Papers. Rare Book and Manuscript Library. Columbia University Libraries. Columbia University. New York.

Starch Studies. Files of Daniel Starch and Staff. Mamaroneck, N.Y.

Statistical Abstract of the United States, 1974. Washington, D.C.: GPO, 1974.

St. Clair, John P. Letter to Fairfax M. Cone. n.d. Box 46. Fairfax M. Cone Papers. Joseph Regenstein Library. Department of Special Collections. University of Chicago Library. University of Chicago. Chicago.

"A Talk with Fax Cone." *Media Agencies Clients,* Apr. 15, 1963, 26. Copy in Box 10. Newton N. Minow Papers. State Historical Society of Wisconsin. Madison.

Tedlow, Richard S. *New and Improved: The Story of Mass Marketing in America.* New York: Basic Books, 1990.

Thurston, Ken. Memorandum to Fairfax M. Cone. Nov. 8, 1957. Box 44. Fairfax M. Cone Papers. Joseph Regenstein Library. Department of Special Collections. University of Chicago Library. University of Chicago. Chicago.

―――. Memorandum to Fairfax M. Cone. Nov. 14, 1957. Box 44. Fairfax M. Cone Papers. Joseph Regenstein Library. Department of Special Collections. University of Chicago Library. University of Chicago. Chicago.

Tobey, Ronald, Charles Wetherell, and Jay Brigham. "Moving Out and Settling In: Residential Mobility, Home Owning, and the Public Enframing of Citizenship, 1921–1950." *American Historical Review* 95.5 (1990): 1395–422.

"The $250 Million Flop." *Time,* Nov. 30, 1959, 87–88.

Vatter, Harold G. *The U.S. Economy in the 1950's.* New York: W. W. Norton, 1963.

Wallace, David. "Background and Objectives of the Edsel Panel Study." Apr. 1961. Box 16. Paul F. Lazarsfeld Papers. Rare Book and Manuscript Library. Columbia University Libraries. Columbia University. New York.

Warnock, C. Gayle. *The Edsel Affair.* Paradise Valley, Ariz.: Pro West, 1980.

White, B. S. Memorandum to Fairfax M. Cone. Dec. 10, 1957. Box 46. Fairfax M. Cone Papers. Joseph Regenstein Library. Department of Special Collections. University of Chicago Library. University of Chicago. Chicago.

White, Lawrence J. *The Automobile Industry since 1945.* Cambridge, Mass.: Harvard University Press, 1971.

Whiteside, Thomas. "The Man from Iron City." *New Yorker,* Sept. 27, 1969, 47–48+.

Wiebe, G. D. "Is It True What Williams Says about Motivation Research?" *Journal of Marketing* 22.4 (1958): 408–11.

Williams, Robert J. "Is It True What They Say about Motivation Research?" *Journal of Marketing* 22.2 (1957): 125–33.

Winston, C. D., Jr. Memorandum to Fairfax M. Cone. Oct. 18, 1957. Fairfax M. Cone Papers. Joseph Regenstein Library. Department of Special Collections. University of Chicago Library. University of Chicago. Chicago.

 POSTWAR WHITE GIRLS' DARK OTHERS

Adam Rebel's tale of interracial love, 1954.
(Courtesy of the Library of Congress)

MY interest in white girls growing up in the 1950s derives from a curiosity about the postwar roots of the social movements of the 1960s, particularly the women's liberation movement. This interest is undeniably autobiographical as well since I was a white girl growing up in the fifties. I want to make sense of how it was possible for young white middle-class women who had grown up in the apparently stultifying gender culture of domesticity to have become feminists. Not simply as individuals but as a generation, many white middle-class girls who were taught that their goals in life were to become wives and mothers ambivalently internalized these values and sometimes rejected them outright. More specifically for this essay, that rebellion's racial meanings interest me.

In the following pages I synthesize eclectic and assorted evidence of a racial dimension to white middle-class girls' explorations of, even resistance to, mainstream cultural gender expectations. This story is part of a long history, not confined to postwar America but constitutive of American culture as a whole, of white identification with and objectification and appropriation of black culture. In effect, it explores a small piece of the history of the centrality of black culture for whites (Morrison). It also entails an intersection of race and gender themes. The importance of black culture is particularly interesting after World War II given the invisibility of black people in the dominant culture; clearly, something was happening among white youth of the period. But public and collective acknowledgement of desire for African American culture came only in the sixties. In the fifties it was articulated and explored privately despite notable exceptions such as the widespread adulation by white female rock 'n' roll fans for Elvis Presley, a white man imitating a black man. Far from being an invisible border culture, African American culture was at the center of white American life and imagination, where youth, southern civil rights activists, and jazz and rhythm and blues artists were key players.

The story also brings together an eclectic array of sources. Much of the evidence is retrospective, characterized by understandings of the postwar period that were shaped by women's experiences in the sixties and seventies, especially the feminist movement. Personal, cultural, and political experiences changed much about white middle-class women, like myself, and the way we saw the world, including our own pasts. This essay, then, reveals as much about how women of my race, generation, and class have constructed the fifties through feminist lenses as it does about the "real" self-consciousness of girls at the time. I am doubtful, however, that there is a problematic rupture between these representations; the continuity of fifties girls' preoccupations both with issues the women's liberation movement raised and with adult concerns is striking.

This is an interpretation of the fifties, then, that employs a strategy of treating as primary sources writings, including fiction, of women who look back on that time from adult perspectives that are dramatically different from those of their adolescence. At the same time, several novels written during the fifties are considered as evidence of a racial thematic in the sexual imaginations and lives of white girls. Except for *Peyton Place*, I do not know how many people, and more pertinently white middle-class girls, read these novels. Nevertheless, I argue that these cultural products are suggestive of an important racial subplot in postwar white girls' lives. Together with rhythm and blues and retrospective accounts of racial desire, they suggest fertile, and unexamined, terrain.

THE POSTWAR CONTEXT

I begin by contextualizing the subject in postwar frames: prosperity, anti-communism, fear of aliens, whites' interest in blacks (who can be considered among the numerous aliens white Americans worried about), and rigid definitions of femininity. I then consider the attraction of darkness for postwar white girls.

Briefly, despite mass media representations of stability and calm, the fifties was a time of transformation and transition. The period is characterized by shifts from production to consumption, from saving to spending, from city to suburb, from blue- to white-collar employment, and from an adult to a youth culture. The fifties consolidated central elements of the society we live in today; what seemed remarkable then is commonplace now. Corporate expansion and consolidation, advertising and mass media, militarism, information technology, automobiles, higher education, mobility, and style are today recognized as central structuring elements in American society. For those of us born in the forties and after, it is often difficult to recognize the magnitude of postwar changes since we take so many for granted.

Furthermore, there was a pleased consensus that America was the richest and most successful nation on earth, a nation where all citizens could anticipate living the good life. That good life was defined by a well-equipped house in the suburbs, a new car or two, a good white-collar job for the husband, well-adjusted and successful children taken care of by a full-time wife and mother. Leisure time and consumer goods constituted its centerpieces; abundance was its context. White skin was a criterion for its attainment.

For many, including many in the working class, the standard of living spiraled upward. Numerous Americans were more comfortable and secure than their parents had ever been and than they could have imagined themselves during the depression; they anticipated more of everything: money, consumer goods, leisure, education for their children, satisfaction. In short, for many white families it was indeed a good time. The upbeat theme of the postwar period was prosperity. Social analysts, academics prominently among them, congratulated themselves on a nation capable of almost anything.

From a gender perspective, the period was a paradox. Women continued to enter the labor force, while other indicators—prosperity, expansion of higher education, democratization of the family, and increased emphasis on sexual pleasure for married women—also suggest growing autonomy and equality for women after the war. Yet the fifties was politically and culturally conservative, particularly regarding gender and family issues, making these difficult years for women. Just as conditions for their emancipation reached fruition, notions of women's place narrowed.

For young, white, middle-class women, the era offered liberating possibilities masked by restrictive norms. These women grew up and came of age in a time when new lives beckoned while prohibitions against exploring them multiplied. The narrowness of the gender norms in the midst of boom times, and potentially more independent lives than their mothers' lives, led to girls' exploration. Curiosity about race and sex flourished.

In *Deliberate Speed: The Origins of a Cultural Style in the American 1950s,* W. T. Lhamon Jr. asks, "Why was the mid-fifties the precise moment when black culture should have become an apt symbol for the way millions of nonblacks wanted to be in the world?" (39). Kobena Mercer explores the white "postwar democratic imaginary," "*What is it about whiteness that made them want to be black?*" (432). Lhamon answers, not entirely satisfactorily, with the suggestion that whites began to see themselves positioned like blacks, as victims and dupes of the status quo: "Mainstream citizens only started acknowledging their latent black values once they began sharing the doubts and began feeling the lack of control blacks had long known. Then many parts of the mainstream sped toward black culture deliberately" (39–40).

Numerous recent interpretations of postwar popular culture, not to mention earlier work like Nathan Huggins's *Harlem Renaissance,* suggest that black culture was appropriated by whites in the service of their own needs. I include my own work on white middle-class girls in the fifties here, although I believe commentators often formulate the story too crudely (*Young;* "The 'Other' Fifties"). To return to *Deliberate Speed,* for example, Lhamon, discussing the Beat writers, remarks that Allen Ginsberg's poem "Howl" articulated how the Beats "depended on black culture to fix their needs," that Kerouac and other Beats repeatedly "wish[ed] they were Negroes," and that they used the Negro, and jazz in particular, as metaphors for their needs (72). Black critics have remarked as well on Mailer's *The White Negro* and other appropriations (and imitations) of black culture in the postwar period, most notably of rhythm and blues, and most spectacularly in the phenomenon of Elvis Presley.[1]

Not evidently linked, but linked nonetheless, to what Mercer calls young whites' "dis-identification with the position ascribed to them in racist ideologies" (433) is the cold war campaign against communists outside and within American borders (and against those who were believed to have transgressed borders, like the Rosenbergs, by collaborating with foreign enemies). Political, class, sexual, and racial outsiders fueled white middle-class imaginations. Literal and figurative boundaries were important in the fifties, a period in which distinctions between "them" (foreigners and deviants) and "us" flourished. Such distinctions were also very much about "them," black people, and "us," white people, particularly as the struggle for integration intensified. Internationally, the borders of the United States became a central metaphor in the fears of invasion by communists. In popular culture, aliens often circumvented frontiers by invading from the sky. This was captured in the plethora of science fiction films in which alien pods and blobs invaded and destroyed everything we cherished. Andrew Ross suggests that George Kennan's containment thesis seems a more relevant prescription for domestic than for foreign policy. He points out that the policy anticipates "the Red Scare that generated much of the postwar hysteria about aliens, bugs, microbes, germs and other demonologies of the Other that pervaded the culture and politics of the fifties" (47).[2]

The political and sexual repressions, the Red Scare, and the feminine mystique (the title of Betty Friedan's 1963 best-selling book exposing the relentless cultural pressure on middle-class women to become mothers and housewives and the frustration that resulted) were often connected in the public mind. The teenage heroine of a novel about the period pithily states the connection: "The truth was I feared sperm almost as much as I feared Communism" (Alther 57). Fears of communism and female sexuality melded, leading to a policy of containment for both (Rogin chap. 8). Michael Rogin argues that American history is based on a paradoxical duality in which the alien and foreign "other," the disowned and negative American self, is split off and demonized as the enemy. He calls attention to the "creation of monsters as a continuing feature of American politics by the inflation, stigmatization, and dehumanization of political foes" and suggests that American identity has been constructed "against racial, ethnic, class and gender aliens."[3] "Aliens" of color were of great interest to young white people; curiosity, attraction, identification marked girls' explorations.

Kobena Mercer notes the postwar "appropriation and articulation of black signs as an iconic element in the cultural expression of oppositional identities within white society" (430) and refers to a "dis-affiliation from dominant self-images, a kind of strategic self-othering" (432). Race, according to Mercer, became a site for the making and remaking of meanings; whites were engaged in "transracial identifications" and a "collective dis-affiliation from the American Dream" (433). More specifically for our purposes, for girls this "collective dis-affiliation" is apparent in the countercultural influences such as rhythm and blues, rock 'n' roll, working-class style and behavior, the Beats, and unacceptable boyfriends, all of which were employed to subvert dominant notions of white femininity.[4]

It is helpful, then, to think of postwar culture as a culture of containment, with women and black people its objects (E. May). From this perspective, American politics and culture were structured by a defense of masculinity and whiteness; the changes that accompanied the formation of an advanced capitalist society were perceived and experienced as threats from those outside American borders and from those who had been excluded within those borders, women, blacks, homosexuals. White male fear of the loss of hegemony produced discourses about gender and race in which women and black people were to be kept separate and contained (despite or because of the 1954 Supreme Court decision outlawing segregation in public schools and the growing participation of white middle-class women in the labor force). Anxiety over the loss of separate spheres and the integration of the sexes and races was articulated in the celebration of whiteness and traditional domestic femininity, always linked in American culture. Black, female, and homosexual containment took place under cover of an ideological consensus constructed to stave off the claims of those who had been excluded.

FEMININE MYSTIQUE CRITIQUE

The centerpiece of the containment of women, the feminine mystique, was a white middle-class nuclear family with a full-time dependent mother and wife and a breadwinner, head-of-household father and husband. White middle-class girls were preparing for this future, a future represented as the ultimate fulfillment for women. But percolating underneath and around the dominant harmonious middle-class family image was a great ambivalence some white middle-class girls felt about this expectation (often expressed as ambivalence about their mothers). One girl recalls the suburbs where she grew up and "knew no white, middle-class woman with children who had a job or any major activities beyond the family. . . . During the day, it was safe, carefully limited, and female. The idea that this was all made me frantic" (Snitow 219). In another retrospective fictional account by an adolescent of the fifties, the teenage heroine tells her girlfriend that they have minds like men, which makes them, happily, different from most girls: "That was worst of all, I thought, a life where nothing ever happened. I looked around me and saw women ironing dresses and hanging out clothes and shopping for food and playing mah-jong on hot summer afternoons, and I knew I couldn't bear to spend my life that way, day after drab day, with nothing ever happening. The world of women seemed to me like a huge, airless prison where things didn't change. Inside it, I thought, I'd turn gray and small and shrivel up to nothing" (Rivers 23).

The life plan set out for these girls was unacceptable to them. Their society's expectations and, closer to home, those of their parents, did not coincide with their own yearnings. "I couldn't stand girls who wanted to get married and have engagement rings. I knew I was different, and I was glad," recalls one young woman who became a beatnik (Wallechinsky 398). Janis Joplin, in Port Arthur, Texas, during the fifties, expressed a more earthy version of these sentiments. She described herself as "just a plain overweight chick. I wanted something more than bowling alleys and drive-ins. I'd've fucked anything, taken anything. I did" (Dalton 147). Letters to Betty Friedan from this generation provide evidence of girls who felt trapped in the grip of the feminine mystique. They rebelled against the bourgeois respectability and timidity of middle-class conventions built around narrow domestic gender expectations.

Disaffected teenage girls longed for something significant in their lives. "Authentic," "genuine," "real" were words used repeatedly. The culture of the period did not provide them with a sense of being real. They felt that being sheltered, virginal, and female (the first two characteristics equivalent to the third for middle-class white girls) precluded the experience of meaningfulness. The sense that the culture was rife with hypocrisy, with everyone keeping up appearances (by keeping up feminine appearances) in one form or another, generated a yearning for genuine feeling. So did the smallness of their futures.

In *Minor Characters,* the chronicle of her infatuation with Jack Kerouac and the Beats, Joyce Johnson, who grew up in Manhattan and was a student at Barnard in the fifties, writes: "Moving back and forth between antithetical worlds separated by subway rides, I never fully was what I seemed or tried to be. I had the feeling I was playing hooky all the time, not from school, but from the person represented by my bland outward appearance" (41). She writes of herself, Jack Kerouac, and his book *On the Road,* "The 'looking for something' Jack had seen in me was the psychic hunger of my generation. Thousands were waiting for a prophet to liberate them from the cautious middle class lives they had been reared to inherit" (137). For Johnson, Greenwich Village and the Beats "seemed to promise . . . something I'd never tasted in my life as a child—something I told myself was Real Life. This was not the life my parents lived but one that was dramatic, unpredictable, possibly dangerous. Therefore *real,* infinitely more worth having" (29–30). A younger girl echoes Johnson's impatience: "Do you understand? We were hungry for experience, for some kind of real life, for some way to tap our energy" (Mulherin 637). And another young woman: "The basic awareness grew that truth, whatever it was, was something we had all our lives been protected from. Reality had been kept in quarantine so we could not become contaminated" (Maslow 174).

To find themselves, girls had to leave their families behind. Janis Joplin says of her adolescence:

I was raised in Texas, man and I was an artist and I had all these ideas and feelings that I'd pick up in books and my father would talk to me about it, and I'd make up poems and things. And, man, I was the only one I'd ever met. There weren't any others. There just wasn't *anybody,* man, in Port

Arthur. . . . I mean, in other words, in the Midwest you got no one to learn from because there's not a reader down the street you can sneak off and talk to. There's nobody. Nobody. I remember when I read that in *Time* magazine about Jack Kerouac, otherwise I'd've never known. I said "Wow!" and split. (Dalton 162)

Growing up in England, Sheila Rowbotham echoes her American sisters. She describes how her image of the ultimate man was based on a mixture of James Dean, Marlon Brando, and the Beats, a man of few words but intense emotions, expressed through a grunt or a flick of the eye, always on the run. Such a friendly psychopath, she hoped, would notice that under her "healthy exterior" she was "in fact suitably intense and fraught for the most extended and crazed imagination" (*Women's Consciousness* 16). Rowbotham describes herself: "I picked up an insistence on direct experience and feeling. I was inordinately suspicious of reason and analysis. Only moments of intense subjectivity seemed to have any honesty or authenticity." Above all she wanted "intense experiences where everyone spoke of intense subjects and *never* said 'pass the bread and butter'" ("Revolt in Roundhay" 208).

DARKNESS AND DIFFERENCE

Central to the story of the fifties is the powerful influence of black culture, seen most clearly in jazz and rhythm and blues, and the "deliberate speed" in Lhamon's terms, with which whites approached and adopted "black values." White rebels, and here I include the white girls who sought authenticity and experience, and artists, notably the Beats, were drawn to black people and black culture, often in racist and exploitative ways exemplified in Norman Mailer's *The White Negro*. But beyond Greenwich Village and bohemian enclaves, in the rest of America the denial of the black contribution to white culture thrived. It was especially obvious in the effort to whiten rhythm and blues for a white teen audience and in the general project of creating a white popular culture. The effort was, however, accompanied by its opposite, curiosity and enthusiasm on the part of young whites. George Lipsitz makes the point that working-class and black cultural forms became a model for middle-class youths in the fifties. The slang, dress, and music of black people, ethnic minorities, and delinquents had a great impact upon white middle-class youth, some of whom defected to that culture, many of whom wanted to ("Against the Wind" 99–132). Others, too, suggest that the youth culture "had as much to do with interracial affiliations and fantasies of sexual mobility as it had to do with the old containing walls of class divisions and groupings" (Ross 64) and that the cultural revolution that can be said to have begun in the fifties was in essence a "kind of 'trickle up' process of cultural diffusion" (McAdam 143).

Joyce Carol Oates's *Because It Is Bitter, and Because It Is My Heart,* is a novel, from a sociological perspective, about the destructiveness of black-white relations, of racism, in the fifties. The life of Iris, its adolescent white heroine, intersects with that of a black male teenager with whom she falls in love and whom she cannot forget. She is drawn to black people, especially black men. In a way the story is about the forbiddenness of that relationship, the intertwining of racial and sexual tensions, and about the cruel annihilation of hope and possibility black people experience at the hands of whites. But it is also the story of the girl's construction of black people and blackness, and thus of whiteness. At one point, anguished by her own lack of genuineness, of her own reality, she says, "If I was colored . . . I'd know who I was!" (93). Throughout this painful book, Iris is interested in black people, silently sides with them—one of her teachers notes that despite her appearance of goodness and her good grades, she sides with the outlaws—and can find little meaning or feeling in her white life. "*I love you, I would die for you,*" she says of the young black man she cannot give up (with whom she has no relationship), "*You are the only real thing in my life*" (291).

In Lynn Lauber's *White Girls,* another white teenage heroine explores her relationship to black people. Loretta is very interested in them. She likes driving through the black neighborhood. She identifies with black people and is acutely, even guiltily, aware (as were many young middle-class white people) that in her world they appear only in the shape of service workers—janitors, maids, garbagemen. She is warned against them. Describing her attraction to Luther, her secret black boyfriend in high school, Loretta wonders how she can explain how he has "captured her imagination": "Surely part of it was that he was forbidden, always over there—on the other side of the sidewalk, with his laughing, white-toothed friends and their lilting, jeering talk. Who could have resisted him?" (9). She feels real (a word that white middle-class girls used often in their characterization of what they were missing) with him and his family. Her own family is unhappy and repressed—her mother disappointed and bitter, her father silent and fearful, both of them thrifty and private. Loretta thinks that she has always "been drawn to the elegance of blacks" (10). She "thought that they must have been subjugated, like women, because they were so clearly superior. She did not know why or how she had come to think these things, but she thought them anyway, and didn't mind throwing away whatever reputation she had by being with Luther. Already she'd found a note taped on her locker that said 'Nigger Lover,' and there would probably be worse in the future" (156). How are we to understand this? It is significant that Luther and his mother are in their own ways also interested in Loretta.[5] It is not simply a one-way process. But if Loretta's love for Luther is too complicated to be described as racist, it cannot be denied that her appreciation of black people and of Luther is in many ways based on her deprivations. He has been constructed as a life raft, an alternative to her narrow-minded family and her restricted horizons.

In a third fiction example, Anne River Siddons's novel, *Heartbreak Hotel,* the blond homecoming queen, a sorority girl at a small Southern college, disengages from the racist and sexist culture in which she had been brought up, rejecting domesticity and virginity. She falls for a slightly older man, described as hairy and dark, who is committed to racial equality and integration. She sleeps with him although she will not have sex with her fraternity boyfriend, whom she is expected to marry. Maggie eventually finds her way to Greenwich Village, center of jazz and Beats, a common ending or fantasy for nonconformist girls. In both *White Girls* and *Heartbreak Hotel,* the white middle-class heroine gets pregnant by her dark lover. At the turning point in *Heartbreak Hotel* when Maggie consciously breaks from southern racist norms and—less directly—feminine gender expectations, she sees a black man apprehended by the police: "I had the funniest feeling when I stood there looking at the Negro. I felt like I was looking at myself" (165).

Here the racial component at the heart of the postwar cult of domestic and dependent femininity is obvious.[6] Domesticity as middle-class women's one true calling kept white women separate, and thus pure. The suburbs and towns in which girls were expected to live their lives were white and feminine; women and children were segregated from men and people of other races (except for the black maids employed by middle-class, even lower middle-class, families). Although she knew nothing about him and he was only an image to her, Maggie identified with the black man because she understood that she was, in her own way, trapped, her options narrowly defined and oppressive. "Throwing away" their reputations, these young, white, and privileged women opted for escape from the boundaries that confined their class, sex, and race. That escape involved a longing for a different, more "genuine" life and in some cases a genuine effort to listen and learn.[7]

I want briefly to draw attention to several fifties texts that corroborate racial themes found in retrospective fiction. Two pulp novels (paperback and costing twenty-five and thirty-five cents, respectively) entitled *Stable Boy* and *Houseboy* directly engage racial issues, specifically white female desire for black men. The front cover of *Stable Boy* announces, "Kitty Couldn't Stay Away From the Barn" (not surprising given her name) and "Their Lust Knew No Barrier, Their Passion No Wall"; unsurprisingly, in large letters on the back cover: "The Animal in Her. . ." (Rebel). The story is of frustrated white women (unable to contain the carnal in themselves) who cannot stay away from the black stable "boy"—one even dies in his arms at the moment of climax. *Houseboy* is about a young white girl who gives herself to the black "houseboy," is fascinated and "strangely excited" by him, but feels that her passion makes her so "bad" that she kills herself (Fairbank). Both take place in the South; the women are very white and are tormented or killed by their desire; the men too are destroyed. These pulp novels bluntly confront heterosexual racial themes that retrospective accounts explore more gingerly. The plots are about white women who cross feminine gender boundaries by acting on their sexual attraction to black men. Their ambivalence, fear, torture even, create the tension; the women know they are breaking taboos but cannot help themselves. They always pay (as do the men). In the retrospective material, they do not, at least not to the same extent. The women accept their own desire and act on it to free themselves from restricted feminine scripts.

And there is *Peyton Place* by Grace Metalious. The hardcover edition was a bestseller in its year of publication (1956) and moved into second place during the next year even as its paperback version was selling an unprecedented three million copies. It was filled with sex and sexual intrigue, notable in a decade celebrated for its situation comedies featuring twin beds for married couples and official chasteness. There are also clear racial subtexts in the book. The source of the town name is a secret because it was named after a black man, Samuel Peyton, an ex-slave who is very black, emigrates to and becomes a successful businessman in France, marries a white French-woman, returns to Beacon Hill in Boston, where he and his white wife cannot find a place to live despite his success, and eventually builds a castle, of which every piece is imported, in New Hampshire, close to the site of where the town grew.

The male sexual hero of the story has a Greek surname and is handsome in a "dark-skinned, black-haired, obviously sexual way." The sexually active girl, who comes from a terribly poor family and whose father rapes her, has "long, dark hair. . . . Her eyes, too, were dark and slightly slanted, and she had a naturally red, full-lipped mouth over well-shaped, startlingly white teeth. Her skin was clear and of a honey-tan shade" (31). Her teacher thinks that if she wore gold hoops in her ears, she would "look like everybody's idea of a perfect gypsy." (Observing the father sexually attacking his daughter, a terrified girlfriend almost faints and as she falls, "the world seemed to undulate over her and around her. She panted with the effort to fight off the blackness that threatened her from every side" [57].) One last example from the fifties plays on the same themes. In Philip Roth's *Goodbye Columbus*, the following dialogue takes place. When Neil telephones college student Brenda for a date, she asks, ""What do you look like?" "I'm . . . dark." "Are you a Negro?" "No" (6). Brenda is middle class and Neil working class, both are Jews. The mixture of working class and masculine darkness reappears, amalgamating different and dark. For WASPs, Jews were dark, exercising a fascination for Christian girls. Even in this story, Jewish Brenda is effectively a WASP, so successfully has she assimilated. In postwar America, assimilation entailed becoming white; Brenda has succeeded and Neil is trying, his difference undoubtedly one of his attractions.

In these fifties texts sexuality is coded as dark or black with white "good" women drawn to black or dark men, or sexual women represented as lower class and dark. Interracial sex, and almost all of it involves white or fair women with black or dark men, then, as in the retrospective fiction, is simultaneously forbidden and desired and almost always a disaster for all concerned (pregnancy, abortion, or death for the women and often death for the black men). In fact, it must always be kept in mind that black mens' lives were literally at risk in liaisons with white women, a fact that inevitably underscores the privileged ignorance of white girls' fantasies and behavior. In the midfifties, fourteen-year-old Emmett Till was brutally murdered in Mississippi for talking to a white woman in a store. Racist realities faced by black men, women, and children serve as a chilling check on any gendered construction of whiteness that utilizes blackness. And yet the fantasies and relationships occurred and are significant from every perspective. Despite, or because of, the danger for everyone, white girls' and women's desire for dark or different men is represented as powerful and as an escape from conventional (asexual) feminine scripts. All the texts portray white, privileged women desiring difference in the search for an authenticity they could not find at home.

ROCK 'N' ROLL

Rock 'n' roll was central to the white teenage experience of the fifties. Ironically, packed into the phrase "rock 'n' roll," which came to be a symbol of rebellious white youth, is the history of the attempt to tame the music from which it derived, rhythm and blues, for white audiences. The story of rock 'n' roll as the badge of postwar white teenage culture is another racial story, one in which black and minority music was adapted and transformed, some would say appropriated and distorted, by white record companies and white artists into music deemed suitable for white adolescents. Here is one more version of whiteness constructed against blackness, of a herculean effort to contain, transform, even erase black culture from white life. At the same time it is a story, as Eldridge Cleaver suggests, of the embrace of black music and dance by white youth: "The white youth of today have begun to react to the fact that the 'American Way of Life' is a fossil of history. What do they care if their old baldheaded and crew-cut elders don't dig their caveman mops? They couldn't care less about the old, stiffassed honkies who don't like their new dances: Frug, Monkey, Jerk, Swim, Watusi. All they know is that it feels good to swing to way-out body rhythms instead of dragassing across the dance floor like zombies to the dead beat of mind-smothered Mickey Mouse music" (38).[8]

From this perspective, rock 'n' roll was not simply a top-down enterprise but a contested cultural terrain (Lipsitz, "Against the Wind," "Land of a Thousand Dances"). Black culture, through music, was the dialectical accompaniment, the alter ego, to white middle-class teenage life. Like the early civil rights movement that penetrated the consciousness of white America with dramas of bus boycotts and school integration, rock 'n' roll was a racial subtext in postwar America. Its ambiguity—mainstream but potentially disruptive, part of the dating ritual but encoded with sexual and racial meaning—hints at the complexity of young whites' enthusiasm for rock 'n' roll. In the words of Gerald Early, "Those were the years . . . in which America recognized, and cringed before, the social reality . . . of a miscegenated culture in which, beneath the mask of inhuman and racial etiquette where everyone supposedly was as separated as the twin beds in the bedroom of nearly every 1950s TV sitcom, there lurked an unquenchable thirst for mixing. And the 'new' popular music helped to expose the false separation of America from itself, by revealing the culture's essential fusion all the more inescapably" (38).

Two accounts run parallel, then. One is the effort to create white "rock 'n' roll"—even the term itself was manufactured by a white man—from black rhythm and blues. The purpose of this, Nelson George argues, was to dull the racial identification and make young white consumers more comfortable by producing music that seemed more "universal." George refers to rock 'n' roll as "white negroism" (67). Sanitized white cover versions of black records were central to the effort to maintain segregation, protect white youth (specifically white girls) from the sexuality of black music, and make huge profits for white record companies and artists (who often stole from black artists). Elvis Presley was the centerpiece of this success.

The other account is of the unprecedented interest, obsession even, of white youth with black music, which could be heard on black radio stations and later on a few white radio stations, played by daring white disc jockeys like Alan Freed. Lipsitz suggests that privileged youths, "looking for alternatives to the secure but stifling and limited sexual roles and identities of middle class life" were able to "begin experimenting with cultural forms that challenged sexual repression, racial oppression, and class oppression" ("Land of a Thousand Dances" 280). Janis Joplin remembers, "They were playing that fifties crap on the radio. . . . It seemed so shallow, all oop-boop. It had nothing. Then I heard Leadbelly and it was like a flash. It *mattered* to me" (Dalton 38).

Two Jewish sisters who lived on Long Island secretly went to rock 'n' roll shows organized by Alan Freed in New York City and Brooklyn. "The groups came on in some of the most amazing clothing Susan and Lorraine had ever seen—shimmering outfits, parodic variations on the blandest of formal attire. The Isley Brothers were Christmasy in bright red tuxedo jackets with shiny green satin lapels" (Katz 93). The author describes how the girls "felt the show leave the stage and flow like lava into the audience. The music encircled the girls from Harbor Isle as young people danced in the aisles beside them. The show was a purity of sensation that resonated inside them, pulsing, expansive, full of joy. For Lorraine the enthralling spectacle was enhanced by the presence of black people—the *schvartzes* her grandmother and father talked about. They were all around her. She watched black girls sway to and fro and tried to move like they did" (93).

Despite or because of the racism to which Lorraine was exposed in her family (she had "heard her father refer to black people—the best, wisest, most spirited, and noblest varieties of Americans, in her opinion—as *schvartzes* and even 'Mau-Maus'"[127]), she is enthralled and begins to date "exotic boys in leather jackets," "dark-skinned boys with names like Julio and Jesus, who spoke accented English, wore crosses, were graceful and uninhibited on the dance floor, and seemed to regard Ellen and Lorraine with the same awe the girls had for them" (128).

Gerri Hirshey, a white woman whose life was changed by black music, writes, "When soul was at its peak in the 1960s, an entire generation was trying to get out of its post-Eisenhower self. Soul blew a huge hole in *Leave it to Beaver*-land. It was untrammeled, emotional, *different* music" (xii).[9] Such experiences reflected the need and ability of the younger generation to find alternatives to the limited options available in middle-class life. Elinor Lerner writes, "For teenagers like myself, there was a clear distinction between life before rock and roll and the world which had been changed by the music" (332). Rock 'n' roll, she says, created a sense of "alienation, rebellion, and affirmation/community." Rock challenged traditional and official American culture because of its multiracial influences and contacts. James Brown's father, much like Eldridge Cleaver, suggested that young white folks "run *away* from America" (Hirshey xvi), meaning white middle-class America. The cultural duality of the music, simultaneously mainstream and subversive, innocent and dangerous, meant the music was both safe and potentially disruptive, more effective perhaps because of its ambiguity. Rock 'n' roll offered "visions of independence, excitement, danger, as well as temptations and promises of a life which included models other than that of the nuclear family, white house and picket fence" (Lerner 332).

I want to conclude this section on rock 'n' roll by pointing to "color-coded" features of fifties youth culture that especially impacted on girls. Reproducing the adult culture's dualism of light and dark—with its profound and unacknowledged racial meanings—obvious in fair movie stars, models, and beauty standards, dissident white girls chose darkness. Sometimes they *were* dark because of their immigrant backgrounds (and many American girls spent a good deal of grooming time attempting to disguise or alter this aspect of themselves). The "good" approved teen culture was light and white, the threat black. Jazz and rhythm and blues were the subtext for the fifties drama of "good" versus "bad" teens; only whitened versions of black rhythm and blues were acceptable for white teenagers. It was a white time in America; success was represented in the burgeoning postwar media, on television, in advertising, and other forms of popular culture in white terms, assimilation only the most obvious example.[10] Black people were practically invisible in the mass media and when they were not their portrayal was racist, as in the *Amos 'n' Andy* and *Beulah* television shows. Michele Wallace, a black woman, writes, "I . . . grew up watching a television on which I rarely saw a black face, reading Archie and Veronica comics, Oz and Nancy Drew stories and *Seventeen* magazine, in which 'race' was unmentionable" (41). The assimilationist ideology proposed that America was a welcoming melting pot into which everyone could and would be incorporated. Erasing one's difference, assimilating, was a sign of Americanness. And assimilation meant passing for white. Beauty standards were white. So were models of the family and gender. Deviants and doubters, often dark or swarthy in representation, were outcasts.

It is far from irrelevant, then, that hoods and "bad girls" wore black—black leather jackets, boots, and belts—and in comparison were represented as darker than innocent, suburban teens. Dissenters, or aliens in the central cities, were, felt, or were imagined to be dark. Hoods were not the only ones in black; the Beats wore black. Black clothes signified you were Beat or bohemian: black turtleneck shirts, black stockings, black sunglasses. An adolescent remembers, "I just wanted to be a beatnik. I quit wearing pink and orange and always wore darker colors. I was one of the first people in Charleston to get dark stockings. I was in a shop once and a girl goes, 'Look, Mommy, that lady has white arms with black legs'" (Wallechinsky 397). And another young woman's attire is described: "For an evening of poetry or folk music in Greenwich Village Lorraine wore a black cotton turtleneck, black tights, and black flats, and carried a tiny black pocketbook" (Katz 147).

In Alix Kates Shulman's *Burning Questions,* the fictional heroine Zane recounts the tale of white middle-class girls in her school sponsoring a rummage sale in a poor black section of Babylon, Indiana. She recognizes that certain color combinations were forbidden in her town, considered breaches of taste called "loud, gauche, stupid, Italian, Jew," and yet the black people who filled the rummage sale "consistently violated these simple, basic rules. . . . Their very skin and hair violated Babylon minimal rules of decorum" (29). Here Zane points to a fact of American cultural life in the fifties. "Different was wrong. The wrong attitude, the wrong amount of hair . . . the wrong color skin . . . the wrong clothes from the wrong stores, made you unfit for Babylon" (15). Black clothes, even black skin, bright colors, long hair signaled deviance. A fixation on grooming, cleanliness, on controlling the body thrived. It helped to be fair in all ways: skin, hair, eyes, and disposition. Pastels and fair and light skin and hair were linked to being a "good" girl.

Darkness and difference were coupled in postwar America. For middle-class white girls, whose behavior and aspirations were so narrowly circumscribed, evenings like Lorraine's at the Brooklyn Paramount—hearing and dancing to rhythm and blues, the thrill she gets from the sensuality of the music, her attempts to dance like black girls dance, her identification with dark people and dates with dark boys—express the desire for a life that breaks with their own, for a genuineness they could claim as their own, even as it was not. Darkness, whether in the form of rock 'n' roll or boyfriends or fantasies, offered girls danger and models that broke with "the nuclear family, white house and picket fence" (Lerner 332).

CONCLUSION

I have been asking whether black people figured in white girls' imaginations in ways that facilitated, imagined or real, escape from white middle-class expectations.[11] Given that most middle-class white teenagers had little opportunity to know black people, it seems likely that they, girls included, were not learning from black culture, considering it from its own perspectives, according it a subjectivity separate from their perceptions. Some white girls used the sensibilities of darkness as a way out of boredom and restlessness. They were drawn to black music and difference—delinquent and dark boyfriends, working-class, Beat, and bohemian lovers, jazz and rock 'n' roll—because they were inappropriate and forbidden, because they seemed "genuine" and "real." Oates's heroine is so preoccupied with black people that "glancing down at the whiteness of her skin she feels a sensation of vertigo, a physical sickness, as if this whiteness were the outward symptom of her spirit's etiolation, a profound and unspeakable not-thereness" (155). Iris may be an extreme case but "otherness" was of interest to young white people and racial difference was part of the "other fifties" many of them sought. By projecting their own needs and desires onto those who were different, white youth often remained as ignorant and in many cases as racist as they were when they began to be interested. But was the relationship simply voyeuristic and objectifying?

I do not believe so. The attraction of blacks and black culture for whites also took black culture into account; young white girls were genuinely interested. A process was underway that led to the social movements and culture of the sixties. Young people in the fifties were learning about white culture by appreciating black culture; if they were racist in their ignorance, they were also drawn respectfully, and rebelliously, articulating "black signs as an iconic element in the cultural expression of oppositional identities within white society" (Mercer 432). Ironically girls' explorations often reproduced their feminine positioning as subordinates and sex objects, although they positioned dark male "others" similarly. But they were simultaneously active agents in the rejection of racial and gendered meanings of a femininity meant to confine them. While their desire could be described as the objectification and use of an "other" culture, it encompassed more than that, its opposite in fact, an appreciation and empathy that went public only in the next decade.

In the midst of the great postwar celebration of white suburban domesticity and wholesomeness, of virginal white teenagers at the sock hop, white girls began to explore differences that were supposed to be invisible and found meaning that was absent in the paths set out for them. Blackness, darkness, exerted the pull it did because the denial of difference was so central to conceptions of whiteness. From this perspective, whiteness was a color defined by blackness or, rather, its denial. These young women sensed the deprivations that segregation of all kinds imposed, recognizing that they suffered from a whiteness so hegemonic that most white people with whom they came in contact never seemed to notice it.

If whiteness in postwar American culture is framed as a question, an issue to be examined rather than assumed, then the invisibility of difference on which it was premised was interrogated by white girls. Their interest in rock 'n' roll, in black or dark boyfriends, in vaguely androgynous men, and in Beat culture and Beat men (white outsiders who were themselves drawn to black culture), was an acknowledgment of black culture and black life and provided them with alternative visions of masculinity and femininity, of identity, and of heterosexuality.

The appeal that subcultures and people marginal, sometimes oppositional, to mainstream white culture held for postwar white girls raises two kinds of questions. The first concerns the exoticization of blacks by whites, specifically, the ways in which, in W. T. Lhamon's words with which I began, whites "depended on black culture to fix their needs," or more charitably perhaps, in Kobena Mercer's words, about how and why the "collective dis-affiliation from the American Dream" took shape as "transracial identifications" and "strategic self-othering." The second links the appeal and its exploration as a prefiguring of white feminine rebellion in the next decade. In that moment of white imitation, identification, appropriation, objectification, and longing lies a key to the tightly linked racial and gender meanings that lie at the heart of American culture.

NOTES

I would like to thank Joel Foreman for encouragement, information, and editorial advice.

1   The project of considering whiteness in relation to blackness, and it *was* black that was the "other" racial group in postwar America, is not innocent. It threatens to recreate the invisibility of black people by constructing black people as phantoms of whites' imaginations. In a review of Gunnar Myrdal's *An American Dilemma* (1944), a book that shaped postwar academic debates about race in America, the novelist Ralph Ellison remarked that black people often seem to exist in the "nightmarish fantasy of the white American mind," thereby denying reality to African Americans. Ellison articulates the dangers a project such as this skirts: construction of black people as phantoms of whites' imaginations, exoticizing and stereotyping them as the "other" that will save whites (82). It jeopar-

dizes whites' ability to acknowledge black people's existence, subjectivity, and contribution on blacks' own terms. And, finally, considering whiteness in relation to blackness can erase black people's experience of racism. Thus a project that problematizes whiteness requires simultaneous and vigilant recognition of the reality of black people's lives. See Frankenberg for further discussion.

2   See Guerrero chap. 2, especially p. 68, for a discussion of racial coding of monsters in Hollywood films.

3   Rogin xiii, xiv. See Patterson for an articulation of the argument that American democracy was and is based on slavery and racism.

4   White articulation of meaning, and resistance, in racial terms is central to any explanation of American life. In individual and collective change there is a long history of white "transracial identifications" in which postwar white girls are only a chapter. Meaning in right-wing terms is as saturated with race, perhaps even more, by the self-conscious defense of white power through racial oppression.

5   Young whites and blacks were interested in each other. This appears to be an off-limits area of study in postwar and sixties America. For example, mutual interracial heterosexual attraction caused serious problems in the youthful civil rights movement of the early sixties, particularly in the Student Non-Violent Coordinating Committee (SNCC). The difficult feelings these relationships generated influenced the development of the Black Power movement and of separate white and black feminisms, a topic I am currently studying.

6   See Lanser for a fascinating and provocative racial interpretation of Charlotte Perkins Gilman's essay "The Yellow Wallpaper" that bears on my points here. She asks, "Is the wallpaper, then, the political unconscious of a culture in which an Aryan woman's madness, desire, and anger, repressed by the imperatives of 'reason,' 'duty' . . . and 'proper self-control' . . . , are projected onto the 'yellow' woman who is, however, also feared alien?" (429). Lanser's interpretation of the story suggests that the constricted meaning of white femininity for an early twentieth century upper middle-class white woman in a racist society shaped her images of escape in racial (and racist) terms. Again, the subjectivity of the "yellow other" is invisible. See also Torgovnick and Hawthorne.

7   See Pratt, who criticizes herself for identification with victims and her use of them to mourn for herself: "Then I understood that I was using Black people to weep for me, to express *my* sorrow at my responsibility, and that of my people, for their oppression: and I was mourning because I felt they had something I didn't, a closeness, a hope, that I and my folks had lost because we had tried to shut other people out of our hearts and lives" (40).

8   Cleaver was writing about the sixties, but the trend he described began in the fifties.

9   For more on the impact of black music on white girls, see Douglas, especially
    chap. 4, "Why the Shirelles Mattered."

10 Marge Piercy writes that these years "represented the last gasp of WASP histo-
    ry as history: the history of the affluent white male Western European and lat-
    terly American presence in the world given to us as the history of humankind;
    Western European culture of the better-off sold as Culture." She continues, "Even
    the lawns were Christian" (114).

11 The evidence suggests it was black men who occupied white girls' imaginations
    but in fact there is very little "evidence" about any of this and even less about
    how black women figured in white girls' imaginations. At a time when white
    middle-class suburban women were baking casseroles and chauffeuring their
    daughters to ballet lessons and the daughters were preoccupied with popular-
    ity and appearance, and when there were few inspiring white female political
    figures, it was impossible not to register the black girls and women in the news
    who were courageous political heroines. The images, for example, of Rosa Parks
    and the maids and babysitters walking to work rather than taking segregated
    buses during the long Montgomery bus boycott, teenage girls integrating Lit-
    tle Rock High School, and Autherine Lucy integrating and getting expelled from
    the University of Alabama provided striking contrasts to middle-class white
    women's concerns. So did rhythm and blues artists.

WORKS CONSULTED

Alther, Lisa. *Kinflicks*. New York: New American Library, 1975.

Babcox, Deborah, and Madeline Belkin, eds. *Liberation Now!: Writings from the
    Women's Liberation Movement*. New York: Dell, 1971.

Beal, Frances M. "Double Jeopardy: To Be Black and Female." In *Liberation Now!:
    Writings from the Women's Liberation Movement*. Ed. Deborah Babcox and Made-
    line Belkin. New York: Dell, 1971. 185–97.

Breines, Wini. "The 'Other' Fifties: Beats and Bad Girls." In *Not June Cleaver: Wom-
    en and Gender in Postwar America, 1945–1960*. Ed. Joanne Meyerowitz. Philadel-
    phia: Temple University Press, 1994. 382–408.

———. *Young, White, and Miserable: Growing Up Female in the Fifties*. Boston: Bea-
    con, 1992.

Cleaver, Eldridge. *Soul on Ice*. New York: Dell, 1968.

Dalton, David. *Piece of My Heart: The Life, Times, and Legend of Janis Joplin*. New
    York: St. Martin's Press, 1985.

Douglas, Susan J. *Where the Girls Are: Growing Up Female with the Mass Media*. New
    York: Times Books, 1994.

Early, Gerald. "One Nation under a Groove." *New Republic,* July 15–22, 1991, 30–41.

Ellison, Ralph. "*An American Dilemma:* A Review." In *The Death of White Sociology.* Ed. Joyce A. Ladner. New York: Random House, 1973. 81–95.

Fairbank, Walton. *Houseboy.* New York: Pyramid Books, 1953.

Ferguson, Russell, Martha Gever, Trinh T. Minh-ha, and Cornel West, eds. *Out There: Marginalization and Contemporary Cultures.* Cambridge: MIT Press, 1990.

Frankenberg, Ruth. *White Women: Race Matters.* Minneapolis: University of Minnesota Press, 1993.

George, Nelson. *The Death of Rhythm and Blues.* New York: Pantheon Books, 1988.

Goodman, Mitchell, ed. *The Movement toward a New America.* Philadelphia: Pilgrim Press, 1970.

Grossberg, Lawrence, Cary Nelson, and Paula Treichler, eds. *Cultural Studies.* New York: Routledge, 1992.

Guerrero, Ed. *Framing Blackness: The African-American Image in Film.* Philadelphia: Temple University Press, 1993.

Hawthorne, Susan. "The Politics of the Exotic: The Paradox of Cultural Voyeurism." *NWSA Journal* 1.4 (Summer 1989): 617–29.

Heron, Liz. *Truth, Dare, or Promise: Girls Growing Up in the Fifties.* London: Virago, 1985.

Hirsch, Marianne, and Evelyn Fox Keller, eds. *Conflicts in Feminism.* New York: Routledge, 1990.

Hirshey, Gerri. *Nowhere to Run: The Story of Soul Music.* New York: Penguin Books, 1984.

Huggins, Nathan Irvin. *Harlem Renaissance.* New York: Oxford University Press, 1971.

Johnson, Joyce. *Minor Characters.* Boston: Houghton Mifflin, 1983.

Katz, Donald. *Home Fires: An Intimate Portrait of One Middle-Class Family in Postwar America.* New York: HarperCollins, 1992.

Ladner, Joyce A. *The Death of White Sociology.* New York: Random House, 1973.

Lanser, Susan S. "Feminist Criticism, 'The Yellow Wallpaper,' and the Politics of Color in America." *Feminist Studies* 15.3 (Fall 1989): 415–41.

Lauber, Lynn. *White Girls.* New York: W. W. Norton, 1990.

Lerner, Elinor. "Response to Robin Roberts." *NWSA Journal* 2.2 (Spring 1990): 329–37.

Lhamon, W. T., Jr. *Deliberate Speed: The Origins of a Cultural Style in the American 1950s.* Washington, D.C.: Smithsonian Institution Press, 1990.

Lipsitz, George. "Against the Wind: Dialogic Aspects of Rock and Roll." *Time Passages: Collective Memory and American Popular Culture.* Minneapolis: University of Minnesota Press, 1990. 99–132.

————. "Land of a Thousand Dances: Youth, Minorities, and the Rise of Rock and Roll. In *Recasting America: Culture and Politics in the Age of Cold War*. Ed. Lary May. Chicago: University of Chicago Press, 1989. 267–84.

Maslow, Ellen. "Storybook Lives: Growing Up Middle Class." In *Liberation Now!: Writings from the Women's Liberation Movement*. Ed. Deborah Babcox and Madeline Belkin. New York: Dell, 1971. 171–76.

May, Elaine Tyler. *Homeward Bound: American Families in the Cold War Era*. New York: Basic Books, 1987.

May, Lary, ed. *Recasting America: Culture and Politics in the Age of the Cold War*. Chicago: University of Chicago Press, 1989.

McAdam, Doug. *Freedom Summer*. New York: Oxford University Press, 1988.

Mercer, Kobena. "'1968': Periodizing Politics and Identity." In *Cultural Studies*. Ed. Lawrence Grossberg, Cary Nelson, and Paula Treichler. New York: Routledge, 1992. 424–49.

Metalious, Grace. *Peyton Place*. New York: Julian Messner, 1956.

Morrison, Toni. *Playing in the Dark: Whiteness in the Literary Imagination*. Cambridge, Mass.: Harvard University Press, 1992.

Mulherin, Kathy. "Memories of a Latter-Day Catholic Girlhood." In *The Movement toward a New America*. Ed. Mitchell Goodman. Philadelphia: Pilgrim Press, 1970. 634–41.

Oates, Joyce Carol. *Because It Is Bitter, and Because It Is My Heart*. New York: Plume Books, 1991.

Patterson, Orlando. "Toward a Study of Black America." *Dissent* 36 (Fall 1989): 476–86.

Piercy, Marge. "Through the Cracks: Growing Up in the Fifties." *Parti-Colored Blocks for a Quilt*. Ann Arbor: University of Michigan Press, 1982. 113–28.

Pratt, Minnie Bruce. "Identity: Skin Blood Heart." In *Yours in Struggle: Three Feminist Perspectives on Anti-Semitism and Racism* by Elly Bulkin, Minnie Bruce Pratt, and Barbara Smith. Ithaca, N.Y.: Firebrand Books, 1984. 9–63.

Rebel, Adam. *Stable Boy*. New York: Beacon, 1954.

Rich, Adrienne. "Disloyal to Civilization: Feminism, Racism, and Gynephobia." *Lies, Secrets, and Silences*. New York: W. W. Norton, 1979. 275–310.

Rivers, Caryl. *Virgins*. New York: Pocket Books, 1984.

Rogin, Michael. *Ronald Reagan: The Movie*. Berkeley: University of California Press, 1987.

Ross, Andrew. "Containing Culture in the Cold War." *No Respect: Intellectuals and Popular Culture*. New York: Routledge, 1989. 42–64.

Roth, Philip. *Goodbye Columbus*. New York: Bantam Books, 1959.

Rowbotham, Sheila. "Revolt in Roundhay." In *Truth, Dare, or Promise*. Ed. Liz Heron. London: Virago, 1985. 189–211.

———. *Women's Consciousness, Man's World*. Baltimore: Penguin Books, 1973.

Shulman, Alix Kates. *Burning Questions*. New York: Alfred A. Knopf, 1978.

Siddons, Anne River. *Heartbreak Hotel*. New York: Ballantine Books, 1976.

Smith, Lillian. *Killers of the Dream*. New York: W. W. Norton, 1978.

Smith, Valerie. "Split Affinities: The Case of Interracial Rape." In *Conflicts in Feminism*. Ed. Marianne Hirsch and Evelyn Fox Keller. New York: Routledge, 1990. 271–87.

Snitow, Anne. "Pages from a Gender Diary: Basic Divisions in Feminism." *Dissent* 36 (Spring 1989): 205–24.

Spelman, Elizabeth V. *Inessential Woman: Problems of Exclusion in Feminist Thought*. Boston: Beacon, 1988.

Torgovnick, Marianna. *Gone Primitive: Savage Intellects, Modern Lives*. Chicago: University of Chicago Press, 1990.

Wallace, Michele. "Modernism, Postmodernism, and the Problem of the Visual in Afro-American Culture." In *Out There: Marginalization and Contemporary Cultures*. Ed. Russell Ferguson, Martha Gever, Trinh T. Minh-ha, and Cornel West. Cambridge, Mass.: MIT Press, 1990. 39–57.

Wallechinsky, David. *Class Reunion '65*. New York: Penguin Books, 1986.

West, Cornell. "The New Cultural Politics of Difference." *October* 53 (Summer 1989): 93–109.

Joel Foreman ━━━

Three

MAU MAU'S AMERICAN CAREER, 1952–57

L IKE "megaton," "Sputnik," and
"black power," "Mau Mau" was
one of the notable signifiers circu-
lating internationally in the 1950s. Its
first documented appearance in the
1948 records of the British East African
police (Rosberg 331) was unremarkable at
the time, foretelling neither the postcolonial future nor the explosion of American
interest when news agencies first reported
the 1952 Mau Mau revolt against white rule
in Kenya. Carried along first by news reportage, then by a best-selling novel, and finally by a Hollywood film, Mau Mau caught and
held "the imagination of the American public" (Weisbord 185) for five years.[1]

Because Mau Mau was a completely new
signifier, postwar Americans—who knew very
little about Africa[2]—made sense of it by pro-

Hollywood's version of the 1952 Mau Mau
rebellion in British East Africa.
(Courtesy of the Library of Congress)

78

jecting onto it homegrown fears and desires. Consequently, two general tendencies, each with its own distinct ideology, shaped the accounts of Mau Mau. One, manifesting racist fears and resistance, signified a resurgence of deplorable African savagery; the other, the desire for equal treatment and freedom from colonial authority, signified an emancipatory political movement grounded in legitimate grievances. The former signification was useful to proponents of white supremacy who wished to maintain the unifying force of a colonial hegemony. It emphasized the tropology of terror and fixed public attention upon images of assassination, primitive oath takings, and blood rituals; assaults by trusted servants upon their Euro-settler employers; mutilated livestock; and bodies of victims—both black and white—hacked by Mau Mau pangas (a machete-like agricultural tool). In contrast, the emancipationist account explained the Kenya conflict in terms of problematic colonial practices:[3] land redistribution policies that enabled a small group of Euro-settlers to control twelve thousand square miles of productive land while over a million Kikuyu owned only two thousand; an apartheid government that produced a "reformed" legislative council of five blacks (representing 5 million Africans) and fourteen whites (representing forty thousand Euro-settlers); and episodic political repression that included the 1940 banning of the Kikuyu Central Association and the 1949 quelling, without redress of grievances, of a massive general strike.

The correctness of these divergent representations is not so much at issue here as is the history of the struggle to define the Mau Mau signifier in America.[4] That history is inscribed in texts circa 1952–57, and in what follows I draw from that corpus three textual instances of contention and appropriation. In the first, the ideological forces of 1952 faced off in the arena shared by the weekly magazines *Time* and *The Nation*. In the second, Mau Mau migrated into the domain of fiction when Robert Ruark, a well-known Scripps-Howard writer of five weekly columns for almost two hundred newspapers (Moley 96), authored the best-selling 1955 novel *Something of Value*. In the third, Hollywood acquired the screen rights to the story, which Richard Brooks, notable for his success with *Blackboard Jungle* (1955), revised for a 1957 film version.

DURING the first week of October 1952 the Mau Mau signifier made its public debut in a series of ill-prepared assaults that killed one white settler and resulted in the call for a military state of emergency. On October 20 *Time* magazine registered this event in "Kenya: SOS." Its lead paragraph is a classic instance of the colonial effect on cross-cultural representation: "In Kenya Colony's dusty highland capital of Nairobi (pop. 120,000), a quarter-mile-long queue of jumpy white settlers lined up last week to buy rifles and shotguns. White vigilantes patrolled their lush coffee plantations; two battalions of the King's African Rifles, supported by armored cars, deployed for action. The cause of all the commotion was the Mau Mau (rhymes with bow-wow), an African secret society whose savage warriors have pledged themselves in blood to drive the white man out of Africa" (40). Given shape within the prevailing colonial discourse, the *Time* story typifies the way the triumvirate of American mass weeklies—*Time, Newsweek,* and *Life*—represented the Mau Mau during the years of the emergency. The story's governing trope attributes the cause of the African-European conflict to only one of its two antagonists. Organized in this way the narrative encourages its readers to identify with the industrious white settlers who had resorted to the use of firearms to protect the hard-won gains of their labor. The orderly way in which they lined up, the "lush" abundance of their plantations, the disciplined reaction implied by the synecdochal "rifles": all these details represent a just, defensive response to an unreasoned force located at the other end of an opposition. Those who had created the problem, characterized as a "commotion" and thus seemingly without serious political consequence, were primitive[5] Africans who had succumbed to the brutal impulses issuing from the heart of their darkness. They, the Mau Mau, were both childishly insignificant, as was suggested by the derisory equation of the Mau Mau and "bow-wow,"[6] and to be feared, because of their atavistic use of blood pledges. The combination of immaturity and terror situated the Mau Mau at the negative pole of the savage/civilized binary opposition, one that the U.S. public had seen acted out frequently in filmic encounters between whites and peoples of color in the American West.[7] The generic elements of the western—a wilderness, the bloodthirsty primitives, the irrational slaughter of innocents, the noble white defenders of law and order—are deployed in the account of the Mau Mau: Africa was like the frontier, the Mau Mau were like "Indians," the Kenyan Euro-settlers were like cowboys and sodbusters. Much of this is made explicit by a *Time* story titled "Kenya: Frontier War." It opens as follows: "Kenya last week was like Dakota Territory in the days of Sitting

Bull" (35). Several years later, this comparison would also occur to Bosley Crowther, whose review notes that the Richard Brooks version of *Value* "has the character of a film about Indians and white settlers" (24). Both examples demonstrate the way Americans readers saw Mau Mau through preexisting categories and drew the signifier within a network of specifically American meanings.

The resulting representation of Mau Mau had specific ideological effects. First, it simplified and dramatized a complex sociopolitical phenomenon, thereby exciting readers without motivating change. Second, it confirmed existing stereotypes about African behavioral patterns, thereby avoiding a fresh and serious examination of the racial and economic grievances behind the East African insurrection. Third, it promoted American readers' identification with the British and precluded a similar involvement with the Mau Mau, thereby legitimating the former's view of the emergency and completely excluding the latter's from consideration.

In the four years following the appearance of "Kenya: SOS," *Time* published thirty-one additional articles on the Mau Mau, few of which diverged significantly from the ideological routine set at the inauguration of the series. Updating the specific facts and personalities of the moment, the typical article includes a description of a Mau Mau atrocity (usually a decapitation of an innocent victim), details of various "primitive" behaviors (e.g., the wearing of bracelets of flesh stripped from tortured victims), body counts, news of British triumphs, and the quoted comments of white settlers or British functionaries. The last is most notable because, as we will see, the absence of the voice of the Mau Mau is indicative of a hermetic circle,[8] a virtually impermeable boundary that prevented the participation of the Mau Mau in the construction of their American representations[9] and facilitated the process by which they were demonized. They were, to all intents and purposes, an enemy, a status that made it virtually impossible for their voices to be heard by the correspondents for mainstream American publications such as *Time*.

The policy whose reciprocal logic deprived the Mau Mau of a voice in the construction of its American representations and legitimated the British position is indicative of the systematic bias operating throughout the *Time* series. Whereas the Mau Mau are described as savages, terrorists, practitioners of mumbo-jumbo, thugs, Kukes, blood drinkers, butchers, pagans, and screaming tribesmen, the British are pictured as valiant, famed, soldierly, successful, brave, able, and innocent. Even the descriptions of killing are not exempt from this discrepancy. The British conduct military operations; the Mau Mau indulge in terrorism. Moreover, the descriptions of British kills efface the details of bodily damage and emphasize martial skill and technological prowess. In contrast, the accounts of Mau Mau violence commodify the terrors of mutilation and dismemberment. Thus one typical report focuses on a band of naked Mau Mau women who decapitated a man and showed his head to "his widow before slowly strangling her. . . . Then they hacked her four children to pieces" ("Slaughter in Kenya" 30). In such reports, the machete-like blade (the panga) that served as agricultural tool and weapon is invested with a sense of fascinated horror that is wholly contrary to the treatment of British weapons. In an article that singles out a British soldier who "bayoneted eight Mau Mau," the point seems to be that death meted out with European weapons in a just cause is praiseworthy. "'I was lucky,' said the soldier. 'I happened to be well placed'" ("The Darkening War" 38).[10]

What is repressed and marginalized in *Time* is amplified and brought to center stage in *The Nation,* a small alternative publication with a readership of 40,000 that challenged the antagonistic modes of colonial thought and presented a case for African self-determination. Whereas *Time* deployed strategies that encouraged its readers' identification with the white residents of Kenya, *The Nation* attempted to legitimate the political desires of the Mau Mau. Whereas *Time* reinforced the fear of the uncontrolled primitive and the related fear of the devastation and appropriation of developed property, *The Nation* addressed another set of concerns: equal rights and opportunities, justice and dignity, the importance of the vote, the fear of state repression by the bureaucracies of the Right, and the desire for a social program that would improve education, provide wage assurances and better housing, eliminate discrimination, and institute local control of the land and of government. In other words, *The Nation*'s representation of the Mau Mau was a projection of the publication's own humanitarian concerns, concerns it was believed could be addressed by the institution of a social program that protected, expanded, and extended middle-class and labor rights.[11]

An examination of the ten Mau Mau articles published by *The Nation* between November 1952 and July 1956 may well start by considering what, in relation to *Time*'s reportage, is a most notable omission: not a single article contains a decapitation, a hacking, or any description whatsoever of Mau Mau

"savagery." That this editorial policy was fashioned in opposition to the practices of the popular press is confirmed by a complaint that "the failure of the
press to give adequate coverage to the fifty-eight day trial of [Mau Mau leader
Jomo] Kenyatta—one of the major political trials of recent years—was in glar-
ing contrast to the space it has devoted to reports of the terror." As an alternative, *The Nation* provides a critical treatment suited more to a "social crisis"
("First Korea, Now Kenya" 337–38)[12] than to an outbreak of unmotivated primitivism. Issuing from an anticolonial posture, the critique stresses social and
economic analysis of the insurrection's underlying causes, focuses on the abrogation and abuse of human rights, and humanizes the Kikuyu. Moreover, the
credentials of the writers who produce this critique indicate significant involvements with indigenous African interests: George W. Shepard Jr., who authored
the first and last articles in the series, was "general manager of the Federation
of Uganda African Farmers" ("Kenya: African Storm Signal" 407); St. Clair Drake
"shared an apartment with Mbiyu Koinange, London representative of the
Kenyan African Union" ("The Terror That Walks by Day" 490); Elizabeth E.
Hoyt "spent some time among the Kikuyu tribe in 1951 while . . . on a Ful-
bright" ("Dark Road in Kenya" 550); and Keith Irvine "was the first white student to attend Achimota College on the Gold Coast" ("New Crisis in Kenya:
Adventure in Imperialism" 74). Given these involvements and the editorial
dispositions of *The Nation,* it is not surprising that the Mau Mau articles are
in toto a plea for African self-determination.

The two articles that close the series are quite explicit about this point.
In "New Crisis in Kenya: Adventure in Imperialism," Keith Irvine critiques
the East African Royal Commission Report (a proposal that would unify Kenya, Tanganyika, and Uganda) as a moment in "the new chapter now opening
in the history of British East African colonialism" (74). Irvine argues that the
report's recommendations would consolidate white financial control of Kenya, further deprive the Africans of their claim to the land, reduce them to a
"wage-earning basis," and destroy tribal and religious traditions. His conclusion: "What is envisaged is not the indigenous development of a new society so much as the imposition of an alien form of life from above" (75). George
Shepherd's "The End of the Mau Mau Rebellion" presents similar concerns.
Published late in 1956 when the Mau Mau were no longer a threat, the article provides a summary view of the emergency and notes with considerable
satisfaction that "British officials are busy instituting reforms which they were

unwilling to give prior to the outbreak of violence" (8). Among the reformers is Michael Blundell, who is identified as a member of "a more or less liberal group that favors multi-racial government." As an alternative to the "apartheid" proposed by another group of settlers, Blundell's proposed multiracial government strikes Shepherd as a positive, though problematic, step toward the goal of African independence. The reason to worry about the settler politician, Shepherd writes, is that he has "said more than once that the time would come when the Africans would have to be told 'so far and no further.'" Shepherd is heartened nonetheless by events and believes that the "corner has been turned" and the stage set for "Africans to gain power and justice through political means" (9).

In keeping with what amounts to a policy of support for African self-liberation, many of *The Nation's* Mau Mau articles adopt a rhetorical strategy that humanizes the Kikuyu and gives them opportunities to be heard in the West. "Kenya: African Storm Signal," the first essay in the series, highlights the trial of Jesse Kariuki, the vice president of the Kenya African Union, and treats it as an instance of the abridgement of due process: "The trial was held in secret. The defendant was denied the basic right to confront his accusers, and after he was declared guilty, the government still debated the pros and cons of making the evidence public" (Shepherd 408). To appreciate the full significance of this representation, we must first note the stark contrast between it and the images of the Kikuyu in *Time,* where the question of legal rights is never raised. Second, consider that the Kariuki case assumes that legal privileges accorded to Americans should also apply to Africans. In the act of accepting that assumption, the reader identifies with Kariuki and regards him not only as a fellow human but also as one who should be treated as though he were the subject of a democracy.

Yet other efforts to humanize the Kikuyu include the story of a student who comes to the United States to get a university degree and must contend with the efforts of the immigration service to deport him because he had written letters years earlier calling for better education for the Kikuyu. *The Nation* is at pains to point out the irony here, namely, that an interest in the promotion of education for Africans (usually regarded as a means to self-improvement and civility) should mark a person as a possible communist (Drake 490–92). In "Dark Road in Kenya" Elizabeth Hoyt directly engages the notion that the Mau Mau are a communist front and actually quotes an avowed Mau Mau who claims to be disinterested in communism and whose remarks seem to indicate that he does not even know what communism is. As with the narrative of Jesse Kariuki, these accounts were designed to break down the imagined differences that separated Americans from Africans.

AS I noted earlier, the appropriations of the Mau Mau signifier allow us to isolate two discursive tendencies in fifties America: one, exemplified by the *Time* reportage of the Mau Mau, operated in the service of an ideological unity that maintained segregation within the United States and colonial exploitation without. The other tendency, represented by *The Nation,* actively resisted the totalizing colonial forces and served the formation of a new cultural identity, one that was more inclusive and egalitarian, extending to global "others"—if only in principle—the democratic rights of Americans.

The mass weeklies' distribution of these opposed points of view created a community of readers that numbered in the millions and for whom Mau Mau was a signifier powerfully charged with suasive energy. In effect, the first moments of Mau Mau's American career created a market that would be exploited in succeeding years. Robert Ruark was a central figure in this exploitation. Having already achieved modest success with one fiction situated in Africa, *Horn of the Hunter* (1953), he published in 1955 a novelistic account of the Kenyan antagonism. Entitled *Something of Value,* the novel quickly demonstrated the commercial power of Mau Mau, was selected for the Book-of-the-Month Club despite the dissenting opinion of one judge who found the book "shocking" ("Caveat Emptor" 108), became the nation's number two best-seller behind Françoise Sagan's *Bonjour Tristesse,* and remained in print through 1980. As we will see, the novel's fictionalized accounts of the Mau Mau and the British are profoundly shaped by the same discursive forces that informed *Time's* reportage.

The barriers that precluded dialogue between Robert Ruark and the Africans he represented were formidable. He did not speak the languages of the Kikuyu, nor is there any evidence to indicate that he ever associated with the Kikuyu people outside of the privileged compounds of the white visitor. Moreover, having been raised in North Carolina in the twenties and thirties, Ruark had been subject to the American color bar and its apparatus of separation and racial devaluation, and this also proved to be an impediment to any desire he might have had to identify with the Kikuyu. It comes as no surprise that Ruark's reflexive response to the Mau Mau signifier reproduced the division that typically separated Western observers and the African "other" and sustained the colonial point of view. This happened despite his self-regard as a racially open-minded person. Ruark's obituary writer quotes him on this point: "'I was . . . toted up to boyhood by a former slave. My playmates were Negroes as were my hunting friends and fishing friends.'" Yet the readings of his own contemporaries counter that in *Value* he had "loaded the dice against the negro" ("Robert Ruark Dead in London" 31).

The validity of this charge is quite evident from what Ruark writes about his research. In the foreword to the novel, he distributes thanks to eighteen members of the Kenyan community. All of them are European; most are "personal friends" (*Value* x). The first people on the list, Harry and Mickey Selby, had a kinship relationship with Ruark, who agreed to be their son's godfather. Moreover, Harry Selby, "one of the most sought-after of Kenya's professional white hunters" ("Season for Safari" 78) and a man "active in counter-Mau Mau operations" (Ruark, "Your Guns Go with You" 10), probably served as a model for Ruark's central character, Peter McKenzie. This set of real and imaginary relationships provides us with a picture of Ruark's extensive involvement with the white settler community, a social fact that clearly shaped his view of the Mau Mau. One reviewer of the novel critiques just this problem. Ruark, he writes, "has identified himself passionately with the Kenya settlers' state of mind" (Davidson 448).

As a consequence of his isolation from the indigenous African community, Ruark's constructions of the mind and manners of the Kikuyu and the Mau Mau are either generalized fabrications produced by imaginary reformations of book accounts or compelling descriptions of real deprivations seen from a distance. The latter, as for example Ruark's description of the Nairobi slums, issue from an alienated observer who is disgusted by what he sees, attributes the sight to the debased and savage impulses of the African, and dissociates himself and his culture from any responsibility for cause or effect. We will see more of this later.

The other kind of research Ruark conducted was text based and here too his identification with the settler point of view led him to conclude that Europeans were the authorities to be consulted. He was attracted to the work of Elspeth Huxley, a writer who has been described by one contemporary Kikuyu as a "racist apologist for European settlerism in Kenya" (Ngugi Wa

Thiong'o, *Writers in Politics* 17). He disliked Jomo Kenyatta's *Facing Mount Kenya,* the sole acknowledged African source, which, Ruark writes, "was important chiefly for its biased view of his own Kikuyu people" (*Value* x). Elsewhere Ruark, echoing *Time,* condemns Kenyatta because he "is by no means his own man. He was educated abroad, boasts of spending several years in Moscow, is married to a white woman" ("Your Guns Go with You" 12). In these judgments we can see the workings of a subjectivity that pulls all discourses, even those containing the voice of the "other," into a tightly unified substantiation of colonial positions. The one potentially contrary force—Kenyatta—loses its deconstructive potential because it is assimilated as a distortion of the factual situation. For the "facts," Ruark looks to the British Africanist Louis Leakey's short treatise *Mau Mau and the Kikuyu,* a report that issues from the position of objectivity affected by the colonial observer. The scene Leakey shares with Ruark is quite conservative: the injustice, inequality, and repression associated with the color bar are regrettable but minor concerns. The real problem is the "speed of progress" that "made a part of the population unbalanced in their outlook and thus paved the way for movements like Mau Mau, in the hands of an unscrupulous few" (85).

Whereas Leakey uses metaphors drawn from developmental psychology to account for the Mau Mau, Ruark draws his from disease and the supernatural. Thus moderation and local explanation give way to invective and global generality as Ruark claims that the Mau Mau movement was a "symptomatic ulcer of the evil and unrest which currently afflict the world" (*Value* ix). The overdetermined body politic image condenses several categories of negativity—physical corruption, demonism, communist subversion, and Third World unrest—and indirectly reveals the successful efforts of the "colonial government . . . to portray Mau Mau as an irrational force of evil, dominated by bestial impulses and influenced by world communism" (Furedi 4). The image appealed to many American readers for whom the traditional links between cleanliness, Christianity, democracy, and social order (and the binary opposites of these terms) had been reasserted by conservative discursive forces at the outset of the cold war. The fact that Jomo Kenyatta had spent significant time in Moscow was enough to suggest that the movement was tainted by Soviet expansionism. That it was "evil" and filthy was evidenced by Mau Mau atrocities and initiations that required the ritualistic consumption of human fluids and the commission of sexual perversities.[13]

"To understand Africa," Ruark writes, "you must understand a basic impulsive savagery that is greater than anything we 'civilized' people have encountered in two centuries" (*Value* ix). The statement produces two effects. First, it places the reader in the familiar position of the enlightened and rational observer of the primitive "other." The second effect, a rather ironic one, depends upon the invocation of the powers of the intellect. Ruark enjoins the reader to "understand" savagery by noting that it cannot be understood. Because it is an "impulsive" action of a mindless body, "savagery" defies reason and can be accounted for only by relegation to the realm of the inexplicable. Thus Ruark calls upon reason to deny its own analytical power when confronted with allegedly precivilized and irrational human behavior.

This subversion of reason is but another of the symptoms of the opposition of African and European. By consigning the Mau Mau to a category that precludes analysis, by unselfcritically assuming that the European position is reasoned and judicious, the opposition effectively suspends the need to offer any other form of explanation, blocks inquiry into the sociopolitical causes of the problem, and maintains the prevailing power relations. It also makes possible Ruark's claim that his "is not a political book" (*Value* ix) even though it clearly employs dialogue, character, and narrative action to polemicize the Euro-settlers' position. This contradiction is rooted in a fixed assurance that the point of view being presented is utterly true and thus so impervious to detraction that it cannot be limited to the realm of the political.[14]

A brief paraphrase of *Value*'s main conflict and its resolution will help us see that the contrary is the case. The protagonist, Peter McKenzie, is the son of a white settler and a decided advocate of white rule. His constant companion until adolescence is Kimani, a Kikuyu youth who eventually runs away from home and becomes a Mau Mau leader. Peter and Kimani fight on opposing sides during the hostilities and fatally confront each other when Peter tracks the Mau Mau to his mountain lair, kills him in personal combat,[15] and decides to adopt and raise his infant son. Here the political reality of the Mau Mau, and all its attendant frustrations, is translated into an allegory in which Peter and Kimani personify their opposed political orders. The wish-fulfillment ending—McKenzie murders Kimani—empowers the colonial reader and produces considerable gratification by providing a fantasy of domination, one that releases the negative energy associated with the anxieties of the emerging postcolonial world. That Peter thereafter adopts Kimani's infant son extends and complicates the political allegory and its psychic pleasures. As the son of Kimani, the orphan is the living representative of the dead father's identity. Within the order of the imagination the son *is* Kimani, but with a difference. The intransigent and dangerous adult Mau Mau is displaced and repositioned in an imaginary space in which he is transformed into the ideal colonial "other": a helpless, harmless, and malleable child. Authority is restored to the paternal figure of benevolence—McKenzie. His metaphorical child—the African—is wrested from the bind of ignorance, superstition, and savagery. Liberated by the unfortunate, though necessary, deaths of his real parents, the child becomes subject to a European upbringing and the dictates of reason. Throughout this narrative the colonial manages to sustain a moral self-image in which charity coexists with the rightful force of disciplinary power. Thus Ruark presents the adoption as a humanitarian gesture and obscures its character as a self-serving European appropriation of African resources.

Of the many examples that could be cited to demonstrate ideological control over fictive technique in *Value,* the anthropological juxtaposition is especially useful. By novelizing and contrasting ethnographies of the European settler and the Kikuyu, the technique reveals a differential between the writer's representation of his own community and his cross-cultural representation of the Kikuyu.

Ruark's most significant deployment of the technique juxtaposes detailed accounts of Kikuyu and British settler marriages. The biological and cultural equivalences between the two point to a universality of human experience and in some measure promote the experience of cross-cultural intersubjectivity. However, in the final analysis the intersubjective framework loses its potential for advancing an emergent postcolonial subjectivity because it foregrounds and intensifies a negative difference rather than a set of positive similarities. The occasion for this juxtaposition is the marriage of Peter McKenzie's sister, Elizabeth, to one Jeff Newton. After describing the beginning of these ceremonies, Ruark shifts the reader's attentions to Karanja, the head man on the McKenzie farm and the father of Kimani (the yet-to-be Mau Mau leader who will be killed by Peter). Karanja is not participating in the festivities because he is in prison. But stimulated by the sentimental realization that the Newton-McKenzie bonding is in progress, he remembers his own courtship and marriage. This recollection, followed as it is by a return to the Newton-McKenzie wedding, provides a powerful ideological counterpoint.

Karanja's wedding ceremonies provide us with an example of the process by which Ruark imaginatively enters and constructs the African "other." When we read the words and the thoughts attributed to Karanja, or any other of Ruark's Kikuyu, we participate in a discursive formation whose materials have been drawn not from the Kikuyu representations of Kikuyu experience but from European versions that have been filtered through the conceptual grid of the colonial. Thus Ruark's Karanja is the project of an alienated observation point, one that is both physically and psychologically outside of the community it claims to comprehend.

In this fashion Ruark manipulated, both culturally and historically, the position of a midcentury reader. First, the reader observes the behavior of the inferior "other" from a site of cultural elevation; second, the spectacle, presenting itself as an episode in the spectator's own natural prehistory, reinforces the reader's sense of superiority. The cost of this inflation is borne by the Kikuyu, who are depersonalized and perceived as cultural puppets and animalized humans. Another Western benefit of the colonial, this psychic exploitation uses the colonized to enhance the reader's sense of freedom, individuality, and personhood.

These intellectual and emotional gratifications are byproducts of the logic of primitivism that, when taken to final conclusions, produces the physical equivalent of alienation, i.e., disgust. As the narrative approaches the focal point of the Kikuyu marriage, its sexual consummation, Ruark's description of the couple's reproductive activities strips away the cultural overlay that links them to a human community. Isolated in the wilderness, unconstrained by reason and culture, they become animals: Karanja's wife is likened to a zebra, Karanja to a bull. It is not at all unusual for erotic encounters in fiction to employ figures drawn from animal nomenclature in order to signify passion. These figures usually function to draw the reader into the circle of arousal and enable a vicarious participation that dissolves the barriers between the reader's self and the fictive characters. But the opposite effect is produced by Ruark's contrivances. The specific device that inhibits a positive vicarious response is the body of Karanja's mate. Whereas the female body is usually fetishized as the desired object of the Western gaze, the body of the Kikuyu female is antithetical to conventional notions of beauty: Karanja's nameless and voiceless spouse is overloaded with adipose tissue and is smeared with animal fat. Running counter to Western preferences in anatomy and olfactory adornment, both particulars signify colonial disgust at the evolutionary inferiority of the Kikuyu. The Western standards that produce this judgment remain unavailable to critique. For Ruark, they appear to be a natural ground. Locked outside the Kikuyu subjectivity, both by choice and circumstance, he produces images that are alienated and best exemplified by the spectacle of Karanja's "snorting" entry into his mate and his multiple "mounting[s]" (126–27) as they work at reproductivity.

By contrast, the description of the Newtons' matrimonial rituals comes from within cultural practice. It follows from and exploits experiences and conventions that have been lived by Ruark and his readers. It does so first and foremost by structuring more fully articulated characters whose involvement with ritual and tradition appears to be a matter of personal decision. Rather than stereotypes moving along a fully determined track, Jeff Newton and Elizabeth McKenzie display their awareness of the traditions that they choose to enact: their participation seems to be the expression of voluntary and individualized decisions. In addition, they are endowed with a wide range of emotional responses as they move through the various ceremonies. The dialogue between husband and wife is extensive and seems to escape formulaic control. The whole section is filled with tangential details and unplanned behaviors that seem to escape the imposition of culture and tradition. The readers enter the personal musings and the interiority of husband and wife as Elizabeth's gentle lust emerges in a Freudian slip and Jeff anticipates with some anxiety the honeymoon night.

Although the narrative works toward the marriage coupling, the actual performance is withheld from the reader. Instead the reader is treated to an anticipatory display of the bridal body which, in strong contrast to Karanja's Kikuyu woman, has been cleansed by a bath and posed with anterior lighting to reveal beneath diaphanous garments the outline of a conventionally well-formed feminine figure. This erotic synecdoche displaces the mechanics of coital love and produces the kind of genteel and inoffensive stimulation appropriate for hero and heroine in the best-selling fiction of the fifties.

The juxtaposition of the Newtons and the Karanjas has two corollary effects: first, it maintains the distance between the reader and the Kikuyu even as, second, it generates empathy for the white settlers. Moreover, this strategic and ideological disposition of elements prepares for a chain of emotional manipulations effected later in the novel when Kimani's Mau Mau troop (convincingly established as the savage "other") assaults the Newton family (convincingly established as good people) and kill all, including two children, but Elizabeth. This pattern of alienation and identification carries forward to the end of the novel, where it performs its final function by aligning the reader's emotions with Peter McKenzie when, partly as an act of retribution, he murders Kimani.

I have ended this part of my argument by focusing on the reader because I want to emphasize the political power of Ruark's fiction. As a discursive and ideological fact, Kimani's murder acts out a desire to master the disturbing forces of the emergent postcolonial world. The narrative implicates the reader in this struggle and efficiently generates negative oppositional energies whose resolution is dictated by the logic of violence. Although there were alternatives, murder—the elimination of conflict through the elimination of the "other"—becomes the final, very gratifying, solution for the problems of cultural opposition. This imaginary and intensely personalized containment parallels what was happening in the real-world efforts of the British to hunt down, kill, incarcerate, and convert the Mau Mau.[16] Ruark's mass-medium contribution to this effort constructed the scene of conflict inside the imagination of numerous readers and enabled them to participate in it. Participation is, by definition, never neutral. By personifying the conflict in the characters of Peter McKenzie and Kimani and organizing the sympathies and antipathies of his readers, Ruark actively reproduced the cultural resistance to the formation of a multicultural social order, what he has one character in *Something of Value* refer to as the "age of the glorified wog" (94).

THE film takes a very different ideological stance, mainly because Richard Brooks was placed in charge of the $300,000 screen rights ("Author Robert Ruark" 73). He concluded that Ruark was wrong about what was happening in Kenya ("The New Pictures" 124)[17] and produced a film whose representation of the Mau Mau signifier is ideologically aligned with *The Nation*. Keeping Ruark's title, characters, and much of his plot, the film, starring Sidney Poitier and Rock Hudson, shifts the novel's political orientation by replacing the novelist's colonial perspective with an emancipatory view of Mau Mau.

A brief description of Brooks's film involvements in the forties and fifties produces a litany of concerns associated with a liberal ideology. His screen-adapted novel *The Brick Foxhole* (1947) focuses on the murder of a homosexual. *Brute Force,* a 1947 screenplay, deals sympathetically with convicts driven to escape by a cruel warden, and *Storm Warning* (1950) is about a town terrorized by the KKK. For his directorial debut in *Crisis* (1951) Brooks treated moral issues associated with Latin American fascism. His most famous film of the decade, *Blackboard Jungle* (1955), offers a sensitive treatment of race and racism. The film Brooks worked on immediately before *Something of Value, The Last Hunt* (1956), is no less sensitive with respect to the human relationship with the animal world and has to be considered one of the few environmentally conscious films of the decade. Given these credits, and the ideological assumptions they imply, it is not surprising that Brooks reworked Ruark's story into a film that struggles to revise, rather than reaffirm, the tradition-bound signifying chains of colonial discourse.

The narrative events located at the open and close of both novel and film illustrate the character of Brooks's revisions. In the beginning of Ruark's novel the teenage Kimani is mock-killed by Peter McKenzie in a hunting game that anticipates Kimani's murder at the end of the book. For the opening of the film, Brooks stays within the framework of a generic youthful encounter but transforms its ideological significance: In two short scenes the boys collaborate to win a soccer game and then compete in a friendly broad jump. The segment concludes with their hands, black and white, clasped in amity. Brooks also follows Ruark by ending the film with Kimani's death, but it is not the result of McKenzie's murderous intent. To the contrary, McKenzie struggles through much of the film to prevent such a fatal close. He is the agent for a negotiated settlement between the British and the Mau Mau and he even risks his life in a preliminary jungle encounter with Kimani in an attempt to work out the terms of a surrender. One gung-ho vindictive white settler comes close to the truth when he calls this McKenzie a "black liberator."

As one element in a discursive formation, Brooks's McKenzie organizes (much of the time) the conditions of the possibility of a postcolonial subjectivity. The formation replaces the binary antagonisms of Ruark's novel and substitutes a principle of egalitarian relations. Put another way, the McKenzie of the novel relates to the Mau Mau Kimani across a gap that cannot and should not be bridged, and thereby perpetuates the master-slave relationships of the colonial world. The McKenzie of the film identifies with Kimani, seeks out the points of resemblance between them, and invests the Mau Mau with the signs of a common humanity. Thus the circuit of energy that links the spectator and the film enables the spectator to experience vicariously a multicultural identity.

A summary of the film's concluding scenes reinforces this point. After a year or more of hostilities, McKenzie manages to meet Kimani, who has become a Mau Mau general. They negotiate a settlement, but due to circumstances beyond McKenzie's control, Kimani and his people are ambushed as they try to comply with the armistice. Kimani flees with his infant son and is tracked by the anguished McKenzie, who wants to explain that the ambush was not an act of betrayal. No longer able to trust anyone, Kimani tries to kill McKenzie, but falls into a pit where he is impaled on sharp stakes. With his last words the dying Mau Mau leader asks McKenzie to give him his son and to bury them both, but Peter refuses, saying he will raise the child and thus create a better world.

As elsewhere in the film, here the filmmaker's ideological revisions of the novel display an intersubjective consciousness at work. Brooks transforms Ruark's savage Mau Mau into a tragic victim and McKenzie becomes a peacemaker, rather than a murderer, who almost dies because he will not fight back when Kimani assaults him. These changes challenge the conventional colonial antagonisms in that the spectator enters into the experience of the Mau Mau leader, an extremely rare moment in the filmic representations of Africans in the Hollywood films of the fifties. The medium of the spectator's entry is the pathos generated by the narrative circumstances described above in concert with Kimani's demeanor, his physical appearance, and (among other considerations) his commitment to monogamy and parenthood.

The final product is a very positive equation between Mau Mau and Kimani. There is, however, a third element—the self of the spectator—that must be included in the equation because of the audience's emotional involvement with Kimani. That involvement is an identification: an extension of the self into the "other" and a collapsing (if only temporarily) of the distinction between the two. So a more accurate rendering of Brooks's Mau Mau, a rendering that emphasizes the intersubjective character of the signifier, depends upon our ability to imagine a cognitive realm in which the Mau Mau signifier, the Kimani filmic image, and the spectator's sense of self overlap and interpenetrate. Like The Nation's Mau Mau, Brooks's Mau Mau signifies the possibility of racial equality and interdependence in a postcolonial world.

Up until its closing moments the Brooks film works to construct and sustain this possibility, at which point the narrative reverses its ideological polarity and reveals how much it is constrained by the same discursive forces that shaped Robert Ruark's novel. Consider the killing of Kimani. Although Brooks changes the circumstances of the Mau Mau's death, thereby pointing out once again that he is not bound by the Ruark text, he still follows the novelist and kills off Kimani. Many other options were available. For example, Brooks could have eliminated the chase scene and allowed Kimani to raise his son and continue the revolution another day. Surely such an ending would have been too severe a test of the audience's ability to identify with a black man. More palatable is a concluding vision of justice and equality that conceals the reiterated core values of a conservative white hegemony.

Brooks manages this balancing act by making Kimani's death a self-inflicted tragedy: Kimani digs the pit in which he is finally impaled and his fall happens when he tries to kill the unresisting McKenzie. Thus McKenzie is absolved of culpability and the Mau Mau is designated as the tragedy's causal agent. As both victim and agent, Kimani, like Oedipus, is designed to elicit intense feelings of pity from the spectators. Moreover, these pleasures of tragic sorrow may be enjoyed without the spectators having to feel that they are implicated in Kimani's demise; it is unfortunate but it is also Kimani's own fault. The fact of the matter is, however, that Kimani's death is a convenience: it eliminates any future problems involved with the Mau Mau's adjustment to a new social order. While Kimani lives, negotiations are required. Once he is dead, unequivocal power reverts back to the white man. The spectators do indeed respect Kimani, care for him, and regret his loss, but they are also relieved because his death eliminates the Mau Mau's disruptive power and restores the familiar, and therefore comforting, social equilibrium that prevailed before the uprising.

This emotional ambiguity also appears in McKenzie's refusal to respect Kimani's final wish—that his living son be buried with him. As seen from the perspective of the fifties, the refusal is a humanitarian decision that properly values the life of the child more than the authority of the father; from a postcolonial perspective, it is a denial of the Mau Mau's right to self-determination, a denial that reproduces the cultural domination against which Kimani rebelled earlier in the film when his father was imprisoned for sanctioning, according to Kikuyu practice, the death of an infant. What is at stake is the authority of Africans to govern their own affairs despite European disapproval. McKenzie's intervention may appear to represent an enlightened reverence for life unless we interpret it, as I think we should, as another instance of a colonial will to power that claims superior knowledge and disregards the stated self-interests of the "other." In Kimani's case the self-interest is his desire to spare his child the agony of life in a colonial order. McKenzie's decision to oppose Kimani displaces the Mau Mau's rightful paternal authority, breaks the intersubjective relationship that prevailed during most of the film, and gives way to the resurgent ideological force of the colonial code. As with Kimani's death, the spectators are allowed to balance conflicting points of view. They can participate vicariously in the European domination of the affairs of the African "other" and they can feel that doing so is morally justified.

Though muffled and contained by an ideologically purposeful sentimentalism at the end of the film, the Mau Mau signifier in Brooks's *Something of Value* represents a radical call for an order of black self-determination that had the potential to discomfit a mass audience in the fifties. Just as the narrative of Kimani's life displays a developing consciousness of the legitimacy of black problems, his death is a white wish fulfillment and an ideological repression. The discursive forces that produced such an equivocation were responding simultaneously, on the one hand, to the claims for justice and equality and, on the other, to the claims of a deeply entrenched, though beleaguered, white supremacy. As with Kimani's death, the forces of repression would win the fifties struggle to deny the Mau Mau signifier both in the imagination of the American public and in the highlands of East Africa. Yet this denial would only be temporary. In the sixties Kenya would become an African nation and in America people like Rap Brown, Stokely Carmichael, Malcolm X, and Huey Newton (all proponents of black self-determination, black power, and the revolutionary uses of violence) would become the objects of public fascination in much the same way Mau Mau had in the previous decade. Mau Mau did not die. It was transformed.

NOTES

1   The *Reader's Guide to Periodical Literature* and the *International Index to Periodicals* are useful references in this matter. Both list full entries from 1952 to 1955

and then show a tapering off: one reference in the former for 1961, one in the latter for 1960, and none thereafter.

2   For a discussion of the paucity of American images of Africa in the fifties see Staniland 19–56.

3   For a brief overview see Newsinger.

4   For an account of Mau Mau as a history of distortions, see Lonsdale. For current views of Mau Mau, see Cleary; Edgerton; Gordon; and Throup.

5   Marianna Torgovnick writes, "Primitives exist at the 'lowest cultural levels'; we occupy the 'highest,' in the metaphors of stratification and hierarchy commonly used by Malinowski and others like him. The ensemble of these tropes—however miscellaneous and contradictory—forms the basic grammar and vocabulary of what I call primitivist discourse, a discourse fundamental to the Western sense of self and Other" (8). See also JanMohamed.

6   For another equation between Mau Mau and animal see "Kenya: The Meow-Meows."

7   For a provocative view of encounters between Americans and various "others" see Rogin.

8   For the voices of the Mau Mau, see Barnett; Kariuki; and Ngugi Wa Thiong'o, *The Trial of Dedan Kimathi.*

9   Said generalizes this point: "Without significant exception the universalizing discourses of modern Europe and the United States assume the silence, willing or otherwise, of the non-European world" (50).

10 See Baldwin for a proud account of one American's participation in the British security program of torture and summary execution.

11 Martin Staniland's judgment about American views of Africa applies as much to *The Nation* as it does to *Time:* "American visitors and commentators did see what they knew and judged what they saw according to what they valued— behaving like so many mirrors walking down bush paths" (2). For a similar use of the mirror image, see Cooper.

12 For a specific critique of *Time,* see "Once upon a Time, Inc."

13 "Kenya: Mau Mau Terror" concludes with a description of an oathing ritual: "A cup of blood of a freshly killed goat is passed seven times around the head of an initiate. Sometimes he has to bite the goat meat seven times, or take seven sips of the blood—often with the goat's eyeballs floating in it" (49).

14 Davidson (449) takes issue with this mystification of Mau Mau. See Gunther for a fifties treatment of the Mau Mau that, in contrast to *Value,* carefully lays out the sociopolitical complexities of the movement.

15 JanMohamed notes that the "elimination of the offending natives" (67) is typical of the plot structure of colonial texts.

16   For a lurid account of the atrocities committed by the British in their efforts to contain the Mau Mau, see Baldwin.

17   See also "Into Africa's Depths." The reviewer notes that Ruark "is known to be less than pleased with the movie version." His comment, "These kids struck out in the humor department" (115).

WORKS CONSULTED

Alpert, Hollis. "SR Goes to the Movies: Kenya Violence." Rev. of *Something of Value*. *Saturday Review*, May 18, 1957, 36.

"Author Robert Ruark: Jungle and Jingle of a Best Seller." *Newsweek*, Aug. 29, 1955, 73–76.

Bakhtin, M. M. *The Dialogical Imagination*. Ed. Michael Holquist. Trans. Caryl Emerson and Michael Holquist. Austin: University of Texas Press, 1981.

Baldwin, William. *Mau Mau Man-Hunt: The Adventures of the Only American Who Has Fought the Terrorist in Kenya*. New York: Dutton, 1957.

Barnett, Donald, and Karari Njama. *Mau Mau from Within*. New York: Monthly Review Press, 1966.

Brett, E. A. *Colonialism and Underdevelopment in East Africa: The Politics of Economic Change, 1919–1939*. New York: NOK, 1973.

Byars, Jackie. *All That Hollywood Allows: Re-Reading Gender in 1950s Melodrama*. Chapel Hill: University of North Carolina Press, 1991.

Carothers, J. C. *The Psychology of Mau Mau*. Nairobi: Government Printer, 1954.

"Caveat Emptor." Rev. of *Something of Value*, by Robert Ruark. *Time*, May 2, 1955, 108.

Chinweizu, Onwuchekwa Jemie, and Ihechukwu Madubuike. *Toward the Decolonization of African Literature*. Nigeria: Fourth Dimension, 1980.

Cleary, A. S. "The Myth of Mau Mau in Its International Context." *African Affairs*, no. 89 (1990): 227–45.

Clifford, James. *The Predicament of Culture: Twentieth Century Ethnography, Literature, and Art*. Cambridge, Mass.: Harvard University Press, 1988.

Cooper, Frederick. "Mau Mau and the Discourses of Decolonization." *Journal of African History* 29.11 (1988): 313–20.

Crowther, Bosley. "Screen: Racial Conflict." Rev. of *Something of Value. New York Times*, May 11, 1957, 24.

"The Darkening War." *Time*, Mar. 8, 1954, 38.

Davidson, Basil. "Man and Beast in Kenya." Rev. of *Something of Value*, by Robert Ruark. *The Nation*, May 21, 1955, 448–49.

Drake, St. Clair. "The Terror That Walks by Day." *The Nation*, Nov. 29, 1952, 490–92.

Edgerton, Robert B. *Mau Mau: An African Crucible*. New York: Free Press, 1989.

"First Korea, Now Kenya." *The Nation*, Apr. 25, 1953, 337.

Friedenberg, Daniel. "The Mau Mau Terror." *The Nation*, Oct. 19, 1953, 10–11.

Furedi, Frank. *The Mau Mau War in Perspective*. London: James Currey, 1989.

Gordon, David. *Decolonization and the State in Kenya*. Boulder: Westview Press, 1986.

Greenblatt, Stephen. *Shakespearean Negotiations: The Circulation of Social Energy in Renaissance England*. Berkeley: University of California Press, 1988.

Gunther, John. *Inside Africa*. New York: Harper and Brothers, 1955.

Hoyt, Elizabeth E. "Dark Road in Kenya." *The Nation*, Dec. 13, 1952, 550–53.

"Into Africa's Depths." Rev. of *Something of Value. Newsweek*, May 13, 1957, 115–16.

Irvine, Keith. "New Crisis in Kenya: Adventure in Imperialism." *The Nation*, July 23, 1955, 74–76.

JanMohamed, Abdul R. "The Economy of Manichean Allegory: The Function of Racial Difference in Colonial Literature." *Critical Inquiry* 12.1 (1985): 59–87.

Kariuki, Mwangi. *Mau Mau Detainee*. Nairobi: Oxford University Press, 1975.

"Kenya: Frontier War." *Time*, Feb. 23, 1953, 35.

"Kenya: Mau Mau Terror." *Newsweek*, Oct. 20, 1952, 49.

"Kenya: The Meow-Meows." *Time*, Nov. 3, 1952, 36.

"Kenya: The Night Visitors." *Newsweek*, Feb. 9, 1953, 42.

"Kenya: S.O.S." *Time*, Oct. 27, 1952, 40.

Kenyatta, Jomo. *Facing Mt. Kenya: The Tribal Life of the Gikuyu*. New York: Vintage Books, 1962.

Leakey, Louis. *Mau Mau and the Kikuyu*. London: Methuen, 1952.

Lonsdale, John. "Mau Mau's of the Mind: Making Mau Mau and Remaking Kenya." *Journal of African History*, no. 31 (1990): 393–421.

McCarten, John. "The Current Cinema." Rev. of *Something of Value. New Yorker*, May 18, 1957, 94.

Moley, Raymond. "Good-by, Mr. Ruark." *Newsweek*, Dec. 11, 1953, 96.

"The New Pictures." Rev. of *Something of Value. Time*, May 20, 1957, 124–25.

Newsinger, John. "Mau Mau—Thirty Years Later." *Monthly Review* (May 1985): 12–21.

Ngugi Wa Thiong'o. *The Trial of Dedan Kimathi*. London: Heinemann, 1976.

———. *Writers in Politics*. London: Heinemann, 1981.

"Once Upon a Time, Inc.: Mr. Luce's Fact Machine." *The Nation*, Feb. 18, 1956, 134.

"Robert Ruark Dead in London; Author and Columnist Was Forty-Nine." *New York Times*, July 1, 1965, 31.

Rogin, Michael. "Kiss Me Deadly: Communism, Motherhood, and Cold War Movies." *Representations* 6 (Spring 1984): 1–36.

Rosberg, Carl, Jr., and John Notingham. *The Myth of "Mau Mau": Nationalism in Kenya*. New York: Praeger, 1966.

Ruark, Robert. *Something of Value*. Garden City: Doubleday, 1955.

———. "Your Guns Go with You." *Reader's Digest*, June 1953, 8–12.

Said, Edward. *Culture and Imperialism*. New York: Alfred A. Knopf, 1993.

Schaub, Thomas Hill. *American Fiction in the Cold War*. Madison: University of Wisconsin Press, 1991.

"Season for Safari: American Gun and Camera in Africa." *Newsweek*, Feb. 28, 1955, 78–81.

Shepherd, George W., Jr. "The End of the Mau Mau Rebellion." *New Republic*, July 9, 1956, 8–9.

———. "Kenya: African Storm Signal." *The Nation*, Nov. 1, 1952, 407–8.

"Slaughter in Kenya." *Time*, Nov. 2, 1953, 30–31.

Staniland, Martin. *American Intellectuals and African Nationalists, 1955–1970*. New Haven: Yale University Press, 1991.

"That $300,000 Novel." *Newsweek*, Apr. 25, 1955, 116.

Throup, David. *Economic and Social Origins of the Mau Mau, 1945–53*. Athens: Ohio University Press, 1988.

Torgovnick, Marianna. *Gone Primitive: Savage Intellects, Modern Lives*. Chicago: University of Chicago Press, 1990.

Weisbord, Robert. *Ebony Kinship: Africa, Africans, and the Afro-American*. Westport, Conn.: Greenwood Press, 1973.

Whitfield, Stephen J. *The Culture of the Cold War*. Baltimore: Johns Hopkins University Press, 1991.

Part Two   Television

Horace Newcomb —

 **THE OPENING OF AMERICA**
Meaningful Difference in 1950s Television

Milton Berle, host of *The Texaco Star Theater*, 1948–53.
(Courtesy of the Library of Congress)

M
Y earliest memory of television comes from 1951. I sat
one night in the company of
men and boys, on boxes and a few
scattered chairs, in the showroom of the local hardware store,
distributor of television sets.
We gathered there to watch the
Joe Louis–Ezard Charles prize
fight that would determine
the new heavyweight cham-
pion of the world. Charles
won.

I was nine years old, living with my mother, father,
and sister in Sardis, Mississippi, a town of about two
thousand citizens. We did
not own a television re-

ceiver set, few among those two thousand did. But we sometimes watched with neighbors, and our use of the new medium was as part of a wider pattern of interaction with popular entertainment. Radio, movies, even comics were never shunned in our household and, for the most part, rarely criticized. Some might say this was because there was nothing in that entertainment to challenge, subvert, alter, or enlighten us in any way that would make close monitoring necessary. But such a view overlooks the ways in which television expanded our world and with that expansion challenged it in unexpected and, doubtless, unplanned ways.

Soon after the Louis-Charles fight my family purchased a television set and we watched the fights on many Friday nights. We watched drama and comedy, live and filmed, variety shows and performances, amateur hours, game shows, children's shows (available for all audiences in prime time), some baseball in the summer, news (I remember seeing American troops on retreat in Korea in the winter, a terrible sight for youngsters whose lives had already been defined in large part by World War II), atomic bomb explosions, Bishop Sheen or Billy Graham, old Tarzan movies, and on and on.

I invoke these memories not to call up nostalgia as an analytical device. Rather, I want to suggest that careful historical grounding in place, society, and culture should encourage us to avoid quick generalizations about television, to forego some of the most widely perpetuated versions of its history, and banish some of the most simplistic notions about its social and cultural roles—its broadest "effects," if you will.

The situation in which I first experienced television can best be described, despite previous and long-standing experience with radio and movies, as that of a "closed culture." Heavily circumscribed by theology, religious practice, and the translation of religious belief into everyday ethical and political action, that culture was still always fundamentally defined by regional identity, and that identity by race. That is why the gathering of white men and boys, watching two black men fight hard against one another with their fists, is so vivid a memory. Television intruded into my culture, offering me a perspective on the world at large that I rarely found in other media, other forms. I, and others, took up many aspects of that broader perspective and knew that our lives were changed. For these reasons I have never accepted a great many easy explanations about the way television insinuated itself into the life and culture of twentieth-century America. And this is why I reconsider here the role of television in the 1950s.

THE clichéd master narrative of the American fifties—bland, controlled, complacent, commercial—has perhaps been related more forcefully to television than to any other aspect of expressive culture. This is so because television is seen not merely as reflecting this view or even as solely engendering these characteristics. Rather, the history of the medium itself in this decade is considered emblematic of all the fifties stands for. That history is chronicled—by television and social critics during the fifties and by media historians since then—as an epic of decline and loss, of a failure of nerve, of a promise turned to lies. Television was touted as a technological wonder that could transform the nation in some vague and undetermined manner into a postwar utopia. It displayed the landscape of a newer, brighter America. But by the end of the decade that landscape had degenerated into the vast wasteland that has become an acceptable paradigm for television history.

For the medium, this overall decline was from the heights of live, televised drama to the depths of filmed programming. The shift of locus from New York to Hollywood was itself sometimes written as a passage from Parnassus to Babylon, and the products of that sorry locale were deemed the evidence of exiled labor, toiling in the interests of false gods. Erik Barnouw's standard history of television surveys the transformation in many ways. For example, he presents it as a general condemnation of a particular genre, the western, in a particular industrial formation, the telefilm. "Although many fine films throughout film history have dealt with internal character conflicts, such conflicts were seldom important in telefilms. Telefilms rarely invited the viewer to look for problems within himself. Problems came from the evil of other people, and were solved—the telefilm seemed to imply—by confining or killing them" (214).

Barnouw was quick to link this commentary on a particular program type to a larger purpose. Citing a psychologist who argued that westerns give "the viewer a feeling of security that life itself cannot offer" (Dichter, qtd. in Barnouw 214), Barnouw added: "In Dichter's view the western seemed to serve the same emotional needs as consumer goods, and their alliance was presumably logical" (214). The implications of failure are intended to be clear.

A more complex and sophisticated analysis, representative of a newer form of television history, begins on a different tack. "Regarding the often-claimed intrinsic virtues of live versus film television drama . . . I remain agnostic," says William Boddy in his outstanding history of policy, industry, and criticism, *Fifties Television*, "and likewise skeptical of the unqualified superiority of 'Studio One' over 'The Untouchables,' or of a typical Rod Serling script for 'Playhouse 90' over one written for 'Twilight Zone'" (8).

But even this study ends in a more familiar manner, its rhetoric suggesting one more version of a narrative of lost opportunities: "The devaluation of television writers and critics, the shrinking of the aesthetic promise of the medium they had celebrated just a few years earlier, and the growing rigidity of program formats, acceptable dramatic subjects, and desired audience targets convinced many critics inside and outside the industry that prime-time television's weaknesses were inherent in the commercially supported system of broadcasting" (253).

Acknowledging the force of these received views, some newer histories are, nevertheless, challenging them. Lynn Spigel, in her carefully detailed analysis of how we came to understand, indeed, came to live with television, suggests that the shifts in the first decades of television were far more complex than the narrative of decline would have it. Her discussion of the domestic situation comedy offers an example of this kind of analysis.

In its earliest manifestations, the family comedy provided viewers with more than just an idealistic picture of themselves at home. A refraction rather than a reflection of family life, the domestic sitcom appealed to viewers' experiences in postwar America and, above all, their fascination with the new television medium. The self-reflexive genre wedded everyday life to theatricality, revealing the artifice entailed in staging domesticity for television cameras. In the process, it offered viewers a sense of imaginary transport, promising to carry them into the homes of familiar television neighbors, who lived in a new electronic landscape where the borders between fiction and reality were easily crossed. (180)

Even the historical data, however, cannot overcome larger theoretical formulations in which television functions as a kind of cultural monolith, the dark mirror of America's fateful union with commercial forces, a mirror that either distorts or obliterates politics and political activity in the cultural service of capital's pervasive strategy. One of the clearest expressions of such a view is in Nick Browne's essay "The Political Economy of the Television (Super)Text." There he links the political economy of television to its narrative economies, arguing that television's organization of schedules colonizes our lived experience, substituting consumer products for real solutions to problems found in our actions or in our fictions, and draining citizens of public life and will. It is this overall schedule, rather than any one program, form, or genre, that accomplishes such ideological work in the cultural sphere: "Placement of a program with respect to the time of day, the day of the week, in relation to what precedes it on the same network, and what it plays against on the others, is the framework not only of popularity, but, I submit, determines format and reception as well. The schedule determines the form of a particular television program and conditions its relations to the audience" (588).

Clearly, all these linkages were established, to a degree, in radio. They are characteristics of American commercial broadcasting in general rather than of television in particular. Significantly, however, the rhetoric with which they are applied to television suggests again the tendency to explain the newer medium in dire terms. Yet, despite Browne's own pessimistic conclusions regarding television's sociocultural functions, the approach he suggests is marvelously insightful and has, to my knowledge, never been taken up as a serious strategy for understanding the history of the medium. Here is his challenge:

> The history of the text of television can be made significantly available by a study of the logic and organization of the slots and formats that compose the framework of the television schedule. The schedule organizes the terms of television's disparate programming in the overall economy of the television world. . . . The selection and arrangement of these program types, night by night, week by week, year by year, through the competitive strategies of the networks, compose the more or less orderly megatext of television. The schedule, we might say, *represents* the comprehensive text of television. (589–90)

I believe that Browne's argument that the television schedule constitutes a "supertext" and the history of that schedule a "megatext" suggests a workable plan for constructing television history. But I do not accept the negative determinist assumptions that undergird it. These assumptions fit and reinforce notions of the "decline" of television in the fifties and match all too easily the conventional explanations of television's early development. In this essay I wish to explore alternative explanations of some of these issues and of some aspects of fifties television.

For example, in reconsidering conventional accounts of the decline of television we must begin with the recognition that notions of the "Golden Age of Television" rely on a very limited set of examples and a particular evaluative scheme that honors particular aesthetic choices. The focus on psychological realism of so-called "ordinary" characters, on contemporary settings, on nonformulaic narrative structures, and, for most early television critics, on probing particular types of social problems elevated some of the early live dramas on television into exemplary texts. Barnouw's clutch of titles from the midfifties is typical:

> The Philco-Goodyear series offered [Paddy] Chayefsky's *Holiday Song* (1953), *The Mother* (1954), *Bachelor Party* (1955), and *A Catered Affair* (1955); Robert Alan Arthur's *Man On A Mountaintop* (1954) and *A Man Is Ten Feet Tall* (1955); Horton Foote's *A Young Lady of Property* (1953); Gore Vidal's *Visit To A Small Planet* (1955). The Studio One series came up with Reginald Rose's *Thunder On Sycamore Street* (1954) and *Twelve Angry Men* (1954). The Kraft series had Serling's *Patterns* (1955). (159)

This is an impressive list indeed, particularly given that all of these works also appeared in print and several in film or on Broadway. But when compared with the number of hours of television programming already in place, these "memorable," touchstone texts are small in number—and judging from subsequent programming trends, perhaps smaller in influence.

Still, there are several points to be made here. The "narrative of decline" that characterizes much historical and critical, but also popular, discourse surrounding fifties television was never solely or simply directed at the way in which telefilm drove out live television drama. Throughout his history, for example, Barnouw also levels his critique at increasing pressure to produce "acceptable" programming, even within these writer-driven, theater-like, live productions. He recounts increasing pressure from sponsors for works that were not pessimistic, works more suitable as contexts for advertisers' purposes. Moreover, he cites pressures brought to bear from political quarters during the McCarthy period, pressure intended to cleanse these serious television productions of any potentially subversive notions. It is easy enough to see that the sort of live programming praised by critics often included works that were critical of some conventional notions of "proper" Americanism, therefore doubly unsuitable as the ground on which American advertising, and thus American commerce, could flourish. In short, his account of television's "fall" into regularized, standardized, predictable narrative forms is grounded in a wider perspective on American social history and can be used to undergird Browne's assumptions about the regularization of experience. These views combined would suggest that the early period of television history was one in which the intended, or merely unreflective interactions of institutions—networks, regulators, program suppliers, advertisers, sponsors—gradually were integrated into the more cohesive system described by Browne.

What such an account does not offer, however, is any way of understanding that other programming forms were available throughout this early period and were always capable of presenting, in different ways, some of the same issues, ideas, conflicts, and contradictions that had lain on the surface of the "Golden Age" dramas. Moreover, the standard account cannot fully explain varieties of audience experience and choice without somehow, explicitly or implicitly, laying blame on that audience. It is true, for instance, that live programming venues were selected as "Outstanding Drama Series" during all these middecade years. But from 1953 to 1955 *I Love Lucy* and *Dragnet* (another telefilm series prototype and *Lucy*'s only serious rival in popularity) were the most widely viewed television series. In other words, filmed, standardized, formulaic programming was already in place and winning audience loyalties even as critics, historians, writers, some directors and producers, and some policymakers began to lament the decline of a different form of television.

Another aspect of Barnouw's argument is central here, an aspect that again provides strong support for Browne's notion of a "supertext." In this construction of the history another form of decline in the fifties is played out in the reduction of choices available to viewers. Admitting that some mix of programming was always available, even in the earliest years of television, the critique is directed against the turn to telefilm as the dominant mode of production. Choice here is defined in terms of the availability of "original" works for television, most often live drama, mixed with "lighter" filmed entertainment such as *Lucy*, with variety programs, some sports programming, and so on. By the end of the decade, this view suggests, "everything" was the "same," meaning that it was produced in Hollywood on film. The oft-cited "glut" of westerns is often used as evidence for this "sameness." As I will show later, this formulation of "choice" severely constrains any close analysis of television programs and assumes an audience unable to distinguish among versions and instances of genre, form, and formula.

I begin, following Browne's suggestions for a history of the schedule, by applying Browne's overview to some aspects of television programming in the fifties, but I examine his notion of the "supertext" quite differently. The difference lies in a fundamentally different set of assumptions. I have presented this other way of exploring television as one that considers the medium as a "cultural forum," a notion developed in 1984 with Paul Hirsch, and one I continue to find a strong explanation of television textuality (Newcomb and Hirsch). Briefly put, the notion of television as a cultural forum rejects any concept of the medium, in its American, commercially supported form, as monolithic and uniform. Granting that television is a central site of hegemonic struggle, we argue that the achievement of ideological domination in the expressive, cultural sphere is far more difficult, in moments both of production and reception, than theory would often admit. From this perspective, then, television is considered as a rich, varied, and internally contradictory text, and these contradictions are expressed at every level, within single programs, within series, within and among genres. While it has been suggested that such a model may be too generous in its imputation of conflict and contradiction, other evidence supports our view. Historically based textual analysis, such as that offered by Spigel, and more careful audience analysis suggest it is more difficult to make a case for a consensual hegemony in television than for degrees, often high degrees, of difference—ideological, aesthetic, cultural.

In this essay, then, I will accept the fact that networks, advertisers, and programmers struggled to position their products and their audiences in a firm alignment, using primarily filmed material by the end of the decade to create a more manageable production and programming practice while attempting to create a more manageable audience. But I will focus my analysis on the difficulty of this process, on the internal distinctions among form, genre, time slot, weekday. And I will add to this basic description a closer analysis of several programs from the fifties that exemplify, in the form of single episodic texts, this struggle for meaning and significance. In these programs the struggle is carried out in the more overtly emotional contexts of narrative, spectacle, and self-reflexive instruction about the nature of television.

HERE is the Monday night program schedule for network television at the beginning of the 1951–52 season.

7:30	ABC	*Hollywood Screen Test*		
	CBS	*News*	7:45	*Perry Como*
	NBC	*Those Two*	7:45	*News*
8:00	ABC	*The Amazing Mr. Malone*		
	CBS	*Lux Video Theater*		
	NBC	*The Paul Winchell Show*		
8:30	ABC	*Life Begins at Eighty*		
	CBS	*Talent Scouts*		
	NBC	*Voice of Firestone*		
9:00	ABC	*Film*		
	CBS	*I Love Lucy*		
	NBC	*Lights Out*		
9:30	ABC	*Film* (continued)		
	CBS	*It's News to Me*		
	NBC	*Robert Montgomery Presents*		
		(replaced by *Somerset Maugham Theater*)		
10:00	ABC	*The Bill Gwin Show*		
	CBS	*Studio One*		
	NBC	*Montgomery/Maugham* (continued)		
10:30	ABC	*Studs' Place*		
	CBS	*Studio One* (continued)		
	NBC	*Local Programming* (McNeil 854)		

Clearly the programming reflects a greater mix of types and formats than would be available at the end of the decade. Some of the options demonstrate television's constant search for audience acceptance and its experimentation with conventional formats and formulas. *The Amazing Mr. Malone,* for example, was based on a radio series centered on a Chicago criminal defense lawyer that had premiered in 1948. *Life Begins at Eighty,* also taken from a radio show, appeared first on NBC, then ABC, then Dumont, then back to ABC and lasted until 1956. McNeil's encyclopedia describes it as a venue in which "a panel of octogenarians dispensed advice on topics submitted by viewers" (406). *Talent Scouts,* originated by Arthur Godfrey on radio and often relying on familiar guest hosts, is a self-explanatory programming category, again illustrating the resilience of some specific types. But *The Bill Gwin Show* (another one-season phenomenon) asked couples from the studio audience to act out scenes suggested by song lyrics (94). On reflection it seems unsurprising that contemporary program developers frequently mine television history for suggestions. Such a program might, drawing on the range of MTV offerings, be quite popular today.

Such connections, however, are not the main point of exploring, even in brief description, these "forgotten" programs that existed alongside the more memorable ones. Rather, I wish to indicate that by including in prime time both *The Bill Gwin Show* and *The Paul Winchell Show,* in which the famous ventriloquist and his equally notable dummy, Jerry Mahoney, performed at a level often thought suitable for children, early television was far more varied, appealed to a broader spectrum of audiences, was more contradictory than it often appears in conventional descriptions. True, the live theater presentations listed in this schedule offered, on occasion, glistening grist for the "Golden Age" myth mill. But those who made music with knee-bent hand saws on the *Ted Mack Amateur Hour* or the boxers who battled fifteen-round championship bouts or *Treasury Men in Action* or *TV Teen Club* were equally at home in the lineup.

Moreover, it seems clear that this mixture of forms, formats, genres, and venues was neither culturally nor ideologically homogeneous. An aspect of the "amateur" pervaded a great many of these early presentations. Even the live dramatic productions were often crude narratives, confined to enclosed spaces, focused on individuals not for psychological purposes, but for ease of presentation, so they could be easily captured by an equally crude technology. And they were often filled with technical errors that made them laughable even at the time. That all this fascinated, appealed to, and finally tutored a mass audience in the habits and regularized definitions of "television" is doubtless true. I make no claim here that television was offering radical alternatives to dominant perspectives, though in any given television drama that might indeed be the case. My argument is that varying perspectives, drawn from or related to variances in class, region, ethnicity, taste, experience, and other markers, appeared regularly, and that television, from its earliest periods, was shot through with a range of difference.

Consider this claim in light of one television program, the most popular television program during the early fifties—*The Texaco Star Theater,* better known by its later title, *The Milton Berle Show.* The episode I discuss here aired April 2, 1951.[1]

The Texaco corporate logo, the familiar five-pointed star, rises from before the camera. Behind it, rushing onto the stage to the flood of music are the Men of Texaco, a singing group in neatly pressed uniforms, military style garrison caps, polished shoes—the garb of the well-dressed filling station attendant of the day. Their song extols the quality of their work in caring for "your" car. Then they shift into spoken rhyme to introduce their star, Milton Berle, the last line of their intro describing him as the one "whose jokes are prehistoric."

On this cue Berle, in a caveman suit, strides onto the stage carrying a dummy female over his shoulder. He flings the dummy aside and rushes into the audience and slashes about with a rope "vine." He attacks the orchestra. He steals a fur coat from a woman in the audience, puts it on, struts back to the stage, makes jokes, then retreats behind the curtain as a commercial is presented by his announcer, Frank Gallup.

After the commercial Berle does a stand-up routine filled with simple jokes, then introduces Ethel Waters, a black star of the Broadway hit *Member of the Wedding,* who will sing. Waters performs a medley—"Heat Wave," "Memories of You." The camera catches her in a series of strong medium shots and close-ups. At the end of the medley she steps off stage. Berle calls her back to take a bow. Berle does more jokes, then introduces celebrities in the audience, among them Ezard Charles, new heavyweight champion of the world. He also introduces members of the New York Yankees baseball team, who appear in a skit with Berle. The skit is followed by another stand-up sequence filled with sexually suggestive jokes, clearly built upon and reminiscent of vaudeville.

Joe E. Browne makes one of his first television appearances and comedian-singer Rose Marie offers an extraordinary impression of Jimmy Durante and is joined on stage by several other Durante impressionists.

Frank Gallup intros a commercial by bringing Berle's salary onto the stage—in a bus driver's change belt. Berle continues to play off this gag and the show breaks down completely before Gallup gets to finish with good words about Texaco.

Berle introduces Tony Martin, elegant in his tuxedo, elegant in his performance of "Begin the Beguine." Then Berle asks Martin to perform "Tenement City," a remarkable number that takes up almost ten minutes of the show. Joe E. Browne plays "John Doe," who wanders into a working-class tenement neighborhood filled with "brotherly love." A tableau vivant motif comes to life as the music takes us into the world of "The Postman," "The Ice Cream Man," and "Mrs. Cohen and Mrs. Kelly." "Mrs. Cohen" makes wonderful Irish stew, "Mrs. Kelly's" gefilte fish is the best to be found. "The Gossip," "The Cop," "The Organ Grinder" are each introduced musically.

Then, from the side of the stage a young black male, perhaps twelve or fourteen years old, steps to the center. He sings "Somewhere over the Rainbow." His voice is huge. His presence powerfully engaging. The "neighbors," his "audience," rave and applaud as he completes the song and disappears back into the "street scene." The skit closes and Berle adopts his "Uncle Miltie" persona, singing a good-bye song to all his nieces and nephews to end the show.

In all, it is a packed hour. By today's television standards, the technique is crude, fundamental. The skits seem overly long, tedious at times. But for me, the most memorable aspects of the entire program have to do, again, with race.

Neither Ethel Waters nor the young singer of Judy Garland's song are called to Berle's side for conversation as the white performers are. Indeed, the young man who sings "Somewhere over the Rainbow" remains nameless, a member of the chorus who has been assigned center stage for a few moments. Those moments stand out, as does Waters's number, because it is 1951, because Ezard Charles is in the audience. Barnouw on Berle: "He was impertinent, but never politically risky" (117).

With such generalizations, there is no allowance for context. In Sardis, Mississippi, in 1951, it was not only the racial aspects of the show, but the slightly off-color jokes, the introduction of baseball stars, "in person," that carried political implications. The potential rupture of social and cultural boundaries was present in such moments. I would suggest that a true understanding of television in the fifties might more profitably consider contexts and connotations such as these than accept the quick explanation of historians and critics whose cultural assumptions, distinctions, definitions, and ri-

gidity are worn so confidently. The fact that television continued and extended radio's role in creating a massive, instantly available "market" for consumer
goods equally available in postwar America is well noted. What is less often
recognized is the "political risk" that came with television's, perhaps unintended, creation of a nation, a culture in communication with itself. All that
had been presented before as spectacle, as event in the movies now became
familiar and intimate in the domestic sense of those terms. These vaudevil-
lians, these black faces, were no longer "out there," requiring a public, if often
clandestinely so, visit. One could now experience previously unavailable,
even forbidden, pleasures at home. Small wonder that protests against television rose in conjunction with the spread of the medium, protests that continued, but soon dwarfed, those previously mounted against other forms of
popular entertainment.

The Texaco Star Theater and other variety shows remained popular
throughout the decade. In many ways they were a model, a microcosm, of
network television. Jugglers here, jokes there, a small talking mouse thrown
in for a change, popular singers, actors, dancers performing for "us" rather
than in the context of a narrative, all of which could be translated into a
western here, a detective there, a range of families in a domestic comedy,
doctors, lawyers, all of them competing for our time and attention, reorganizing heroism and melodrama, gender roles and power relations into a
specific generic format. As often pointed out, few of these offerings challenged, in an overt manner, the prevailing points of view. But they did offer
a level and range of styles, motifs, ways of behaving, ways of speaking, ways
of dressing and eating and working not fully shared until that time. And in
some moments, the challenges and changes were raised to a self-conscious
level that doubtless infuriated the political watchdogs of the day. A 1952
episode of The Goldbergs illustrates.

As usual, Molly Goldberg (played by Gertrude Berg in a script written
and produced by Berg) opens the show with a personal commercial. She has
been to RCA's Exhibition Hall and introduces John William Streeter, a historian of science at Franklin Hall in Philadelphia, to explain "television inter-
ference"—and to explain why RCA has dealt with the problem with its new
Magic Monitor Circuit System. For Molly Goldberg this is a wonder. "Oy,
what did RCA do for the world?" Such moments, commercials blended into
narrative or introduction, were common in early television and reflect instruc-

tional strategies through which America came to accept such commercial underwriting as totally normal broadcasting practice.

An even more illuminating sequence comes later when husband Jake announces that his Uncle Berish will be staying with them for a few days. This makes problems for Molly's Uncle David, who lives with the family. David begins to feel unwelcome because special considerations are made for Berish. Berish, for example, brings his goldfish with him and they must be fed regularly, the little cuties named "Schopenhauer, Shakespeare, and Julius Caesar. I used to have Karl Marx, but I had to give him away."

The episode is filled with references to Kafka, Nietzsche, Einstein, and Huxley. And when the charming argument between the two uncles becomes heated, David yells, "Don't have opinions," and Berish cries out in response: "Where am I? America, USA. Free speech is free opinions, don't take my opinions away from me." Not to be bested, David retorts, "You were a bookbinder. Does that mean you know what's in the books? Did you read one page?" And we move into a discussion of Shakespeare.

I do not cite this episode as a sort of ideological debate occurring regularly in this or other television programs. In fact, I cite it because of its distinction, because in 1952 it might have stood out as much as it did in 1993 when I viewed the tape, when I realized that this episode aired *after* Philip Loeb had been hounded off the same program by political monitors of broadcasting and some years before his tragic suicide. *The Goldbergs* is often cited as atypical, as precisely the type of television driven off the air by the shift to Hollywood, to telefilm, to more homogeneous, regularized forms. But that assumption, too, needs closer analysis.

A Saturday night schedule from the end of the decade (1959–60) demonstrates very clearly some of the changes that had come about.

7:30	ABC	*Dick Clark*
	CBS	*Perry Mason*
	NBC	*Bonanza*
8:00	ABC	*The High Road*
	CBS	*Perry Mason* (continued)
	NBC	*Bonanza* (continued)

8:30 ABC   *Leave It to Beaver*
      CBS   *Wanted Dead or Alive*
      NBC   *The Man and the Challenge*

9:00 ABC   *The Lawrence Welk Show*
      CBS   *Mr. Lucky*
      NBC   *The Deputy*

9:30 ABC   *The Lawrence Welk Show* (continued)
      CBS   *Have Gun Will Travel*
      NBC   *Five Fingers*

10:00 ABC   *Jubilee, USA*
      CBS   *Gunsmoke*
      NBC   *Five Fingers* (continued)

10:30 ABC   *Jubilee, USA* (continued)
      CBS   *Markham*
      NBC   *It Could Be You* (McNeil 862)

Now the mix is more constrained, but still a range of forms is clearly represented. Moreover, an examination of the entire week in which this schedule appears reveals substantial opportunities for varied selection or program types. It also reveals that on some nights westerns outnumber all other forms by an enormous margin. The question, however, for Barnouw, for other historians, for policymakers such as Newton Minow is whether or not similarities of this sort reduce the range of possible enjoyment and interaction, of ideology and critique, of meaning and engagement sought with more conventional definitions of "quality," "variety," "significance," and "risk."

My example here is *Have Gun, Will Travel*. In some ways it is an easy choice with which to illustrate ideological conflicts, for this program often dealt with issues of social significance, with the defense of the oppressed, with the overthrow of authority. Nevertheless, the particular plots are sometimes quite powerful and revealing of what went on in a great many westerns, as well as in other types of programming.

Have Gun, Will Travel centered on the exploits of Paladin (Richard Boone), a gun-for-hire who also exhibited the most elegant traits fostered by education, enlightenment, wealth, travel, and cosmopolitan experience. Making his home in the Carleton Hotel in San Francisco, he scanned newspapers from around the West in search of interesting possibilities for his talents. When he found such a story, or when someone heard of him, he wired his card— the image of a chess knight and the motto that gave the show its title. He then changed from the elegantly attired gentleman into the black-clad gunman and rode off to pursue his profession.

In the episode I examine here, the assignment comes differently. Hey Boy, a Chinese employee of the Carleton who attends Paladin, misses several days of work and is replaced. Paladin goes into the Chinese community to find him, meets his sister, and learns (after considerable complication) that Hey Boy, referred to in the Chinese community by his correct Chinese name by both Paladin and the Chinese characters, has gone to the railhead where his brother works as a laborer. The brother has written that an evil foreman steals wages from Chinese workers, feeds them tainted food, and otherwise abuses them. Hey Boy later receives another letter informing him that his brother has been killed in a construction accident. In the work camp Hey Boy has threatened the life of the foreman and now languishes in jail. The foreman drops charges against him. Recognizing a plot in which Hey Boy, when released, will be killed, Paladin sees that he remains incarcerated.

He then goes to the workers' camp for the central scene in this narrative. There he challenges the workers to stand up for their rights. He speaks Chinese and drinks from their single water dipper. But he exhorts them in English. "You eat slop. You live like slaves. One of your brothers is killed. Then you lick the boots of the man who killed him." The foreman appears and tries to force Paladin out. They fight, and of course the foreman is beaten. Throughout he refers to the Chinese laborers as "little monkeys."

When the workers rise up and demand that the foreman be turned over to them Paladin offers a predictable, but no less effective speech. They, too, must live under the law, must allow the authorities to take care of such situations. Two workers step forward to testify and the sheriff arrests the foreman.

There is certainly no call for rebellion or revolution here, no charge against the order of dominant authority. But I suggest that such programming, contrary to Barnouw's generalized historical assumptions about westerns, about telefilm, about Hollywood products, and about television, was indeed politically challenging, even politically risky. For all its final acceptance of dominant perspectives, it suggests here and repeatedly throughout the series that in its approved, socially ordered form, the dominant system fails over and over on crucial issues. Only the outsider, the intervening hero who privileges the spirit of the law over its institutional form, is able to restore an appropriate order in which race, class, and gender must not be reasons for discrimination. Moreover, what Barnouw and other generalizing historians and theorists often overlook is that most of the westerns and a great many other programs presented on telefilm were in fact anthologies. Their content may have been set in specific times and places, but the issues faced in those programs were widely varied. Their heroic interventions may have been, in formal terms, repetitive, but reaching the conclusions required explorations of character that exceed conventional "good guy–bad guy" formulas. And to overlook that Richard Boone's Paladin was as different from James Arness's Matt Dillon and from all the other central characters in westerns is to deny the very aesthetic such critics profess with regard to "good drama." It is true that these characters were male heroes, but the style and definitions of those elements varied widely and significantly.

If nothing else, the content and distinctive factors of such programs suggest explanations for why the ideological challenges of the sixties emerge, in spite of a system of popular culture too often characterized as structurally conservative and monolithic. As conventionally explained, television was complicit in retarding social ferment, the consideration of social alternatives, real social change. My argument is that social alternatives, personal and systemic, were always available in television, whether or not they contributed in a direct manner to social action. In the details and particulars of television programming we find a process of social ferment. Happy endings and commercial breaks may have served as stoppers on the jugs, but the brew of social action was putting pressure on from the inside. Many further examples are possible. The point is that surrounding the safe and careful sounds of Lawrence Welk were the slapstick and blue humor of Red Skelton, the sophisticated, deadpan style of Peter Gunn, the zaniness of Lucy. Even in the suburban confines of *Father Knows Best*, most plots developed along lines of social discourse, asking over and over, Why should things be the way they are? The answer—Because that is how we hold it all together—necessarily involved the repeated questioning of gender roles, family structure, the nature of authority that drove episode after episode of that series. These were the issues, controversies, debates, and contradictions that were coming into homes across the nation.

The domestication of drama alters the manner of experience from that of the movies. In the theaters, on the special occasion of leaving the home for a night at the movies, such narratives may have drawn audiences in for a few hours of contemplation. When versions of those same narratives came into the home, in ongoing series with familiar characters, with conflict and contradiction forming night after night of plot and character, the ratios of influence were altered. I suggest they have yet to be fully accounted for—or even acknowledged—by many leading television critics and historians.

SUCH concerns raise the largest question and return us to Browne's argument that it is the overall schedule, firmly in place by this time, that regulates our experience and ideological sense of society and culture. Any accomplishment of this work, however, is dependent, again, on an audience unaware of its choices or of what is being "done to" it. Clearly, I have presented no detailed analysis of the schedule here. Such a historical analysis is beyond the scope of a single essay. (Any examination of the history of American television schedules in the various encyclopedias of the medium, however, offer ample evidence of difference if the user avoids prior assumptions that "all TV is the same.")

Still, from the point of view of the forum model, the generic differences alone among programs offer viewers substantially varied ways of experiencing and considering the world. The range of programming selected by audiences shows movement among those possibilities, attendance to alternate representational structures, and enjoyment of different types at the same time. Closer analysis would show specific plots and styles as significant in that process. Even toward the end of the decade, during the period in which westerns dominated the schedule and thereby limited viewer choices, we should note that millions of viewers were watching other programs instead of and in addition to the westerns. For the "monolith" argument to hold, such distinctions must be considered meaningless.

On the face of it, then, Browne's argument, that the modification of social experience into a regularized pattern of expectation and fulfillment that matches industrialized society, is undeniable. Any further argument that this pattern overrides all other differences is highly suspect, however. This is particularly the case when we realize that television, from its earliest periods, tutored its audiences not only in regularity, consent to commercials, gender-specific genres, and scheduling practices but also in self-reflexive, parodic, self-critical viewing strategies.

To illustrate this final point I will use another fifties program. Again, I make no claims of general audience response or unwavering cultural pattern. Rather, I will show how one very popular program treated itself and television without condescending to a mass audience.

Like many other domestic situation comedies, *Make Room for Daddy* offered a soothing view of the traditional family, content with basic values of the home—warm, comforting, and designed along lines of gender authority. As Lynn Spigel has shown, however, it was a family of self-conscious performers, as removed from ordinary experience in some ways as the westerns and detective shows that may have surrounded it at any given time (149). The episode I present here raises that level of performance to new heights, and I argue that it presumes an audience extraordinarily sophisticated in its understanding of television, the constructed nature of the medium, indeed, the contrived, artificial, remote-from-experience nature of the schedule itself.

As the episode opens Danny Thomas, who plays a television-nightclub comedian on the show, waits for a call from his agent. He will learn whether or not he has been selected for a big special on CBS. He is sure he will not be selected. "They always get Benny or Hope. This time they'll get Como." One of his daughters wants Como. His son butters him up for a new bike, telling him how much better he is than Como, but when Thomas refuses the bike, his son stalks out of the room explaining that everybody likes Como.

Word comes from the agent—Benny got the show. Thomas rants and raves about Benny. "He gets everything from me. He's my nemesis. Ricky Nelson will retire before Benny." The doorbell rings; Jack Benny is at the door. Thomas falls over himself in flattery, explaining why Benny should have the show. A series of jokes explores Benny's popularity. "You fold you hands and say 'Well,' then you stare at them for two minutes and they get hysterical." Thomas believes it is black magic. Benny asks, "You think I'm in league with the Devil?"

Later, Thomas falls asleep and dreams that Benny meets with the Devil, played by Gale Gordon. Throughout this sequence the jokes are all about show business, television, agents, the networks. Benny convinces the Devil to sign Thomas to the same type of contract that Benny has. Benny goes to Thomas and closes the deal. All Thomas has to do is utter "Gee" and audiences will melt with laughter. The phone rings. Thomas's agent tells him he has the CBS show. "Gee!" he exclaims—and his wife collapses into peals of laughter. Ecstatic, but skeptical, Thomas thanks Benny, but suggests that "supernatural things don't happen, do they Jack?" Benny roars out a peal of devilish laughter. Worried, Thomas asks again, "Who would sell his soul to the Devil and be condemned to Hell?" Benny replies, "I did—and it's Heaven."

Thomas wakes with a start, terribly relieved that it was all a dream, of course. The doorbell rings and Thomas answers. It is Jack Benny. He has talked the network into giving Thomas the show, and he has brought the show's sponsor. He steps aside and Gale Gordon, sponsor as Devil, appears. Thomas runs away with, "You're not gonna get my soul," as the two men stand puzzled in the doorway.

None of these jokes could work without an audience alert to what networks are, how agents work, what sponsors contribute to the process—and what they demand in return from both performer and audience. Obviously, an argument can be made that this is the most subtle form of co-optation, that one must watch the program to get the joke, be an "insider" in order to be fully implicated in "the schedule" and victim of it. But such arguments oversimplify processes of cultural interaction. This small bit of conventional fiction offers a perspective, a place to stand, from which to participate. It also offers, as do many other television programs, a critique of that same platform. A careful, extended history of television in the fifties would show, I believe, many other instances that offered similar perspectives on television and on every other aspect of American social and cultural life.

I also believe such an analysis would show that this medium had, by the end of the decade, become the central organizing medium in American social experience. Ratios of influence from literature, film, music, information, education, and religion were all altered by its presence, but hardly obliterated. By the end of the fifties it was impossible, even if one criticized or chose to withdraw from the use of television, not to be implicated with and within it. The dominant version of television history sees such implication as a seamless web of social control with television's programming a bland mush of identically inferior entertainment, its audiences duped into uncritical consumerism. As stated at the beginning of this essay, such a "story" fits neatly with other representations of the fifties. Both narratives oversimplify. Just as the reevaluation of the fifties has begun in many fields, so our understanding of television in that decade is being reexamined. The perspective of time, the resources of both video and print archives, a concern for detailed analysis rather than simplistic, overgeneralized pronouncements that do little more than carry out specific hegemonies and cultural agendas, all promise that a full history of the period will show a society caught up and swept along by a new medium. But that society was no less complex, no less complicated, conflicted, and contradictory than any other.

With this knowledge perhaps we can face more confidently a new period of electronic communication, a period that succeeds "the network era" with promise of changes as exciting, and as profoundly troubling, as those brought by "television." Perhaps, if we know the fifties better, we will be better able to deal with these new possibilities more carefully, more rationally, and more critically. The psychic, ideological, social, and cultural landscapes of America were profoundly altered by the new medium in the fifties, but we are probably no worse, and perhaps better off, for it. Television is not the devil to which we bargained away our cultural soul.

NOTE

1   Videotapes of all of the television shows discussed here are available for viewing at the Museum of Television and Radio, New York.

WORKS CITED

Barnouw, Erik. *Tube of Plenty: The Evolution of American Television*. Rev. ed. New York: Oxford University Press, 1983.

Boddy, William. *Fifties Television: The Industry and Its Critics*. Urbana: University of Illinois Press, 1990.

Browne, Nick. "The Political Economy of the Television (Super)Text." In *Television: The Critical View*. Ed. Horace Newcomb. 4th ed. New York: Oxford University Press, 1987. 585–99.

McNeil, Alex. *Total Television: A Comprehensive Guide to Programming from 1948 to 1980*. New York: Penguin.

Newcomb, Horace, and Paul Hirsch. "Television as a Cultural Forum: Implications for Research." In *Television: The Critical View*. Ed. Horace Newcomb. 4th ed. New York: Oxford University Press, 1987. 455–70.

Spigel, Lynn. *Make Room for TV: Television and the Family Ideal in Postwar America*. Chicago: University of Chicago Press, 1992.

David R. Shumway ➤

Five — WATCHING ELVIS
The Male Rock Star as Object
of the Gaze

Elvis Presley on *The Ed Sullivan Show,* 1956–57.
(Courtesy of the Library of Congress)

W HILE the 1950s
are usually under-
stood by the gener-
al public as placid, even
"tranquilized," to quote Robert Lowell, much research suggests that the period was instead a time of significant social
and cultural transformation. Of
course, changes during the fifties in film and popular music are
generally well known, but what
these might reveal about changes
at a deeper social level have not
been explored much. My essay
looks at the visual aspects of Elvis
Presley's performances as an indication of fractures in the seemingly solid edifice of traditional gender roles.

The decade is most often described as the period in which gender definitions reverted to prewar "normalcy," a reversion that is sometimes characterized as imposing even more rigid limits than had been typical during the twenties and thirties. But recent studies by historians such as Beth Bailey and Barbara Ehrenreich have suggested that there were important changes in the construction of sexuality and gender during the fifties and that these changes produced cultural tensions and anxieties. One change was the development of what has been called "a highly sexualized society" in which "the number of explicitly sexual references in the mass media doubled between 1950 and 1960." Yet it was a society that continued to demand that "teen and preteen girls . . . be not only 'good' and 'pure' but to be the enforcers of purity within their teen society" (Ehrenreich, Hess, and Jacobs 11). Thus conditions would seem to have been ripe for these girls to participate in communal fantasies that were at once sexually charged but not sexually explicit. Such fantasies are the stuff that fueled Elvis's rise.

But it was not just teens who felt confusion; there was a widely perceived crisis of gender roles. Changes in the social relations of the genders doubtless produced this crisis. During the war a large number of women entered what had been a primarily male work force and thus threatened the definition of masculinity, as did the increasing number of men who found themselves in jobs and in a home life that did not permit them to exhibit such traditionally masculine qualities as power, dominance, aggression, and ambition (Bailey 98). These changes permitted and were abetted by an increasing awareness of the constructedness of gender spread by popularized versions of Freud. The result was a perception of the "fragility of gender" given expression in a deluge of articles about a "crisis of American masculinity" that in turn often seemed to be caused by a crisis in femininity.

These crises were attributed to two causes. The first had to do with the changing roles men played in American society. Previously, masculinity had been identified with independence and aggression, and it had been given its own spaces in society, the many forms of work and leisure that excluded women. According to Bailey, however,

in the postwar era Americans were coming to grips with changes in their economy and society that, they feared, had rendered "traditional" masculinity obsolete and threatened the vitality of American culture. In the world of the corporation, the "organization," men needed different qualities to succeed. Teamwork, conformity, cooperation, the "social ethic"—these were functional behaviors for corporate success. But they were traditional *feminine* behaviors—the antithesis of aggressive masculinity. To continue to provide well for his family, many feared, a man would have to act like a woman. (104)

But it was not just men's roles that were changing. In spite of the postwar ideological effort to return women to traditional roles (Friedan), there were more married women in the labor force during the fifties than before the war. As more women entered the economy, critics charged "that women were robbing men of their masculinity by adopting masculine (aggressive) roles." These changes threatened three perquisites the American male had assumed as his right: his role as economic provider, his separate subculture of work and leisure, and his aggressiveness, the definitive character of masculinity itself. As Bailey notes, there is a crisis of femininity implicit here: "the fragility of gender was the root of the trouble. The necessary barriers had broken down and women were exercising too much power—whether by stifling masculinity or by assuming masculine traits themselves" (105).

The very perception that gender roles are fragile made Elvis's transgressions both all the more threatening and a cultural force that others would exploit. Elvis transgressed gender boundaries in several ways, but it is my contention that his most troubling transgression was to call attention to his body as a sexual object. This transgression initiated a certain kind of visual presentation of male rock 'n' roll stars that I call feminization. Not all rock stars exhibit themselves in this way, but enough have—and they represent a relatively wide spectrum of rock forms—that feminization cannot be regarded as merely an accident of individual expression. To say the rock stars have been feminized is to say that in their appearance and performance they have violated traditional male gender codes by adopting some that have been considered normally female codes. But feminization does not, as Marjorie Garber contends, render Elvis a transvestite. Transvestism, or female impersonation, might be seen as one extreme toward which feminization has developed, but the phenomenon on which I will focus here is not mainly a matter of cross-dressing. Elvis and other feminized rock stars retain many traditionally male characteristics in their appearance and behavior. They remain, for example, aggressive and even violent in their performances. Thus such cross-dressers as David Bowie or Boy George should not be understood primarily as examples of feminization, although the phenomenon might explain the conditions for their public acceptance. Transvestite rock has been more directly influenced by gay subcultures.

In describing Elvis's feminization, my aim is to try to account for the process in terms of a violation of a gender distinction that is at least as fundamental as dress, but much more subtle: my claim is that Elvis became feminized because he displayed his body as a sexualized object. I thus disagree with Garber's position that all blurring or breaking of gender boundaries can be understood in terms of a "transvestite continuum" (353–54). Though Garber claims to want to challenge the binarism of the gender system, her continuum seems rather to reproduce it, for all violations of the gender code are read as part of an attempt to imitate or masquerade as the other gender. The transvestite makes an effort to appear as gendered differently from his or her anatomy. The feminized rock star does not pretend to be a woman, but rather takes up some of the markers usually reserved for women. As a result the rocker is perceived as feminine because of the rigidity of the gender system; were it not so rigid, he might have been perceived as redefining masculinity. Moreover, unlike the transvestite, the rock star may or may not be aware that he is transgressing gender codes. Elvis, I think, was largely unaware that his performances violated a gender boundary. That may be because Elvis's violation was not so much his behavior, but the relation of that behavior to the gaze, a relation Elvis may not have comprehended, though later rock stars seem to have made explicit use of it.

Some of Garber's case for Elvis as a cross-dresser does refer to his costumes—his use of eye shadow, his fifties gold lamé suit, and his seventies jumpsuit. But much of it rests on the perception of Elvis's feminization. As she puts it, "critic after critic notices that his sexuality is subject to reassignment. . . . This male sex symbol is insistently and paradoxically read by the culture as a boy, a eunuch, or a 'woman'—anything but a man" (368). The issue, as we will see, is even more complicated than Garber makes it, since Elvis is often perceived not merely as a man, but as something of a superman. But in spite of this, Elvis has been feminized. His biographer Albert Goldman offers the most extreme expression of this, providing Garber with an image of Elvis in his Las Vegas jumpsuit as a transvestite successor to Marlene Dietrich (368). Goldman himself describes Elvis's post-army appearance on a television program with Frank Sinatra as "queer. . . . When he confronts the smaller but more masculine Sinatra, Elvis's body language flashes, 'I surrender, dear.'" Goldman's view is suspect because he is an "Elvis debunker"[1] and because his reading reflects the perceptions of 1981 far more than it does those of 1956. If few in the fifties perceived Elvis as a "woman," he did seem in some odd way feminine to them.

I understand the gaze as a power relation or as a sign of that relation. One instantiation of male dominance exists in the unequal exchange of looks that men and women direct at each other. As many theorists have argued and empirical studies have demonstrated, men gaze at women far more often than the reverse (Henley 160–66). This fact of social behavior is represented, enacted, and reinforced in all forms of visual media. The propensity for male film characters to gaze at their female counterparts is well known, and feminist film scholars since Laura Mulvey have argued persuasively that the camera's gaze usually duplicates the male character's so that the female is the object of the viewer's gaze as well. And we also have the history of painting and still photography, especially advertising, in which women's bodies are displayed to sell everything from women's clothing to motor oil. As John Berger puts it, "Men look at women. Women watch themselves being looked at" (47). The power relations implied in this gaze are not a matter of voyeurism, at least not as it has been defined in the psychoanalytic tradition. It is not the illusion of a surreptitious control that the gaze enacts; it is rather a direct assertion of dominance. The gaze is a gesture that, in modern American and European societies, is similar to gestures in animal social groups that mark and reinforce their hierarchical relations.

The gaze does more than merely assert simple dominance, however. By demarcating the female body as sexual, the structure of the gaze is central to the construction of sexuality. It is not just the one-way direction of the gaze that matters, but that the female body is gazed at precisely as a sexualized object. My point here is that to be gazed at as a sexualized object is to be put into a role that until recently only women have played in our culture. As Steve Neale has observed, when males are presented as the object of an erotic look, as Rock Hudson is in Sirk's melodramas, the male's "body is *feminized* . . . an indication of the strength of those conventions which dictate that only women can function as objects of an explicitly erotic gaze" (14–

15).[2] The image or persona that many male rock stars present in performance is the product of the same process of feminization. In other words, these stars have been constructed by dominant relations of visibility.

The cinema, however, is a place where rupture in these relations could occur. Merely to be represented, to act in a film, is already to step over to the other side of the gaze. Most male stars in Hollywood cinema have avoided feminization by controlling the look within the filmic narrative and by enacting traditional masculinity in other ways. Rudolph Valentino, however, does represent a rupture in visual relations. His appeal, according to Miriam Hansen, depends "on the manner in which he combines masculine control of the look with the feminine quality of 'to-be-looked-at-ness.' . . . To the extent that Valentino occupies the position of primary object of spectacle, this entails a systematic feminization of his persona" (12–13). Outside of his films, in photographs and performances as a dancer Valentino was even more feminized because in these he lacks the masculine control of the look and his body becomes solely the object of the gaze (Studlar). Like later rock stars, however, Valentino insisted on his masculinity even to the point of challenging to fight those who questioned it.

But Valentino is the exception rather than the rule. We can find instances of male stars' bodies as objects of the gaze in the films of the classic period, but they are not common. Clark Gable, for example, does something of a striptease for Claudette Colbert in *It Happened One Night,* but this scene must be read against his dominance, in visual and all other relations, in the rest of the film. Only faces of male stars are regularly the objects of the camera's gaze during the classic period of Hollywood, yet the convention dictates that a male face will appear to be watching someone else, revealing spiritual depth, or demonstrating intellectual activity. Cary Grant may have defined a certain image of the handsome male, and as such was certainly an object of desire, but he did so seemingly without our noticing anything in particular about his body except his face.

Jon Savage points out that, after Valentino, James Dean is the next instance of a major male star who is presented as the object of the gaze and who, like Valentino, became the object of cult worship. Dean in *Rebel without a Cause* was the "uncanny enactment of 'the passivity of the adored object' that was the new condition of stardom. Masculinity was now being defined by the female gaze." But it is precisely "masculinity" that is put in question by this relationship. Savage describes Dean's sexuality in that film as "highly androg-ynous," which is to acknowledge Dean's feminization (144). That both the Sal Mineo and Natalie Wood characters seem to take Dean as an object of desire could only reinforce this feminization. If being the object of the female gaze is feminizing then, *a fortiori,* so is being the object of the male gaze.

Valentino, Dean, and Elvis are routinely described as androgynous, but that problematic term deserves a bit of digression. A simple definition of the term is the combination of male and female in one being, and the dictionary gives "hermaphroditic" as a synonym. But the latter term is most often ap-plied to the existence of both male and female genital organs in the same individual, whether such an arrangement is functional and biologically nor-mal, as in earthworms, or is a nonfunctional abnormality, as in humans. Androgyny, on the other hand, is most often applied to the appearance and, less frequently, the behavior of people, and thus concerns secondary sexual traits such as beards or breasts. Yet the term is often used as if physical fea-tures beyond these were also sexually differentiated. Thus Valentino is said to have a feminine face, while Elvis Presley and Mick Jagger are said to have female eyes or lips. In this conception, androgyny seems to be, like hermaph-roditism, a kind of birth defect. Dean's androgyny, however, does not fit this model. His face and body are quite ordinary in their appearance and his blue jeans and T-shirts are usually makers of masculinity; nor is his behavior ste-reotypically feminine. It is rather that Dean's body is displayed for others, that it has "to-be-looked-at-ness" that leads us to experience him as androg-ynous. Similarly, a rock star's lips become a gender marker because of the way they are constituted in visual relations.

Valentino and Dean were cult objects, but their on-screen sexualization is relatively subtle. Neither prepare us for Elvis Presley, who was a fan of both, nor does Frank Sinatra, who had a following of teenage girls in the forties. Because Elvis's androgyny, like Dean's, cannot be ascribed to dress or to what we would ordinarily call feminine gestures, it can only be produced by his position within the structure of the gaze. Yet the passive/active opposition that has been held to structure the politics of looking in narrative films can-not operate in the same way in the concert setting. The singer is both active and passive, an object of adoration and at the same time someone engaged in demanding physical work. To be the object of mass adoration confers a sense of enormous power on the star. That power compensates to some extent for the lack of the control of the look, but it does so only ambiguously, for as Sue Wise has pointed out, the star is precisely an object of his fans and is thus in their power (397). Moreover, "to be a performer is to be at one's most vulnerable" (Henley 167). Unlike most male stars, but like Valentino and Dean, Elvis consistently revealed that vulnerability.

The major factor in Elvis's feminization, however, was the sexual suggestions of his dancing. This dancing was a source of great shock when it was first presented on national TV. Yet it is important to keep in mind that when Elvis was performing in small clubs in the South, his dancing provoked no outrage. Even his first TV appearances on the Dorsey brothers' show, which included some of his dancing, produced little outcry, perhaps because the shows were seen by smaller audiences or because Elvis's dancing was shot from a high angle, lasted for only a short time, and was relatively tame. But with Elvis's first appearance on the *Milton Berle Show,* things began to change. The cameras met Elvis's performance of "Hound Dog" head-on and he gave the audience a little peek at what they might have witnessed in a Beale Street club. The reaction of both professional critics and self-appointed guardians of morality was swift and harsh. The public outcry nearly caused NBC to cancel Elvis's next scheduled appearance on the *Steve Allen Show.* Rather than cancel the appearance, the network devised a plan to contain Elvis. Allen dressed him up in tails and had him sing "Hound Dog" to a live basset hound. Later in the same year, Elvis was restrained by court order from making any offensive gyrations on stage in Jacksonville, Florida. Early in 1957, in what was Elvis's third appearance on his show, Ed Sullivan insisted that Elvis be photographed only from the waist up.

Why did Elvis's dancing cause such outcry? In the history of mass culture, Elvis may be the first male star to display overtly and consistently his body as a sexual object. Precursors, such as Valentino, whose dance performances and still photographs were read in much the same way, reached relatively few viewers when compared either to Valentino's more conventional film roles or to Elvis's television performances. Fred Astaire, Gene Kelly, and other film dancers also bear comparison to Elvis, and Steven Cohan has argued that song-and-dance men were feminized as a result of the way they displayed their bodies before the camera. Yet Astaire and his ilk never produced the cultural anxieties that Elvis did. While the dancer's body is much more the object of the gaze than that of the dramatic leading man, he is not presented as the object of an explicitly sexual gaze. In part this is because a song-and-dance man like Astaire usually played a conventional male role in the films in which he danced. More important, however, the dancing itself is a highly conventionalized spectacle, the performance of which is understood as an art or craft of which the dancer is master. Moreover, the dancer's body is usually covered in formal wear or other conventional garb, making it much less the object of the gaze than is the male ballet dancer's. In fact, the song-and-dance man's dance diverts attention from his body as a sexual object, perhaps in the same way that athletic contests display men's (and women's) bodies without such display usually being perceived as sexual.[3]

But if Elvis represents a break with male performance in mass culture, that does not mean that he invented the style of performance he displayed. On the contrary, there is good reason to believe that Elvis's dancing, like his singing, was an adaptation of black performers' styles. T-Bone Walker and Wynonie Harris are often mentioned as precursors. Harris's producer, Henry Glover, said that "when you saw Elvis, you were seein' a mild version of Wynonie" (Tosches 37). Some who knew Elvis in his pre-recording days say that he learned his style from performers on Memphis's Beale Street: "He would watch the colored singers, understand me, and then got to doing it the same way as them. He got that shaking, that wiggle, from Charlie Burse . . . right there at the Gray Mule on Beale. Elvis, he wasn't doing nothing but what the colored people had been doing for the last hundred years" (Robert Henry qtd. in Marcus, *Dead Elvis* 57). The question of just what if anything Elvis did bring to this style can probably never be settled because the black musicians whom he imitated were seldom filmed. But that is my point. Black blues musicians were part of a subculture; their music did reach a mass audience, but their live performances did not. What distinguished Elvis's performances was that they were televised and, in the cases of the Berle and Sullivan shows, that they were watched by enormous audiences consisting mainly of whites who had never seen rhythm and blues singers perform.

It was not just the size or racial composition of the audience that is significant here, however. The context in which Elvis performed gave the dancing he learned from black performers a new meaning, as did the persona that he developed in collaboration with Colonel Tom Parker and the entertainment industry. It is first worth considering what that persona was not. Elvis did not present himself as a typical blues or rhythm and blues figure. Elvis did not cultivate the image of a sexual athlete or lady-killer as Wynonie Harris, Robert Johnson, and Muddy Waters had in different ways. The lyrics to the latter's most famous songs—"Mannish Boy," "I'm Your Hoochie Coochie Man," "Rollin' Stone," "I'm Ready"—are celebrations of the singer's sexual prowess in which he brags about both his conquests and his abilities. There is not a hint in these songs of the vulnerability characteristic of many blues songs, including those of Johnson. Johnson's persona developed less in his lyrics than in his behavior and in the legends that spread after his death. By virtue of his reputed pact with the devil, Johnson *was* the hoochie coochie man whom Muddy Waters merely sang about. Elvis, on the other hand, was in his early years the antithesis of such Faustian characters. The lyrics of his major early hits almost invariably present a wounded or vulnerable lover— "Heartbreak Hotel," "Don't Be Cruel," "I Want You, I Need You, I Love You," "Love Me Tender." Big Mama Thornton's "Hound Dog" was in her version the female equivalent of a Muddy Waters song. Elvis's version, on the other hand, does not transform the material back into the male original (as Rufus Thomas had in "Bear Cat"). Elvis's "Hound Dog" is best understood as an inspired piece of scat singing or as a novelty song, sexual in attitude or presentation but not in content. The failure to occupy an unambiguous male subject position here corresponds to other, less subtle violations of the gender system we will find in Elvis's visual presentation.

Elvis borrowed his performance style from another kind of blues—that of the singers and shouters who had fronted for bands—but he did not imitate their personas either. Wynonie Harris, for example, was explicit about the image he used to attract women: "I play to create impressions," Harris said. "Woman can get stirred up by a man who seems cruel, ornery, vulgar, and arrogant" (Tosches 40). Charlie Gillett describes the performances of blues shouters such as Harris and Joe Turner as "intimate, relaxed, loaded with sexual references and suggestive plays on words." "But it wasn't just the words—the whole character of the shouted blues was adult, in the tone of voice used by the singers, the assumptions behind the songs, and the sophistication of the musical arrangements" (139, 137). Although Elvis may not have been understood mainly as a teen performer at first, it quickly became apparent that teenagers would be his major market. Cause and effect are hard to disentangle here, and we cannot safely assert either that Elvis's persona was designed to attract his teen audience or that the audience was attracted to a persona that emerged without conscious design. In any case, some elements of Harris's style—orneriness, vulgarity—doubtless appealed to teens and we find these in Elvis's performance. Nevertheless, Elvis does not come across as cruel in spite of the aggression of his performances, and he certainly does not seem the sophisticated and insinuating adult.[4] Innocence, rather, is the dominant characteristic of the Elvis of the fifties. That quality has been apparent to many interpreters of his music, for example, Peter Guralnick on "That's All Right," Elvis's first release from Sun Records: "It sounds easy, unforced, joyous, spontaneous. It sounds as if the singer had broken free for the first time in his life. The voice soars with a purity and innocence" (28).

This side of Elvis may have gotten lost in the late sixties when the first generation of rock critics described him as if he were the white incarnation of the bluesman's sexuality. This reading of Elvis ignores not only the image he presented in his music but his larger public persona as well. "The official Elvis," as Guralnick observes, is marked by "modesty, . . . deferential charm, [and] the soft-spoken assumption of commonsense virtues" (24). One sees this Elvis much in evidence in the TV appearances of the period, in the still photos, and in the interviews. And, there is a particular sense of vulnerability to Elvis, especially in the way he responds to various figures of authority, such as television host Steve Allen. On Allen's show, Elvis was disciplined by being made to perform as clown and he responded to the humiliation with perfect submission. Compare Mick Jagger's mocking expression while singing bowdlerized lyrics to "Let's Spend the Night Together" on the *Ed Sullivan Show*. Unlike the Rolling Stones or the Beatles, Elvis always seemed to play the good son to the show business fathers, respecting their authority rather than mocking or challenging it.

Whether or not this official Elvis is a contrivance, it fit perfectly Colonel Tom Parker's plans for the star. As various accounts of the career assert, Parker's goal was to make Elvis a pop singer. It would, after all, have been impossible in 1955 for him to want to make Elvis a rock 'n' roll star, since such a career path did not yet exist. Thus if the teen audience was to be Elvis's base, the peak he would try to reach would be a mass audience of the white middle class of all ages. His early, unsuccessful appearance in Las Vegas is a testimony to that plan as is the mixture of material Elvis recorded, including an album of Christmas songs. Such a career plan precluded Elvis from producing a persona to match his rhythm and blues performance style and may have contributed to perceptions of his feminization.

Elvis's performance style must be understood in terms of the social and cultural environment that would produce such a career plan. The mass audience had a very narrow range of expectations about male sexuality and it did not include any overt form of self-display; that mode was reserved for women. But television would also change the perception of the sort of performances a Wynonie Harris or a T-Bone Walker might perform in a nightclub. In a club setting, there is more interaction between the audience and the performer, and the performer is less the center of attention. The patrons may be more engaged in other activities than they are in watching the musicians, and their own dancing especially would render the performer more a part of an event than the event itself. Even in a concert setting—which was relatively rare for blues or rhythm and blues performances—a singer or band leader is at most the focal point of attention, but he or she never consumes the entire visual field. On television, however, the performer becomes not merely the center of attention, but often its sole object. In other words, as a television performer, Elvis was the object of a much more focused and intense gaze than his predecessors had been. Elvis was not merely introducing a style with which whites were unfamiliar, but using that style under conditions that transformed its cultural significance.

Contemporary commentators reveal by their descriptions of Elvis that they are aware that this display violates gender codes. The terms in which Elvis's performance was discussed are ones usually applied to striptease: "bumping and grinding." By the middle of 1956, the time of the Berle show performance, he had already been given the nickname "the pelvis," a name which of course means what it does not say. But what is it that is not being said? The standard answer is "the phallus." But unlike performances by some later male stars, in these TV performances at least the penis itself is not emphasized.[5] Elvis's costume, which always included a jacket, hides, rather than displays, his genitals. Sue Wise offers an explanation of the phallocentrism of much writing about Elvis: "what he represented must be the phallus—after all, it must have been something rather wonderful to produce this reaction in girls, and what is more wonderful than the phallus? Lead bar in his trousers or no, when these male writers saw him on stage they saw a 'weapon' of 'heroic' proportions, for how else could he have this effect on women?" (397).

The writers Wise quotes offered their analysis in the late sixties, however, so they may at best reflect the way adolescent male fans of the fifties might have interpreted Elvis. What contemporary adult audiences saw in Elvis's performance was not the parts but the whole. His motions suggested intercourse, and his performance was read as a public display of "sex." Elvis thus put the "sex" that the name rock 'n' roll described explicitly into his performance. But in presenting himself as an object of sexual incitement or excitation, he violated not just Victorian morality—which was no longer hegemonic—but more importantly the taboo against male sexual display. In violating this taboo, Elvis became, like most women but unlike most men, sexualized. As Frigga Haug and her collaborators have illustrated, women are routinely sexualized as the result of their socialization under patriarchy. Various parts of women's bodies—e.g., hair, legs, breasts—become loci of sexualization; women's fashion always calls attention to these features, which are presented for the male gaze, and thus mark the woman as a sexual object. While women are the most sexually marked group, some men are marked in different, lesser degrees. Gay men are perhaps the most marked, but black men are more sexually marked than white men. This last point suggests that if a black man had performed on television in the same way as Elvis, he might not have been met with the same response.

But there is one aspect of these early television performances that might have caused the largely white audience to be even more outraged had the performer been black: the pictures of white teenage girls seemingly losing control under the influence of the performer. Considering this counterfactual example might lead us to recognize one limitation of Wise's reading of Elvis that treats the narrative of Elvis's power over his female fans simply as a way of denying those fans' power. It is true that the narrative renders the Elvis phenomenon "unthreatening" to men, but only to those who identify with Elvis. Elvis's "effect" on young girls threatened those men who assumed that young girls needed to be protected both from sex in general and from its expression in questionable characters like Elvis in particular. His supposed effect on his audience is an essential element in the construction of Elvis as the object of the gaze. According to one narrative, Elvis made his "pelvic gyrations" a regular part of his act after female members of his audiences screamed and applauded at them (*Elvis '56*). Photos of one of these early performances show young women in various states of rapture while watching Elvis perform. When Elvis is featured on major national TV programs, the audience becomes part of the show. In the Berle performance, the film cuts between the stage and the audience, the latter presented not as a large mass of indistinguishable faces but of particular faces whose response tells us of the excitement the performer is generating. This editing also reinforces—or perhaps reifies—Elvis as the object of a specifically sexual gaze. It is not just an audience, of which each viewer is a member, that is watching Elvis. Rather, television or newsreel viewers experience Elvis as the object of the gaze of the (almost exclusively female) individuals who scream, faint, and otherwise enact ecstasy. This representation of Elvis is formally equivalent to the shot/reverse shot editing that structures the gaze in narrative cinema. It becomes a standard trope of the representation of rock and will be repeated numerous times during the British invasion of the sixties

Now it may seem that the logic of my argument would lead inevitably to the claim that these girls who watch Elvis are masculinized by their place in the visual hierarchy. But the pictures themselves prohibit one from following this logic. The point will be made clearer if we compare these screaming, ecstatic teenage girls to the familiar representations of male audiences watching striptease. The latter enact voyeurism; rather than expressing their desire, and thus their lack of control, these men sit impassively or they make jokes to relieve the embarrassment of experiencing sexual excitement in the company of other men. Thus the very expressiveness of these rock fans defines them as female, whatever they are read to be expressing. Often it was that most "female" of all emotions, hysteria.

The visual relation between fan and star under these conditions is ambiguous. The star remains an object of the fan's gaze and thus is vulnerable to her, but the fan's visible response is seemingly produced by the star and thus is in his control. This ambiguity made Elvis all the more threatening, for he seemed, like alcohol, to cause girls to lose their proper inhibitions. This reading of Elvis and his fans can only come from the outside, for the fans themselves do not feel driven. Wise describes her Elvis as a "Teddy Bear" for whom she felt affection rather than desire (395). While Wise's construction of Elvis is suspect as a general account of his female fans' response to him—especially since she is writing as a lesbian—her insistence that we take account of the fans' subjectivity is salutary. She argues that Elvis was "an *object* of his fans," rather than the subject that both adult opponents and male adolescent fans assumed him to be (397). In fact, fans do behave as if Elvis and other rock stars are objects over which they exercise some control. Simon Frith argues that "the power struggle between stars and fans is what gives concerts their sexual charge" (167). The rock star becomes a fetish, not in the psychoanalytic sense, but in the root sense of an object believed to have magical power. To the fan, the star as fetish has power for her, not over her. How else do we explain the enormous market for trinkets carrying names or likenesses of Elvis or other stars? In Elvis's case, the process has gone so far that he now quite literally is becoming deified.

Elvis was not the only rock star to have violated gender codes in the fifties. Little Richard emerged from the gay subculture to be billed as the "queen of rock 'n' roll." But Richard's race made him less threatening, not only because black men were already more sexual, but also because the color line kept him out of the center of public attention. Furthermore, consciousness of Richard's sexual orientation was low among the white teen audience for his work. The gay themes of his lyrics were either expunged ("Tutti-Frutti") or lost ("Long Tall Sally") on the straight audience (see Lhamon 92–96). Elvis's example created new possibilities for male performers, but it took a few years for these possibilities to be realized. Perhaps the first expressions were the teen idols, which the entertainment industry marketed as "safe Elvises." Performers such as Frankie Avalon, Bobby Rydell, and Fabian were essentially male pinups, that is, objects to be gazed at, but little in their behavior or appearance—except their passivity—realized the feminine position this placed them in. They were safe because their sexualization was relatively minor, and their appeal was explicitly likened to the "matinee idols" of the cinema. Yet this comparison does not adequately reflect the passivity that the role of teen idol entailed. Without fictional roles with which they could be identified and even without great success at making or selling records, the teen idols were little more than objects to be gazed at.

CONCLUSION

Elvis needs to be understood as a product of the troubled construction of gender and sexuality during the fifties. But his cultural significance cannot be understood in the context of that moment alone. His violation of gender codes inaugurates a pattern of historical development that later male rock stars will enact. The Beatles represent the next significant moment of feminization. Beatlemania is best understood as a reprise of the reaction to Elvis but on a much greater scale. The Beatles did not call attention to their bodies as Elvis had, but their long hair, worn in bangs, was widely perceived as feminine. "What was most shocking and deeply appealing about the Beatles was that they were, while not exactly effeminate, at least not easily classifiable in the rigid gender distinctions of American middle-class life" (Ehrenreich, Hess, and Jacobs 34). One contemporary commentator observed that some of the Beatles mannerisms were "a shade on the feminine side, such as tossing their long manes of hair," but Ehrenreich, Hess, and Jacobs note that such adult commentators missed the point: "the Beatles' androgyny was itself sexy. . . . To Americans who believed fervently that sexuality hinged on *la différence,* the Beatlemaniacs said, No, blur the lines and expand the possibilities" (35).

If the Beatles represent a mild form of the feminization of rock stars, the career of the Rolling Stones illustrates the full development of this phenomenon. Mick Jagger has described himself as being like a stripper: someone who performs in a sexually charged way, but who, of course, does not feel that charge himself when he performs, since it is precisely performance, work, routine (25 X 5). What this comparison suggests is the high degree to which Jagger was conscious of feminization. Yet the early Stones' performances (1964–65) were also sexually tame compared to those of Elvis. Their dress may be shabby and disrespectful of concert convention, but it does not violate gender codes. In 1966, however, ten years after Elvis's first TV appearances, the Stones did a promotional photo session in drag. Soon after, in the video for "Jumpin' Jack Flash," several band members appear heavily made up; with his puffed-out hair and bug-eyed sunglasses, Brian Jones looks distinctly like Leslie Gore. Jagger's facial expressions, which are the camera's most constant subject, recall those of the stereotypical Hollywood vamp. And while previously Jagger's dancing was restrained, here he begins to repeat and embellish Elvis's pelvic movements. Jagger's open shirt and tight pants together with the camera's much tighter hold on his body sexualizes him even more than Elvis had been. Furthermore, Jagger's jeans are tight enough to make the bulge of his penis plainly visible. Does the era of cock rock begin exactly at the moment of transvestite rock? This combination reappears with a vengeance in heavy metal.

In the years that followed, the Stones continued to develop the feminine implications of being the object of the gaze. The Stones, for example, seem to have been the first males to perform in lingerie, when during their 1972 tour, Jagger wore a white, gossamer jumpsuit that was almost a body stocking. By 1976, Jagger and Ron Wood were flirting with each other on stage and engaging in mock sex—they were performing "Star Fucker"—while the stage props included a giant inflatable phallus. But here we recognize the phallic rock associated with Elvis is not only explicitly adopted by the Rolling Stones but also is already being ironized.

The Stones' innovations provided most of the material for the conventions of heavy metal, including leather, lace, and the baring of skin. But where the Stones' performances, at least in the beginning, were transgressive and thus represented alternatives to the dominant modes of gender construction, heavy metal has become simply a mirror of such construction in American culture, the point, as I read it, of Penelope Spheeris's *The Decline of Western Civilization, Part 2*. Metal costumes combine markers of both masculine and feminine sexuality—epitomized by outfits best described as leather lingerie—so that while they sexualize the body, they do so in terms of a new set of conventions in which the feminine is once again subsumed by the masculine. Metal performers have thus completely recuperated the gender breakdown that early performers had suggested. Heavy metal's themes of violence and power, which its performers enact on stage, make it clear that the spectacle still can be powerful. Furthermore, this power seems to have reobjectified female heavy metal fans, whose own exhibitionism turns the performers into voyeurs. In our contemporary culture anyway, boys will be boys even when they are dressed like girls.

The fifties marked the beginning of a shift in the representation of gender in mass culture, a shift that doubtless reflected the growing realization of gender as a cultural construction. At the moment, men's bodies are far more often objects of the erotic look than they were in the fifties. In fashion photographs, for example, the male torso seems to have become almost as commonly photographed as the female. These photographs and other evidence suggest that men now more routinely watch themselves being looked at. Nevertheless, the dominant relations of looking remain in place. While contemporary Hollywood cinema avails itself of the greater range of possibilities for treating men as erotic objects that rock 'n' roll has in part created, women's bodies remain far more frequently displayed for the camera. Men continue to control the gaze in film and in the culture even if they are now more often also its object.

NOTES

I am indebted to fiction writer Lynne Barrett from whom I have borrowed the idea of the male rock star as object of the gaze. I would also like to thank Joel Foreman, Paul Gripp, Jean Sieper, Paul Smith, and Kristina Straub for comments and suggestions that have contributed significantly to this essay. A brief version of my argument was first presented in "Rock & Roll as a Cultural Practice," from which several paragraphs of this essay have been adapted.

1   Garber does not seem to understand the cultural significance of the insults Goldman directs at Elvis's masculinity. Such insults are a staple of working-class male culture and an expression of homophobia. She writes as if Goldman were also celebrating transvestism, when his goal is in fact to castrate Elvis, to deprive him of his cultural power.

2   See Byars for an extended discussion of gender in fifties melodramas that supports Neale's position.

3   This is not to say that athletes cannot present themselves as objects of the sexual gaze, as Andre Agassi has done. Moreover, as male bodies have become more often the object of the sexual look in the culture at large, male athletes may be more likely to be understood as such objects.

4   I am speaking mainly of Elvis's television performances from the fifties. There is a cruel side to the characters that Elvis played in some of his films, but even here, however, cruelty is never the dominant impression.

5   There are stories about Elvis stuffing his pants to make himself look well endowed, but the television performances reveal none of this. Garber recounts one of these and her commentary on it reveals a consistent flaw in her argument. She claims that the use of a "prosthesis" is part of Elvis's transvestism in which "the phallus itself becomes an impersonator—and, moreover, a female impersonator, for only a female would lack a phallus and need a substitute" (366–67). If we step back just a bit from Lacanian theory, we might be able to read the surface text here. That Elvis is trying to be more male does not make him female, any more than a woman with a padded bra or breast implants is rendered male by their use. If there is anything feminine in the use of a phallic prosthesis, it lies in the breaking of the taboo against male self-display.

WORKS CONSULTED

Bailey, Beth L. *From Front Porch to Back Seat: Courtship in Twentieth-Century America*. Baltimore: Johns Hopkins University Press, 1988.

Berger, John, Susan Blomberg, Chris Fox, Michael Dibb, and Richard Hollis. *Ways of Seeing*. London: BBC; Middlesex: Penguin, 1972.

Byars, Jackie. *All That Hollywood Allows: Re-Reading Gender in 1950s Melodrama*. Chapel Hill: University of North Carolina Press, 1991.

Cohan, Steven. "'Feminizing' the Song-and-Dance Man: Fred Astaire and the Spectacle of Masculinity in the Hollywood Musical." In *Screening the Male: Exploring Masculinities in Hollywood Cinema*. Ed. Cohan Hark and Ina Rae Hark. London: Routledge, 1993. 46–69.

Ehrenreich, Barbara, Elizabeth Hess, and Gloria Jacobs. *Re-Making Love: The Feminization of Sex*. Garden City, N.Y.: Doubleday, 1986.

Elvis '56. Videotape. Produced by Alan Raymond and Susan Raymond. Media Home Entertainment, 1987.

Friedan, Betty. *The Feminine Mystique*. New York: Dell, 1963.

Frith, Simon. *Music for Pleasure*. New York: Routledge, 1988.

Garber, Marjorie. *Vested Interests: Cross-Dressing and Cultural Anxiety*. New York: Routledge, 1992.

Gillett, Charlie. *The Sound of the City: The Rise of Rock 'n' Roll*. New York: Dell, 1972.

Goldman, Albert. *Elvis*. New York: McGraw-Hill, 1981.

Guralnick, Peter. "Elvis Presley." *The Rolling Stone Illustrated History of Rock and Roll*. 3d ed. Ed. Anthony DeCurtis and James Henke, with Holly George-Warren. New York: Random House, 1992. 21–36.

Hansen, Miriam. "Pleasure, Ambivalence, Identification: Valentino and Female Spectatorship." *Cinema Journal* 25.4 (1986): 6–32.

Haug, Frigga, et al. *Female Sexualization: A Collective Work of Memory*. London: Verso, 1987.

Henley, Nancy. *Body Politics: Power, Sex, and Nonverbal Communication*. Englewood Cliffs, N.J.: Prentice-Hall, 1977.

Lhamon, T. H. *Deliberate Speed: The Origins of a Cultural Style in the American 1950s*. Washington, D.C.: Smithsonian Institution Press, 1990.

Marcus, Greil. *Dead Elvis: A Chronicle of a Cultural Obsession*. New York: Doubleday, 1991.

———. *Lipstick Traces: A Secret History of the Twentieth Century*. Cambridge, Mass.: Harvard University Press, 1989.

Mulvey, Laura. "Visual Pleasure and Narrative Cinema." In *Feminism and Film Theory*. Ed. Constance Penley. New York: Routledge, 1988. 57–68.

Neale, Steve. "Masculinity as Spectacle: Reflections on Men and Mainstream Cinema." *Screen* 24.6 (1983): 2–16.

Savage, Jon. "The Enemy Within: Sex, Rock, and Identity." In *Facing the Music*. Ed. Simon Frith. New York: Pantheon, 1988. 131–72.

Shumway, David R. "Rock and Roll as a Cultural Practice." *South Atlantic Quarterly* 90 (Fall 1991): 753–69.

Spheeris, Penelope, dir. *The Decline of Western Civilization, Part 2: The Metal Years.* New Line Cinema, 1988.

Studlar, Gaylyn. "Valentino, 'Optic Intoxication,' and Dance Madness." In *Screening the Male: Exploring Masculinities in Hollywood Cinema.* Ed. Cohan Hark and Ina Rae Hark. London: Routledge, 1993. 23–45.

Tosches, Nick. *Unsung Heroes of Rock 'n' Roll.* New York: Scribner's, 1984.

25 X 5: The Continuing Adventures of the Rolling Stones. Videotape. Produced by Andrew Solt. CBS Music Video Enterprises, 1989.

Wise, Sue. "Sexing Elvis." In *On Record: Rock, Pop, and the Written Word.* Ed. Simon Frith and Andrew Goodwin. New York: Pantheon, 1988. 390–98.

Donald Weber ▬

Chapter
Six

Six

MEMORY AND REPRESSION IN EARLY ETHNIC TELEVISION
The Example of Gertrude Berg and *The Goldbergs*

I N January 1949, after almost twenty years of sustained popularity on radio, the family series known to millions of American listeners as *The Goldbergs* made the transition to the "new" world of television, where, on Monday nights at 9:30 (EST) on CBS, it continued to dramatize the various crises, comic and serious, in the life of perhaps the most famous Jewish family in America. "The Goldbergs March On" (59) is how *Life* magazine described the show's passage from radio to TV a few weeks into its first season, and it pictured Gertrude Berg (1899–1966)—the show's famous creator, writer, and star—sur-

Gertrude Berg as Molly Goldberg of *The Goldbergs*, 1949–53.
(Courtesy of the Library of Congress)

144

rounded by mountains of radio scripts, evidence of the show's long and distinguished earlier incarnation as a daily radio serial second only to *Amos 'n'
Andy* in longevity and national affection.

"*The Goldbergs* has now been converted to television," *Life* announced,
"and may go on forever" (59). In fact the show went on to a troubled history
(one of its stars, Philip Loeb, was blacklisted in 1950 and eventually fired).
It was on and off the air, in different formats, with different networks and
corporate sponsors over the next five years; finally, by the fall of 1954, under the title *Molly,* the show ended a truncated season (April–October 1954)
on the Dumont Network and had its last sequence of airings in syndication
during 1954–55. Thus like so many early fifties television programs that featured ethnic family life (including *Life with Luigi, Bonnino,* and *Mama,* about
a Scandinavian family in turn-of-the century San Francisco) along with heavily ethnic-inflected variety shows (most famously *Texaco Star Theater* and *Your
Show of Shows*), *The Goldbergs* disappeared from television by the midfifties,
at the threshold of what George Lipsitz terms the arrival of "ethnically neutral" (72) programming. By "ethnically neutral" Lipsitz refers to shows like
Ozzie and Harriet, Father Knows Best, and *Leave It to Beaver*—programs that
took for granted the arrival of suburban family life. This displacement, Lipsitz argues, in effect drained "ethnic" content from prime time as it signaled
the new hegemony of national networks in shaping the content of television
programming, thus replacing previous corporate sponsorship of shows with
the centralized authority of the network itself.

The Goldbergs tried to adjust to these postwar demographic-economic
shifts as Berg dutifully moved her television family from Tremont Avenue in
the Bronx (where for years her character Molly had ritually presided over
her tenement windowsill, giving homespun advice to her neighbors) to the
suburban enclave of Haverville (the "village of the haves," in David Marc's
nice formulation [51]), but the transition proved short-lived; the show's
"march" from radio through television's golden age did not survive the dramatic structural transformations that had begun to mark American culture
by the end of the decade.

MY task in this essay is a close examination of selected television episodes
of *The Goldbergs* as "texts," which will enable me to address a number of issues in American cultural and ethnic studies currently engaging students of

television and popular culture: the agency and impact of early ethnic television in the legitimizing process of emergent, postwar commodity capitalism;
the agency and role of ethnic "memory" in this dynamic of critical reception
(including the formation of audiences often theorized as "resistive," oppositional readers/viewers) and cultural legitimation; the meaning of memory,
specifically Jewish memory, in Berg's imagination of Jewish-American family life (from the thirties to the fifties); and, finally, the ways Berg's Jewish
middle-class imagination determined what she felt could or could not be represented about Jews on television—the issue, that is, of how ethnic memory
("the textured layers of immigrant experience [48]," in Lipsitz's formulation)
at times inspired, at times *contained* the content and tone of *The Goldbergs*
on television. Before I address these issues, however, let me locate the sources of Berg's famous alter ego, Molly Goldberg, by discussing the popular
modes of Jewish-American cultural expression against which she fashioned
her ideal of ethnic wisdom and unqualified familial love. In addition, let me
establish the contexts for a reading of *The Goldbergs* on television by briefly
describing her early career as radio auteur (including a sampling of her listener responses) in the thirties.[1]

As to the origins of the Goldberg family, Berg drew on her own family,
especially her grandparents and children, as inspiration for Molly's husband,
Jake, and their children, Samily and Rosily (*Molly and Me* 174–94). Berg's
father owned a small Catskill hotel, and during the summers Berg would try
out various sketches and routines that eventually ended up in *The Goldbergs*.
Berg's imagination of Molly's character, and of Jewish family life in general,
fashioned in the late twenties, was constructed, as various early newspaper
and popular magazine articles about her point out, in apparent negative response to the often raw, raucous, uncivil world of Jewish dialect humor, represented by early vaudeville comedians like Monroe Silver (who recorded a
series of "Cohen on the Telephone" albums in the twenties—comic monologues featuring the mishaps of a recent immigrant confronted with the
strange ways of the host society) and in the wickedly satirical sketches of the
now obscure dialect artist Milt Gross, whose work in the *Sunday World* (also
in the late twenties) garnered a sizable audience. Dialect humor in general
flowered in American popular culture at this historical moment; its stars included vaudeville performers like Fannie Brice (among her recordings was a
variation on Silver's routine called "Mrs. Cohen at the Beach") and Sophie

Tucker (the "red hot mama" who included in her repertoire a number of bawdy, double entendre–filled, Yiddish-inflected ballads). In 1930, soon after what a newspaper termed her "meteoric success in the radio world," Berg explained that her own portrait of Jews and Jewish life issued from an uneasy reaction to "Jewish types portrayed on the stage," a tradition within American popular culture which, she confessed, "was very revolting to me" (Jaffe).[2]

What must have revolted Berg about the Milt Gross material (by the fifties one could speak, derogatively, of a "Milt Gross" style of dialect humor) was how the mangled Yiddish-English discourse in his humorous sketches (and strange drawings—Gross was also a fairly primitive cartoonist) rendered immigrant family life as unsavory, as an endless screaming match between lazy, streetwise children and shrill, quick-to-holler-and-hit immigrant parents. Gross was notorious for his Yiddish parodies of various American tales and legends ("Cuttsheep of Miles Standish" or "Sturry from Hurratio Halger") rendered in a thick dialect and often filled with hilarious malapropisms ("I should geeve gradually a dife in de wodder, I should rull her on a berrell she should be rusticated," narrates Gross's "Hurratio Halger," about his providential saving of the banker's daughter) (*Dunt Esk!!* 207).

In retrospect, Gross's two collections, *Nize Baby* (1926) and *Dunt Esk!!* (1927), may have offended some of his (Jewish) readers' assimilationist sensibilities; perhaps they were made to feel embarrassed by how awkward and "uncivilized" Jews sound in his unbuttoned parodies. Perhaps, too, they heard (at some level) tones of a darker world beneath the raw generational exchanges (often leading in Gross's work to physical violence and filial flight) in brutal sketches filled with the mocking, sardonic humor subversive both of the authority of the family and of the dominant culture. Above all, troubled readers in the late twenties (perhaps like Berg herself) may have sensed the anarchic potential of Yiddish dialect humor (and probably of most effective dialect humor in general, from Finley Peter Dunne's Mr. Dooley to Langston Hughes's Jessie Semple), which in Gross's art explodes American mythologies through the overturning linguistic power of parody. At some level, that is, Gross's richly comic, but harsh immigrant landscape is the lowbrow version of Henry Roth's utterly unsentimental, harrowing canvas of immigrant coming-of-age, *Call It Sleep* (1934), in which Yiddish is rendered as a lyrical English and English is represented in severely fractured, disjointed, often incomprehensible street Yinglish. In both instances success (material and spiritual) in America proves illusory, and the immigrant myth of middle-class arrival is denied—at least in Roth's demystifying vision—by the terrifying figure of the vengeful father who, feeling himself a failure in the New World, takes his smoldering rage and swelling paranoia out on his bewildered, innocent son.

By contrast, Berg's career in radio and television amounts to a gigantic effort to soften the jagged edges of historical alienation through the supremely maternal figure of Molly Goldberg and her special accommodating stance—a vision of a loving family, of interdenominational brotherhood, of middle-class ideals, of the harmonies of *American* life, indebted to the ideals of both immigrants and American founders (in the television show, ovals of Washington and Lincoln grace the wall of the Goldbergs' Bronx apartment). Above all, Berg's representation of host-culture experience, in contrast to the harsh world imaged in *Call It Sleep,* is that of family life unconflicted, untainted by New World irony and despair (the bitter tones that nourish the parodic sensibility). When Gertrude Berg first imagined, in the midtwenties, a radio series about Jewish family life in America, she titled it *The Rise of the Goldbergs* and constructed her vision of ethnic striving as a testament to the wonder-working powers of the American dream, a daily chapter in the saga of hope and perseverance that struck a profound answering chord in the hearts and minds of what soon became her millions of listeners during the Great Depression.

The popular response to the radio *Goldbergs,* as gleaned from selected extant letters, was overwhelmingly enthusiastic. "The nation's ear," announced the fan magazine *Radioland* in 1934, was "attuned to the conversation of the best known family in America" (Maxwell 72). For example, the show's initial sponsor, Pepsodent toothpaste, reported to Berg that *The Goldbergs* received 3,302 letters during May 1932, of which 2,838 were complimentary, while only 11 voiced objections (W. W. Templin to Berg, June 17, 1932, Correspondence Scrapbook 1, 1931–32, Berg Papers). "We certainly admire the ideals this family stands for, and the way they reach the inner and higher feelings of us all," wrote a devoted listener in 1931; "the Goldbergs are to the mind what Pepsodent is to the mouth—they both leave a clean, wholesome feeling not to [sic] soon to be forgotten" (Correspondence Scrapbook 1, 1931–32, Berg Papers).

Distilling from the surviving testament to the show's popular reception, the voices of Berg's listeners convey a rare, immediate sense of just how accessible, how compelling Berg's construction of the Jewish-American family as *American* family proved to be. *The Goldbergs* appears to have truly inspired its audiences during the Great Depression, filling an affective void: the show literally became a surrogate family, surrounding households across the country in the thirties with the familiar sounds of middle-class experience, with the comforting message of middle-class ideals.³ If in some sense (following historian Warren Susman) the cultural moment of the thirties can be viewed as a time when people sought to embrace a soothing explanatory narrative or myth or ideology in the face of an uncertain future (160), then *The Goldbergs* performed its cultural work as an agent of social cohesion, offering a utopian dream ("they present life as it should be," wrote a woman from Oklahoma City in 1933 [Correspondence 1933, Berg Papers]) to a nation reeling from economic rupture and social dislocation. The figure of Molly, we might say, inspired faith—and faithful listeners—during an interval of spiritual doubt and historical uncertainty.

About the virtually unqualified, positive reaction to her characters Berg was genuinely surprised; potential network executives had at first been skeptical about the appeal of such an "ethnic" show. Interestingly, though Berg labored to modify the extremely distasteful dialect tones of *Nize Baby*, what remains striking about the early *Goldbergs* scripts is just how heavily "ethnic" they in fact are. Listen, for example, to a sample of one of Berg's earliest-penned exchanges between Molly and Jake:

JAKE: Molly, your soup is feet for a kink.
MOLLY: You mean a president. Ve're in Amerike, not in Europe.
JAKE: Oy, Molly, Molly, soon ve'll be eating from gold plates.
MOLLY: Jake, d'you tink it'll taste better?
JAKE: Soch a question?   (*Molly and Me* 179)

This exchange, which Berg performed for Edward R. Murrow on *Person to Person* in 1954 and repeated again in her 1961 autobiography, *Molly and Me*, already marks the imagination of Berg's central characters: Jake, always seeking a fuller material existence; Molly, always tempering his impulsive desires with a down-to-earth reality check designed to remind him, and her listeners, about the spiritual costs of acquisition. Or listen, only a few months into the depression, to what the nation heard, in the following conversation between Molly (spelled "Mollie" in early scripts) and Jake from the fifteenth episode of *The Goldbergs*, titled "Sammy's Bar Mitzvah":

MOLLIE: You know, Jake, ull de pipple vhat goes arount saying dat in life is more troubbles dan plezzure is ull wrong—I tink so.

JAKE: Bot everybody says so—even de beegest writers.

MOLLIE: Oy, dat's because dey didn't found out de secret.

JAKE: Aha! so you found it, ha?

MOLLIE: Yes, Jake. Dun't leff. Maybe I'm a plain peison, and I dun't ridd vhat de high writers is writing, bot by myself I found out de whull secret.

JAKE: So tell me too.

MOLLIE: You see, Jake, it's true vhat in life is lots of trobbles. Bot de come, dey're here, you go through vid dem, and findished.

JAKE: Nu, so dat's de secret?

MOLLIE: Not yat. Bot de goot tings, de plezzures, is never findished. Dey're ulvays vid you—it not outside, den inside.

JAKE: How's dat?

MOLLIE: Because ull you got to do is cloise your eyes—vhat am I talking?—not even cloise your eyes—unly tink, and ull de nicest fillings, de best experiences in your life is beck again, and even more lovely dan before. You can live it ull over again! . . .

JAKE: Your secret can't vork for everybody, Mollie. Maybe unly far drimmers like you.

MOLLIE: Nu, be a drimmer! Dat's de secret, see?

Here, it seems to me, is a Yiddish-inflected dialect offered as a (conscious?) counter to the unsavory model of Milt Gross (yet in places Berg appears to draw directly on Gross's characteristic style, even his mode of spelling); here is a warm, homey Yinglish designed to address the emotional and psychological needs of its audience during the winter of the country's Great D/depression. Although it is impossible to recover fully *The Goldbergs*'s audience in the early thirties, Molly's fervent voicing of the dreamer's unflappable, progressivist vision must, at some level, have reverberated in the hearts and minds of listeners across the country. And if Molly's uplifting rhetoric in fact had an impact, its power may have been linked to her social position as newly arrived American visionary, revoicing, recapitulating the country's innermost ideals of cosmic optimism and resilient striving. Thus what was "sedimented," to recall Lipsitz's key word, layered in the early radio *Goldbergs,* and perhaps extracted by her American listeners—some of whom would structure their lives around a ritual "appointment" with Molly—is a rich deposit of national ideals filtered through the imagination of her faithful, New World immigrant dreamer. Berg's Molly, that is, loomed in the popular imagination as the keeper of the immigrant/American dream through the act of utterance: her visionary Yinglish enacts, indeed testifies, to the promise of the American myth. Thus in direct contrast to (in Berg's view) the degrading, ethnic-literary caricatures of Milt Gross, Berg's Molly strives to speak, if not with the pure "American" inflections of the dominant culture, then with immigrant tones that nevertheless revoice national ideals. Berg constructs, I want to emphasize, a rhetorical world against "ungenerous" parody, against—can it be called?—"un-American" irony. In the linguistic universe of Molly Goldberg, *drimm* = dream.

In addition to working against popular stereotypes, Berg envisioned *The Goldbergs* from its beginnings as a radio show as a repository of ethnic memory. Thus at another sedimented level the show mined the memories of its Jewish listeners; for some it may have assuaged shame and anxiety over social marginality and difference; for others it may have aided in the therapeutic release of long-suppressed or simply forgotten ethnic feelings. One listener from Brookville, Indiana, after hearing a Yom Kippur show in October 1935, wrote Berg a thank-you note on behalf of the two Jewish families in town: it "touched our hearts as it was so real and reminded me of years gone by" (Oct. 3, 1935, Correspondence Scrapbook 4, 1935, Berg Papers). Writing about the same broadcast, a young woman from Los Angeles admitted that although she was "a modern Jew of the younger generation," the Yom Kippur show "certainly gave a tug at my heart strings" (Oct. 2, 1935, Correspondence Scrapbook 4, 1935, Berg Papers).[4] Eight years later a man from Cleveland, in response to another Yom Kippur show, thanked Berg because "this series from your facile pen has done more to *set us Jews right* with the 'goyim' than all the sermons ever preached by the Rabbis" (Oct. 1943, Correspondence Scrapbook 7, 1941–49, Berg Papers). And after a Yom Kippur show aired in 1949, a young woman felt moved to respond, "I admire your courage to depict our Jewish life in such a beautiful way" (Oct. 6, 1949, Correspondence Scrapbook 7, 1941–49, Berg Papers).

From the beginning, then, it appears that Berg and *The Goldbergs* performed the cultural work of recuperating Jewish memories and ritual practices (Passover shows were performed throughout the show's tenure as well), presenting, really re-presenting Jewish life to America in ways that made the audience members feel better about their own uprooted condition, more at ease in their New World zion. Ethnic memory in Berg's imaging of *The Goldbergs* is thus cohesive, a bonding ritual designed to defend against (imagined) host culture threat (or ignorance), as well as a defense against disabling nostalgia. Indeed, as if to compensate for her self-confessed "lack of Jewish training" in her private life—Berg's own speech, we should note, was mannered and precise and thus she was, more or less, performing ethnic memory for her audience—Berg redressed the religious balance in art by incorporating religiously "authentic" shows that rendered Jewish rituals and liturgy in the warmest, most affecting light.

Yet Berg, always self-conscious about "host" culture reception, also carefully monitored the "Jewish" content and tone of the show. In a 1956 interview, about the time *The Goldbergs* had run its course on television, Berg enumerated those subjects she deemed inappropriate for representation on her show, a revealing litany of prohibited themes: "You see, darling, I don't bring up anything that will bother people. That's very important. Unions, politics, fundraising, Zionism, socialism, inter-group relations, I don't stress them. . . . After all, aren't such things secondary to daily family living? The Goldbergs are not defensive about their Jewishness or especially aware of it." "I keep things average," Berg confessed in the same interview; "I don't want to lose friends" (Freedman 359–60). Or, as the case of Philip Loeb reveals, make trouble. Loeb made trouble for Berg, for he symbolized, by his political behavior—which in the forties included support for the integration of baseball, among other "subversive" causes—all that Berg's imagination of Jewish life, really Jewish history in America, sought to repress. Loeb's listing in *Red Channels* in the summer of 1950—an exposure that would prove fatal to his career—"brought up" (to recall the anxious language of the *Commentary* interview) an alternate, dissenting relation to the dominant culture that Berg—given her status in the popular imagination as matriarch of *the* America-embracing, middle-class ethnic family—could not, finally, be associated with.[5]

Berg, we recall, created *The Goldbergs* to "set us Jews right" and labored to portray Jewish family life as the incarnation of the American way before the judging gaze of the host culture; by the late forties and early fifties Berg/ Molly was the symbol of the rising Jewish middle class, the figure who not only recapitulated the experiences of many women among her viewers/listeners ("You symbolize for them the lives that they have lived," a 1942 letter from the director of a Jewish old-age home wrote to Berg [July 14, 1942, Correspondence Scrapbook 6, 1939–41, Berg Papers]) but perhaps the most visible mediating link between the host culture and the affective life of the Jewish middle class. And that mediating role was, above all, "to keep things average" and not make trouble.

So, for example, even in the potentially dangerous sphere of landlord-tenant relations—the would-be subject of an early TV *Goldbergs* called "The Rent Strike"—the potential exposure of real class inequities, the arranging and implementing of a rent strike in the Goldbergs' Bronx building is contained through Molly's office as *fixerke*,[6] which eliminates the need for collective action. As the story unfolds, Papa Jake, played by Loeb before the blacklist, is outraged by yet another rent increase and adamantly refuses to accept the landlord's demand (Loeb, by the way, is so animated, so fiery in this role that his agitated presence virtually overwhelms Berg's performance). The crisis dramatized in "The Rent Strike" is resolved in the end, however, not by tough landlord-tenant negotiation but rather through Molly's distinctive mode of reconciliation: her domestic art of cooking. Seeking to save the day, she bakes a cake especially for the landlord, since it happens to be his birthday. Uncle David (a Goldberg extended family member and also, by virtue of his heavy Yiddish accent, the show's most "ethnic" character) squeezes lemons for lemonade as an offering to the landlord's wife, in order to soften her, and thus her husband, on the issue of the rent increase. In the end the gift of food, and Molly's generous heart, overcome the threat of a Bronx tenement rift; "A landlord is also a person," Molly declares, as the episode closes in harmony and reconciliation.[7]

It may be that Berg's evasion of taboo political themes (in the case of "The Rent Strike," issues of power and property) together with her conscious avoid-

ance of subjects keyed, at least in some segments of the American imagination, as overtly "Jewish" (e.g., "unions," agitating for social justice) contributed to the enormous popularity of *The Goldbergs* on television. Swerving
further from Jewish memory, even the series' representation of religious ritual became attenuated by the early fifties. Berg continued to do shows with
religious themes, such as "Yom Kippur," which was virtually identical to an
earlier radio program, but on TV its theme focused more on the unbreach-
able bond between father and son than on the spirit of the sacred holiday
itself. Unlike the radio segments, the TV *Goldbergs* declined to render the
forms and rituals of Jewish religious observance. Even the plot of the Passover show for television avoids addressing the meaning of the holiday; instead, it concerns the mildly funny comedy of how many extra portions of
gefilte fish Molly needs for a continually mounting number of guests she hears
will attend the Seder. (By the early fifties, Berg's notes on these particular
scripts indicate that other, nonreligious shows replaced those with religious
themes.)[8] Thus it may be that the TV audience for *The Goldbergs*—and now
I mean its Jewish-American viewers—needed the social-religious-political
repressions implicit in Berg's litany of prohibited themes. It needed, in the
early fifties, the figure of Molly to help ease the cultural-historical transition
into the middle class.

Indeed, what marks the television version of *The Goldbergs* is the show's
anticipation—indeed, expression—of what the sociologist Herbert J. Gans,
in 1956, labeled "symbolic Judaism," a term he later enlarged into "symbolic ethnicity"—a religious-cultural outlook linked to the fifties phenomenon
of middle-class arrival. "As a result of the pressures, the training, and the
rewards offered by American society," Gans observed, "traditional Judaism
has ceased to be a living culture for the second-generation Jew. Parts of it,
however, have remained active in the form of habits and emotions; these are
now providing the impetus for a new 'symbolic' Judaism still in the process
of development" (425). *The Goldbergs,* in light of Gans, proved to be the perfect televisual medium "mirroring" this new class because it avoided the
messier history of immigrant life. Of course to speak of television's "mirroring" dimension, as Todd Gitlin and other students of television culture remind us, simplifies the complex dynamic of legitimation and resistance ("how
popular culture can simultaneously subvert and reproduce hegemony," in T. J.

Jackson Lears's succinct phrasing [1405]). The themes and issues represented—or not represented—on *The Goldbergs* actively shaped, and were shaped
by, the real aspirations of at least some portion of its implied audience: a new
ethnic middle class looking to the dominant culture as an authorizing, legitimating sphere.[9]

Gertrude Berg joined in the distinctively fifties work of cultural legitimation through the performance of ethnic memory. As Lipsitz has shown, early ethnic television reveals a powerful disjunction between "sedimented"
memory and emergent commodity culture. "Network television," writes
Douglas Kellner, "became the voice of corporate capitalism and the instrument of its hegemony" (45). But more than the voice of the network boardroom, it was the voice of Molly Goldberg that sanctioned the new consumer
culture. Listen, for example, to Berg's TV pitch for Sanka Coffee, a monologue
that prefaced the episode of *The Goldbergs* broadcast on April 24, 1950:

> I'm just going over the recipe I used today. I made a cake—wait, you'll
> see it. I hope I didn't put in too much flour—it will be heavy. A recipe
> means ingredients . . . the right ingredients never fail to bring the right
> result, whether it's a cake or a house or a disposition . . . I mean it. If for
> instant, you are a person that should not drink coffee with caffeine in it
> and you do so regardless you know what happens . . . disturbed sleep—
> irritability—and do I have to tell you what irritability can do to the com-
> plexion of your family life? Don't ask. . . . I am already a Sanka drinker
> since time immemorial and I have never stopped thanking my friends that
> recommended Sanka to me. I am not asking you to thank me. I am only
> asking you to switch. That'll be my thank you . . . from you to me.

The language of Berg's commercial for Sanka coffee reveals in powerful ways
the corporate appropriation of immigrant residues; the tones and rhythms
of immigrant life, although in a noticeably diluted form, are summoned to
spur and sanction the purchase of commodities in response to Molly's authorizing voice. The ritualized invocation of "Don't ask," in this commercial
context, resonates with terrific irony. In Gross's 1927 *Dunt Esk!!* this famous
immigrant phrase bespeaks a weary but knowing exasperation with the comedy of ghetto life; by 1950 the expression has become a cute rhetorical utter-

ance designed to win consumer confidence. Even Molly's mild malaprop "for instant" highlights the attenuation of the once lively language of the dialect artists (unless Berg intended this as a pun on a type of coffee).[10]

The advertising format of Molly's opening monologue was eventually dropped from *The Goldbergs;* in the show's last incarnation, *Molly,*[11] the opening shots, before the actual plot commences, depict the white-breaded landscape of suburbia—cars cruising slowly down Main Street, a picture of a water tower, manicured lawns. Yet in these post-Loeb episodes, Berg offers her viewers a Molly less sure of her mediating, negotiating abilities; a Molly whose identity is often challenged by the less ethnic, new suburban, commercial world of the fifties. Her efforts at personal and familial incorporation remain in uneasy dialogue with the lure of that New World's monetary rewards. This cultural tension is richly inscribed in two key Haverville episodes, each screened in the fall of 1955, titled "Social Butterfly" and "Molly's Fish."

"Social Butterfly" followed "Moving Day," an episode about the family's transition from tenement to suburb. In "Moving Day" Molly sells off all the Bronx furniture, even Rosalie's piano, to buy new furnishings for Haverville; at the end of the show only ovals of Washington and Lincoln remain in the empty foyer, symbols of immigrant residue (specifically, the family's host-culture adoration of American icons) that survive—indeed oversee—the Goldbergs's urban evacuation.

"Social Butterfly" opens with Molly anxiously preparing to "receive," as she terms it, the stream of new neighbors who, according to the authority of the etiquette manuals she has consulted, will be calling on this particular night—it is, after all, the end of their first week as emigrants to Haverville ("That's the regular procedure when new people move into the neighborhood," she explains to her family). Papa Jake (now played by Robert H. Harris) assures Molly that their community will take her "to their hearts like Tremont Avenue." In her "hostess gown," Molly worries about Uncle David's (played by Eli Mintz) exposed suspenders and reminds her son, "Sammy, darling, did you put on your college pin?" To Molly's extreme dismay no one appears this night, except the town fire chief selling raffles (he enlists Jake and Uncle David to join the volunteer fire department). Eventually Molly gives up any hope of "receiving," and the opening scene ends with the surprise arrival of a huge "good luck" horseshoe wreath, sent by the old Bronx crowd, a token of her past life—a symbol that leaves Molly with the ache of bittersweet memory for the world she has left behind. "Not everyone reads etiquette books," Jake gently advises, as the Goldbergs all retire, each chanting the refrain, "Don't be lonesome, Molly."

Determined to make new friends, Molly sets out the next morning to survey the neighborly landscape. Three sharp, unsettling rebuffs ensue. Watching portly Mrs. Carey cleaning her first-floor window (the intimate scene of window-to-window exchange between neighbors has disappeared in the suburbs, replaced by yard-to-yard dialogue), Molly immediately brings up the impertinent (as it turns out) subject of food and dieting. Molly's opening conversational gambit, "We like to eat evidently," is met with a pointed, huffy reply by Mrs. Carey ("I never discuss my eating habits!"), which compels Molly to leave. Next, Molly offers a little boy dressed in a Davey Crockett coonskin hat a chocolate cookie ("I'm the cookie lady," she announces). Next, she encounters Mrs. Peterson (the Goldbergs are evidently the only Jews in Haverville) hanging out her laundry and suggests that Mrs. Peterson visit Jake's new store (Jake has moved up from tailor to manufacturer) to buy a dress wholesale for her daughter's upcoming wedding. "I thought there was a law against wholesale selling to retail customers?" Mrs. Peterson questions in reply and in extremely sharp language rebuffs Molly's offer. It turns out that her husband sells dresses retail in town; Molly's offer appears, therefore, as "not very ethical." Finally, as if matters could not get any worse, the little boy's mother shows up to scold Molly for giving her son chocolate cookies; of course he is allergic to chocolate—she expects him to have a toxic reaction any minute.

Thus the plot of "Social Butterfly" involves three social snubs, three blows to Molly's self-esteem, three severe challenges to her identity. In reaction, Molly becomes forlorn, listless; she loses her appetite, even her desire to cook. During this time of trial (Berg portrays Molly as depressed; she is having an adjustment reaction to suburban life) she refuses to relinquish the token of her previous happier life, the Tremont Avenue good luck wreath. "When are you going to throw out that remembrance of your past?" an annoyed—and very hungry—Jake asks. "Never, never" is Molly's answer. In the meantime the family arranges a surprise visit by Mrs. Herman, Molly's closest Bronx neighbor, who forsakes her grandson's birthday party out of concern for her old friend.

In the meantime, too, Molly somehow jolts herself from lethargy and takes action in the kitchen. In a rapid sequence of shots we see Molly preparing

. . . something, in a flurry of kneading, cutting, tasting. As this episode approaches closure Mrs. Herman arrives ("You of *all* people lonesome, Mrs. Goldberg!" she exclaims in disbelief). At the same moment, however, Mrs. Carey rings, to return a pot. Trying to pronounce the words correctly, she confesses that never in all her life has she tasted such delicious food ("Mrs. Goldberg, you genius you," is how she puts her rapt enthusiasm for Molly's culinary art). Struggling to pronounce the exotic words, Molly helps Mrs. Carey by naming the wonderful foods she has bestowed upon her new neighbor: *tsimmes,* gefilte fish, strudel. In the next instant other neighbors arrive at the Goldbergs' door, welcoming Molly (this turns out to be the night prophesied by the manuals—the marking of Molly's arrival in Haverville). Mrs. Peterson thanks Molly for buying a new dress from her husband's store (Molly just happens to be wearing it; "I'm all early American," she proclaims—a wonderfully ironic statement, suggestive of the immigrant desire, voiced with a mild Yiddish-English inversion, to appropriate the genealogical authority of the American founders); Davey Crockett's mother materializes to inform Molly that her son is not allergic to the cookies so could she have Mrs. Goldberg's delicious recipe, please? "Social Butterfly" concludes with Molly "receiving" invitations to speak before the local Garden Club, the Gourmet Club (would Molly give a talk on the preparation of *tsimmes?*), and so on. Seeing her old friend surrounded by animated neighbors Mrs. Herman decides to return to the city, promising Molly, "I'll tell the Bronx how busy you are!"

What remains striking about "Social Butterfly" is how Berg imagines ethnic food as agent of social incorporation; how, that is, the offering of (say) gefilte fish enacts a ritual of integration, of conformity, above all of reassurance. "Traditional foods and ways of eating," remarks an anthropologist of ethnic foodways, "form a link with the past and help ease the shock of entering a new culture" (Kalcik 37). Yet in earlier ethnic literature (especially in the example of Anzia Yezierska's autobiographical fiction), immigrant daughters tend to be revolted by the foodways of the Old World; they are unable to swallow or tolerate the herring and onions their parents feast on— ethnic food in Yezierska generates the nausea of memory in the rising generation. Molly, by contrast, resolves the problem of host culture acceptance (it does not matter whether Mrs. Carey is herself Irish-American; she represents the new suburban turf that Molly's ex-Bronx self seeks to conquer) through what might be called the boundary-crossing power of gefilte fish: the gift of food is again (recall "The Rent Strike") Molly's mode of conflict resolution, indeed (in the new suburban fifties) her only mode of negotiating "otherness." In another context, or era, gefilte fish might have figured as a boundary-making symbol ("a marker of ethnic identity" [Kalcik 38]); but in the television world of Haverville (whose opening filmed sequences have, ironically, the texture and look of the Waspy, "ethnically neutral" shows *Molly* will soon be displaced by) Berg presented a safe story of acceptance and toleration for the new Jewish middle class, thus consolidating a process of "symbolic ethnicity" already underway, if not virtually completed by the midfifties. In the end, a TV situation that might have exposed barriers between people or explored the dangerous territory of Americanization (Kessler-Harris xiii)—the strains of acculturation in the suburban fifties—becomes instead a comical case study of social harmony and leveling though a mode of symbolic ethnicity—the gift of gefilte fish.[12]

Few extant episodes of *The Goldbergs* hover around such taboo subjects as "Social Butterfly." One final example of Berg's imagination of the "mild" tensions between American and ethnic family life may be found in a *Goldbergs* show called "Molly's Fish," an episode that reveals how popular ethnic TV, perhaps still saturated with an immigrant-sedimented sensibility, could offer a potential critique of the dominant—or soon to be dominant—commodity culture of the fifties.

The plot of "Molly's Fish" turns on the desire, on the part of a national supermarket chain (Peter Piper Supermarkets), to mass produce and market Molly's unique and delicious "fish balls," as her gefilte fish are called throughout the episode (indeed, it took two screenings of "Molly's Fish" for me to realize that not once is the term *gefilte* ever mentioned; it is as if the word itself is unutterable, taboo. As is, by the way, the required "matzoh meal" in the fish's preparation—instead it is called "cracker meal." Were these terms "too Jewish" for Berg to name on television in the fifties?). "This fish is commercial!" the store's traveling representative declares; "I can do something with your fish, Mrs. Goldberg." This enterprising dream runs into problems, however, when the scene of production shifts from Molly's kitchen to Chicago, where in a huge, antiseptic cooking area (it is "hospital clean," Molly remarks), overseen by Molly's *goyische* alter ego (the chief food inspector and her legion of turbanned, nurse-like assistants), Molly is invited to create "her" fish—"like mama used to make," in the words of the supermarket chain's agent. The great comedy—and substantial critique—of "Molly's Fish" issues from the bafflement of those in the corporate, high-tech, mass-production-mentality world before the figure of Molly and her ethnic culinary art. Of course no specific recipe exists to guide in the preparation, nor do quantifiable amounts of ingredients. Turning a gigantic food grater, Molly is shown surrounded by a group of cooking aides, armed with clipboards, attentively counting every turn of the machine, trying to demystify the secret of her fabulous "fish balls." Sadly, however, because Molly is alienated from her own kitchen, the result is, in the words of one of the corporate designated food tasters, "Not your fish, Mrs. Goldberg."

Perplexed by her failure to duplicate "her" fish in the assembly-line world of Chicago and big business, Molly calls on Mrs. Herman back in the Bronx for the exact numbers. "Who measures?" is the reply. "I cook blind," Molly explains to a boardroom filled with extremely genteel-looking, disappointed executives. But the real explanation for the dilemma involves the limiting, mechanistic, quantifying mentality of the commercial world itself, which literally drains the ethnic flavor out of Molly's sacred fish, subverting (in the process) her domestic sphere.

Yet in the original ending to the script of "Molly's Fish" Berg has Molly return to Haverville dejected, her final conversation with Peter Piper an apology for her poor cooking performance: "From trying you can't build an industry. A fish that's good today and bad tomorrow is not a business. A flash in the pan. That's what I am." But in a flash of cooking revelation (or is it the return to the family that jogs her culinary memory?) Molly is able to make "her" fish once more. Her immediate impulse is to call Chicago ("Jake! David! I did it! I did it! I'm not a flash in the pan. I did it again. It's my fish.") Uncle David, however, has stopped by Peter Piper on his way home and has discovered a new item, a jar of Fanny's Fish Balls. "They got somebody else?" Molly wonders; "They couldn't wait." Of course the commercialized fish proves inedible, and Jake is given the last, comforting word: "Molly, who needs them? Oscar in the Waldorf is also not commercial. He's exclusive like you, Molly." In the original conclusion to "Molly's Fish," then, Molly remains, at the very end, still lured/compelled by the promise, and by the monetary potential, of commodification.

The revised aired TV version of "Molly's Fish" concludes, however, with an adjusted recognition on Molly's part: "A mother is not a corporation," she acknowledges. This insight, in the end, helps her to recover (to her family's delight) the art of making "her" fish. Instead of running to the phone to call Chicago, Molly writes down the recipe for herself. "And what's your decision?" Jake asks, "Are you going back to Chicago?" (there is now no competing line of Fanny's Fish Balls to deter Molly from marketing herself). Molly's reply is an adamant "No. The big world is too big for me, Jake. I found out a mother cooks best where she is needed the most." In the end, some areas of the self cannot be commodified; in this respect ethnic memory—inscribed here in the culinary art/cultural work of making gefilte fish—may at times be able to expose the contradictions of market capitalism (the argument of some theorists of popular television) as it resists incorporation. From this perspective "Molly's Fish" might be said to challenge the strategies of emergent commodity culture that, through the agency of network television, appropriated ethnic memory for the legitimization process itself. "A mother is not a corporation" is thus uttered from within the resisting space opened by the exposure of the commercial imagination's limitations; in turn, Molly's comic negotiations with the new technology of mass production become, at some level, the viewer's as well. At the historical-economic moment when television validated, as it showcased, the new ideology of commodity (here I follow Lipsitz and Kellner), a show like "Molly's Fish," despite Berg's own participation in the rituals of legitimization, challenged the authority of commodity through the empowering memories of ethnic foodways.

THROUGHOUT the fifties and until the end of her career on stage and television, Gertrude Berg continued as a symbol in the popular imagination of the "warm and wise" Jewish mother (O'Connor). Although the world of the ethnic family sitcom had virtually vanished there remained another scene of Jewish-American popular culture, a realm outside the safe, domestic world of Berg's vision of ethnic family life. I refer of course to the overturning, irreverent, uncivil comedy of the rising generation of stand-up comics and TV performers who—contemporaneous with Berg—fashioned a dislodging humor of subversive wit and social criticism unavailable in the ethnic family sitcom (Marc 11–30). *The Goldbergs*, we need to remember, faded from television in the late fifties at the threshold of Lenny Bruce, Shelly Berman, Mort Sahl, the Two-Thousand-Year-Old Man, the young Jackie Mason, and (crucially) the young Philip Roth and Woody Allen. What was taboo, unutterable on *The Goldbergs* was grist for the stand-up comedian. The show's often genial, safe imagination of ethnic experience, its easy assumptions that the new Jewish middle classes could assimilate through an offering of gefilte fish were examined and overturned by the relentless, manic, unhinged, individualized style of stand-up comedy and parody. By the midfifties, if not earlier, the night club stage, not the television screen, became the site for contested readings of the culture. It was, I would argue, a potentially creative, liminal space that could provide "oppositional" readings of the culture for an audience resisting, not only the suburbanized, commodified scene of American culture, but also the domesticated, middle-class Jewish world ultimately symbolized by the television world of *The Goldbergs*.

NOTES

I would like to thank the following family, friends, and colleagues for their responses and suggestions to earlier versions of this essay: Julius Baker, Sacvan Bercovitch, Dan Czitrom, Hasia Diner, Jay Fliegelman, Daniel Horowitz, Amy Kaplan, Michael P. Kramer, George Lipsitz, Leo Madow, Max Novak, Jeffrey Rubin-Dorsky, Jack Salzman, Jessie Weber, and Stephen Whitfield.

1   The Berg Papers housed at the George Arents Research Library at Syracuse University is a vast collection that includes scrapbooks containing Berg's correspondence, general scrapbooks, and scrapbooks concerning specific events in Berg's career, as well as a huge archive of original scripts from all of Berg's shows from the early radio days through Berg's last television show. In addition there are printed materials relating to all aspects of her career. The Margaret Herrick Library at the Academy of Motion Picture Arts and Sciences in Los Angeles collection contains a number of clippings and materials related to Berg, including the original Paramount script for *Molly*. Much of this material has informed this essay.

2   The materials for reconstructing the contexts of Berg's imagination of the Goldberg family are drawn from both printed and manuscript papers contained in the Berg Papers. The following quotation is from a transcript, dated May 30, 1930, released by the Jewish Telegraphic Agency: "Always revolted by the manner in which Jewish characters were portrayed on the stage and screen and in literature, she put her writing talent and dramatic genius into a radio sketch which interprets the Jews as she always thought them. . . . In shunning the broken English dialect of Jewish comedians she has created something new"

(Postal). Most commentators at the time also noted the contrast between Berg's own normative speech and Molly Goldberg's heavy accent: "She even looks like Molly ought to look, though she does not speak like her" (Kassell 419). In his biography of Fannie Brice, Herbert Goldman claims that Berg virtually stole her trademark "Yoo hoo, Mrs. Bloom" from Brice's "Mrs. Cohen" routine (136).

3   For example, here is a woman writing about *The Goldbergs* from Oklahoma City in January 1933: "There is not a thing about the 'Goldbergs' I can find to criticise, for they present life as it should be. . . . We like the democratic and friendly feeling they have for Jew, Gentile and Catholic. . . . 'Molly' is a beautiful character, an example to all wives and mothers, and her philosophy is practical for our every day living. . . . We like their patriotism, their constructive, charitable acts, their sympathy for friends in pleasure or trouble. In fact, we cannot imagine any portrayal of family life more perfect" (Correspondence 1933, Berg Papers). Similar responses to the radio *Goldbergs* can be found in the Berg Papers. They suggest just how truly exemplary a figure the American listening public found Berg's construction of Molly.

4   These letters were in response to *The House of Glass,* a serial about a family who runs a Catskill hotel (modeled, of course, on her own family history) that Berg wrote and starred in (as Bessie) in the midthirties, in between radio runs of *The Goldbergs*. The script of this episode is in the Berg Papers.

5   A brief account of the Loeb affair: In the summer of 1950 Loeb was listed in *Red Channels,* the blacklist Bible of the networks and sponsors. After much debate with CBS and General Foods, Loeb was fired by Berg (although Berg at first tried to keep him on the show) in January 1952, and *The Goldbergs* eventually returned to TV that spring with three new sponsors (paying for three fifteen-minute segments a week) on NBC. Bitter, exhausted, burdened with tremendous personal debts, hounded by the IRS, Loeb committed suicide in September 1955. Berg kept a separate scrapbook of the flurry of newspaper accounts of the Loeb affair, but she does not mention the incident in either the 1956 *Commentary* profile, the interview with Edward R. Murrow, or her autobiography. Milton Berle, who often had Berg play Molly on his *Texaco Star Theater* (according to the archives, there was even some talk of making the Goldberg family a regular feature of Berle's variety show [Spigel 149]), writes in his autobiography, although "I screamed and pleaded . . . I could never get my good friend John Garfield on the show [Berle refers to 1950, after *Red Channels* appeared]. And I couldn't even get an explanation of why I couldn't have Gertrude Berg on, even though she had her own television success with *The Goldbergs* at the time." Loeb, Berle goes on to say, "a loveable man, saw his whole career shrivel to nothing" (293, 294). In a letter to the *New York Times,* Harriet Berg Schwartz, Berg's daughter, writes

in defense of her mother's actions during the time of the blacklist: "My mother would not go along with this injustice."

6   I borrow this term from Angoff ("The Goldbergs" 20) In another essay on the show Angoff observes, "I have found the simpler the people, the less complicated, the more they are likely to enjoy 'The Goldbergs,' and that the *ersatz* intellectuals, especially the females, tend to look down upon it" ("Jewish Humor" 12). Angoff's implicit claim, that class position, especially of women viewers in the early fifties, shaped response to *The Goldbergs,* is probably impossible to establish. Beyond the nostalgia for some today of watching Berg perform Molly, women viewers tend to find Molly a powerful character. We should recall that Berg controlled the show, including dealing with sponsors, lawyers, and actors, for twenty-five years. "There is, also, the professional Gertrude Berg: a hardheaded, realistic woman of great talent, with restless energy and a driving ambition" (Poling).

7   Compare Lipsitz, speaking of "rent strikes by tenants in *The Goldbergs*" as potentially "resonant" with "class consciousness" (59). *The Goldbergs,* however, is thoroughly middle class—in style, tone, content, and characters. In light of the video and manuscript evidence it seems clear that *The Goldbergs* ultimately cannot fit into Lipsitz's model of working-class ethnic television.

8   By contrast, a Passover show broadcast on radio (Apr. 3, 1939) includes Passover liturgy sung in Hebrew and the sound of a rock smashing through the Goldbergs' window. Constructions of such anti-Semitic behavior could not have been displayed on television in the midfifties.

9   On the subject of Jewish American life during Berg's tenure as radio-TV auteur (a rich, complicated interval too vast and varied to engage fully in this essay) see the classic texts by Glazer and Moore, and new important interpretations by Feingold, Shapiro, and Joselit.

10 The Sanka ad is in Berg's own hand in Radio and T.V. Scripts, 1950, Berg Papers. When the show returned to TV, with a new Papa Jake, in the spring of 1952 among its new sponsors was Necchi sewing machines, for whom Berg wrote—and performed as Molly—the following monologue: "To retire means to stop . . . who wants that. . . . Always keep in the march of time . . . with one foot forward. . . . My motto is be as modern as tomorrow. . . . And with my Necchi machine I brought the future into my life" (Apr. 11, 1952, Radio and T.V. Scripts, 1952, Berg Papers). On the relation between "ethnic" memory and commodity legitimation see Lipsitz.

11 Note the continuing emptying out of "ethnicity" over time in Berg's career, from Maltke Talnitzky (the original name she chose for Molly Goldberg [*Molly and Me*

175]) to *The Rise of the Goldbergs* to *The Goldbergs*, to *Molly,* and finally, by 1961, to Mrs. G of the short-lived TV series *Mrs. G Goes to College* (the "G" standing for "Green," itself truncated from some unspecified, more overtly "ethnic" source.

12   Significantly, a late episode of *Mama*, "The Hansens' Rise in the World" virtually repeats this theme. Mama senses that she is accepted into the snooty "Bayside Ladies Culture and Conversation Club" because, she comes to realize, "they like my recipes."

WORKS CONSULTED

Angoff, Charles. "The Goldbergs." *Reconstructionist,* Dec. 24, 1954, 1922. Copy in Printed Materials, Box 5. Gertrude Berg Papers. George Arents Research Library. Syracuse University. Syracuse, N.Y.

———. "'The Goldbergs' and Jewish Humor." *Congress Weekly* 18.9 (Mar. 5, 1951): 12–13. Copy in Published Materials, Box 5. Gertrude Berg Papers. George Arents Research Library. Syracuse University. Syracuse, N.Y.

Berg, Gertrude. *Molly and Me.* New York: McGraw-Hill, 1961.

———. Papers. George Arents Research Library. Syracuse University. Syracuse, N.Y.

Berle, Milton. *Milton Berle: An Autobiography.* New York: Delacorte Press, 1974.

Feingold, Henry L. *A Time for Searching: Entering the Mainstream, 1920–1945.* Baltimore: Johns Hopkins University Press, 1992.

Freedman, Morris. "The Real Molly Goldberg." *Commentary* 21 (Apr. 1956): 359–64.

Gans, Herbert J. "American Jewry: Present and Future." *Commentary* 21 (May 1956): 422–30.

Gitlin, Todd. "Prime Time Ideology: The Hegemonic Process in Television Entertainment." In *Television: The Critical View.* 3d ed. Ed. Horace Newcomb. New York: Oxford University Press, 1982. 426–54.

Glazer, Nathan. *American Judaism.* Chicago: University of Chicago Press, 1957.

"The Goldbergs March On." *Life,* Apr. 25, 1949, 59–62.

Goldman, Herbert. *Fannie Brice: The Original Funny Girl.* New York: Oxford University Press, 1992.

Gross, Milt. *Dunt Esk!!* New York: George H. Doran, 1927.

———. *Nize Baby.* New York: George H. Doran, 1926.

"The Hansens' Rise in the World." *Mama.* 1957. Videotape. T86 1128. Museum of Television and Radio. New York.

House of Glass. Script of Episode 25. Oct. 2, 1935. Radio and T.V. Manuscripts, 1935. Gertrude Berg Papers. George Arents Research Library. Syracuse University. Syracuse, N.Y.

Jaffe, Jean. "This Is Molly Speaking of the Rise of the Goldbergs." Ms. Correspondence Scrapbook 1, 1931–32. Gertrude Berg Papers. George Arents Research Library. Syracuse University. Syracuse, N.Y.

Joselit, Jenna Weissman. *The Wonders of America: Reinventing Jewish Culture, 1880–1950*. New York: Hill and Wang, 1994.

Kalcik, Susan. "Ethnic Foodways in America: Symbol and the Performance of Identity." In *Ethnic and Regional Foodways in the United States: The Performance of Group Identity*. Ed. L. K. Brown and K. Mussell. Knoxville: University of Tennessee Press, 1984. 37–65.

Kassell, Hilda. "An Off-Stage View of Molly Goldberg." *American Hebrew and Jewish Tribune*, Oct. 21, 1932, 419. Copy in Published Materials, Box 5. Gertrude Berg Papers. George Arents Research Library. Syracuse University. Syracuse, N.Y.

Kellner, Douglas. *Television and the Crisis of Democracy*. Boulder: Westview, 1990.

Kessler-Harris, Alice. Introduction. *Bread Givers*. By Anzia Yezierska. New York: Persea, 1975. v–xviii.

Lears, T. J. Jackson. "Making Fun of Popular Culture." *American Historical Review* 97 (Dec. 1992): 1417–26.

Lipsitz, George. "The Meaning of Memory: Family, Class, and Ethnicity in Early Network Television." *Time Passages: Collective Memory and American Popular Culture*. Minneapolis: University of Minnesota Press, 1990. 39–75.

Marc, David. *Comic Visions: Television Comedy and American Culture*. Boston: Unwin Hyman, 1989.

Maxwell, Perriton. "The Mother of the Goldbergs." *Radioland* 11 (Mar. 1934): 40–41, 53, 71–72. Copy in Printed Materials, Box 2. Gertrude Berg Papers. George Arents Research Library. Syracuse University. Syracuse, N.Y.

"Molly's Fish." *The Goldbergs*. Jan. 5, 1956. Videotape. VA2004. UCLA Film and Television Archive. Los Angeles.

"Molly's Fish." Script. Radio and T.V. Manuscripts, 1955. Gertrude Berg Papers. George Arents Research Library. Syracuse University. Syracuse, N.Y.

Moore, Deborah Dash. *At Home in America: Second-Generation New York Jews*. New York: Columbia University Press, 1981.

"Moving Day." *The Goldbergs*. Sept. 22, 1955. Videotape. 2591 T. UCLA Film and Television Archive. Los Angeles.

O'Connor, John J. "This Jewish Mom Dominates TV, Too." *New York Times*, Oct. 14, 1992, C20.

"Passover Program." *The Goldbergs*. Apr. 3, 1939. Recording. R86:0791. Museum of Television and Radio. New York.

"Passover Program." *The Goldbergs*. Apr. 18, 1949. Script. Gertrude Berg Papers. George Arents Research Library. Syracuse University. Syracuse, N.Y.

Person to Person. Gertrude Berg Interview. Hosted by Edward R. Murrow. June 4, 1954. T269. National Jewish Archive of Broadcasting. Jewish Museum. New York.

Poling, James. "'I'm Molly Goldberg.'" Clipping in Gertrude Berg File. Margaret Herrick Library. Center for Motion Picture Study. Motion Picture Arts and Sciences Academy. Los Angeles.

Postal, Bernard. "The Story of Gertrude Berg, Author and Actor." *Jewish Toronto Canada*, Oct. 5, 1934. Copy in Scrapbook 1934. Gertrude Berg Papers. George Arents Research Library. Syracuse University. Syracuse, N.Y.

"The Rent Strike" (alt.: "The New Landlord"). *The Goldbergs*. Sept. 5, 1949. Videotape. T7650. Museum of Television and Radio. New York.

"Sammy's Bar Mitzvah." *The Rise of the Goldbergs*. Feb. 26, 1930. Script. Radio and T.V. Scripts, 1930. Gertrude Berg Papers. George Arents Research Library. Syracuse University. Syracuse, N.Y.

Schwartz, Harriet Berg. Letter. *New York Times*, Nov. 11, 1990, E16.

Shapiro, Edward L. *A Time for Healing: American Jewry since World War II*. Baltimore: Johns Hopkins University Press, 1992.

"Social Butterfly" *The Goldbergs*. Sept. 29, 1955. VA1913 T. Videotape. UCLA Film and Television Archive. Los Angeles.

Spigel, Lynn. *Make Room for TV: Television and the Family Ideal in Postwar America*. Chicago: University of Chicago Press, 1992.

Susman, Warren I. *Culture as History: The Transformation of American Society in the Twentieth Century*. New York: Pantheon, 1984.

"Yom Kippur." *The Goldbergs*. Oct. 3, 1949. Script. Gertrude Berg Papers. George Arents Research Library. Syracuse University. Syracuse, N.Y.

Part Three — Film and Gender

David Van Leer

Seven

WHAT LOLA GOT
Cultural Carelessness on Broadway

S TUDENTS of popular cul-
ture have long debated the
relations between unso-
phisticated texts and the societies that produce them. In
optimistic American formulations—of, say, the myth-
and-symbol critics—pop-
ular literature is treated
as "an objectified mass
dream" in which "the
individual writer aban-
dons his own personali-
ty and identifies him-
self with the reveries
of his readers" (Smith
91). The success of nine-
teenth-century dime
novels or of twentieth-

Figure 2. Gwen Verdon as Lola.
(Reprinted with the permission of Margaret Fehl
and the Billy Rose Theatre Collection, New York Public
Library for the Performing Arts, Astor, Lenox, and Tilden
Foundations. Photograph by Fred Fehl.)

171

century slasher films marks their ability to speak directly to the dreams (or the nightmares) of their audiences. For more skeptical European theorists—like those of the Frankfurt school—the passivity of the audience makes this very dream fulfillment suspect, with the "culture industry" functioning as opiate and instrument of indoctrination (Adorno; Benjamin).

Subsequent scholars have challenged both the elitism of such intellectualized readings and the uniform image of culture they foster. The process by which an author identifies with "his" audience is not only painfully sexist. The very notion of a shared "mass dream" presumes that mass to be homogeneous and inert, leaving little role for conflict or opposition to the dominant ideology. To represent a more dynamic interplay between popular texts and their readers, contemporary critics have downplayed consensus and emphasized instead the tensions within culture: whether through exploring the "cultural work" by which texts resolve the unpleasant "hard facts" of modern life (Fisher) or by focusing on moments of "category crisis," in which failures in cultural definitions reveal the overlap among apparently discrete categories (Garber).

I wish to approach the question of oppositional readings from a slightly different direction—to locate resistance not at sites of transformative crises but as underlying the very unanimity on which consensus critics build. Cultures are as interesting for what they think is not a problem as for what they think is, and the very absence of anxiety can epitomize for subsequent generations the limitations of a previous age. The works that I isolate trade comically on stereotypes not yet called into question. In the very casualness of their discriminatory assumptions—racist, sexist, classist—they measure not crisis but complacency, the fact that no one cared to challenge what now seem obvious errors. But such indifference is itself a symptom of weakness, for the complacency of the dominant culture also encourages what we might call "cultural carelessness." At sites of complacency, where discipline is relaxed, the very confidence that allows a culture blindly to assume its control permits oppositional voices to undermine that control undetected. And in the carelessness that attends confidence, these apparently discriminatory representations can actually become occasions for a variety of minority voices to speak with comparative freedom.

The possibility of discovering oppositional voices within the carelessness of the dominant culture seems especially important in charting the continu-

ity of homosexual culture. Embracing the self-respect that attends open affirmation, gay liberation of the 1960s and 1970s tended to undervalue the less
confrontive techniques of previous generations of homosexual artists. Believing "coming out" to be the only viable political option, activists stigmatized
everything else as "hiding," as if before 1969 all homosexual history took
place in a "closet." Yet whatever its taboos against public declaration, the
decade of the 1950s in fact afforded considerable opportunity to examine
conventional norms covertly, and many authors explored in popular genres
the alternative lifestyles banished from high culture. The overconfidence of
the fifties prepared the way for the crisis of 1969, and these early challenges
to that cultural hegemony are both an important part of our homosexual
heritage and an implicit corrective to the middle-class Waspishness of the gay
"clone" culture that followed.

TO exemplify the possibility for opposition within the conventional, I wish
to focus on the ambiguities of a single piece of cultural carelessness—Gwen
Verdon's showstopping performance of "Whatever Lola Wants (Lola Gets)"
from the 1955 Broadway musical *Damn Yankees*, filmed with Verdon in 1958.
Although not artistically innovative, *Damn Yankees* does unintentionally raise
questions about the relation between masculinity and sexual desire. And in
its very *in*ability to answer these questions it permits a dialogue among play,
performers, and audience on complex issues about cultural positioning and
articulability.

The musical is a modernization of the Faust legend, with a script by the
novelist Douglass Wallop and producer-director George Abbott and music by
Richard Adler and Jerry Ross. Joe Boyd, an aging real estate broker, sells his
soul to Mr. Applegate (aka the devil) in return for leading his hometown
baseball team, the Washington Senators, to victory over the New York Yankees. Fearful that he may not like the deal, Boyd insists on an "escape clause,"
which will allow him to break his contract on a given day. Leaving his wife,
Meg, in the belief that he will return to her shortly, the middle-aged Boyd is
transformed into Joe Hardy, a twenty-two-year-old natural athlete, who joins
the Senators and quickly becomes a national hero. But celebrity does not
compensate for the loss of domesticity. Joe returns home and rents a room
from Meg, without telling her who he is. To protect his interests, Applegate
tries to distract Joe with his top home-wrecker, the witch Lola. The ploy fails,

and Lola becomes more interested in protecting Joe than in seducing him. Applegate tries to discredit Joe further by spreading the rumor that he had taken a bribe while playing in the Mexican league under another name. The rumor leads to a hearing at which Meg saves Joe by falsely swearing to have known him as a youth. But during the trial, the deadline passes for activating the escape clause, and Joe sadly joins Lola in eternal damnation. In one last attempt to outsmart Applegate, Lola drugs the devil so that Joe can at least play the final game to clinch the pennant. Angry at being outwitted, the devil transforms Lola into a hag and in the last play of the game changes Hardy back into Joe Boyd. Freed from the devil's power, Boyd makes the winning play and returns to his wife to live happily ever after.

The success of the show derives less from its plot or score than from the talents of rising comedian-dancer Gwen Verdon, who made Broadway history near the end of the first act with her performance of "Whatever Lola Wants." The dramatic situation is simple. To distract Joe from his wife, Applegate introduces the witch Lola into the men's locker room to seduce Joe. While Applegate hides behind the lockers, Lola offers herself to Joe as his greatest fan. At first she appeals to him for protection and is unable to climb off a bench without his assistance. When Joe remains politely oblivious to the sexual invitation in Lola's professed helplessness, she turns bully, trying to cajole him into passion with a seductive song and dance:

Whatever Lola wants
Lola gets
And little man, little Lola wants you.
Make up your mind to have no regrets,
Recline yourself, resign yourself, you're through.
. . . .
You're no exception to the rule,
I'm irresistible, you fool, give in! . . . Give in! . . . Give in![1]
(Abbott 91–92)

The scene is curious from a number of angles. Most obviously it is totally unnecessary to advance the plot. Never does Lola present a sexual threat to Joe or a viable alternative to Joe's wife. Instead the dance floats freely in the musical as a moment of pure performance—a declaration of coming-of-age by choreographer Bob Fosse and actress Gwen Verdon, both of whom

Figure I. Mary Martin's furry strip tease in *Leave It to Me*. (Reprinted with the permission of the Billy Rose Theatre Collection, New York Public Library for the Performing Arts, Astor, Lenox, and Tilden Foundations. Photograph by Van Damm.)

established their star credentials with this number.[2] It is this narrative freedom that makes the scene so theatrically pleasing and interpretively rich. One need not care about *Damn Yankees* to enjoy the sequence, and that very looseness invites a wide range of readings. I want to isolate three aspects of the dance for special consideration—its characterization of desire and its use of ethnic and of sexual stereotypes to reinforce that representation.

The number is a variation on the traditional striptease. The striptease's relation to sexual desire is itself, of course, ambiguous. It is unclear that sexual availability is necessarily an aphrodisiac, especially when availability is read wholly in terms of visibility. Perhaps the tease was always within quotation marks, performing passion without proffering it. This distancing theatricalization is compounded by Broadway's ironic and finally duplicitous relation to the strip. Legitimate theater rarely alludes to stripping without implicitly distinguishing that low performance tradition from its own self-conscious artistry. If the striptease may occasionally leer, its Broadway counterpart almost always smirks. The touchstone performance here is Mary Martin's stage debut, her rendition of Cole Porter's "My Heart Belongs to Daddy" in the 1938 musical *Leave It to Me* (figure 1). Wearing a thick fur coat, which invited fetishistic fantasy but also allowed her to appear to take off clothing without actually being unclothed, Martin sang Porter's suggestive lyrics about a sugar daddy in her characteristically chaste, white voice and clipped enunciation.

Many subsequent shows repeated this Broadway convention of the enacted, de-eroticized strip—*Pal Joey* (1940), *Flower Drum Song* (1958), *Guys and Dolls* (1950), Marilyn Monroe's iconographic performance of "Diamonds Are a Girl's Best Friend" in the 1953 film version of *Gentlemen Prefer Blondes,* and Verdon's own Broadway debut as a soloist, the "Garden of Eden" sequence from *Can-Can* (1953). The tradition reached its logical conclusion four years after *Damn Yankees* with *Gypsy* (1959), a musical about the relation between burlesque and Broadway, and one ending with a fantasy striptease by Mary Martin's chief theatrical rival, Ethel Merman.

Mary Martin, *Guys and Dolls,* and Marilyn Monroe (at least) are implicated in Gwen Verdon's performance of Lola's strip. But the excessive quotations buried in the performance free Lola's strip from traditional Broadway cynicism. Our awareness of the performance as a performance, however pleasurable, forces us to consider the seduction as a process and our relation to it as voyeurs. In the traditional Broadway striptease, whether or not individual viewers are excited by disrobing, the audience is encouraged to act as if titillation were beside the point—to distinguish themselves as theatergoers from the crude vaudeville patrons, often shown onstage hooting in excitement. In *Damn Yankees,* however, audience sympathies are more complex. Narratively, of course, we want Joe to reject Lola. At the same time, Joe's aloofness forces us to realize that unlike Joe we derive pleasure from the dance. In the movie version of the scene, the camera calls attention to the spectatorial complicity of both Joe and audience by aligning itself visually with neither position. Rarely do we see Lola's performance head on, either from Joe's standpoint or from our own. Instead we get shots over Joe's shoulder or ones that move diagonally across the horizontal frame of the screen (an implicit proscenium arch)—shots that include the process of watching as part of the image.

The audience's uncomfortable relation to the strip is compounded by the ambiguity of the body language with which Verdon presents Lola's offer. Some of the dance's gestures might be seen to imitate traditional sexual movements—hip swings, wrist and ankle flips, slow sensual turns. But the minimally mimetic character of these gestures is overshadowed by their baroque heightening, and what we remember is the stylization and not the movements they imitate. Such gestures, of course, were to become Bob Fosse's personal trademark and his way of distinguishing his work from the more naturalistic and classical movements of previous choreographers such as Agnes de Mille and his own mentor Jerome Robbins. Even this early in his career, before such gestures came simply to signify "Fosse," they are more theatrical than erotic. At the very least, it would be hard to identify any sexual equivalent for the most bizarre of these movements—Verdon's hunched diagonal cross, her arms swinging like an elephant's trunk.

This desexualization of eroticism is most obvious in the dance's conclusion. The final step—a traditionally balletic if somewhat athletic backward arch—is simply theatrical, and a clear bid for applause. More interesting is Lola's movement at the number's climax. After a section of hyperactivity, Verdon freezes to recapitulate the (ungrammatical) refrain: "I always get what I aim for / And your heart'n soul is what I came for." For these lines she adopts a stationary stance with feet spread and hands on hips (figure 2; see p. 171). Her position is anything but inviting. The line itself suggests not desire but competition. It is delivered neither to Joe nor out front to the audience, but is sung three-quarters to emphasize the character's self-preoccupation. To this extent, it recalls not the furry intimacy of Porter's fetishistic tease but the megalomania of another Mary Martin stance—her 1954 show-stopper as an androgynous Peter Pan announcing that "[S/he] Gotta Crow" (figure 3).

The tension between Lola's statement and Verdon's stance calls into question exactly what the claim claims. "I always get what I aim for / And your heart'n soul is what I came for" is, of course, one of the dull Faustian puns with which the script abounds. It further underlines the shallow irony of the scene. Lola will not get Joe, as she would easily understand if at this moment rather than turning away she looked at him to see his visible disinterest. But it also raises larger questions about the character of desire and of the "self" that desires. First, Lola's boast too easily links up desires and events. The projection forward in time by which we identify our goals is not the same as the tracing backward by which we identify how we ended up with what we got. If we get it, we must in some sense have "aimed" for it, or at least aimed at it. But that sort of historical necessity is not the same as desire, any more than the fact that we get what we deserve proves that we get what we want. More fundamentally, Lola's boast obscures the very ambiguity of motives that keeps this show going. As the plot makes clear, there may be a difference between why Lola came and where she aims, between why she came and why

Applegate has her come, even between where she aims and where she wants to strike. And if the audience is never quite sure what constitutes the "whatever" of Lola's wants, we suspect our uncertainty mirrors her own confusion about her motives.

THE Lola scene, then, dramatizes an ambivalence about intention, a submerged pun on "desire" that exploits the discontinuity between discursive strategies and psychological needs—the question of what Lola really wants and whether she desires desire. The artificiality of Verdon's dance suggests Lola's deviousness while simultaneously underscoring more general ambiguities concerning desire itself. By putting Lola's seduction so clearly within ironic quotation marks, Verdon challenges the notion that externalized actions reflect deeper internal motives called "needs" or "desires." For her Lola, there is only surface and gesture, without underlying character or essence.

In its theatricality, the dance points to what recent feminist theory has called the "performative" aspects of sexuality, the degree to which all gender is "masquerade" and "drag."[3] For Lola, as for postmodernists, desire is not a psychological condition but a cultural act. Yet the sequence does more than simply dramatize the cultural construction of emotions. Verdon's theatricalization of desire is filtered through two additional performances—of ethnic identity and sexual preference. It is the cultural specificity of these secondary theatricalizations that most distinguishes the scene from the traditional Broadway striptease. In using ethnicity and sexuality to explicate Lola's relation to gender, the show unintentionally raises questions about the degree to which the three categories share the same cultural space.

The use of ethnic difference is the more explicit—and the more troubling. To seduce Joe, Lola dresses in an outlandish costume (topped with a ridiculous floral headdress), calling herself "Senorita Lolita Rodriguez Hernando, Miss West Indies of 1957." Throughout the scene, though nowhere else in the musical, Verdon speaks in the clichéd dialect of the Hollywood spitfire ("en leetel men, leetel Lo-la wan-chu"). This second masquerade underlines the theatricality of gender by doubling the performances, with Lola standing in the same relation to Lolita that Verdon stands to Lola. Yet the two forms of difference are not truly equivalent, and in treating them as identical, the show makes ethnicity an extension of gender, and subordinate to it. The ethnic motif has no special effect of its own on Lola's audience: Joe and Applegate so fully accept the conflation of gender and ethnicity that they seem not to notice Lolita's difference from the Anglos around her.

Lola's music is as ethnicized as her performance, drawing on elements of the habanera, the tango, and the bolero. Latin rhythms influenced popular music in the United States at least as early as the midnineteenth century, when Louis Moreau Gottschalk incorporated Puerto Rican and Cuban elements into his otherwise Chopinesque piano pieces. This appropriation accelerated in the early twentieth century, with Irene Castle's and Vernon Castle's popularization of the tango—from Argentina by way of Paris—and continued with similar importations of (among others) the Cuban rumba, the Afro-Cuban mambo, the Afro-Brazilian samba, and the hybrid chachacha, probably a variant of the Cuban danzon (Roberts). Throughout the thirties, forties, and fifties, mass-culture performers like Carmen Miranda, Desi Arnaz, and especially Xavier Cugat were successful proponents of this Latinized music in Hollywood and on the band circuit. Broadway regularly imitated the trend. After a somewhat slow start with Cole Porter's rumba "Begin the Beguine" (*Jubilee*, 1935), by the fifties Broadway was filled with Latinized hits: Leonard Bernstein's "Conga!" (*Wonderful Town*, 1953); his tango "I Am So Easily Assimilated" (*Candide*, 1956); Mark Charlap's "Captain Hook's Tango" (*Peter Pan*,

1954); Jule Styne's "Mu-Cha-Cha" (*Bells Are Ringing,* 1956); Mary Rodgers's hybrid "Spanish Panic" (*Once upon a Mattress,* 1959); and of course the tango "Hernando's Hideaway," from Adler and Ross's *Pajama Game* the year before *Damn Yankees.*

Although part of an ongoing commercialization of Latin music, Lola's song is more offensive than most in its use of stereotypic images. Some ethnic stereotyping always occurred whenever Latin rhythms were used to suggest exoticism, sensuality, and romance. On Broadway the ethnicity of such moments was usually understated: an innocent Anglo was simply taught a new "foreign" dance step, with greater or lesser success; or the cast suddenly appeared, dancing at a club like Hernando's Hideaway, a Chinese restaurant with a salsa band. In *Damn Yankees,* however, the specificity of the Lolita persona attributes to ethnicity distinct, negative characteristics. Finding no pleasure in this aspect of performance, Lola characterizes Lolita as a sexual chore, her "standard vampire treatment" (Abbott 64). More generally the script's conflation of seduction and ethnicity trades on the cliché of Latin sexual voraciousness and the irresistibility Lola claims in her song becomes a property of her Latinness. Such characterizations set up a dichotomy between American purity and Latin degeneracy, one by which even the damned Lola can demonstrate her essential innocence. When during the seduction Lola begins to admire Joe's fidelity to his wife, Verdon registers this character shift by a momentary return to her normal Lola voice. Such shifts from a Latin accent into an American one identify Spanish as the language not only of seduction but also of deceit and adultery, leaving English as the sole domain of fidelity and family values.

Similar negative stereotyping attends the scene's linking of seduction and homosexuality. Questions about sexual orientation are never very far from the surface in the Faust legend. Contemporary charges against the historical Faust conflated attacks on his necromancy with accounts of his molesting male students. The first high literary treatment—Christopher Marlowe's *Tragical History of Doctor Faustus*—is not just the work of a notoriously gay playwright but itself sexualizes the relation between Faust and Mephistopheles. Most subsequent readings—Goethe's *Faust,* Thomas Mann's *Dr. Faustus,* and especially his son Klaus Mann's *Mephisto*—admit of homoerotic readings (Kaufman 13–21).

In *Damn Yankees* such issues are largely centered in the devil, Mr. Applegate. Throughout the script, Applegate is described with words that in the fifties were coded as gay. At his first appearance, he is said to be "slight" and "dapper" (Abbott 11). His apartment in the second act is characterized as "flamboyant" (Abbott 128). Similarly his costuming emphasizes his deviance. His closely cropped hair is an affectation of youthfulness frequently associated with gay men; and his red pocket handkerchief simultaneously alludes to his demonic origin and the traditional emblem of postwar homosexuality. As Lola's strip works to masculinize (or at least desexualize) her, so Applegate's costumes feminize him (figure 4).

With the encouragement of this visual coding, the script reads Applegate's demonic intentions as a form of displaced sexual desire. Throughout the musical, Applegate tries to woo Joe to the joys of demonism by expressing contempt for both women in general and marriage in particular. He explains this hatred in terms of the ways in which wives always muck up his plans. Indeed both Meg and Lola do foil his attempts to trap Joe's soul. Yet his expression of this misogyny in snide one-line wisecracks drawn from the camp tradition tends to underscore its sexual dimension. This gay "bitch wit" is particularly evident in his relations to the reporter Gloria. In her desire to expose Joe's dishonesty, Gloria is the only character in the show to aid Applegate in his plans for Joe's damnation. Yet Applegate's relation to her is purely antagonistic, and she is in fact the subject of his nastiest asides, most of which deal with her unfeminine behavior.

The gay coding of Applegate is heightened by the choice of Ray Walston to perform the role—both on Broadway and in Hollywood. Walston is not gay-identified, but his slight body type and somewhat wooden line delivery made him well suited to roles that emphasized strangeness. Although Applegate is Walston's only award-winning performance, his other roles equally exploit his traditionally unmasculine physical type. He first became known for his portrayal of Luther Billis in *South Pacific*, a chorus lead whose most extended scene is the song "Honey Bun," a drag performance complete with grass skirt and coconut-shell breasts. Later Walston played one of the more homophobic parts of the post-*Psycho* sixties, the transvestite cosmetician of *Caprice* (1967). And his most widely seen characterization, while not explicitly gay, was both misogynistic and bizarrely otherworldly—the title role in the television situation comedy *My Favorite Martian* (1963–66).[4]

It is in light of this gay coding that we must read the sequence following the "Lola" number—the devil's brief parody of it. Angry that Joe has gone off with his wife, Applegate appears from behind the lockers to critique Lola's performance. Objecting that "your methods are old-fashioned," he contemptuously reprises a few measures of her seduction. Like Lola's dance itself, this very brief coda works on a number of levels. One would not want to miss Lola's instantaneous loss of accent in her conversation with the devil or Applegate's characterization of performance as employment—his willingness to grant to Lola the very job-oriented sensibility he finds so unfeminine in Gloria. But I want to focus on a single aspect of this scene—its relation to the camp tradition of quotation and female impersonation.

The imitability of female performance always, of course, calls attention to the constructed character of gender identity. At the end of *Gentlemen Prefer Blondes*, for example, Jane Russell can become "Marilyn Monroe" through reprising in a platinum wig Monroe's "Diamonds" number.[5] In *Damn Yankees*, however, the imitation is across gender lines. The mini-reprise asks us to imagine Applegate momentarily as a woman. Although the script has already coded the devil as gay, Walston refuses to adopt those performance styles most closely associated with gay gender-crossing. Studiously avoiding the falsetto voice traditionally used in drag representations of women, he sings entirely in his own register, reproducing neither Lola's intonations nor her accent. His movements transform the dance back into a bump-and-grind, with only the arm thrown across his shoulder even glancing at the irony of the drag review. His fury incapacitates him, and the scene ends with him petulantly stamping his feet. The joy the audience feels in Verdon's performance of gender is denied Walston's performance of homosexuality, which appears merely childish and impotent by comparison. It is not Lola's method but Applegate's that is "old-fashioned."

Damn Yankees represents the theatricality of desire by reading ethnicity and homosexuality similarly in terms of performance. There are in the "Lola" scene at least four revisions of normative sexuality—Latin performance, Verdon's burlesque of those performance traditions, drag performance, and Walston's de-ironization of those traditions. In these revisions the musical flirts with a whole set of demeaning cultural stereotypes—foremost among these, the primitivization of Latin culture as natural and exotic and the dismissal of gay male culture as flamboyant and infantile. These limitations cannot be explained away. Yet the carelessness with which the show reproduces the sexism, racism, and homophobia of its culture exposes the vulnerability of those assumptions. The moments when the show thinks itself most in control of its stereotypes are often those when traditional values have actually been suspended. And in the performance's conflation of gender, ethnicity, and sexuality this complacent dance becomes a potential site for rethinking the meaning of all three.

Gender stereotyping is the most obviously threatened, and by the very linchpin of the show's commercial success—the presence of Gwen Verdon. Verdon's personality is as disruptive as it is entertaining. Although Verdon was a successful performer on Broadway, *Damn Yankees* is her only screen success, and one of her few film appearances. In general her talents were felt too hyperbolic for the greater intimacy of the screen, and when her other stage triumph *Sweet Charity* (1966) was filmed in 1969, the role went to Shirley MacLaine, who was overtaxed by the part's singing and dancing. In Verdon's Lola, we get not simply the performance of a first-rate dancer and a comic singer of considerable charm. We get a female image that, unlike MacLaine's, was not primarily directed at a male sensibility. By the time *Damn Yankees* was filmed, Verdon was not so young as MacLaine was in *Sweet Charity* and not so traditionally attractive. Moreover, Verdon's limitations themselves make space for an even more unusual female performer—Shannon Bolin, who played Meg on both stage and screen. As with many dancers, Verdon's considerable talents do not extend so far as lyric singing, and in *Damn Yankees* all the romantic songs had to be given to Joe's wife. But since Meg need not dance or flirt, the part went to an unprepossessing woman over forty, whose chief performance strength was a rich singing voice. The part was, and is, unusual in its notion of type, and Bolin herself won praise but no further roles.

Any show built around Verdon is likely to require an imaginative relation to fifties gender categories, and *Damn Yankees* in fact offers more interesting women's roles than most Broadway musicals. Not only Lola but even Meg and Gloria actively advance the plot as do none of the ballplayers, including Joe. More strikingly, the musical is one of the few not to have a love story at its center. Although the marriage between Meg and Joe unifies the plot, it occupies little of our attention. The women are more fully characterized by their jobs than by their sex lives. When her husband disappears, Meg quickly becomes financially self-supporting by taking in boarders. Gloria is a reporter whose interest in ballplayers is not sexual but professional. As for Lola, of course, sex is her job. Whatever its effect on Joe Boyd, the devil's pact frees the show's women from economic and emotional dependence on men.

This innovative characterization of women undercuts the apparent celebration of baseball as a bastion of masculinity. The very carelessness with which the show reproduces contemporary clichés about the "unbeatable" Yankees reveals how professional baseball was striving to mythify a middle-class notion of masculine achievement at the very historical moment when that notion was being eroded. Although paying lip service to the traditional dichotomy in which Joe and baseball stand for masculinity and Meg and home for femininity, the show is unable to sustain it. None of the women fulfills the stereotype of wife and mother with any precision, while Joe's teammates, inept athletes with comic physiques, speak not for skill or even brute strength but (in the show's other hit song) for "Heart."

The show's inability to sustain its masculine/feminine dichotomy is clearest in the publicity department's uncertainty about how to represent Verdon herself. The show's most famous advertisement offered the image of the un-

Figure 5. The original publicity poster.
(Reprinted with the permission of the Billy
Rose Theatre Collection, New York Public
Library for the Performing Arts, Astor,
Lenox, and Tilden Foundations.
Photograph by Gene Cook.)

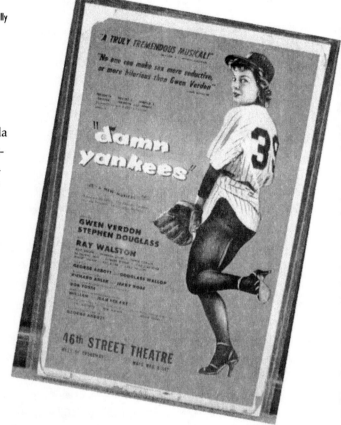

dressed, desexualized Lola
and (again) alluded in image and layout to a simi-
larly masculinized use of
Mary Martin's Peter Pan
the year before. But, in
fact, the first poster for
the show challenged
more directly the tra-
ditional characteriza-
tion of baseball as
masculine (figure 5).
Here an image of
Lola in a baseball
uniform—the
badge of masculine
empowerment—feminizes her
more than any of her more explicitly seductive female
clothes in the show proper. The subsequent repression of this photograph
suggests that even the show's creators understood how such an image might
erode the show's complacent faith in the masculinity of sports.

Similar tensions complicate the show's use of ethnicity. The score under-
mines the script's stereotypes by the musical respect it affords them. Whatever it thinks of its Latin origins, "Lola" is after all the show's finest song.
The traditional theatrical striptease satirizes its source—most commonly, as
in *Gypsy* or Monroe's "Diamonds," through the parodic accompaniment of
the blaring trumpet and crude percussion licks. "Lola," however, does not
trivialize its rhythmic impulses but instead employs complex orchestral effects
that allow the music to seduce even as Lola does not. Nor is Adler and Ross's

score monochromatic in its appropriation of Latin rhythms. The parodic use of Latinness in the striptease is modified by the later use of the mambo in the dance number performed to celebrate the team's winning streak and by the return of a domesticated form of tango in the love duet between Joe and his wife.

The musical also makes surprising concessions to ethnic politics. The libretto is preoccupied with place and with cultural differences among American cities—New York, Washington, Hannibal, Providence. The national pastime of baseball fosters regional competition and antagonism. This disunity within the states raises implicit questions about what lies without. Some of these questions are made explicit. The rumor about Joe's dishonesty in the Mexican league invites the audience to think about the moral implications of such an ethnicized "bush" league. Even the show's title can function as a pun, directing its damnation not only at a New York baseball team but (in Spanish) at American political intervention more generally. A musical that appears to engage in cultural appropriation alludes in its title to the epithet by which Latin America traditionally reviled the United States as culturally and politically imperialist—"Yanquis."

Such ambiguities are compounded whenever the show links ethnicity to its equally ambiguous gender representations. Gender revisions defuse ethnic stereotyping most at the moment that most fully equates the two—the Lolita caricature itself. As first conceived, the scene is racist: authors, directors, and actors all assume that for Broadway's largely white middle-class audience the humor of the spitfire stereotype will more than override its prejudice. Yet in some ways such prejudice only makes explicit the racial inequities in all ethnicized music. Most bandstand and Broadway performances presuppose Anglo superiority in silently assuming their audiences' understanding of and entitlement to ethnic materials. Some appropriations—including "Hernando's Hideaway"—make no mention of the rhythms' origins; and in *Wonderful Town* Rosalind Russell (as Ohioan Ruth McKenney) actually teaches the conga *to* Brazilians. In Lola's dance, the racist distinction between Latin voraciousness and American purity at least acknowledges that ethnic groups might be significantly different. By depicting Joe's moral superiority to Lolita, the show inadvertently admits that Lolita knows some things Joe does not.

The very complacency of such ethnocentricity also leaves unresolved interesting inconsistencies in the scene's representation of ethnic identity. There is, of course, an implicit contradiction between the two ways in which ethnicity is used. As a stage accent, Lolita's Latinness stands for fraud, against the authenticity of Lola's Rhode Island origins. Yet, as irrepressibly sexual, Lolita symbolizes the exotic's access to original innocence, a natural shamelessness lost through acculturation. The tension between the Latin as true and this Latina as false is compounded by the fact that, though offered as irresistible, Lolita's Latinness is in fact resisted. The seduction fails, of course, because Joe loves only his wife. The easy triumph of marital fidelity, however, does not of itself explain the failure of Latin irresistibility, and if we intuitively know that Meg will win we must still consider the implications of Lola's defeat. Her failure might suggest that the so-called irresistibility of Latin sexuality is a myth, the racist construction of white middle-class culture. The scene might believe that, though Latin sexuality exists as something truly different, ethnic difference resides not in essential primitiveness but in the Latin's different cultural relation to sexuality, a cultural difference that would not speak to the very WASP Joe.

Verdon's own indifference to her failure, moreover, permits an even more radical reevaluation of ethnic sexuality. A very talented dancer and comedian, Verdon was physically incapable of the voluptuousness of a Monroe. Casting this skinny pale actress, however momentarily, as a sultry Latina only compounded the joke of her own sexlessness. To maintain audience sympathy and avoid self-parody, Verdon does not distance herself from her character, but places Lolita in control of the joke. In so doing she extends the musical's ironic approach to gender to its ethnic stereotyping as well. The same performativity that puts Lola in charge of her seduction allows Lolita to control her ethnicity. Verdon's Lolita is not a cartoon spitfire but a figure of playful knowledge and power. She exploits the theatricality of Latinness to destabilize ethnic caricature, much as Verdon uses dance to explode clichés of female desire.

In treating ethnicity and gender as comparable acts of performance, then, *Damn Yankees* is even more perceptive than the most sophisticated and sympathetic of the Latin musicals, Bernstein's *West Side Story* (1957). Although that play's Puerto Ricans are psychologically complex, they are still primitives, characterized by their rhythmic syncopation and flashy colors. The Sharks dance with unexamined naturalness the exotic dances of their native culture. They can be passionate, tortured, conflicted, and angry, but not self-reflective or ironic. By mixing Latinness with other sexual performances—like those of Betty Boop or of teenagers on the telephone—Fosse and Verdon suggest the self-consciousness with which Lolita performs all sexual activities, both "natural" and borrowed. Their Latina is not trapped by stereotypes but revels in them. She celebrates the irony by which Latin sexuality understands and underscores its own artificiality. More performing than performed, this Lolita refuses to win or lose at sex and instead envisions seduction simply as an entertaining game.

JUST as the intersection of gender and Latin sexuality opens a space for rethinking the musical's ethnic stereotypes, gender ambiguities complicate the work's crude use of homosexuality. Though unadmirable, the devil is in the play a figure of considerable power and, as in many Faust stories, he upstages the hero. When Walston won New York's Tony award for his performance, he won as best leading actor, not supporting actor. To attribute homosexuality to so strong and unconflicted a character is an advance over many cold war representations. The relation between Applegate and Lola reinforces this sexual revisionism. Traditionally, of course, witches are the devil's concubines. Although, in his misogyny, Applegate predictably shows only professional admiration for Lola's sexual skills, the two are emotionally coupled, and their fights stand as the show's sole sexualized moments. While not homosexual, their exchanges suggest that gender relations need not take the culturally sanctioned form of heterosexual marriage.

The real threat to heterosexuality, however, is not Applegate, but Joe Hardy. Joe is a difficult and finally a thankless role. The play's moral center, he remains pure despite his demonic pact. His goodness, however, is passive, and his refusal of temptation looks like the absence of desire. He cannot express passion in his scenes with his wife because a fifties audience would be made uncomfortable by a young actor's making love to a woman over twenty years his senior. Similarly Lola's seductions are fun for the audience only if they have no effect on Joe himself. Rather than recognize and refuse temptation, Joe must ignore it, denying that temptation is tempting, even as Lola and the audience revel in the fantasy of being bad.

On Broadway, the virility of Stephen Douglass's Hardy made his sexual reticence incomprehensible, and his four-square masculinity derailed the show's more ironic approach to desire. It is in portraying the absence of passion that Tab Hunter's movie performance works so well. During the striptease, Hunter remains oblivious to Lola's offer, politely observant but uninvolved, as if uncertain of what she wants (or what she wants him for). When, for example, Lola throws off her shirt, his gaze dutifully follows the inanimate piece of clothing and ignores the flesh she has stripped bare. The performance is not psychologically realistic: after many years of marriage, Joe Boyd/Hardy cannot claim sexual innocence. But Hunter's blandness eliminates any threat of moral transgression that might interfere with our pleasure in Verdon's performance.

The exploitation of Hunter's innocence depends on the overlap between the ambiguities of the role of Joe Hardy and the ambiguities of Hunter's position in Hollywood as invisible gay man. The movie asks us to believe the contradictory propositions that a certain sexual situation would be by definition irresistible and that in one particular case a man resisted it. It then uses Hunter's inability to represent heterosexual passion to finesse that contradiction. Wherever the tensions between masculinity and morality increase, so does the homosexual subtext. The setting of Lola's failed seduction implicitly recognizes that locker rooms are traditional sites of homoerotic tension. The film underscores this irony by having Hunter first appear in the scene clothed only in a towel. He is more fully sexualized (and more nude) than Verdon ever is, and the scene really involves complementary teases—Hunter's dressing and Verdon's undressing.

By using Hunter's passionlessness to leaven the character's moral and physical superiority, the film trivializes homosexuality as an emotional vacancy verging on imbecility—the absence of passion, rather than passion for a nontraditional object choice. Even while merchandising Hunter's boyishness, energy, and blondness, the film implicitly devalues these traits as stereotypically homosexual. Encouraging audiences to believe naively in the possibility of sexual disinterest, for skeptical (savvy) viewers the film offers as alternative the probability that this particular sexual disinterest has a simple though unspoken cause. "Innocence" in this context functions, like "bachelor" in the nineteenth century, as a euphemism for homosexuality. Perplexed by Hardy's fidelity, audiences are invited to translate feelings of moral inferiority ("I don't know how he can resist that") into sexual complacency ("We all know what that means").

Whether directed at Tab Hunter, Montgomery Clift, Anthony Perkins, or (in a different way) at Rock Hudson, James Dean, and even Cary Grant, sexual innuendo and sight gags often accompany the use of gay male performers to represent an ideal of heterosexual male sensitivity.[6] Despite the film's sneers, however, Hunter is a surprisingly appealing homosexual, especially compared to the stereotypic Applegate. Hunter's Joe is not, like Walston's devil, "coded" gay. Yet, without crudely distinguishing Walston's "playing" gay from Hunter's "being" gay, we can read the two more neutrally as contrasting ways of playing gay in the fifties. Walston represents the visible "queen," a campy homosexual who openly fulfills social stereotypes. But, as Hunter's performance and career suggest, there can also be a homosexuality which, while not exactly "closeted," is only visible negatively, in the absence of heterosexual emotions and affects. Walston's devil is defined and damned by the heterosexual norms he inverts. Hunter's Hardy is simply something else, to which such social strictures do not apply.

In hinting at Hunter's homosexuality, the movie trades on homophobic stereotypes to disguise irregularities in plot and characterization. Thinking to profit from the cultural taboo against homosexuality, however, the filmmakers only silence themselves, while affording Hunter indirect access to power. The film cannot actually mention homosexuality. Open examination of Joe's implied deviance would undermine the show's idea of faithfulness. Adultery threatens the generation's morality less than the admission that not all marriages are built on heterosexual passion. Moreover, while the filmmakers are trapped by their silence, Hunter is liberated by his. His refusal to explain his preferences—to Lola and his fans—indicates comfort with his social compromises: he does not explain his sexual orientation simply because he does not think it needs to be explained. Even his "innocence" and "blandness" may be strategic. By adopting certain clichéd forms of homosexual behavior, Hunter can use to his own advantage the very cultural stereotypes meant to stigmatize him, obscuring his wants as fully as Lola/Lolita does hers.

Though undemonstrative, Tab Hunter's performance is then surprisingly necessary to the success of *Damn Yankees*. Not only does his marketability as a Hollywood star permit the casting of relative unknowns in the other key roles. His restraint and dramatic inexpertise sanction the hyperbole of Verdon's and Walston's star turns. His unselfconscious underplaying is even at times better served by the camera than their calculated overacting. Most important, it is his point of view that lies at the center of the film. In one sense the characters perform for (or even at) a passive immobile Joe. In another, however, Joe's consciousness actively shapes and controls how those performances appear to the audience. Although grounded in the moral sensibility of his alter-ego Boyd, the movie spends most of its time with Hardy. And in the show's conflicting injunctions to watch Lola and return to Meg, the audience regularly finds itself caught in the middle, sharing with Hunter in his gay bemusement.

At this point we must reconsider exactly what is the devil's pact in the show. In contracting trivially to win at baseball and more generally to recapture youth, Joe Boyd abandons conventional culture for a neutral territory in which moral absolutes become merely performative possibilities. As is customary in such utopias—from Shakespeare's forests on—transformations move across sexuality, and the heterosexual Boyd becomes a homosexual Hardy as easily as Rosalind becomes a boy in *As You Like It*. Joe's transformation invites us to rethink the more general ambiguity of sexual identity in the musical. The reporter Gloria plays a relatively small role, leading one dance number and sponsoring the investigation into Joe's alleged dishonesty. Nevertheless she leaves her mark. As a woman more interested in work than love, she is regularly teased by the devil and the team manager for her inability to perform wifely duties. This teasing, however, always accepts her lack of sexual interest in the players, whom her reports objectify and demasculinize. As with Joe Hardy, her sexual disinterest is explained in ways that complacently reaffirm cultural stereotypes: sexually repressed, she substitutes work for men. But as with Joe Hardy, the carelessness of the explanation raises more troubling questions. Is her mannishness a defense against perceived insufficient femininity or one more nontraditional sexual performance? If working is truly a man's job, does Gloria appropriate other masculine activities? Although the show avoids these questions, and surely does not code her as lesbian, the failure to provide Gloria with a convincing heterosexual psychology leaves open the possibility that she has a commonplace homosexual one.

A comparable silence complicates the seduction scene with which we be-gan. The show takes the seduction lightly, teasing Joe's sexual reticence and laughing at the absurdity of Verdon's performance. But rather than reduce that performance to a caricature of normative sexuality, we might think about it on its own terms—not as parody but as a new form of sexual pleasure. Verdon's lack of voluptuousness redefines what constitutes sexual appeal. The strip that from one angle seems to desexualize her from another angle liberates her from the control of male voyeurism. At the end of the song her competitive, aggres-sive pose is not really asexual. It rejects desire as possession to reembrace it as power. And while the show's producers surely had no interest, however im-plicit, in activating the lesbian subtext in its gender characterizations, it is also true that Lolita's sexual dominance anticipates rather closely some affirmative images in contemporary lesbian S/M culture.

Joe's passionlessness, then, lies at the center of the musical's cultural com-placency. The show invites us to indulge in fantasies of youth, celebrity, in-fidelity, even miscegenation, incest, and damnation. This moral holiday is authorized by Hardy's stability—the possibility that a character offered such temptations would merely long for age, home, and Meg. Joe stands in for the shared consciousness of the decade, those unstated but purportedly univer-sal cultural and moral norms against which we measure the deviance of wom-en, devils, Latins. The problem with such moral rectitude is not that it could not exist but that it would have no identifiable characteristics if it did. All discriminatory dichotomies—female/male, black/white, Latin/Anglo, gay/straight—are defined primarily in terms of the supposed deficiencies of the disempowered half. "Male," "white," "Anglo," and "straight" only take on meaning reflexively through their lack of the traits that make the other cat-egories inferior. As a role, Joe Hardy has no performable characteristics of his own.

So long as shared cultural assumptions are not challenged—so long as audiences accept Joe's fidelity to Meg as sufficient explanation for his pas-sionlessness—then the indefiniteness of his values passes unnoticed. Once they are called into question, however, it becomes clear that the show can-not defend its universal truths. And when the producers try to establish their validity negatively—through invidious comparisons with unwanted femi-ninity, Latinness, and homosexuality—they actually provide those minori-ty cultures a voice in the very process meant to ostracize them. The careless-

ness with which the show characterizes the culture's shared wants is epitomized by the ambiguity of Lola's unspoken "whatever." At first the ambiguity seems trivial. Since we all know what she is after ("what that means"),
speaking is unnecessary. The unsaid is simply sex. But as faith in shared
cultural assumptions breaks down, the meaning of the unsaid broadens.
"What we all know" is transformed into competing ways of knowing and
the growing sense that we do not know what "that" means at all.

"Whatever Lola Wants (Lola Gets)" presents itself as a scene of comic
double failure: Joe is stupid because he does not respond and Lola is stupid
because she wants him to. The film approaches it as well as the traditional
sexual misalliance between the deluded heterosexual woman and the closeted gay man. Such comic readings, however, depend on normative standards
of sexual behavior—the truths universally acknowledged that all women
want husbands and all men want women. They are the point of view of the
devil, or of the male heterosexuality that he upholds through his very attempts to subvert it. Minorities performing the scene can overturn this discriminatory reading simply by redefining the "whatever" of desire so care-
lessly left unspecified. In their performances, desire does not fail but is
instantaneously gratified. The unspoken represents less some goal to be
reached than the process of reaching it. Lola's desire is performance as dance;
Joe's, performance as innocence. Both are fulfilled, despite the devil's plot.

Through sketching the contradictions and lapses in a very commercial
work, I hope to have suggested a model for a minoritized reading of difference. The compromises demanded of high-cultural representations of sexuality—those, for example, of Tennessee Williams or William Inge—are well
known. At its closely watched borders, dominant ideology strictly limits what
can be said about cultural difference. Mass-market fare like *Damn Yankees,*
however, may provide instances of cultural carelessness, during which minority voices can speak more openly. By focusing on the intersections among
various minority positions—the ways in which "others" come bundled together—we may be able to loosen the majority's stranglehold on discourse.
Bracketing questions of vertical power, we can learn to talk more horizon-
tally about interrelations between minorities. Such stories, even if negative,
afford a means of escaping the traditional paradigms of minorities as dam-
aged and victimized, to expose parallel weaknesses in careless ideologies. And
in the process these horizontal accounts allow us to construct, as does Lola's

dance, a narrative in which the Yankees do not win—in which they do not even appear on stage.

NOTES

An abridged version of this argument appeared as the first half of the final chapter of my book *The Queening of America: Gay Culture in Straight Society* (New York: Routledge, 1995), 157–202. © 1995. Used with permission of Routledge, Inc.

1   Lyrics from *Damn Yankees* written by Richard Adler and Jerry Ross Copyright 1955, Frank Music Corp. All Rights Reserved.
2   The number is not, of course, the literal debut of either performer. A seasoned chorus member, Verdon had upstaged the female lead with her specialty dance in *Can-Can* two years earlier. But *Damn Yankees* was her first attempt to carry a show by herself. Fosse was not only an experienced dancer. He had successfully choreographed Adler and Ross's *The Pajama Game* the season before. *Damn Yankees,* however, was his chance to prove that his former triumph with "Steam Heat" had not been a fluke, or (as some cynics had suggested) the uncredited creation of *Pajama Game's* co-director, the celebrated choreographer Jerome Robbins.
3   The contemporary literature on these issues is enormous. The classic statement on masquerade is Riviere. For modern reformulations, see Heath and Doane. For theoretical readings of performance and drag, see Butler, *Gender Trouble* and "Imitation," and the essays reprinted in Case.
4   Walston replaced Myron McCormick, the original Billis, in the early fifties and performed the role when the musical was filmed in 1958. Before his personal triumph as Applegate, he gave unremarkable performances as well in Rodgers and Hammerstein's *Me and Juliet* (1953) and Harold Arlen's *House of Flowers* (1954). For a scathing account of his drag performance in *Caprice*, see Russo 54, 162.
5   Monroe's performance lies at the center of debate on gender performativity and the female gaze (Arbuthnot; Turim). Insufficient critical attention, however, has been paid to Jane Russell's imitation of that performance.
6   For the fullest exploration of this duplicity, see Meyer. For more general treatments of male homosexuality and spectatorship, see Dyer, Neale, and Miller. The scholarship on lesbian spectatorship is enormous. For important statements (that review as well previous arguments), see de Lauretis, "Sexual Indifference" and "Film and the Visible," and White.

WORKS CONSULTED

Abbott, George [Richard Bissell], and Douglass Wallop. *Damn Yankees.* Music and lyrics by Richard Adler and Jerry Ross. New York: Random House, 1956.

Adorno, Theodor, and Max Horkheimer. *Dialectic of Enlightenment.* 1947. New York: Continuum Books, 1975.

Arbuthnot, Lucie, and Gail Seneca. "Pre-Text and Text in *Gentlemen Prefer Blondes.*" In *Issues in Feminist Film Criticism.* Ed. Patricia Erens. Bloomington: Indiana University Press, 1990. 112–25.

Benjamin, Walter. "The Work of Art in the Age of Mechanical Reproduction." *Illuminations.* New York: Schocken Books, 1969. 217–51.

Butler, Judith. *Gender Trouble: Feminism and the Subversion of Identity.* New York: Routledge, 1990.

————. "Imitation and Gender Subordination." In *Inside/Out: Lesbian Theories, Gay Theories.* Ed. Diana Fuss. New York: Routledge, 1991. 13–31.

Case, Sue-Ellen, ed. *Performing Feminisms: Feminist Critical Theory and Theatre.* Baltimore: Johns Hopkins University Press, 1990.

de Lauretis, Teresa. "Film and the Visible." In *How Do I Look?: Queer Film and Video.* Ed. Bad Object Choices. Seattle: Bay Press, 1991. 223–84.

————. "Sexual Indifference and Lesbian Representation." In *Performing Feminisms: Feminist Critical Theory and Theatre.* Ed. Sue-Ellen Case. Baltimore: Johns Hopkins University Press, 1990. 17–39.

Doane, Mary Ann. *Femmes Fatales: Feminism, Film Theory, Psychoanalysis.* New York: Routledge, 1991.

Dyer, Richard. "Don't Look Now: The Male Pin Up." *Screen* 23.3–4 (Sept.–Oct. 1982): 61–73.

Erens, Patricia, ed. *Issues in Feminist Film Criticism.* Bloomington: Indiana University Press, 1990.

Fisher, Philip. *Hard Facts: Setting and Form in the American Novel.* New York: Oxford University Press, 1985.

Fuss, Diana, ed. *Inside/Out: Lesbian Theories, Gay Theories.* New York: Routledge, 1991.

Garber, Marjorie. *Vested Interests: Cross-Dressing and Cultural Anxiety.* New York: Routledge, 1992.

Heath, Stephen. "Joan Riviere and the Masquerade." In *Formations of Fantasy.* Ed. Victor Burgin, James Donald, and Cora Kaplan. London: Methuen, 1986. 45–61.

Kaufman, Walter. Introduction. *Goethe's Faust.* Ed. Walter Kaufman. Garden City, N.Y.: Doubleday, 1963. 13–21.

Kuklick, Bruce. "Myth and Symbol in American Studies." *American Quarterly,* no. 24 (1972): 435–50.

Mast, Gerald. *Can't Help Singing: The American Musical on Stage and Screen*. Woodstock, N.Y.: Overlook Press, 1987.

Meyer, Richard. "Rock Hudson's Body." In *Inside/Out: Lesbian Theories, Gay Theories*. Ed. Diana Fuss. New York: Routledge, 1991. 258–88.

Miller, D. A. "Anal *Rope*." In *Inside/Out: Lesbian Theories, Gay Theories*. Ed. Diana Fuss. New York: Routledge, 1991. 118–41.

Neale, Steve. "Masculinity as Spectacle: Reflections on Men and Mainstream Cinema." *Screen* 24.6 (Nov.–Dec. 1983): 2–16.

Pronger, Brian. *The Arena of Masculinity: Sports, Homosexuality, and the Meaning of Sex*. New York: St. Martin's Press, 1990.

Radway, Janice. *Reading the Romance: Women, Patriarchy, and Popular Literature*. Chapel Hill: University of North Carolina Press, 1984.

Riviere, Joan. "Womanliness as a Masquerade." *International Journal of Psychoanalysis*, no. 10 (1929): 303–13.

Roberts, John Storm. *The Latin Tinge: The Impact of Latin American Music on the United States*. New York: Oxford University Press, 1979.

Russo, Vita. *The Celluloid Closet: Homosexuality in the Movies*. Rev. ed. New York: Harper and Row, 1987.

Smith, Henry Nash. *Virgin Land: The American West and Symbol and Myth*. Cambridge, Mass.: Harvard University Press, 1970.

Turim, Maureen. "Gentlemen Consume Blondes." In *Issues in Feminist Film Criticism*. Ed. Patricia Erens. Bloomington: Indiana University Press, 1990. 101–11.

Wallop, Douglass. *The Year the Yankees Lost the Pennant*. New York: W. W. Norton, 1954.

White, Patricia. "Female Spectator, Lesbian Specter: *The Haunting*." In *Inside/Out: Lesbian Theories, Gay Theories*. Ed. Diana Fuss. New York: Routledge, 1991. 142–72.

Willis, Paul, with Simon Jones, Joyce Canaan, and Geoff Hurd. *Common Culture: Symbolic Work at Play in the Everyday Cultures of the Young*. San Francisco: Boulder Press, 1990.

Jackie Byars —

THE PRIME OF MISS KIM NOVAK
Struggling Over the Feminine in the Star Image

Kim Novak, 1960.
(Courtesy of the Library of Congress)

THE star image known as "Kim Novak" was first created in 1953, when Rita Hayworth walked out on Columbia studio head Harry Cohn and he, in turn, selected Marilyn Pauline Novak from among the studio's contract players, had her made over by Columbia's image experts, renamed her, and proposed her for Stardom. Her first assignments (*Pushover, Phffft!* and *Five against the House*) established her as a sex symbol and a strong competitor for Marilyn Monroe. Cohn then awarded her prize roles in several Columbia productions (*Picnic, The Eddy Duchin Story, Jeanne Eagles, Pal Joey,* and *Bell, Book, and Candle*), and for remuneration, he twice "loaned" her out (for roles that would both inflect and inflate her star image), first to Otto Preminger (United Artist's *The Man with the Golden Arm*) and then to Alfred Hitchcock (Paramount's

197

Vertigo). Kim Novak has been described as the last studio-produced star, and the fact that Harry Cohn was a guiding presence through the height of Novak's career—in effect, co-authoring her star image—would lend this notion some credence. In fact, Richard Lippe—in the most important (if not the only) previous article on the star image Kim Novak—lists as a primary motivation for his analysis the fact that "Novak's image, from the outset, foregrounds the manufacture process which is obscured to varying degrees in the construction of most star images" (5). However, Lippe flatly states that Novak almost immediately attained stardom, ignoring the significant distinction between stars (celebrities) and Stars (cultural icons).[1] Although these films made Novak a box-office rival to Marilyn Monroe, audiences of the period never validated Novak as a Star, as they did Monroe, who cultivated her status as a sex symbol while Novak problematized hers.

As Richard Dyer has suggested, following Francesco Alberoni, stars are not produced by studios; they are social phenomena (Dyer 6; Alberoni; Reeves). The powers that be in the film industry have the capacity to propose candidates for stardom but lack the power to validate the candidate, to christen an actor a Star; that power resides with film audiences. Dyer describes the phenomenon of the star image as a structured polysemy in which various elements can either reinforce each other or exist in opposition/contradiction. Film audiences have tended to make Stars of actors whose star images are ideologically coherent; it is these actors who become cultural icons, Stars like John Wayne. The various elements of the star image John Wayne—"his bigness, his association with the West, his support for right-wing politics, his male independence of, yet courtliness towards, women"—reinforce one another (Dyer 72). In some star images the tension between contradictory elements is successfully negotiated or masked, as in the case of Marilyn Monroe. Until the later years of her career—when the contradictions within the star image threatened to fragment the image—innocence and sexiness effected a "magical synthesis" of opposites (Dyer 30). However, there are some candidates who never achieve Stardom because the tensions that exist within their star image are painfully evident; they are relegated to a lesser rank (star with a small *s*). Such was the case with Kim Novak.

During Novak's (not always happy) collaboration with Harry Cohn, her roles—and, as a result, her star image—foregrounded tensions over gender construction, rather than masking them. Cohn's first casting decisions placed

Novak in Monroe-type roles (*Pushover, Phffft! Five against the House*), but he fairly quickly changed his casting strategy. Cohn was probably correct when he attributed her box-office success to the choice roles he awarded her in the mid- to late fifties. In 1956, when Boxoffice declared Novak the number one star in the United States, Cohn commented, "The success of Novak is due to great pictures. Any girl who gets six pictures like Novak got has got to be a star. We've got twelve to fifteen million dollars invested in her" (Haspiel 79). What was particularly unusual about Novak's brief stardom was that her star image drew its power not from ideological cohesiveness but from ideological struggle. Cohn seems to have recognized this fact, and the roles he assigned Novak took advantage of it. But after Cohn's death during the filming of *Bell, Book, and Candle*, Novak began to be typecast. Never comfortable with the attempt to make her into a sex symbol, she later complained, "They were wanting sex symbol and all the glamorous Marilyn Monroe kind of things. And I was in that same old role over and over, and I was just really frustrated" (Forsberg). The attempt to fit Kim Novak into the Marilyn Monroe mold—an attempt Cohn had clearly abandoned—was doomed to failure, as was her candidacy for lasting Stardom. Marilyn Pauline Novak and, as a result, the star image she and Harry Cohn co-authored, were too complex for Stardom.[2] A quintessentially fifties figure—and the embodiment of conflicting versions of femininity—Novak was an all-American beauty at a time when the category itself was beginning to be called into question. Her star image was a conflicted one, and her roles and performances expressed a resisting structure of feeling that only later became articulated in the ideological struggles over femininity during the sixties.

OUTLAW EMOTIONS AND A NEW STRUCTURE OF FEELING

The second great wave of American feminism surprised many by seeming to erupt from nowhere in the sixties, but looking back it is not so hard to see that the seeming eruption was not an eruption at all but rather an increasingly explicit response to the social, cultural, and economic changes that occurred in the United States during the fifties.[3] During World War II, women who had never before worked outside their homes were encouraged to do so, in support of the war effort, which accelerated change in defining the "appropriately feminine." But in the wake of the war, when returning military men flooded the work force, the U.S. government, trade unions, and the popular press joined forces in a campaign to persuade women that their "proper place" was married, raising children, and working only in the home. The dominant trend toward early marriage was encouraged by popular publications emphasizing that women outnumbered men in the United States (Byars 92). In many ways, the entertainment industries and their products (such as films) only slightly less overtly supported this attempt to maintain femininity and female sexuality as naturally subservient to male definitions and desires.[4]

However, the expected easy victory for this patriarchal campaign was thwarted by an amorphous, unorganized, and powerful force, a force evident in many of the Hollywood films of the period. Although it was undoubtedly true that many, if not most, studio-produced films of the time reinforced the messages of the campaign, many of these films also carried messages that challenged its ideological agenda, often quite subtly. I have previously drawn on Raymond Williams's notion of "structures of feeling" to describe the still preemergent and unarticulated force that, during the fifties, prevented that expected victory and prefigured the ideological struggles over gender that became explicit in the sixties (56–57). Williams described a structure of feeling as a historically specific quality of social experience embodied in and given expression through the implicit tensions often noted as "an unease, a stress, a displacement, a latency: the moment of conscious comparison not yet come" (130). One way of thinking of structures of feeling is to see them as preemergent ideologies straining for but not yet attaining articulation; Alison Jaggar, who argues persuasively that emotions are in part social constructions, offers another, complementary way of seeing them—as configurations of "outlaw emotions" that challenge the hegemony of dominant groups (159). Jaggar identifies as outlaw emotions those that are incompatible with dominant perceptions and values. Race, class, and gender are only the most obvious of the divisions in our society that produce groups of people whose experiences and emotions challenge those of people who inhabit groups that are dominant:

> People who experience conventionally unacceptable, or what I call "outlaw," emotions often are subordinated individuals who pay a disproportionately high price for maintaining the status quo. The social situation

of such people makes them unable to experience the conventionally pre-scribed emotions: for instance, people of color are more likely to experi-ence anger than amusement when a racist joke is recounted, and women subjected to male sexual banter are less likely to be flattered than uncom-fortable or even afraid. When unconventional emotional responses are experienced by isolated individuals, those concerned may be confused, unable to name their experience; they may even doubt their sanity. (160)

When such isolated individuals begin to share their "outlaw" emotions with other, similar individuals and to collectively begin the process of reevaluat-ing the status of these emotions, they constitute the basis for a subculture and for emergent and oppositional ideologies. They may be, in Jaggar's words, "politically because epistemologically subversive" (160).

Outlaw emotions and the structures of feeling into which they are orga-nized achieve signification far more subtly than residual, dominant, or emer-gent ideologies, so as a result, their participation in the hegemonic process is more difficult to identify, but they "may provide the first indications that something is wrong with the way alleged facts have been constructed," and acknowledging outlaw emotions helps make it clear "that what are taken generally to be facts have been constructed in a way that obscures the real-ity of a subordinated people, especially women's reality" (161). The tensions that can be identified—most frequently through hindsight—when outlaw emotions become configured into a structure of feeling speak in, through, and around aesthetic forms and conventions, exerting palpable pressures and setting limits on experience and actions. In fact, it is in aesthetic forms and conventions that we can often find the first evidence of a new and widely experienced structure of feeling, and a primary aesthetic form in the cinema is the star image, a media text (not a real person) that is constructed through the intersection of promotion, publicity, films, and commentaries or criticism (Dyer 68).

Richard Lippe analyzed the interaction of biographical, critical, and jour-nalistic writings with Novak's films to suggest the complexity and ambigu-ity of that star image, arguing that the Novak star image is "relevant to fem-inist concerns," that it is "in a certain respect, progressive," and that it "hinges on disrupting female stereotyping," but he significantly understates the case (Lippe 5). Structures of feeling strain for articulation in star images like that of Kim Novak, and through the lens of that star image—particularly as it was manifested in her performances in the best of the roles awarded her during her association with Harry Cohn—we can see potent evidence of that structure of feeling that so successfully resisted the attempt to restrict "women's place." In Novak's performances in certain of these roles, this resisting structure of feeling came perilously close to overt articulation, and it is hardly surprising that after Cohn's death, less imaginative film executives avoided this danger—repeatedly trying to homogenize the Kim Novak star image by pigeonholing the actor in roles dependent on her status as a sex symbol (to the point that, eventually, she went into semi-retirement).

THE CONSTRUCTION AND RECONSTRUCTION OF "KIM NOVAK"

Dyer suggests that the star image is a complex totality that has a temporal dimension, a structured polysemy that is constantly in process (Dyer 72). We can freeze one moment of that image for synchronic analysis. We can, for instance, profitably examine a single role in a single film to uncover the various voices that speak in and through it, showing how those voices reinforce or contradict one another. This essay examines six of Novak's films from the fifties, showing how the films—through her roles—foregrounded conflicting constructions of femininity and how her performances heightened conflict and exhibited the difficulty of being a young, unmarried woman in the America of that time. With each new role, an actor reformulates her star image; the star image—like a narrative—unfolds over time, with each new event (role) restructuring our perception of the image and its past. This essay also focuses on the development of the Kim Novak star image, which even in its "failure" to achieve Stardom, most fully realized its potential while Harry Cohn was alive and shepherding its progress. The most striking aspect of this star image, however, is the consistency with which it expressed not ideological coherence but contradiction.

Prior to her association with Cohn at Columbia—during and for a brief period following junior college—Marilyn Pauline Novak worked as a model in her hometown, Chicago. She then toured the country demonstrating refrigerators as Thor's Miss Deep Freeze and settled in Los Angeles in the summer of 1953. There she landed walk-on parts in a couple of RKO films (*The French Line* and *Son of Sinbad*) before screen-testing at Columbia, where executives noted her limited acting experience but were impressed by her "star quality," her looks (Haspiel 74–76). The studio packaged and coached her and began production on the star image that was to be known as Kim Novak.[5]

Novak's first two roles for Columbia placed her in the company of the well-known stars Fred MacMurray (*Pushover*, 1954) and Jack Lemmon (*Phffft!* 1954) and established her reputation as a Marilyn Monroe clone with a box-office draw. During this period, the sensual power of her screen presence was expressed in a relatively uncomplicated if already self-conscious sexuality.[6] Richard Lippe dismissed her next film, *Five against the House*, arguing that it "didn't significantly develop her image" (8). He described the character as simply the nondescript and conventional love interest of one of the film's "important" male characters. His dismissal indicates an insensitivity to the difficulty of that conventional part, a difficulty Novak teased out in her performance. The fairly predictable plot does focus on five college men who set out to rob a casino in Reno. One man's "love interest," Kay—a nightclub singer in a college town—ends up going along and even becomes central to the plot's resolution, but neither the plot nor its resolution was significant in the construction of the Kim Novak star image.

As Kay, the only significant female character in the film, Novak negotiated and embodied contradictory constructions of femininity, and her character acknowledges their incompatibility, in terms of fifties morality. The role was overdetermined by the distinctions between "town and gown," between the exchange value of chastity and the lure of sexual desire, and between naiveté and sexual experience, distinctions that divided women into the marriageable and the nonmarriageable. Such a distinction was significant in the fifties, when a family-centered culture was America's bulwark against fears of economic depression, against the insecurity produced by the atom bomb, and against fears of communism; during this period, the pressure to marry and form nuclear families was overwhelming (May 13). Marriage was the film's primary subtext, and the contrast among the moments in the film that featured Novak's character shows how her role embodied the "potential wife/ sex kitten" dichotomy more frequently referred to as the "virgin/whore" dichotomy. Most actresses specialized, embodying one category or the other; Elizabeth Taylor specialized in playing the virgin who became the happy wife, while Gloria Grahame cultivated the sensual slut. Novak's star image was a balance, a play between the categories, and in this role, that balance

becomes explicit. Her performance as Kay accentuated the difficulty of experiencing those outlaw emotions—the simultaneous desires for passionate
sexuality and security—and by the perceived impermeability of the boundaries that enclosed and separated the categories "sex kitten" and "wife."

The film first sets up Kay as the sex kitten, on display as a nightclub singer
in a low-cut black dress with rhinestone spaghetti straps that keep falling
off her shoulders. Kay croons romantic ballads and fondles the vertical poles
that decorate her stage, causing a minor character, struck dumb by her powerful sensuality, to ignore his date. This aspect of her character is reinforced
in a following scene. As Kay exits the shower in her dressing room, her suit-
or Al (Guy Madison) enters the room, which is framed by her right leg. She
dries her leg, which is bent into its most alluring shape (that shape encouraged by high heels) when she goes up on her toes as she leans into a chair.
She is, in this shot, reduced to a body part. She *is* an erotic object, that sensual sex kitten she seemed on stage, and she knows it.

Novak's full-figured body was difficult to disguise, even when she was
costumed primly in a suit, as she was in other scenes, scenes in which she
reveals her lack of naiveté as well as the outlaw emotions inspired by her
conflicting desires. She knows that she's attractive, and she likes male attention, but she has also learned how problematic that attention can be for a
woman who ultimately wants love, marriage, financial security, and a family. She tells Al, "I've been dating college boys since I was old enough to be
noticed by them. It's no trick for a girl to be busy in a college town." But she
has also learned the difficult lesson that college boys seek sexual favors from
"townie" girls but do not perceive them as marriageable: "There's something
about being away to college makes for lasting love affairs which are forgotten the minute graduation's over."[7] Still, although—as an ex-serviceman on
the GI bill—Al is not a typical college boy, Kay knows that if she were to seem
sexually experienced the sound of wedding bells would be silenced, even for
him. Although women were increasingly expected to be passionate as wives,
premarital passion was definitely outlawed.

Kay reveals both a self-awareness of her physical attributes and her desire to marry, but she also reveals her fears of being rushed into marriage,
fears that—in this pro-marriage period—must be subdued: "I may look like
the blonde bombshell that's been every place and done everything, but I'm
not. And all these big emotions are wonderful, but they just kind of scare

me, too." As fifties plots would have it, Kay has to choose. For Al, it is now or never. Al wants to marry, and, impatiently, he wants to marry *now*. Not only is Al a male character in a patriarchal society (and, as such, draws on the power his position entails), but he also embodies the dominant trend— toward early marriage. Kay's fear of allowing herself to be swept by a passionate romance into a quick marriage represents an outlaw emotion. The possibility of remaining a spinster was unthinkable among Americans of this time, who highly valued the nuclear family based on a heterosexual married couple.

Because divorce was equally unthinkable, Kay's fears may be seen as justified; nevertheless, her resistance to being rushed into marriage—and her resistance to Al's male desires—must be sublimated. Given his ultimatum, Kay follows the multitude who married quickly in the fifties, and she and Al head (with the other potential bandits) off to Reno and into the rest of a wacky plot, resolved happily only through the strength of character shown by Kay and Al. Although Novak's character was featured in only a few scenes, we can see in this character—faced with choices common to women of the fifties—an uneasy embodiment of the tensions between sexual desire, the desire for marriage, and the knowledge that giving into the former before the latter was surely "inappropriate." This part and Novak's performance were far from insignificant; they laid the groundwork for the intricacies that would develop in the star image Kim Novak.

Novak's box-office successes prompted Cohn to reward her with her first big role, Madge in the film adaptation of William Inge's Broadway hit *Picnic,* directed by Joshua Logan. This role could not have been more perfect for Novak, whose personal discomfort with her own physical beauty was exactly what the part demanded. Logan observed, "She bears the burden of her beauty as if it were a physical disability" (Peachment). The tension central to Madge—the tension between reveling in the attention received because, as a voluptuous blonde, she so perfectly fit the fifties American social construction "beautiful woman" and the troubling idea that perhaps there is more to life than just being ogled—expressed a still preemergent structure of feeling that would later become central as feminists developed the language necessary for addressing this question. However, although Madge did wonders for Novak's career—*Picnic* reached number six on Variety's Top-Twenty Moneymaker list in 1956, the same year Boxoffice named Novak the number one star in the United States—the role further skewed her star image, ensuring that Novak would never achieve Stardom.

The attention of the other characters in the film frequently focuses on this small town beauty, and the rich and attractive Alan Benson (Cliff Robertson) wants to marry her. But when Alan's unemployed, transient college fraternity brother, Hal Carter (William Holden), arrives in town, hoping Alan can give him a job, tension escalates. Hal cannot keep his eyes off of Madge, and she cannot keep her eyes off of him, either (and the camerawork often implicates the viewer in the agency of her active gaze). In less than a day, Hal and Madge fall in love and leave town—a seemingly straightforward plot but a plot mightily complicated by the camerawork, by Madge's peculiar predicament, by Novak's costumes, and by the actors' performances.[8]

Madge, who works as a clerk in the local five-and-dime, knows that, because of her beauty, menial labor will not be her ultimate fate, but she also knows that marriage to a rich man (with or without romantic love) and a prim-and-proper country-club future can be a prison. When she looks at Hal, Madge sees more than just a hunk. Hal offers her a choice, a way out of the life that has seemed to be mapped out for her. Looking at Hal, Madge sees another way of being; he excites in her the sexual passions that members of "polite" fifties society sublimated, passions that become for her the key to independence and self-fulfillment. Madge's mother, Flo Owens (Betty Field), speaking from the experience of having a husband abandon her and her two young daughters, assures Madge that a union with Hal will only lead to heartache and poverty. But passion (surely an outlaw emotion for a proper young unmarried woman of the time, especially for a woman "destined" for upward mobility) transforms her unfocused gaze, a look that prompted one contemporary critic to observe that Novak "makes a hypnotic trance an eloquent expression" (qtd. in Haspiel 77). For Hal, Madge abandons passivity. In a particularly sensual dance sequence, Madge and Hal gyrate to a slow jazz tune as their eyes consume one another.[9] Clad in a bright pink dress with an amazingly tight bodice that accentuates Novak's lush figure, Madge finds her sexual desires finally awakened, and she is released from the stasis of a life seemingly beyond her control. Having found a direction, Madge acts.

The traditional heterosexual coupling so common to the endings of Hollywood films is implied here, as an aerial shot shows the parallel courses of the freight train Hal has hopped and the bus Madge has boarded. In their parting words they planned reunion, and Novak's prim blue suit visually assures the audience that she will remain chaste until they are married. What makes this particular plot and this particular coupling interesting is that it occurs as the result not of a male character's action but of Madge's decision and her action. Madge harnessed the outlaw emotions that allowed her to reject the "perfect" life to which her beauty had seemed to condemn her, and Novak's performance makes the spectator excruciatingly aware of the pain of yet another conflicted female positioning common among American women of this decade.

Novak's next important role returned her to the realm of sexual labor, where the tensions between sexual desire and the desire to remain marriageable that were central to her character in *Five against the House* once again surface.[10] Cohn rented Novak to Otto Preminger to play opposite Frank Sinatra in his controversial film about drug addiction, *The Man with the Golden Arm*. Like *Picnic*'s Madge, Molly is another strong working-class beauty who desires romantic love and a marriage based on it, but like Kay, Molly embodies contradictory impulses/desires/emotions in order to delineate the boundaries of acceptability (boundaries which, of course, also delineate "outlaw"). Struggling to get by, Molly works as a B-girl who makes her living wearing sexy dresses (glittering and low cut, with off-the-shoulder straps that showcase her bare shoulders) and chatting up men so they will buy drinks in a strip joint. Her discomfort obvious, she painfully inhabits sleaze, and her pain makes it apparent that she is the wholesome and supportive girl-next-door (or downstairs, as the case is here). Compounding contradictions, she is represented as sexually available—first seen leaving her apartment with Johnny, a boyfriend who obviously sleeps over (a common fifties film ploy: associating working-class women with sexual availability and experience, making the likelihood that these women will attain their dreams highly questionable).

Frankie Machine (Frank Sinatra)—returned to his working-class neighborhood after a stint in prison, during which he kicked a heroin habit—finds himself powerfully attracted to the beautiful, sensual Molly. He disapproves of her boyfriend, but he refuses to offer himself as an alternative. Married to the stereotypically weak and feminine but paraplegic Zasha (Eleanor Parker), who is only much later revealed to be clinging and conniving, Frankie tells Molly, "I ain't comin' around no more. You understand?" Of course, she understands. By being available for premarital sex, she has crossed a social boundary, and she understands it very well, however much she desires (as all American women were supposed to) a middle-class and married life.[11] She stares away from Frankie, her bosom heaving softly as he caresses her bare shoulder and insists, "You're a good girl, Molly." "Sure," she responds, abjectly, eyes focused away from him, "real good." And the central question concerning this character (and American women of the period) was, precisely, *what does it mean to be "good"?*

Molly continually negotiates the distance between sexual worker and social worker, sublimating any outlaw emotions and eventually promising to help Frankie—addicted to heroin again—kick his habit cold turkey. She locks him in her apartment and goes to Zasha, who calls her a tramp and will not listen to anything she has to say. The contrast between the nurturing, loving Molly and the irrational, selfish Zasha comes to a head in this scene, when Zasha insists, "*He* put me in this chair." She would rather see him dead than with somebody else. The contrast between Molly and Zasha highlights the "appropriately feminine": nurturing is good, self-interest is bad. Molly *is* a good girl, forced by a bad situation into compromising her nature; compassion *could* be her middle name. Otto Preminger recruited Novak because of it; he described Novak as "the way every American girl would like to look." Every man, he felt, "would like to have a girl like that. She is not too sophisticated. She gives you a feeling of compassion" (Forsberg). The role emphasizes nurturing as primary to femininity, but in doing so, it turns on its head the expectation that sexual experience precludes sympathy, giving an American audience further grounds for considering the film controversial.[12]

Novak's role in the romantic musical *Pal Joey* again explicitly raised the question, "What is a good girl?" but this role answered the question in a significantly less controversial fashion. Cast as Linda English, Novak plays a girl-next-door-type who—like Madge in *Picnic*—has left her small hometown (in this case Albuquerque) to seek her fortune in the big city (San Francisco). The sweetest, most naive of Novak's characters during this period, Linda seems free of outlaw emotions. She wants to be a singer but accepts interim work as a chorus girl (her work in the realm of sexual labor resonates both with her role in *The Man with the Golden Arm* and with her role in *Five against the House*). Once again, Novak plays a character who embodies contradictions and interrogates prevailing gender constructions, but Linda is much more wholesome and naive, and the values she represents are much more closely in line with prevailing ideologies than those associated with Molly in *The Man with the Golden Arm*. However, like Molly, Linda is involved in a romantic triangle (and once again, the male corner of the triangle is played by Frank Sinatra); she is in opposition to (contrasted with) another female character, and here too, as in the case of Molly, Linda's values are the ones that prevail. She competes with the wealthy widow, Mrs. Prentice Simpson (formerly the stripper Vera Vanessa), a character played by Rita Hayworth, for the affections of Joey, an aspiring musician.[13]

Hayworth's Vera is a smart, determined woman, and at least initially, she wins Joey, bankrolling his dream—a nightclub of his own, Chez Joey—in return for sexual favors and unswerving loyalty. No dupe, she perceives Joey's growing attraction to Linda as she watches him watch Linda as she rehearses "My Funny Valentine," Novak wearing a low-cut costume that calls attention to her voluptuous figure while, white and ruffled, simultaneously signifying wholesomeness.[14] Watching her, Joey is so entranced that he does not hear Vera come in and sit next to him. Vera realizes that Linda could be a significant rival and demands that, to protect her investment (and she does not mean money), Joey fire her.

Novak's only other song-and-dance scene results directly from Vera's demand, and the scenes that lead up to it focus directly on that question of "goodness" and "femininity." Because Joey cannot bring himself to fire Linda outright, he tries to force her into a moral bind that will make her quit the show. He reassigns "My Funny Valentine" to another show girl and assigns Linda a strip routine. Linda does quit and then proceeds to get drunk. Although in most cases a woman drinking alcoholic beverages connotes a moral "flaw," an indication of rampaging outlaw emotions, in this film drinking operates differently because Linda—normally a teetotaler—is so wholesome. Drinking here allows Linda to speak the truth. She confronts Joey, agreeing to do the strip routine and confirming what she knows but, sober, would never say: "You were right. I do have good shape. Confidentially, I'm stacked! Bet you thought I wouldn't, didn't you? I bet you even thought that I couldn't. . . . I will!" She flirts with him (and with outlaw emotions), she kisses him, he kisses back, she passes out. The next morning, he reassures her that she did not do "anything" the night before and that, uncharacteristically, neither did he. She is ashamed: "Where I come from, a girl doesn't spend a night on a yacht and stay for breakfast." When he expresses surprise that her mother would let her "come to the big town," she replies, "My mother says a good girl is a good girl wherever she is," even if she does compromise her ethics for the man she loves.

As Linda rehearses the strip routine the music changes from classical to jazzy, and Linda attempts to shift from classy to sexy, accentuating the strip with her undulating body. In a dramatic contrast to the "Funny Valentine" scene, this scene becomes increasingly tense, as Joey realizes her sacrifice and his real feelings. The pace of the editing increases, with medium to full shots of her alternating with extreme close-ups of Joey's eyes as she strips to a lacy, fitted teddy. Once again, Joey is oblivious to Vera, who enters and watches him watch Linda. And she watches as he dramatically calls a halt to the routine, orders Linda to get dressed, and follows her to her dressing room. Joey is apparently quite willing to let other women strip, but Linda is different. She is a "good girl" (not a "good woman"), and at least partially because of her "goodness," he loves her. She cries as he apologizes to her, sealing the fate of Chez Joey and reaffirming the supremacy of the chaste.

In a scene quite similar to the woman-confronts-woman-on-behalf-of-man scene in *The Man with the Golden Arm*, Linda confronts Vera, speaking on Joey's behalf, and Vera makes explicit the contrast between them. This is not the contrast presented in *The Man with the Golden Arm*, a contrast between a nurturing, loving woman on one hand (Molly) and a vengeful, self-centered woman on the other (Zasha). In *Pal Joey*, different constructions of femininity are at stake, constructions based on sexual experience. Linda is naive and virginal, while Vera is sexually experienced and has even used sex to acquire wealth, which she now uses to acquire sex. The "virgin/whore" dichotomy could not be clearer. And the virgin always wins, at least in fifties films. Vera knows it: "It may come as quite a surprise, Miss English, but I do believe there's nothing between you and Joey. That makes you all the more dangerous. He may not know it, but when Joey told you to keep your clothes on today, he played the greatest love scene of his career. I could undress in the lobby of the Fairmont Hotel, and he'd never turn a hair. So you see, Miss English, with you on the scene, I couldn't possibly reopen the club." Fifties conventions and morality dictated the choice—in favor of Linda, whose attempts to control are far more subtle and who is clearly a virgin. People on the outside know why they are there, and Vera understands that the sexual double standard that dominated

American morality during this period would never work in her favor. The film never questions the fact that it will work in Joey's favor; as the man, he has the ultimate authority to direct the narrative.

Linda was unqualified goodness, and even when she flirted with outlaw emotions, she could not embrace them. She was a rare monolithic character among those produced by the Novak-Cohn collaboration. More characteristic—and more classically Kim Novak—were the last two films Novak made during the Cohn era at Columbia: *Vertigo* and *Bell, Book, and Candle*. With these films, Novak's star image is at its contradictory peak; these are the two Novak-Cohn films that most explicitly delineate different versions of femininity in single characters, and in both films, the internal rhetoric of the film posits one version of femininity as superior to the other, while Novak's performance leads to an opposite conclusion. However, although Novak's performance is central to *Vertigo,* although her performance in this film is arguably her finest, and although it remains the most well-known of her films, the credit for *Vertigo*'s quality tends, unfairly, to go exclusively to Hitchcock. Most of the critical attention the film has received has focused on Hitchcock's contribution to the film, with little acknowledgment of the central importance of Novak's performance.[15]

Initially, *Vertigo* would seem to operate similarly to *The Man with the Golden Arm* and *Pal Joey,* positioning Novak's character(s)—Judy/Madeleine—in a romantic triangle with former police officer Scottie Ferguson (James Stewart) and Midge (Barbara Bel Geddes), to whom Scottie was once engaged. But the important romantic triangle involves Judy Barton (Novak), Madeleine Elster (Novak), and Scottie, and the contrast between different femininities embodied in Novak's roles overshadow those Midge portrays. Key to the contrast are socioeconomic class and regional difference.

Novak first appears as the beautiful, sophisticated, troubled, aloof Madeleine, whom Scottie is hired—by Madeleine's husband, Scottie's former schoolmate Gavin Elster (Tom Elmore)—to follow. As he watches her and learns about her, he falls in love. She is blonde, and she is voluptuous, but she wears expensive and well-tailored clothes. She has cultured manners, and she occasionally lapses into a trance (shades of Madge, whose unfocused gaze also expressed her pain). She attempts suicide by jumping into the San Francisco Bay, and Scottie saves her. Finally, tragically, she seems to succeed, jumping from a Catholic mission tower because Scottie, who suffers from vertigo as the result of a traumatic accident involving another police officer, is unable to make it to the top of the tower to save her. A distraught Scottie thinks he sees her everywhere, finally encountering Judy, who has a distinct resemblance to Madeleine but who is also distinct in numerous ways.

We learn that Judy, like *Picnic*'s Madge and *Pal Joey*'s Linda, has come to the big city from a small town (Salina, Kansas), and her midwestern accent, her cheap and tight-fitting clothes (under which, Truffaut and Modleski both note, she is not wearing a brassiere), and heavy makeup (including heavily penciled eyebrows) signify her lack of both sophistication and "beauty." They signal, in fact, that "beauty" is a construct. Tania Modleski points out that she is "the 'original' woman, who will soon be remade (for the second time) into the fully fetishized and idealized, 'constructed' object of male desire and male 'design'" (96). Judy is "natural," but natural in this case means she is her own woman and she exudes raw sexuality (the lack of the brassiere emphasizes this aspect of her being). She looks the way she wants to and wears the clothes she wants to; she is independent. But the desire for independence—for control over her own destiny, not to mention control over her visual image—was an outlaw emotion in a society in which women achieved romantic attachments (the grounds for that all-important state, matrimony) precisely by giving up the power of self-definition. Driven by his passion for Madeleine, Scottie reconstructs Judy, making Madeleine. And we soon learn that Madeleine was for him always a construction. Made over by Gavin Elster, Judy (Elster's mistress) had posed as Madeleine and had participated in the plot to involve Scottie in Madeleine's "suicide" (murder, we learn). We, the spectators, learn this from Judy's point of view—from a flashback and a letter she writes to Scottie, then destroys, unsent.

Obsessed with her resemblance to Madeleine, Scottie pleads with Judy to allow him to make her over and—having failed to make him love her on her own terms (with her own hair, makeup, clothing, and sensuality) and because she loves him—she relents. He visually recreates Madeleine by having Judy's brown hair bleached blonde and styled like Madeleine's hair, by having her makeup redone (reducing heavily penciled eyebrows to lightly penciled, well-plucked arches), and by recostuming her in the very same kind of clothes Madeleine wore. Judy cooperates by shedding her mannerisms and adopting those of a San Francisco aristocrat. Judy is no longer her own woman, now trapped in the signifiers of elegance and feminine beauty entirely defined by men. And the film, through its positing of Madeleine as beautiful and Judy as plain, attempts to privilege one construction of femininity over another. However, Novak, through the power of her performance in the part of Judy, involves the film's spectators in Judy's pain, as she struggles to convince Scottie that she is Judy Barton from Salina, Kansas, and as she then relinquishes, one piece at a time, the signifiers of her self when, step by step, he replaces them with others. The spectator's pleasure in seeing Judy's makeover is at least partially denied, as Novak's performance makes Judy's misery obvious and the flashback from her point of view encourages spectator identification with Judy, subverting the film's effort to constrict the definitions of the feminine and the beautiful.

Similarly, numerous elements of *Bell, Book, and Candle* posit a *single way* of being feminine, while Novak's performance as Gillian Holroyd works to complicate if not subvert the spectator's ability to believe in that way. An independent female sexuality that operates outside marriage, threatening the patriarchal structure, provides much of the film's liveliness but, by its end, must be constrained. Gillian is one of Novak's most delightful characters and one whose outlaw emotions are given free reign, until the very end of the film, when the character undergoes a dramatic transformation, a transformation that makes explicit just how much a threat to the dominant order women's outlaw emotions are/were. Attention to the plot, to visual elements of the performance and camerawork, and to the contrasting femininities presented within the character played by Novak reveal the nature of the threat and this film's response (which can, easily, be read in contradictory ways). As Gillian Holroyd, proprietor of a shop that sells African and oceanic "primitive" art, Novak's character is from the beginning associated with "otherness" (an "otherness" associated with race, through the reference to Africa, and an association of the African with the "primitive"). As the beginning credits roll, the camera moves through the store window and past its discreet, tasteful, painted sign that identifies both the proprietor and the objects for sale. It focuses on one exotic, "primitive" object after the next, finally focusing on a Siamese cat, who jumps from a shelf onto Novak's shoulder; the cat and the woman are to become central characters.

Shortly we learn that Gillian Holroyd is a witch and part of a family of witches. In fact, she is the most powerful witch in her family and, through her store, the witch most directly related to the "primitive" (and therefore, furthest from "civilized" society's norm). The witches, collectively, are associated with "otherness" through representations that position them as beatniks. In the fifties, the "beatnik" was a powerful signifier for "otherness"; beatniks constructed themselves in opposition to dominant groups through their dress, their lifestyle, and their philosophies, and representing witches as beatniks adds the element of intention, of choice—and of the rejection of societal norms.[16] In *Bell, Book, and Candle,* the plot's premise is so bizarre that, at least in the beginning, an intentionally aggressive woman can be seen as charming and likable, if a bit strange. Gillian is smart, powerful, and sensual—defined by herself and no one else. She sets herself apart visually, by dressing in dramatic colors and patterns—generally red, black, or leopard skin—and often going barefoot. She is a practitioner of magic, which is inherently associated with the irrational, therefore out of that mainstream so enamored with rationality. (In order to negotiate the story, the spectator must, at least provisionally, also give into the irrational and believe in magic.) And she is a woman whose anger and whose desire for vengeance—certainly outlaw emotions for a fifties woman—form the premise of a plot that, because of its "outlandishness," can be seen as entertaining. The plot is simple: witch wants boy, boy is engaged to marry witch's college nemesis, witch uses magic to get boy, boy gets got, boy finds out, boy runs away, witch gives up her unique and formidable powers, and boy returns; they embrace. A simple, tidy plot, with a typical Hollywood "happy ending"—a happy ending that reinforces male dominance and outlaws female independence and control.

Looking at Gillian's relationship with her cat, Pyewacket, provides a way to cut through the proliferation of plot complications to understand the film's messages: romantic love is the basis of marriage, marriage is the most desirable state of being, and female independence precludes both. To gain the romantic attention of her new neighbor, Shep Henderson (James Stewart), to lure him away from her college nemesis Merle (Janice Rule), Gillian involves Pyewacket, her "familiar."[17] As Gillian puts a spell on Shep, she visually blends with her cat, Pyewacket. Her heavily penciled eyebrows accentuate her animality, and the blending of cat and woman expresses her "otherness," her primitiveness, and her unconstrained aggression. Staring at Shep, Gillian hums to Pyewacket and leans forward over the cat until the screen reveals half of her face over that of the cat, her face lit from below with a light that becomes cooler, making her look paler and less "natural"—less "human," more "other"-worldly. Medium shots of Shep, taken from the side with naturalistic lighting (which maintain the representation of this character as a normal person), alternate with progressively closer shots of Gillian and Pyewacket, the screen all black, white, and red, lit to make Gillian and Pyewacket seem unnatural. The sound of her humming intensifies, nearly drowning out Shep's babbling about Merle, when suddenly, we cut to an extreme close-up of the cat's face and then to a black-and-white shot from the cat's point of view, indicating that Gillian and the cat are one and that we are seeing from her (their?) point of view. Shep seems oblivious to the changes in Gillian that are so blatant to those of us on the other side of the screen. Abruptly, her humming stops, and he gets up to leave, but when he tries to leave, he inexplicably turns back toward Gillian. Still cradling the cat, Novak holds herself erect, her head back and her body thrust forward, expressing Gillian's confidence and independence. Shep cannot resist. He moves in to kiss her, and unrestrained female sexuality triumphs.

After this point, he is hooked, literally entranced. Shep dumps Merle and engages in a whirlwind two-week romance with Gillian, finally proposing marriage. But a subtext is based on the story that witches who fall in love lose their powers. As much as she may want to, Gillian is not even sure it is possible for her to fall in love, and she does not really want to give up her powers. And she feels guilty that she has gained Shep's affections through magic. She finally tells Shep that she is a witch, that she had put a spell on him, but he only pretends to believe her until he mulls over the stories he has been told about witches. They argue and he tries to leave, but he cannot; she will not let him. Finally, he believes her, and this most rational of men seeks help from Mrs. DePass (Hermione Gingold), the only witch in the area who might possibly be powerful enough to counter Gillian.

Again, Gillian and Shep argue, and he tells her that he plans to move, to return to Merle. She threatens to put a spell on Merle but at this point mysteriously cannot find Pyewacket. A high angle black-and-white shot gives us Pyewacket's point of view, revealing both the cat's separation from Gillian and Gillian's subordination to phallic power. Pyewacket runs away from her, and she realizes that she has lost her powers (not to mention her exuberant independence). Unfortunately, she has also lost Shep.

Two months pass, and Gillian is miserable. So is Shep, who has not returned to Merle after all. Strangely, Pyewacket appears at Shep's office, and

Shep tries to return her to Gillian, whom he finds transformed. Her shop is now called Flowers of the Sea, and she sells seashells and sea-related ornaments. The exotic, the "primitive" (and the powerfully sensual) are gone. Her costuming, makeup, and posture provide visual evidence of her domestication. She wears a demure white dress with long sleeves, a flowing skirt, and a yellow sash (her yellow heels match—now she is even contorting her feet, in contrast to her previous preference for going barefoot). Novak's eyebrows are smaller (less heavily penciled), and she no longer holds her body proudly erect. She has lost Pyewacket *and* that threatening independent female sexuality.

Gillian and Shep get past the strained beginning of their conversation to acknowledge that they are really, truly in love. As they embrace, the film cuts to Pyewacket, who is perched atop a streetlight. As the film fades to black, Pyewacket wails. Now, how much of the ending can we believe? How much of it do we want to believe? Novak's spirited Gillian was a likable witch, and she was fun to see in overt opposition to dominance. The forceful expression of her outlaw emotions gave the plot life, but the conventional Hollywood "happy" ending in the fifties demanded that opposition fold, to be recuperated for (male-) dominant ideology. She was angry that she could not have things both ways, that she could not be both a "witch" (translated: a powerful woman, free to express her anger, free to embark on a sexual conquest) and a "human" (a woman defined by a male-dominated social structure, which—threatened by the power of the primitive and the irrational—demands a demure and subordinate femininity); for femininity, Gillian even had to give up Pyewacket.

Can we read one of the last lines in a way that recasts an ending that seems oppressive? Shep says, toward the end, "Has it been real all along?" Is it possible that she *has* been a real woman all along? That, enticed by the different, the normal, she decided at some level—conscious or unconscious—to change? Or does this lead to an even more disturbing reading—that we all decide—consciously or unconsciously—that the rewards of conforming to dominant expectations outweigh those of independence and personal power? Is that why Pyewacket wails? The ambiguity of the role, the disappointing transformation of Gillian's personality, and the contradictory but credible interpretations to which they lead make this a fitting capstone to the Novak-Cohn collaboration, to the conflicted star image known as Kim Novak.

FIFTIES "FEMININITY"

Each of these six roles reveals conflicting constructions of femininity, conflicting expectations of and pressures on women in fifties America, and Novak's performances made obvious the difficulty of being a young, unmarried woman in that time and place. Her performance as Kay in *Five against the House* embodied an acute awareness of the tension between sexual desire and the taboo against premarital sex while illustrating the fear of spinsterhood and the fear of being rushed into marriage during a period when women and men were under incredible social pressure to marry but when divorce was practically unthinkable. Novak's performance as Madge in *Picnic* also expressed the fear of a marriage without love and passion, even if it allowed for upward socioeconomic mobility, and although the role reinforced the ideology that links romantic love and marriage, it also showed a woman who acted, who rebelled against the social conventions that would have her marry a rich and respectable man rather than the unemployed, working-class man she loves, undermining the notion that women should be passive.

In both *The Man with the Golden Arm* and *Pal Joey*, Novak's characters competed with another woman for the affections of a man (played, in both films, by Frank Sinatra), and in the competition the qualities of "femininity" were spelled out and the question of what it is to be a "good girl" were addressed directly. In *The Man with the Golden Arm*, Kim Novak played Molly, who failed to meet the most obvious criterion; she apparently engaged in premarital sex. But this film, which gained fame because it dealt with a taboo topic—drug addiction—also disrupted the taboo against premarital sex, because Novak's Molly was so pained by the knowledge that she should be considered a social pariah that she overlooked the features that ultimately redeem her character: she was compassionate and nurturing. These qualities were essential to the social construction "the feminine." She had been so troubled by her outlaw emotions that she had questioned her own worth, but in comparison to the self-centered Zasha, Molly's positive qualities shined. In *Pal Joey*, the competition with another woman hinged simply on the question of sexual experience. Novak's character, Linda, was so wholesome, naive, and virginal that, for the most part, she reinforced prevailing ideologies rather than challenging them. Her competition, Vera, had routinely used sex to gain what she wanted. And, of course, Linda "won" the competition; she, not Vera, was a virgin.

In *Vertigo* and *Bell, Book, and Candle,* Novak's characters embodied conflicting versions of femininity within the same character, and in each of these films, Novak's performances subverted the plot's attempt to posit one version as superior to the other. In *Vertigo,* the blonde, aristocratic, sophisticated Madeleine was brunette, working-class, small-town Judy's competition for the affections of Scottie Ferguson (played by Jimmie Stewart, who also played the love interest in *Bell, Book, and Candle*). The film positioned Judy as "less attractive" than Madeleine, and although Judy liked herself as she was, for Scottie's love, she capitulated. Still, she resisted each step of the makeover but always gave in, until she had again become Madeleine—and had surrendered her autonomy. Novak conveyed Judy's misery as she relinquished control of her life to the man she loved, behavior considered appropriate for women in fifties America. In the much more frivolous *Bell, Book, and Candle,* Novak also succeeded in communicating a sense of loss as her character was transformed—ironically, by love—from a vibrant, lively, overtly sexual, powerful woman to the demure, constrained, submissive woman demanded by fifties standards of femininity. That "happy ending" was achieved at the cost of stifling the attributes that made Gillian fun and likable, and after Cohn's death, Columbia executives stifled the ambiguities and complexities that made Kim Novak a star—but not a Star. The star image Kim Novak was thoroughly of its time, and Novak's performances made the tensions of the decade too evident for the ideological comfort provided by Stars.

NOTES

I would like to thank Elizabeth Faue and Jimmie Reeves for the discussions that enriched this essay.

1   When I first saw Lippe's impressive and interesting article, I thought that the essay I was planning to write was unnecessary, that he had already done it. On closer examination, I find that there are differences in our notions of stardom, in our analyses of the Kim Novak star image, and in our focus. Much of his article is concerned with explaining the rise and subsequent decline (in the sixties) of Novak's stardom. I am less concerned with those issues than with using the Kim Novak star image as a lens though which we can see the conditions of American women in the fifties. Nevertheless, because his analysis is thorough and provocative, a dialogue with Richard Lippe crops up occasionally in this essay.

2   With the exception of my analysis of *Five against the House*, this essay deals only
with the most prominent (and easily available) films produced during the period of the Novak-Cohn collaboration, 1953–58: *Picnic, The Man with the Golden
Arm, Pal Joey, Vertigo,* and *Bell, Book, and Candle.*

3   Decades are, of course, very messy things, refusing as they do to be confined to
numbered years. Along with numerous other scholars who study the fifties, I
consider the period to have begun relatively shortly after the end of World War
II and to have ended with the death of John Kennedy in 1963. A near and dear
friend insists, however, that they ended in 1964, with the "British Invasion" (the
arrival of the Beatles and the Rolling Stones on American soil). Decades, like so
many other things, depend on a person's perspective.

4   Numerous historians have documented and analyzed the changing roles of
women in the United States during World War II and in its aftermath. Notable
sources are Anderson, Chafe, Hartmann, Kaledin, May, and Walsh. Connie Field's
documentary film *Rosie the Riveter* dramatically illustrates the overt postwar
campaign to persuade women that working outside the home and that leaving
children in the care of childcare workers was inappropriate, and numerous scholars have illustrated the ways in which the entertainment industries supported
this campaign (see Haskell; Rosen; Walsh; Biskind).

5   Cohn wanted to call the new star image "Kit Marlowe," and the association with
the term "sex kitten" is impossible to ignore. Novak resisted, suggesting Kim
and insisting on keeping her last name (Haspiel 76). Over thirty years later, in
1986, Novak played a character on the television series *Falcon Crest* named Kit
Marlowe (Hill).

6   Lippe's interpretations of *Pushover* and *Phffft!* focus on the emotional vulnerability that characterized Novak's performances, and his readings support the
argument that Novak's performances undermined the attempt to produce a blatant Marilyn Monroe clone, first in *Pushover,* in which her performance subverted the character type in which she was cast—the femme fatale, generally played
as evil—and then in *Phffft!* in which her discomfort with the role of the dumb
blonde challenged the very stereotype upon which her character was based.

7   The awkward grammar emphasized the class difference between the "townie"
girls and the college boys who used them. Awkward grammar—and the attendant working-class connotations—reappears in her role in *The Man with the
Golden Arm.*

8   The major subplot in *Picnic* involves spinster schoolmarm Rosemary Sidney
(Rosalind Russell), who panics over the possibility that she might never marry.
She virtually forces the man she is dating, Howard Bevans (Arthur O'Connell),
to marry her. Rosemary's desperation is an indication of just how powerful the

social pressure to marry was in the United States during this time, pressure expressed more subtly in *Five against the House.*

9   In frames used for a subliminal advertising gimmick, the words "Hungry? Eat Popcorn" are superimposed over Novak (Haspiel 77), taking advantage of and reinforcing Novak's sensuality, played out here through a small town working-class beauty who indulges the visual appetites of both the film's spectators and its minor characters, the townspeople.

10 In between *Picnic* and *The Man with the Golden Arm*, Novak played Marjoram Ulrichs, a wealthy, sophisticated interior designer from Manhattan in the period biopic *The Eddy Duchin Story.* Marjorie intervenes to help the career of a struggling jazz pianist (Duchin, who later became a successful bandleader), marries him, bears his child, and dies halfway through the film. The role was the only serious aberration during the Novak-Cohn collaboration in that it is the only role which embodied no serious tensions over gender construction.

11 Later in the film, Molly and Frankie actively fantasize about being middle-class, playacting in front of a department store window, but their accents and awkward grammar place them always and forever in the working class.

12 Novak's next film, now considered minor (and, as a result, now difficult to obtain), was another biopic, *Jeanne Eagels;* the film emphasized outlaw emotions that directly confronted prevailing values. The categories "female" and "ambitious" were incompatible in the prevailing value-system during the fifties, and Eagels, an ambitious actress who refused to be defined by men, comes off as a harsh character who is ultimately punished. Novak received extremely negative reviews, perhaps at least partially because of the nature of the role itself. Even before the film was released, Cohn cast Novak in *Pal Joey,* in a role that—while still capitalizing on the ideological tensions so evident in Novak's performances—drew her star image back toward the mainstream.

13 The fact that Novak had replaced Hayworth as Columbia's box-office queen was milked for publicity, but a rivalry apparently never developed (Haspiel 80; Lippe 10).

14 The song was dubbed by singer Trudi Erwin.

15 The number of sophisticated readings of *Vertigo* is daunting, and my brief reading adds little, other than a placement within the development of the Kim Novak star image. Because of his mastery of classical cinematic film form, Hitchcock's films have attracted significant attention among film critics and theorists, and arguments over the construction of gender in (and of the gendered spectator of) Hitchcock's films have been central to many recent analyses of *Vertigo* by critics who depend on psychoanalytic theory and whose analyses are heavily formalist. Some of those readings most useful for feminist critics: de Lauretis, Hollinger, Linderman, Modleski, Wood.

16   Only in *Jeanne Eagels* had Novak played a character so far from what was at the time considered mainstream femininity.

17   In both *Vertigo* and *Bell, Book, and Candle,* Stewart plays highly rational good guys who are manipulated by powerful external forces.

WORKS CONSULTED

Alberoni, Francesco. "The Powerless Elite: Theory and Sociological Research on the Phenomenon of the Stars." Trans. Denis McQuail. In *Sociology of Mass Communications.* Ed. Denis McQuail. London: Penguin, 1972, 75–98. Rpt. of "L'Elite irresponsable: Theorie et recherche sociologique sur *'le divismo.'*" *Ikon* 12.40–41 (1962): 45–62.

Anderson, Karen. *Wartime Women: Sex Roles, Family Relations, and the Status of Women during World War II.* Westport, Conn.: Greenwood Press, 1981.

Biskind, Peter. *Seeing Is Believing: How Hollywood Taught Us to Stop Worrying and Love the Fifties.* New York: Pantheon, 1983.

Byars, Jackie. *All That Hollywood Allows: Re-Reading Gender in 1950s Melodrama.* Chapel Hill: University of North Carolina Press, 1991.

Chafe, William. *The American Woman: Her Changing Social, Economic, and Political Roles, 1920–1970.* New York: Oxford University Press, 1972.

de Lauretis, Teresa. *Alice Doesn't: Feminism, Semiotics, Cinema.* Bloomington: Indiana University Press, 1984.

Dyer, Richard. *Stars.* London: BFI, 1986.

Forsberg, Myra. "Once Again, Ready on the Set for Kim Novak." *New York Times,* Aug. 19, 1990, sect. 2, p. 11.

Hartmann, Susan M. *The Home Front and Beyond: American Women in the 1940s.* Boston: Twayne, 1982.

Haskell, Molly. *From Reverence to Rape: The Treatment of Women in the Movies.* 2d ed. Chicago: University of Chicago Press, 1987.

Haspiel, James Robert. "Kim Novak: Yesterday's Superstar." *Films in Review* 13:2 (Feb. 1978): 73–88.

Hill, Michael E. "The Moth and Keeper of the Flame." *Washington Post,* Dec. 28, 1986, Y6.

Hollinger, Karen. "'The Look,' Narrativity, and the Female Spectator in *Vertigo.*" *Journal of Film and Video* 39.4 (Fall 1987): 18–27.

Jaggar, Alison M. "Love and Knowledge: Emotion in Feminist Epistemology." In *Gender/Body/Knowledge: Feminist Reconstructions of Being and Knowing.* Ed. Alison M. Jaggar and Susan R. Bordo. New Brunswick: Rutgers University Press, 1989. 145–71.

Kaledin, Eugenia. *Mothers and More: American Women in the 1950s*. Boston: Twayne, 1984.

Linderman, Deborah. "The Mise-en-Abime in Hitchcock's *Vertigo*." *Cinema Journal* 30.4 (Summer 1991): 51–74.

Lippe, Richard. "Kim Novak: A Resistance to Definition." *CineAction*, no. 7 (Winter 1986–87): 4–21.

May, Elaine Tyler. *Homeward Bound: American Families in the Cold War Era*. New York: Basic Books, 1988.

Metz, Christian. *The Imaginary Signifier: Psychoanalysis and the Signifier*. Bloomington: Indiana University Press, 1982.

Milkman, Ruth. *Gender at Work: The Dynamics of Job Segregation by Sex during World War II*. Urbana: University of Illinois Press, 1987.

Modleski, Tonia. *The Women Who Knew Too Much*. New York: Methuen, 1988.

Neale, Stephen. *Genre*. London: British Film Institute, 1980.

Peachment, Chris. "That's Why the Lady Is a Broad." Sunday Review Page, *The Independent*, Jan. 5, 1992, 22.

Reeves, Jimmie. "Television Stardom: A Ritual of Social Typification and Individualization." In *Media Myths and Narratives: Television and the Press*. Ed. James Carey. Beverly Hills: Sage, 1988. 146–60.

Rosen, Marjorie. *Popcorn Venus: Women, Movies, and the American Dream*. New York: Coward, McCann, and Geoghegan, 1973.

Rosie the Riveter. Prod. and dir. Connie Field. Charity Productions/Direct Cinema Limited, 1980.

Truffaut, Francois. *Hitchcock*. New York: Simon and Schuster, 1983.

Walsh, Andrea S. *Women's Films and Female Experience, 1940 to 1950*. New York: Praeger, 1984.

Williams, Raymond. *Marxism and Literature*. New York: Oxford University Press, 1977.

Wood, Robin. "Fear of Spying." *American Film* 9 (Nov. 1983): 28–35.

KIM NOVAK 1950s FILMOGRAPHY

[** = available on videotape]

The French Line (1953) RKO; directed by Lloyd Bacon; cast includes Jane Russell.

Pushover (1954) Columbia; directed by Richard Quine; cast includes Fred MacMurray, Phil Crey, Dorothy Malone, E. G. Marshall.

Phffft! (1954) Columbia; directed by Mark Robson; cast includes Judy Holliday, Jack Lemmon, Jack Carson.

Son of Sinbad (1955) RKO; directed by Ted Tetzlaff; cast includes Dale Robertson, Sally Forrest, Lili St. Cyr, Vincent Price.

Five against the House (1955) Columbia; directed by Phil Karlson; cast includes Guy Madison, Brian Keith, Kerwin Matthews, William Conrad, Alvy Moore.

**Picnic* (1955) Columbia; directed by Joshua Logan; cast includes William Holden, Rosalind Russell, Betty Field, Susan Strasberg, Cliff Robertson, Arthur O'Connell.

**The Man with the Golden Arm* (1955) United Artists; directed by Otto Preminger; cast includes Frank Sinatra, Eleanor Parker, Arnold Stang, Darren McGavin.

**The Eddy Duchin Story* (1956) (made before *The Man with the Golden Arm* but released after it) Columbia; directed by George Sidney; cast includes Tyrone Power, Victoria Shaw, James Whitmore.

Jeanne Eagels (1957) Columbia; directed by George Sidney; cast includes Jeff Chandler, Agnes Moorehead, Virginia Grey; singing dubbed by Eileen Wilson.

**Pal Joey* (1957) Columbia; directed by George Sidney; cast includes Rita Hayworth, Frank Sinatra, Barbara Nichols; singing dubbed by Trudi Erwin.

**Vertigo* (1958) Paramount; directed by Alfred Hitchcock; cast includes James Stewart, Barbara Bel Geddes, Trudy Ewen.

**Bell, Book, and Candle* (1958) Columbia; directed by Richard Quine; cast includes James Stewart, Jack Lemmon, Ernie Kovaks, Hermione Gingold.

Middle of the Night (1959) Columbia; directed by Delbert Mann; cast includes Fredric March.

Cynthia J. Fuchs

Chapter Nine   SPLIT SCREENS
Framing and Passing in
Pillow Talk

I was aware of the chemistry between us.
We looked good together. We looked like
a couple should look.

DORIS DAY

Rock was seeing numerous men but he
discovered that as a major movie star, it
was increasingly difficult to get laid.

Rock Hudson: His Story

And yet what if the whole point of
celebrity is the spectacle of people forced
to tell transparent lies in public?

EVE KOSOFSKY SEDGWICK

DOUBLE VISION

THE theatrical trailer for *Pillow Talk* described it as "the most sparkling
sex-capade that ever winked at convention." Indeed, the film's endur-
ing reputation as a chic romantic comedy depends precisely on its friendly contentions with prevailing social and sexual norms. Witty and congenial,
this first on-screen teaming of "the perfect pair" Doris Day and Rock Hudson also offers a surprisingly complex portrait of heterosexual romance as a
site of both conflict and conformity.[1] Released in 1959, the film straddles two
seemingly distinct decades, simultaneously looking back to a time known for
its repression and complacency and forward to one with a reputation for
increasing sexual expressiveness and moral apprehension.

Pillow Talk's complexity, its challenge to this division of history into identifiable decades, has to do with its representational simultaneities. As it

"winked at convention," the movie also offered a kind of "double vision," at once clarifying and smoothing over any apparent split between the fifties and the sixties. Partly focused on a give-and-take fluctuation of cultural attitudes toward gender and sexuality, partly on the elaborate performances by which such fluctuations are resisted, the movie displays and even celebrates the unreality of the split; in doing so, it exposes simultaneously social fragmentation and coherence, delineating tensions which, as David Halberstam notes, existed (not so far) beneath the deceptively "placid surface" of the fifties, tensions arising from the confusing demands and opportunities of mass culture. Halberstam writes that this infamously conformist decade was in fact a time when "exciting new technologies were being developed that would soon enable a vast and surprisingly broad degree of dissidence, and many people were already beginning to question the purpose of their lives and whether that purpose had indeed become, almost involuntarily, too much about material things" (ix). While Halberstam argues that troubling questions about public purpose and personal focus were imminent and inevitable in the developing technologies and concomitant "materialism" of the fifties, *Pillow Talk* interrogates the shift in attitudes that came with the sixties, but also underlines the connectedness of the decades, specifically a continuum of sexual identities and emerging politics.

Throughout *Pillow Talk*, neither Jan Morrow (Day) nor Brad Allen (Hudson) are securely positioned, visually, socially, or sexually. Structured as a series of misrepresentations and misinterpretations, the plot is briefly this: straightlaced interior designer Jan and songwriter Brad share a telephone party line. She deplores his seductions of numerous women; he dislikes her self-righteous propriety. Jan is also being (somewhat clumsily) courted by her client and Brad's best friend, Jonathan Forbes (Tony Randall); while Brad and Jan both share their fantasies of ideal relationships with Jonathan, she also makes some confessions to her maid, Alma (Thelma Ritter). When Jan and Brad meet in person for the first time, he poses as Rex Stetson, a polite and exaggeratedly artless Texas millionaire; his naiveté eventually translates to a seeming "gayness," his ruse to seduce Jan, to solicit her desire to "correct" his unmasculine deviance. After a series of farcical misidentifications, they realize their "true love" for each other and marry to confirm that love and close the narrative.

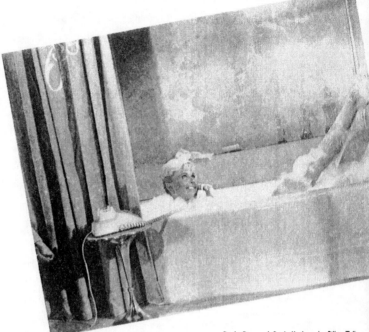

Doris Day and Rock Hudson in *Pillow Talk*.

At first glance, Jan and Brad seem recognizable as "feminine" and "masculine" types (destined to be together), but the film complicates the conflicts and connections of these types by raising questions about the visibility of these gendered and sexual identities, that is, the ways that these identities are measured by "framing" and "passing." Though these terms might appear to be oppositional—framing establishing differences and passing implying their failure—I am arguing that the movie emphasizes their interdependence, insists that any (apparent) disruption of categories depends on the (apparent) maintenance of distinctions between them, a simultaneity mapped onto the interrelations of space, identity, and performance. The framing in *Pillow Talk* is fairly straightforward, such that literal frame compositions indicate the characters' sense of social constraints. Inextricable from its examination of such delineations is the film's exploration of passing into normative social structures (heterosexuality, whiteness, middle-class-ness), as it signifies both conformity and challenge to those structures. Foregrounding the function of identity in passing, as what Amy Robinson calls "a strategy for entrance into representation," the movie also insists on the slipperiness and paradoxical

(Courtesy of the Museum of Modern Art/Film Stills Archive)

nature of this strategy.[2] In passing as a given identity, even one you believe yourself to "be," you must assert a stable, already categorical identity in order to be visible, to be representable; while passing would seem to defy categories, it must adhere to categories as a concept, as well as a means of social and political organization.

If *Pillow Talk* does not exactly dismantle the categories that ground prescriptive heterosexuality, it does challenge the fixity of sex and gender roles through the characters' misreadings of each other's appearance. According to the film's promotional copy, Jan is "a careful career girl who believes in 'singleness'" and Brad is "a carefree bachelor who believes in 'togetherness.'"[3] Much of the film's comedy stems from its what's-wrong-with-this-picture inversion of gendered desire. For instance, seeming to anticipate by three or four years the argument made by Betty Friedan in her *Feminine Mystique,* Jan is a woman whose efforts to define herself through her career are eventually subsumed under the lesson that she will only be fulfilled—a coherent self— when she is married.[4] Even so, to say that the film puts her "in her place" would be reductive, as *Pillow Talk* repeatedly subverts this linear plotline by again and again returning to the question of her and Brad's (and so Hudson's) unconventional ambitions and sexualities. Indeed, its most outrageous "wink" at prescriptive social roles comes in the running joke that Brad is "pregnant."

So, while it might seem that die-hard bachelor Brad (the early, hygienic version of Hefner's "playboy") is defined by his opposite, the marriage-minded career woman Jan (a pert, less risky version of Lana Turner's glamorous, ambitious Lora in Sirk's *Imitation of Life,* also released in 1959), this relation is never stabilized, the definitions remain elusive; Jan's and Brad's identities—performed and received—are less a matter of fixed and freestanding signs (square jaw and stoic demeanor = heterosexual white male; wasp-waist and modesty = heterosexual female) and more a function of their shifting social and formal contexts. These social (diegetic) contexts are expressly mutable spaces that—like the interiors Jan designs—are domestic rooms and offices modified to reflect and contain the increasing speed, anonymity, and technologization of the late fifties; and the formal (extradiegetic) contexts are equally literalized, the split screens that allow viewers to see and know what Jan and Brad do not, namely their "acts" for each other and themselves.

It is significant that these acts are further framed by the promotional apparatus of *Pillow Talk,* by the "celebrity culture" assigning Hudson and Day ordinary but also special and spectacular status. Celebrity culture effects a multiplicity and merging of meanings, again hinging on framing and passing. At once attached to and disconnected from Day's and Hudson's studio-engineered personae, the *Pillow Talk* characters are each a nexus of commodifications, ideals, and secrets, just as stars Hudson and Day are simultaneously atypical ("larger than life") and typical (fan magazines advertised their in-depth looks at the "Dime a Dozen" Hudson and the "Girl Next Door" Day).[5] Their combined celebrity, as a "Hollywood couple," is, as Virginia Wright Wexman writes, created to conform with given gender and sexual codes and embodied by "actors as symbols of romantic desirability" (16). Repeatable and overdetermined, these symbols—these star bodies-as-images—in turn generate social, political, and moral categories, models for audience behaviors and aspirations. And yet, even given its high visibility, celebrity culture is also comprised of secrecy, or more precisely, a well-publicized promise of disclosure. Celebrity, then, obtains in an exchange between audience and performer, a collusion in what Michael Moon and Eve Sedgwick call "transparent lies," where the "private" self is forever available and unattainable, hidden beneath the public image, the surface to be deciphered (227). As Moon and Sedgwick put it, "celebrity itself [is] a level of culture that refuses to keep its place as merely one level among many; as an ontological status that *dis*articulates the intersections among the person, the artist, the fictional character, and the commodity" (227). That is, celebrity works to fragment and "disarticulate" the coherence of particular identities in a public, hypervisible venue, exemplifying and amplifying the fragmentations of identity more generally.

The film's categories of identity are at once familiar and strange, apparently grounded in particular bodies and experiences, but also destabilized by what Halberstam calls "exciting new technologies," those evolving modes of self-representation—the telephone, television, and movies—that were already, even in the ostensibly complacent fifties, challenging fixed measures of identity and identification. Even the most entrenched of these measures, visibility, was becoming threateningly indeterminate: communists or homosexuals were difficult to spot, repressed psychological determinants were driving individual deviances, and social systems (say, institutionalized racism and sexism) were increasingly shown to be constructed rather than "natural" orders.[6] *Pillow Talk*'s most explicit sign of such disruption is the telephone. Since Jan and Brad "meet" over their party line (they literally do not see each other), they continually misapprehend one another according to conditioned expectations and stereotypes, based on incomplete information and faulty interpretation. Evident to us through the film's extravagant visual play across split screens—made possible by the new technology of Cinemascope—their misreadings and performances make the tensions that Halberstam describes quite visible on the film's surface. *Pillow Talk* does not resolve the problem of mercurial identities, but rather exposes its basis in a fear that bodies, however framed and contained, might pass as something they are not.

This fear, of course, presupposes that there is a "baseline" of being, an essential identity that can be disguised or otherwise distorted. As recent queer theory has demonstrated, however, the very idea of an "authentic" or "original" identity is itself a construction, a knowledge system based in visible, embodied differences.[7] Judith Butler argues, for example, that gender "performativity" occurs in repeated images/narratives of gendered and sexual identities, which produce a look of "natural" order. Yet, she writes, this repetition itself "may well be the inevitable site of the denaturalization and mobilization of gender categories" (*Gender Trouble* 31). In other words, the system may be put to work against itself, to expose its artifice and construct-edness. *Pillow Talk,* by exaggerating straight paradigms, challenges these identificatory categories. Moreover, as Butler argues, "Signification is always to some degree out of one's control . . . [so that] specificity can only be de-marcated by exclusions that return to disrupt its claim to coherence" ("Imi-tation" 14). Jan and Brad's misidentifications reframe their mutually expect-ed identity as the ideal white heterosexual couple, as if it is "beyond their control." As an imitation without an original—they "look like a couple should look" (but what can this mean?)—this identity reflects anxieties over cate-gories in the fifties and anticipates their more volatile manifestations in the sixties.

The film shows the precariousness of this couple as an interdependent, shared identity by betraying discrepancies between bodies and identities. The split screens imitate dislocations brought on by technological advances; while the telephone in *Pillow Talk* provides communication and connection be-tween characters, it does so by constructing a series of false identities. In this way, the movie challenges the conventional system of gender and sexual iden-tities—especially those that produce and are produced by celebrity—by underlining the dissonance between public and private performances of "self."

"LIKE A COUPLE SHOULD LOOK"

The film opens with images of discreet raciness, images that adhere to accept-ed limits of sexual representation. A tripartite screen shows a white woman and a white man—anonymous, we see only their nightgowned and pajamaed legs—engaged in coy, sexualized play: pictured on separate screens, in sep-arate beds, they toss brightly colored pillows back and forth so that they accumulate in the empty, central screen. Day sings the title song on the soundtrack: "All I do is talk to my pillow / Talk about the boy I'm gonna marry some day . . . / There must be a pillow-talkin' boy for me."[8]

Her desire is conditioned and contained by conventional, infantalizing language: this "girl" needs a "boy." As the credits close, two screens wipe quickly to the left, leaving only the woman's raised, bare leg, an image that cuts to Day's own leg stretched across the wide screen as she smooths her nylon stocking. The "boy" is introduced by way of the telephone. Jan goes to make a call and overhears a conversation between Brad and a woman, Eileen. Jan interrupts them and Eileen asks who she is. "The other half of my party line," says Brad with obvious aversion. "Just ignore her—she'll go away." Just as Jan lifts the receiver, the screen splits three ways, so that the audience glimpses the breathless woman, Eileen; the object of her affection, Brad; and Jan, whose annoyance at the overstated inanity of their romantic chatter is marked by her rolling eyes, agitated gestures, and frowns.

This breakup of the visual field and narrative displays Jan's frustrations, Brad's duplicities, and Eileen's mediation of their mutual interests. While Jan's sexuality is first underlined by the shot of her leg and then contained by her declarations of modesty and distractedness, Eileen's sensuality is exaggerated: she lounges in a white chaise lounge, openly performing her desire and desirability. Jan, by contrast, resists any similar self-disclosure, such that she is the chaste "answer" to such excessiveness. This chaste image is complicated because Jan's behavior is shown to be at once admirable and pathological, independent and neurotic. Rather than listen to Brad's tedious seduction routine, Jan puts down the phone, tying her dressing gown at the neck and not hearing the ensuing dialogue, whose banality signals to us that Brad and Eileen's romance will be brief. Visually framed (as Brad leans back to the right and Eileen to the left), Jan is trapped both by her own inexpressible longing and by their over-the-top banter. When she picks up the phone, she is caught between them. Seated at his piano, Brad sings, off-key, "You are my inspiration, Eileen . . ." (clearly, Eileen is not much of an inspiration). Demanding that he free up the line, Jan slams down the receiver. Minutes later, she picks it up again, just in time to hear Brad sing the same song, in dreadful French, to Yvette, yet another representation of Jan's repressed desire and Brad's misdirected libido.

These repeated lyrics and situations draw attention to the characters' familiar *roles*, Jan's as uptight "good girl," Brad's as smug "playboy," even Yvette's as romantic decoy.[9] *Pillow Talk* examines the process of repetition and conditioning through its emphasis on talk, chatter, stammering, and, of course, lying (which again and again makes Jan's face flush, while Brad seems quite at ease with his part). Michel Foucault describes the process of attributing and claiming sexual identity as "the nearly infinite task of telling—telling oneself and another, as often as possible, everything that might concern the innumerable pleasures, sensations, and thoughts which, through the body and the soul, had some affinity with sex" (20). But such faith in narrative "truth" is compromised by its assumption that identity inheres in a body that maintains physical and experiential coherence over time. Brad's self-description betrays a comic and disturbing lack of coherence: the lies he tells are also truths. His "task of telling" positions his listeners—Jan, his other girlfriends, and us—so that we can read his sexual identity as a kind of ongoing, repeatable, but also shifting, fiction. Then again, Jan's responses to this fiction construct *her* own excessive "femininity," equally artificial: she judges Brad to be perversely oversexed, properly "unconscious" that she is "in fact" attracted to him in his incarnation as the heterosexually repressed Rex. The borders between fact and fiction are increasingly permeable.

Jan's naiveté is crucial for the film's narrative of pleasurable transgressions. It is the most obvious source of her appeal to Brad (who, according to bedroom farce conventions, seeks redemption in spite of himself), as well as to the audience. Drawing on Day's previous popular personae, all "stable" identities undone over the course of each movie—virginal tomboy (*Calamity Jane*, 1953), devoted mother (*The Man Who Knew Too Much*, 1956), and reliable labor organizer (*The Pajama Game*, 1957)—*Pillow Talk* depicts Jan as an innocent girl-woman with an as-yet-untapped capacity for and interest in sex. Brad, for his part, misconstrues her incipient interest, describing her to Yvette as "some little eavesdropper on my party line. She's always listening in. It's how she brightens up her drab empty life." By remarking her voyeurism, he seems to shore up his charisma and social normality, but his tone is so affected—so frankly "bitchy" and conservative—that their emotional lives look more similar than different.

In other words, while Brad reads Jan, he is also being read by her and, more importantly, by the film's audience, who perceives that he will ultimately be the partner she seeks, accommodating her and our fantasy. So, their exchanges are understandable in multiple and often contradictory ways, such that we attend to his put-downs and her protestations (their conflict) while knowing that they will be proved "wrong" but also "right for each other" (their coupledom). Neither of these readings is fixed at any point. If, as Butler argues, heterosexuality operates "through the regulated production of hyperbolic versions of 'man' and 'woman,'" the resulting ideals are inevitably impossible (*Bodies* 237). If Jan and Brad epitomize such ideals in the fifties, they also illustrate their limitations, offering them as symptomatic of social and political constraints. Or, as Butler puts it, these norms, so exaggerated and repeatable, are "haunted by their own inefficacy" (*Bodies* 237). If *Pillow Talk*'s playboy and virgin are ironic, "wink[ing] at convention," they also expose their cultural production and reception. The masquerades performed by Jan/Day and Brad/Rex/Hudson destabilize boundaries between masculine and feminine, common and perverse, straight and queer. Here, the lines are scrambled.

"BEDROOM PROBLEMS"

Gendered and sexual performances are emphatically in flux in *Pillow Talk*. The identity ascribed to Jan is produced through an exchange among Day, studio publicists, the screenplay, Hudson/Brad, and the film's audiences. Jan traverses several categories of prescriptive "femininity": she is willful, sensitive, ignorant, dependent, and intelligent; she passes as the "perfect," uptight, marriage-minded woman.[10] Her disdain for Brad's rampantly visible sexuality is exposed as bogus by her own misspeaking, the various "slips" that show her "real" sexual predilections and yearnings. During one telephone exchange Brad tells her, "Don't take your bedroom problems out on me." "I have no bedroom problems," she says in a huff, "There's nothing in my bedroom that bothers me." Catching her in an act that suggests simultaneously her repression and desire, he responds triumphantly, "Oh, that's too bad." Jan's reaction—yet again grimacing with discomfort and outrage—shows us that Brad has struck a nerve.

This particular nerve has to do with Jan's unattainable place as autonomous career woman within the fifties heterosexual contract, in that her self-repression is both required and pathologized. The extent of her "problems"—of her needs to be bothered and not bothered at the same time—becomes evident when, early on, she visits the telephone company offices with the hope of getting a private line: the distinction between public/party and private "lines" suggests that her reputation is at issue; Jan's description of her situation suggests that she feels violated by her "party line." She is told that because of the demand, she can only quickly get a private line in the case of an emergency: "If you were to become pregnant, for example, you'd jump right to the top of our list," says the agent, Mr. Conrad. That pregnancy is unquestionably an "emergency" comically emphasizes the social parameters of bodily crises, and the era's medicalization of women's bodies in particular. Jackie Byars observes that in fifties films pregnancy is only "allowed" within the confines of marriage (119). In or out, pregnancy remains a sign of female excessiveness, a realm where men were neither able nor expected to participate, contribute, or understand. Now reconceived as an artificial constraint, the historical conditioning of pregnancy as a medical problem italicizes the confounding mystery and uncontrollability of female bodies and their always-imminent excessiveness to social proprieties.[11] That the movie ends with a final misreading of Brad as pregnant by an excited male obstetrician exacerbates this question instead of settling it. While Brad is, on one level, "feminized" by the doctor's reading and the film's conclusion, his "pregnancy" also lets loose another excessive body, and the anxiety over pregnancy becomes focused not on married or unmarried, but on male or female.

Embarrassed by the mere mention of pregnancy, Jan reasserts her status as self-reliant and single: "I'm not quite ready for that kind of . . . *emergency*." Her coupling with Brad via the party line interferes with her work, certainly, but more disturbingly, it forces her into having "knowledge" of the intimate details of his active sex life (and so incriminates her as a sexual "voyeur"). Looking to exculpate herself by declaring her difference from Brad, she says that she is "on a party line with a sex maniac." Conrad asks her to substantiate this "very serious charge" while shutting his office door, apparently eagerly anticipating the details. Jan lays out the horrifying specifics: "Well, he sings love songs at nine o'clock in the morning!"

Conrad, while taken aback at this revelation, also looks unconvinced that such behavior is by definition offensive or strange. The two-shot in his cubicle shows Jan and Conrad facing off across his desk, and as he occasionally leans in toward Jan, he seems alternately distracted and titillated by the proposition of discussing sexual perversion with a woman. "Has he used any objectionable language on the phone?" Jan says no. "Threats of any nature?" No again. "Has he made immoral overtures to you?" Jan's response—"Not to *me*!"—suggests to the amateur psychologist (Hayden Rourke, who in later years will be better known as the twitchy psychologist Dr. Bellows on television's *I Dream of Jeannie*) that her problem, and the film's critical project, is precisely to uncover her own repressed sexuality, her desire for Brad's attentions and jealousy of the women he does seduce.

Jan's conversation with Conrad—with its escalating innuendo—exemplifies *Pillow Talk*'s examination of split subjectivities, as the characters scrutinize each other, seemingly in search of some stable ground of "meaning" between them. Conrad asks if she's "bothered by this." "Yes . . . I mean no. What do you mean *bothered?*" she responds, leaning toward him (and the camera) as she asks the question. Whether or not Jan is "bothered" becomes the measure of her disorder rather than Brad's. It is clear enough what she thinks Conrad means when she asks him the question: her visible exasperation makes her self-consciousness at once the butt of the joke and the subject of audience sympathy (largely through Day's effective performance). For in confronting such impasses, Jan represents the complexity of women's socialization through language and legal categories, her simultaneous resistance and surrender to these institutional constraints. She can give no "right" answer to Conrad's question about being "bothered": "yes" or "no" both implicate her as interested in and like Brad, whom she has already designated a "sex maniac." Even as she takes on the role of the embarrassed and conspicuously straight woman, Jan is also socially indicted for playing it, trapped in the cubicle with a prying low-level bureaucrat. Bothered first by Brad's insinuations and then by Conrad's questions, she will only be safe from such judgments when she is married. But while both men suggest that the problems are Jan's (as opposed to the dominant culture's, or more specifically, theirs), the audience can enjoy her grumpiness and alarm because we perceive that she has no problems, except, perhaps, with making herself understood by these excitable men.[12]

CONFESSIONS

As functions of audience expectation and participation, the sexual parts played by Jan and Brad collapse the distinction between public and private, a collapse emphasized by the film's insistence that we see what they do not: their private lives are fully visible and their public identities are repeatedly destabilized. When they meet face to face for the first time, their exchange approximates a split screen, but this time Brad overhears *her* conversation. Seated in a swanky restaurant, she's trying to put off the advances of a wealthy client's son, Tony

(Nick Adams). There are mirrors behind them, doubling their images as Brad overhears the young man call her "Jan." Impressed as she walks away from him onto the dance floor—she's wearing a clingy white gown—he thinks to himself (in voiceover on the soundtrack), "So that's the other end of your party line." Determined to "get on friendly terms with *that*," he decides to dupe Jan, assuming a southern drawl and passive demeanor to incite her interest. Much of the humor of his performance depends on viewers' understanding of shy Rex as assertive Brad's opposite; it becomes clear that the role taps some of Brad's "better" qualities and that his warmth, sensitivity, and generosity will be outed by the end of the film. Here Hudson's performance is, typically, both hilarious and revealing; Richard Dyer writes that he "produced a flawless surface of conventional masculinity. Yet it is a surface strangely lacking in force and intensity. It's a sort of parade of the signs of masculinity without any real assertion of it. What's fascinating is the way this quality unsettles the apparently complacent heterosexuality of his films" ("Rock" 30). As Brad-as-Rex, Hudson incarnates a range of "signs," from archetypally "masculine" (the gallant millionaire rancher) to appealingly "anti-masculine" (the shy virgin). At this point, *Pillow Talk* offers a particularly cogent portrait of confusing, multiply sexed positions, as Tony passes out on the dance floor and the congenial Brad (as Rex) comes to the embarrassed Jan's aid: he picks up Tony and slings him over his shoulder. Ironically, for Douglas Brode, this image represents the "All American couple, circa 1959," featuring Jan in her cocktail dress, with gloves up to her elbows, her head cocked as she watches Brad/Rex; he glances back in her direction while carrying a barely conscious Tony (266). With the pretty young man slung over Hudson's shoulder positioned between the two principals, it becomes apparent that this is an "All American" triangle, not a couple at all.

Complications continue as Brad/Rex and Jan display, while seeming to repress, their mutual attraction. After depositing Tony in a cab, Brad/Rex offers to drive Jan home. When he is unable to fit himself into Tony's sports car, the image of Hudson's limbs hanging from the window makes obvious his lack of "fit" inside the role of a conventional suitor. Then, when they take a cab, the split-screen motif assumes yet another form, again suggesting that standard framing cannot accommodate their increasingly tangled relationship: the characters converse politely with one another, while their voice-over narrations disclose their "private" thoughts. Their confessions reify "normal" gender positions but also reinvent them: while making small talk, Jan thinks, "What a marvelous looking man" (the cut from her approving look to the square-jawed Brad marks her position as spectator and his as object); Brad, on the other hand, becomes anxious about his performance, thinking, "I don't know how long I can get away with this act, but she's sure worth a try." When Jan asks, "You married?" (the "woman's" question), she responds immediately to herself (and us), "You idiot! What are you trying to do, scare the man away?" "The man" answers with a respectful, "No ma'am, I'm not" (even as Brad worries to himself that his act will require "some fancy broken field running"). His feint works, for now. Jan is convinced that Rex is the "authentic" gentleman she has been waiting for, especially when comparing him in her mind to the "monsters" Tony and Brad.

The scene, however, makes plain the disjunctions between sexual desire and social propriety. Butler writes, "The subject is . . . never coherent and self-identical precisely because it is founded and, indeed, continually refounded, through a set of defining foreclosures and repressions that constitute the discontinuity and incompletion of the subject" (*Bodies That Matter* 190). Jan and Brad are demonstrably incomplete social "subjects," as they seem forced into ill-fitting roles to attract each other. But more importantly the couple's charade as an interdependent unit—Brad's "masculine" evasions are defined in opposition to Jan's "feminine" yearning for marriage and vice versa—exhibits its incoherence, immateriality, and ironic self-referentiality. They are not "self-identical," but rather acting the prescriptive part of the "Hollywood couple." And again, the joke is manifest to us as we watch them inside this enclosed space, running out of room and small talk. In making asides to themselves and to the audience, Brad and Jan collaborate in a flamboyant performance of heterosexual courtship, in effect "passing" as a straight couple, so that viewers see the machinations for what they are. Even their "true" selves—the worried ones—are plainly acts, undermined by our understanding that they will eventually connect and so complete the heterosexual plot.

SECOND OPINIONS

This plot is both confirmed and contested by the film's secondary characters, who repeatedly comment on its confusions. Jan's misreadings are contrasted with Alma's more knowing response to Brad's sexual spectacle. Perpetually arriving for work late and hung over, Alma is immediately recognizable as more (sexually, sensually) experienced than Jan, but also less "desirable" because of her age and (working) class. The women's exchanges take place in Jan's ultra-white and modern kitchen, the site of her morning preparations (pouring juice or making toast—Jan's domestic activities are limited). Despite her wit and cynicism—or because of them—Alma serves as a warning against Jan's careerism by emphasizing the double bind of her isolation in a male homosocial order and her superficial, elaborately staged femininity.

That she employs a house-cleaner at all obviously denotes Jan's financial, if not social, independence. In her discussion of the "struggle over the meaning of 'Woman'" during the fifties, Jackie Byars argues that women were inculcated into a broad consumer culture, which began, in turn, to address "women's" particular, well-modulated desires (81). Jan exemplifies this shift in her career as a decorator; for in marketing her own "taste" and decorum, the character draws on a growing public appetite for what were previously private and explicitly gendered attributes, for example, the "woman's touch." That her employer, Mr. Pierot, is especially fussy and "feminized" (read: gay) in his inability to cope with a domineering woman client italicizes Jan's "masculine" authority in this particular sphere; further, her use of her professional position in order to exact retribution on Brad—in a horrific decorating job that parodies his "lady-killer" self-image—allows Jan both to operate within gendered limitations (her "feminine" outrage) and to exceed them (her denunciation of Brad's carefully constructed identity as ultra-suave playboy).

As Andrew Dowdy suggests, however, Jan's commitment to her career also implicates her as a "peculiar case of terminal virginity," a condition that, again, has to do with her pathologized repression (183). Alma provides a measure for this "terminal" state. Single and doomed to be forever yearning, she is not "bothered" by Brad at all; she is frankly captivated by his exploits, enjoying them as soap opera, smiling as she imagines herself as one of the many women he seduces ("He's brightened up many a dreary afternoon for me"). Richard Meyer notes as well that Alma's reaction pays particular attention to literalized masculine dimensions: "When size-conscious Thelma Ritter warns the less knowledgeable Day that 'six foot six inches of opportunity doesn't come by every day. When you see it, grab it,' she leaves little doubt that the length of Hudson's body is to be measured as phallus" (260). Meyer argues that in this instance and other repeated references to Hudson's enormity in studio publicity, his masculinity is established in the most prosaic and easily visible terms. His physical excessiveness (he stands at least a full head above anyone in any frame) makes him unique, impressive, and the object of everyone's attention.

At the same time, Alma locates another sort of excess. Dyer argues that alcoholic characters serve as stereotypes to "maintain sharp boundary definitions"; especially important to delineate are those boundaries that are difficult to discern, such as those obscured by homosexuality or alcoholism (*Matter* 16). Alma's behavior (she complains each morning as she rides the elevator, wears an icepack under her hat, and moans when Jan opens the window blinds) designates her deviance, but her "excess" allows her a certain honesty in her dealings with Jan, as well as access to Brad, who takes her out drinking in order to solicit inside information about Jan (not incidentally, Alma drinks him under the table). She advises Jan from the perspective of a social outsider, an older, unmarried woman who has apparently made the "mistakes" that Jan now seems in danger of making. While the society matrons Jan services as a decorator hardly offer more positive models, the foreboding prospect of "spinsterhood" looms more threateningly, visualized in Alma's dowdy coat and shuffling gait. "If there's anything worse than a woman living alone," Alma warns, "it's a woman saying she likes it."[13]

Jan protests vigorously that she does like "living alone," but the film's comedic project is to reveal that she—the confused "modern" woman—does not know what she likes. In this regard she is similar to the overconfident Brad: both are in need of "heterosexualization." The second person to offer advice and to express the principals' desires is Jonathan, Jan's client and would-be suitor and the financier for Brad's latest show. Both Alma and Jonathan mirror the split subjectivities of the central characters. Alma's unrealized but often-expressed interests in sex generally and in Brad specifically correspond to Jonathan's equally loudly declared frustrations, including his pathetic inability to seduce Jan and his more ambiguous overtures toward Brad.[14]

The fastidious, whiny, and insecure Jonathan is a conventional Hollywood fop (the counterweight to Brad's "guy"): he has a therapist and a history of multiple divorces. His interactions with Brad, in which he is decidedly "feminized," further complicate his professed heterosexuality while they provide a measure for "normal" masculinity. Vito Russo writes of this era, that "America's ostentatious fascination with the difference between masculine and feminine behavior and society's absolute terror of queerness, especially in men, continued to be served by the requisite yardstick sissy" (66). In Jonathan, this "yardstick" is at once overtly queer and subversively straight, a problem for the transparent identification of gender and sexuality.[15] His gayness challenges the same heterosexual gender constructs that Brad would seem to confirm.[16] Compared to Jonathan, Brad looks pretty straight. The attraction between them is displaced onto Jonathan's desire for marriage, even as Brad remains committed to "bachelorhood," resisting the fearful desire that Jonathan would personify.[17] Butler observes that "*gender is a kind of imitation for which there is no original*; in fact, it is a kind of imitation that produces the very notion of the original as an *effect* and consequence of the imitation itself"; here, Jonathan's inability to pass as straight, to imitate Brad (or Jan, for that matter) leaves him without conventional romantic recourse ("Imitation" 21). His exaggerated attempts to be "masculine" (as he swaggers and tries to compete with Brad over women, especially Jan) destabilize this gender role as an "original" anything. His exchanges with Brad suggest that the latter is an effect of the former and vice versa.

In one particular exchange, Jonathan describes the perfection and "naturalness" of marriage, which Brad immediately dismisses as horrifyingly routine. Jonathan waits in Brad's living room, an area outfitted for the playboy's conquests (producing instant romantic music, dimmed lights, locked door, and a sofa that converts to a bed, at the touch of a few buttons). Meanwhile, Brad is in the bathroom, preparing for a date (with a woman). The men appear in separate frames, a visual split paralleling their conversation, as they misunderstand and talk past one another. Complaining of his "oppression," Jonathan says, "Some people are prejudiced against me because I'm part of a minority." Brad asks, "What minority?" The obvious answer to this question, given Jonathan's gay affectations and clear admiration for the beautiful Brad, remains, of course, unspoken. "Millionaires," he replies. "You outnumber us, but you'll never get us. We'll fight for our rights to the bitter end. And we've got the money to do it."

Mediating between Jan's and Brad's desires, Jonathan occupies a middle space, not quite gay and not quite straight. Even more vigorously than Jan in the cab, Jonathan plays the "woman's" part to Brad's "man" as they discuss marriage. Like Jan before him, he voices a concern with proper appearances, then encourages Brad to settle down, to "create a stable, lasting relationship with one person." He hopefully adds, "A mature man wants those responsibilities. . . . What have you got against marriage anyway?" Insisting on his stalwart vision of manly, "natural," "original" freedom, Brad asserts that "before a man gets married, he's like a tree in the forest, he stands there independent, an entity unto himself, and then he's chopped down, his branches are cut off, he's stripped of his bark, and thrown into the river with the rest of the logs." Jonathan sighs, "With Jan, you look forward to having your branches cut off."

"NATURAL RESOURCES"

Traditional condemnations of female domesticity and male homoeroticism are closely aligned in this rather alarming but unsurprising image: marriage is equivalent to castration, or more precisely, a married man becomes a woman. Jonathan's use of Brad's "natural" metaphor to express his own "unnatural" desire for castration (here, homosexuality as well as feminization) emphasizes through irony the performativity of heterosexuality and especially its dependence on its "opposite," homosexuality. Brad embodies both ends of this opposition when he plays Rex, perhaps especially during a scene when both Jan and he are in their bathtubs, talking once again on the phone. They mirror one another: she is coy and giggly, immersed in luxurious bubbles; he is flattering and sweet. The split screen allows them to be intimate without seeing each other, their bare feet up against their respective tiled walls, moving closer and closer to each other until they apparently touch: "Every time I see you," he drawls, "I say to myself, we got all kinds of natural resources back home but we ain't got *nothin'* like that!" As he expresses his desire, Brad's branches are clearly at some risk. She encourages him, then becomes demure: "You'll find that most people are willing to meet you halfway." He moves his foot, toe pointed daintily so that it appears to "tickle" hers, and she pulls away with a start.

This moment—which makes Brad and Jan into mirror reflections of each other—visualizes their complicated dynamic, as they transgress from and conform to gendered and sexed expectations. One of the film's central devices for exacerbating and allaying the tension of this dynamic is Brad's ironic commentary on his role as Rex. Early on in her relationship with Rex, Brad calls Jan: "Sharing a phone together, I feel a certain responsibility for you. Now look, take my advice, don't go out with that man tomorrow night. . . . He's a phony." The split screen during this conversation shows him crowded into the upper corner of the frame as Jan smirks, cozy in her bed, secure in her knowledge of Rex's sincerity as opposed to Brad's artifice. "Don't judge other people by yourself," she asserts. That Rex is that self and quite "phony" complicates Brad's position and Jan's response: at last he is telling the "truth," but only because he assumes she will not believe him. At a later point he caters to Jan's anxieties about her own ability to "get a man," making Rex so passive that his sexual identity (and so, hers) comes into question. "He showed me Central Park and then we left," Jan tells Brad, proud of Rex's sexual nonaggression during her evening visit to his hotel room. "Hmm," says Brad. "That's even worse than I thought. . . . Well there are some men who just, uh, they're very devoted to their mothers, you know, the type that likes to, uh, collect cooking recipes, exchange bits of gossip?" "What a vicious thing to say!" she responds. Jan slams down the phone, telling Brad, "You are sick!"

Manifest in Day's physical comedy (her overwrought gestures and expressions), the joke of Jan's overreaction is that her barometer for a gentlemanly norm (Rex) is a spurious one; like her encounter with Mr. Conrad at the telephone office, this exchange puts *her* on the spot as an apparent deviant. Her fuming is ironic and funny, part of the film's jumble of affects and acts, its patently artificial design of normality and sickness. Brad-as-Rex now invites Jan's sexual overtures by pretending to be too "devoted to his mother," a gay performance that is multiply referential and increasingly hysterical. As Dyer observes, "Here is this gay man (Roy Scherer, Junior, Rock's real name) pretending to be a straight man (Rock Hudson) who's pretending to be a straight man (the character in the film) who's pretending to be a gay man (for the sequence or gag in the film)" ("Rock" 31).[18] It is this uneasy and ineffectual repression of subtextual codes that *Pillow Talk* challenges through its comic representations of gayness and straightness: *all* sexual identities are at risk and in motion because they depend on one another for their definitions. In fact, Brad's bind is beginning to resemble Jan's: his nervousness over marriage—which, as he understands it, is a way of being feminized or homosexualized—is an accepted sign of his masculinity, but he must, paradoxically, be married in order to be correctly *hetero*sexual (otherwise he starts to look like Jonathan).

Both Brad's and Jan's dilemmas are produced by the marriage system and remain a roadblock to its/their "fulfillment." The representation of Brad's particular quandary takes two forms, as gayness and as pregnancy. Both "conditions" are represented as threats to the given gender-sex order, and both depend on an unstable dichotomy between visibility and invisibility. Rex's most explicit gay performance—his expressed love of recipes and his mother—takes place at a bar where the focus of the evening's entertainment is precisely an excessive, too visible body, too large to love.[19] While Jan and Brad sit side by side on bar stools at a club called the Hidden Door, she sings along with the piano player, a black woman whose selection is "Roly Poly," a song about an overweight lover: "He measures five feet up and down / And five feet front and back." Envisioning the partner's immense physicality (she can "hardly get [her] arms around him"), the "Roly Poly" lyrics underline the film's concern with bodies that threaten social categories.[20] The most excessive body in the scene is, unsurprisingly, Brad's, as he fidgets and acts out his gayness in an effort to seduce Jan. Ironically, this act is interrupted by Jonathan's appearance at the bar. Just as Jan (conveniently) goes to the "powder room" following her first kiss with Brad/Rex, Jonathan shows up with incriminating photographs taken by a private detective he has hired to follow Jan's new suitor and threatens to expose Brad if he does not "leave town." When Jonathan exits and Jan returns, the singer shakes her head in disgust at Brad, who continues the charade in order to convince Jan to accompany him to a cabin in Connecticut. The observer, whose blackness marks her distance from and excess to the film's overwhelming well-to-do whiteness, serves as Brad's conscience and, in the song she sings as they leave the bar, foretells the deception's outcome: "You lied, you dog, and you'll be sorry."[21]

Brad winks at her, but the moment is strained, marking the film's turning point: from here, the deceit will be discovered (left alone for a moment at the cabin, Jan accidentally finds a copy of his song, "You Are My Inspiration," that had been hidden in Brad's overcoat), and the marriage plot will hurry to its conclusion. When Jan leaves Connecticut with Jonathan (who has followed them to the cabin, arriving just in time to rescue her), she sobs uncontrollably all the way back to New York. Later, Jonathan reports to Brad,

"I never knew a woman that size had so much water in her!" Again, appearances are deceptive.

"UNKNOWN REGIONS"

The film's consideration of this disjunction between bodies and identities culminates in Brad's "pregnancy." Meyer observes that Hudson's appeal was in part premised on his mildness, "the promise to control that big body, the promise not to pounce" (263). In *Pillow Talk,* this "promise" is made in and by Brad's gentlemanly act as Rex. The size and meaning of his body, however, continue to elicit apprehension throughout the film. Brad passes as "pregnant" twice, both times to avoid being literally seen by Jan in Jonathan's office building. Caught in the hallway as she approaches, he ducks into an obstetrician's office, which he mistakes for that of a general practitioner. He pretends that he needs an appointment for an "upset stomach"; the alarmed receptionist informs the doctor, who emerges from his office too late to see the runaway patient, but enormously agitated and titillated at the prospect. The receptionist insists that "he was obviously a psychopath." But Dr. Maxwell disagrees: "What if he weren't? . . . Miss Resnick, medical science still has many unknown regions to explore." Such "unknown regions" pervade the film's multiple instances of passing, their rejection of singular identities and identifications. Recuperated as humor, Brad's pregnancy represents a host of fantastic identity paradoxes, a cascading collapse of distinctions between control and loss of control, homosexuality and heterosexuality, male and female, "original" and "imitation."[22]

The pregnant male gag runs throughout the film, always having to do with the doctor's pursuit of this extraordinary body and connecting Brad's roleplaying to the female version of this "emergency" as an object of medical study. He steps into metaphorical "closets" (specifically, "women's" spaces) whenever he is eluding Jan. After hiding in the obstetrician's office, he then hides in a "ladies room," where he is spotted exiting by Miss Resnick, who again reports him to Maxwell. "Somewhere in this building," the doctor declares, "there may be a man who has crossed a new frontier!" While this crossing is literally into a women's bathroom, it is metaphorically connected to the film's examination of confusing identities and identity politics. And its intersecting narratives of passing, excess, and queerness come together for the last time, ironically yet again, in the consummation of the marriage plot.

On his way to tell Jonathan that he and Jan are expecting a baby, Brad is finally waylaid by the doctor and his receptionist: they try to get him to go with them as he loudly insists they release him. "You don't understand. I'm going to have a *baby!*" "Of course you are," says Dr. Maxwell, smiling and nodding as they drag him off down the hallway, and clearly thrilled that he has finally caught up with the object of his (professional) desire. The "new frontier" of the hystericized male body is now firmly grasped. And as he is carried off, Brad calls for help, "Jonathan! Jonathan!" Rather than offering the expected final image—the straight couple in an embrace—*Pillow Talk* holds out to the end, delivering instead the imagined spectacle of the gay couple that might have been.[23]

NOTES

1   This description of Day and Hudson as "the perfect pair . . . for *Pillow Talk*" appeared on contemporary posters for the film, which was directed by Michael Gordon, written by Stanley Shapiro and Maurice Richlin, and produced by Ross Hunter and Martin Melcher (Day's husband at the time). Day and Hudson were subsequently paired in *Lover Come Back* (Delbert Mann, 1961) and *Send Me No Flowers* (Norman Jewison, 1964).

2   Amy Robinson explains that passing is not "a strategy that evades the dominant terms of representation and the necessities of referential claims of identity [but relies] on the same binary oppositions which ground conventional accounts of the modern subject of a discrete and singular category" ("To Pass/In Drag" 2).

3   A poster for the movie features this caption: "The romantic story of a careful career girl who believes in 'singleness' . . . a carefree bachelor who believes in 'togetherness' . . . and the hilarious things that happen when they tangle!"

4   Joanne Meyerowitz makes the case—a good one I think, and useful for my point that the sixties and the fifties form a continuum of political and social concerns— that Friedan's book was "successful" in 1963 not only because it was "oppositional" to mainstream attitudes toward women's roles but also because it drew "on and reshape[d] familiar themes" already extant in the culture (252).

5   A fan magazine story on Rock Hudson's "hidden life" reveals that he is "a warm, down-to-earth person, a person who is difficult to know because of his fame" (Colbert 53); another is titled "Meet Rock Hudson: He's a Dime a Dozen."

6   For a discussion of the relationship between fear of communism and homophobia, see Corber.

7   See, for example, Burston and Richardson; Butler, *Gender Trouble;* Creekmur and Doty; Doan; Doty; Hamer and Budge; Sedgwick, *Epistemology;* and Wilton.

8   Rappaport's video opens and closes with this song, with the "me" looking for a "pillow-talkin' boy" re-inflected as the male narrator, imagining Hudson as his dreamy object of desire.

9   The appeal and "authenticity" of Rock Hudson are complicated. As Richard Meyer observes, "In Rock Hudson . . . a strapping gay male body closeted its explicit desire for other men while retaining its erotic neutrality towards women, thereby providing a sexual 'safe place' for both sides of his heterosexual audience" (282–83).

10   Day's life has often been depicted as a tabloid spectacle, even in nontabloid venues. For example, Ethan Mordden writes, "Doris Day is a Christian Scientist who loves dogs. Yes. But strange things have happened to her" (248). The fan magazines of the fifties and early sixties similarly painted her several marriages and divorces as inordinate failures, readable signs that this "All American girl," whose appeal to men and women is singular, is at bottom, and secretly, unhappy, and is financially and emotionally abused by "her" men. "Doris is probably the most written about and least known of all the important actresses in Hollywood," writes Helen Hendricks, who quotes *Pillow Talk* producer Ross Hunter: "'For all Doris' effervescence and apparent *joie de vivre,* I sometimes have the feeling that she is busting inside.'"

11   Demi Moore's "infamous" August 1991 *Vanity Fair* cover photo—nude and pregnant—along with its numerous follow-ups, including Moore, naked and body-painted, again for *Vanity Fair* (August 1992) and in Santa's lap (*Vanity Fair,* December 1993), and her husband Bruce Willis, nude and pregnant on the cover of *Spy* (September 1991), generated some controversy, indicating lingering anxieties about the "privacy" of women's bodies when pregnant and discomfort over the relationship between pregnancy and sexuality.

12   Jan's pleasurable resilience is founded in the cross-gendered and sexually playful appeal of Doris Day. Surely, as Judith Mayne writes, the identification and/or projection of lesbianism onto the Day persona is shifting, functioning across different eras or cultures in different ways (163–64). For any of her "authentic" identities is available to us only in her image(s)—as "Doris Day," "lesbian," domestic abuse survivor—necessarily informed by diverse spectator desires, discoveries, and experiences. If her ultra-straightness made her a favorite of fifties fan and women's magazines, Day's well-publicized career-mindedness and success also granted her a reputation for resisting traditional domestic constraints.

Mayne outlines a "critical spectatorship" that is not so much explicitly politicized as much as it is "contestatory," based in a paradoxical relationship between resistance and complicity (164). The critique allowed by such spectatorship is at once historical and ahistorical, a self-conscious "style" (or performance) of reading and making meaning that can concede the categorical usefulness of some impossible-to-ascertain "real" (the always-in-quotation-marks mainstay of tabloid headlines and fan magazine scoops), while understanding the political efficacy of contemporary fictions and fluctuations. Day's occasionally rumored lesbianism is unnecessary for her lesbian iconicity; her sexuality, especially her "virginity," is troubling—and so seductive, titillating—in its independence from "masculine" prescriptions. In the lesbian-camp favorite, *Calamity Jane*, Day's character, Calam, informs her more reserved woman companion—who still believes in the virtues of feminine passivity—"Oh, that's female thinkin', and nothin'll get you into more trouble." Calam's later impersonation of a woman, in a dress at the local dance, is emphatically artificial. Yet, by articulating her dissatisfaction with such "female thinkin'," Calam/Day participates in yet another performance, a kind of (temporarily) resistant tomboy-drag. As Ethan Mordden suggests, "As the frontier heroine who never heard of a dress, Day plays vulgar and dopey, two things she isn't, supplying a new kind of musical comedy fantasy: looks real, but isn't" (247). Lack of "realism" in a musical is hardly news, yet Calam remains an entirely "believable" gender-bender.

13   The film rewards Alma's enthusiastic observance of Jan and Brad's romance by granting her a conventionally happy ending of her own. She and Harry, the elevator man in Jan's building, are on the elevator as Brad carries Jan back to his apartment in a "triumphant," if rather neanderthal, display of coupledom-as-possession. Moved by Brad's bravado, Harry mimics his action, claiming, "That man just inspired me to do something I should have done long ago." He sweeps Alma into his arms, asserting that she needs a "man" to "look after." She responds by saying, "Why Harry, you're so strong," thus settling into her own marriage plot.

14   Brode observes that Randall's increasingly neurotic performance comically caricatures "the decade's executive hero," particularly in his (ironically situated) inability to understand his lack of appeal (267). As if in protest, Jonathan asserts that he has all of the qualities that women would look for: "I'm young, I'm rich, I'm healthy, I'm good-looking. I've got everything!" Including, Jan observes self-defensively, "three ex-wives."

15   See also Dyer on Hudson's queer image: "Rock's pretense does not really undermine *his* heterosexual image, even if he does throw his sexual identity into question. After all, we know he's only pretending" ("Rock" 31).

16 Gayness was certainly readable, even to straight audiences, especially given the purging of government workers during this period, as well as the "educational" material offered by popular magazines (for example, *Redbook*, *Playboy*) of the day, on how homosexuals "acted." See, for example, Corber.

17 Kirby argues that emotional, visceral responses to the movies created "considerable anxiety," particularly in male viewers. Brad's aversion to Jonathan's desires and self-expressions (and presumably that of audience members who "identify with" Brad) are registered in his increasingly gay performance as Rex: fear of being married/female/gay makes the comedy even more "hysterical."

18 Perhaps unsurprisingly, public/media resistance to Hudson's closeted sexuality remains steadfast. The Arts and Entertainment Network's 1993 *Biography* episode about him features narration by Jane Wyman, interviews with Susan St. James and Tony Randall (not, it should be noted, with Day or Elizabeth Taylor, who were very visible during his illness and coming out). The interviews and clips are spliced in such a way that there is no mention of his gayness until the final five minutes (of fifty or so), when the show briefly reports his death from AIDS.

19 Moon and Sedgwick address the question of "outing" fat bodies.

20 Large or potentially uncontrolled bodies repeatedly serve as the film's most visible challenge to social and sexual norms. For example, early on Brad distracts Jonathan from spotting his (Brad's) date with Jan at a restaurant by threatening to fix Jonathan up with a large woman who sits alone at a table. Brad blackmails Jonathan by telling him that he's supposed to be working on songs for the show Jonathan is financing, but is stuck with a date (the woman, whom Brad refers to as "Moose"). Inviting Jonathan to take over on the date, Brad waves and smiles at this woman from behind Jonathan (so that Jonathan is unaware of Brad's manipulation of her response, which is to wave and smile in return). Unnerved by the sight of the woman, Jonathan begs off ("Sorry pal, it's your moose") and leaves the restaurant in a hurry, leaving Brad to continue his evening with Jan.

21 When Jonathan learns that Jan has left Brad miserable, he says, "The great Brad Allen chopped down to size. Floating down the river with the rest of us logs."

22 Day starred in another 1959 movie about male pregnancy anxieties, *Tunnel of Love*, written by Joseph Field, directed by Gene Kelly, and co-starring Richard Widmark, of all people, as Day's suburban architect husband. Unable to get pregnant, the couple decides to adopt. After a drunken loss of memory, Widmark believes, mistakenly, that he has impregnated their assigned social worker (who is giving her child up for adoption). Fearful that the child resembles him (and so will "out" his assumed unfaithfulness), Widmark is increasingly

caught up in a web of much smaller lies over financial transactions and his own identity. Day plays the stalwart but suspicious wife—who does become pregnant by the end—with typical aplomb.

23 Except that the credit sequence alludes to Jan and Brad's marriage and their children. First, one pink and one blue pillow appear, marked with "The" and "End." Then, four more smaller pillows appear on top of one another, alternately pink and blue, each reading "Not quite." That is, no ending is quite stable.

WORKS CONSULTED

Brode, Douglas. *The Films of the Fifties*. New York: Citadel, 1976.

Burston, Paul, and Colin Richardson, eds. *A Queer Romance: Lesbians, Gay Men, and Popular Culture*. London: Routledge, 1995.

Butler, Judith. *Bodies That Matter: On the Discursive Limits of "Sex."* New York: Routledge, 1993.

———. *Gender Trouble: Feminism and the Subversion of Identity*. New York: Routledge, 1990.

———. "Imitation and Gender Insubordination." In *Inside/Out: Lesbian Theories, Gay Theories*. Ed. Diana Fuss. New York: Routledge, 1991. 13–31.

Byars, Jackie. *All That Hollywood Allows: Re-Reading Gender in 1950s Melodrama*. Chapel Hill: University of North Carolina Press, 1991.

Colbert, William. "Rock Hudson: A Great Star's Hidden Life." *Silver Screen* 22:6 (Dec. 1964): 53, 81.

Corber, Robert J. *In the Name of National Security: Hitchcock, Homophobia, and the Political Construction of Gender in Postwar America*. Durham, N.C.: Duke University Press, 1993.

Creekmur, Corey K., and Alexander Doty, eds. *Out in Culture: Gay, Lesbian, and Queer Essays on Popular Culture*. Durham, N.C.: Duke University Press, 1995.

D'Emilio, John. *Sexual Politics, Sexual Communities: The Making of a Homosexual Minority in the United States, 1940–1970*. Chicago: University of Chicago Press, 1983.

Doan, Laura, ed. *The Lesbian Postmodern*. New York: Columbia University Press, 1993.

Doty, Alexander. *Making Things Perfectly Queer: Interpreting Mass Culture*. Minneapolis: University of Minnesota Press, 1993.

Dowdy, Andrew. *The Films of the Fifties: The American State of Mind*. New York: William Morrow, 1973.

Dyer, Richard. *The Matter of Images: Essays on Representation*. London: Routledge, 1993.

———. "Rock—The Last Guy You'd Have Figured?" In *You Tarzan: Masculinity, Movies, and Men*. Ed. Pat Kirkham and Janet Thumim. New York: St. Martin's Press, 1993. 27–34.

Foucault, Michel. *The History of Sexuality: Volume 1: An Introduction*. Trans. Robert Hurley. New York: Vintage, 1978.

Friedan, Betty. *The Feminine Mystique*. 1963. New York: Dell, 1975.

Garber, Marjorie. *Vested Interests: Cross-Dressing and Cultural Anxiety*. New York: Routledge, 1992.

Halberstam, David. *The Fifties*. New York: Villard, 1993.

Hamer, Diane, and Belinda Budge, eds. *The Good, the Bad, and the Gorgeous: Popular Culture's Romance with Lesbianism*. London: Pandora, 1994

Hendricks, Helen. "The Secrets that Doris Day Won't Reveal." *Silver Screen* 28:5 (June 1962): 30.

Hotchner, A. E. *Doris Day*. New York: Morrow, 1975.

Hudson, Rock, and Sara Davidson. *Rock Hudson: His Story*. New York: Avon, 1986.

Kirby, Lynne. "Male Hysteria and Early Cinema." In *Male Trouble*. Ed. Constance Penley and Sharon Willis. Minneapolis: University of Minnesota Press, 1992. 66–85.

Lehman, Peter. *Running Scared: Masculinity and the Representation of the Male Body*. Philadelphia: Temple University Press, 1993.

Mayne, Judith. *Cinema and Spectatorship*. London: Routledge, 1993.

"Meet Rock Hudson: He's a Dime a Dozen." *Screen Stars* 17:2 (Oct. 1962): 47, 60.

Meyer, Richard. "Rock Hudson's Body." In *Inside/Out: Lesbian Theories, Gay Theories*. Ed. Diana Fuss. New York: Routledge, 1991. 258–88.

Meyerowitz, Joanne. "Beyond the Feminine Mystique: A Reassessment of Postwar Mass Culture, 1946–1958." In *Not June Cleaver: Women and Gender in Postwar America, 1945–1960*. Ed. Joanne Meyerowitz. Philadelphia: Temple University Press, 1994. 229–62.

Moon, Michael, and Eve Kosofsky Sedgwick. "Divinity: A Dossier, a Performance Piece, a Little-Understood Emotion." *Tendencies*, by Eve Kosofsky Sedgwick. Durham, N.C.: Duke University Press, 1993. 215–51.

Mordden, Ethan. *Movie Star: A Look at the Women Who Made Hollywood*. New York: St. Martin's Press, 1983.

Oppenheimer, Jerry, and Jack Vitek. *Idol: Rock Hudson, the True Story of an American Hero*. New York: Villard Books, 1986.

Rappaport, Mark, dir. *Rock Hudson's Home Movies*. Videotape. Artistic License/Water Bearer Films, 1992.

Robinson, Amy. "Is She or Isn't She?: Madonna and the Erotics of Appropriation." In *Acting Out: Feminist Performances*. Ed. Lynda Hart and Peggy Phelan. Ann Arbor: University of Michigan Press, 1992. 337–61.

————. "To Pass/In Drag: Strategies of Entrance into the Visible." *Ms.* 1993.

Russo, Vito. *The Celluloid Closet: Homosexuality in the Movies.* Rev. ed. New York: Harper and Row, 1987.

Sedgwick, Eve Kosofsky. *Epistemology of the Closet.* Berkeley: University of California Press, 1990.

————. *Tendencies.* Durham, N.C.: Duke University Press, 1993.

Wexman, Virginia Wright. *Creating the Couple: Love, Marriage, and Hollywood Performance.* Princeton, N.J.: Princeton University Press, 1993.

Wilton, Tamsin, ed. *Immortal Invisible: Lesbians and the Moving Image.* London: Routledge, 1995.

Part Four

Literary and Social Texts

Leerom Medovoi

Chapter Ten   DEMOCRACY, CAPITALISM, AND AMERICAN LITERATURE
The Cold War Construction of J. D. Salinger's Paperback Hero

"Beat" reader of J. D. Salinger's *Catcher in the Rye*.
(Photo by Joel Foreman)

IMAGINING CONSENSUS

UNTIL quite recently, most accounts of American history have characterized the 1950s as an affluent era of broad political consensus and cultural conformity, which then gradually unraveled over the course of the 1960s. Conservatives like Allan Bloom spoke nostalgically of the fifties as a golden age before the fall into anti-intellectual rebellion, moral relativism, and strident promiscuity. Progressives, by contrast, usually branded the fifties, in Fred Cook's words, a "nightmare decade" in which a powerful regime successfully returned women to the home, enforced a social program built on racial inequality, and secured the obedience of youths. For all their differences, both the Blooms and the Cooks agreed that the thirties and the sixties were tumultuous decades of social conflict, while the intervening years of the fifties represent a subdued moment of political quiescence. On both sides of the political spectrum, then, critics took the self-proclaimed existence of consensus and conformity in the fifties for granted.[1]

In the last ten years, scholars have begun to challenge such characterizations of the fifties as a quiet decade. Jackson Lears, for example has explicitly attacked uncritical uses of "the social thought of the 1940s and 1950s—the thought generated by the historical actors themselves—as a guide to understanding American culture and society in the postwar era" (38).[2] Instead, Lears proposed that we understand the so-called consensus of the fifties to have represented a "corporate cultural hegemony" produced by a postwar historic alliance of anti-communist liberal intellectuals, technicians, and bureaucrats, an alliance that obscured what in actuality was a much more complex and conflictual cultural and political landscape.[3] Maintaining the hegemonic representation of fifties America, presumably, required "forgetting" the rise of the Nation of Islam movement, best-selling gay writers, an underground drug subculture, and much more.

One way to challenge the hegemonic historical memory of the fifties would be precisely to write those excluded histories and cultural formations of the decade. Another would be to challenge the assumption that the so-called "consensus" of the cold war was ever stable or univocal, even internally. For the concept of hegemony suggests that the dominant formation itself is heterogeneous, if only because different groups participate in a hegemonic formation for different reasons and negotiate its meaning differently. A hegemony, in the last instance, is little more than the consolidation of an imaginary consensus.

What exactly does it mean to call a consensus imaginary? To take the case at hand, "cold war America" must first be reconceived as a dominant bloc within the nation-state that valorized a shared system of political signs—the various tropes and rhetorics of American democracy as they were relationally defined against the communist enemy. From there, the emphasis must shift from the hegemony's commonality to its multiplicity. By virtue of its heterogeneous composition, that dominant cold war bloc must be recognized as having conferred a range of different meanings and values to that system of signs. Signs are, to be sure, an important site of social struggle between classes or groups who share them. Yet such signs are simultaneously sites for what I am calling the imagining of consensus, the drawing together of different, even conflictual political signifieds, under the aegis of a common signifier.[4]

In this essay, I will explore certain key imaginary qualities of the cold war consensus by considering the debates that shaped the literary reputation of J. D. Salinger's *The Catcher in the Rye* and its teenage protagonist, Holden Caulfield. An analogy between the idiosyncrasies of Holden's speech and McCarthyite rhetoric has been suggested elsewhere by Alan Nadel. I will be drawing a different and broader connection between *Catcher* and its political context by considering the status of "youth" as a privileged cold war trope for American democratic character. Moreover, I will also consider the cultural consequences of this "age" rhetoric as it intersected with the paperback revolution in books that played such a vital role in the rise of teen culture.

Critics who participated in this American youth imaginary often did so for different reasons and imputed to it different political meanings. The apparent consensus of this literary and cultural elite of the fifties was therefore highly unstable and ideologically contradictory. This essay is devoted to the question of why cold war cultural authorities of the fifties came to uphold youth as a figure for the nation. Most studies of the immediate postwar era have emphasized the adult cultural establishment's *hostility* toward the emerging youth culture.[5] As a result, it is sometimes believed that a cold war consensus on the political question of youth did exist, namely one that disapproved of the emerging youth culture. I will suggest that, on the contrary, though the increased autonomy of youths was often feared for its delinquent potential, it was also widely accepted as part of the cold war agenda.[6] As the case of Salinger's novel reveals, cold war cultural leaders at times even defended youth culture's increasingly adversarial tone. The "consensus" regarding youth in cold war America is not to be found in a monolithic position that intellectuals, politicians, and other public figures shared on whether the culture of youths was moving in good or bad directions, a question that in fact was heatedly debated. Rather, "consensus" lay in little more than the cold war hegemonic formation's common adoption of youth as national signifier, a "consensus" whose very thinness continually threatened political fragmentation.

DEMOCRACY AND AMERICAN CHARACTER: A TALE OF COLD WAR
LITERARY NATIONALISM

Perhaps the most striking feature of the critical reception of *The Catcher in the Rye* is the hiatus that elapsed before it became a literary cause célèbre. Holden Caulfield appeared in several sketches in *Collier's* and the *New Yorker* as early as 1945, and *The Catcher in the Rye* was first published by Little, Brown in 1951. It was also chosen by the Book-of-the-Month Club that year as its summer selection, enjoying considerable popular and critical success as a result. *Catcher* appeared high up on the 1951 best-seller lists and was generally praised by reviewers. Nevertheless, Salinger's novel soon faded from the public eye, not to be widely discussed in print again for nearly six years.

During this intervening period, New American Library published a steady-selling, mass-market paperback edition of the novel. Only in 1957 did literary critics within the academy begin to take interest in Salinger's novel. By and large, these were not the more formalistic, conservative New Critics, but liberal scholars associated with the more sociohistorical criticism of the New York intellectual axis of fifties cultural life. Between 1957 and 1963, critics wrote a vast number of essays about *Catcher* and Salinger's subsequent stories. Academic interest then ebbed until, by the sixties, it had slowed to the trickle that it has since remained.

The nature of this relatively brief period of critical fascination with *Catcher* was the subject of a scathing 1976 essay, "Reviewers, Critics, and *The Catcher in the Rye*," by Carol Ohmann and Richard Ohmann. Attacking the various, mostly celebratory fifties interpretations of Salinger's novel, the Ohmanns argued that both *Catcher*'s original reviewers and its subsequent academic critics elided the novel's subtle denunciation of the hierarchical class system in the United States. Instead, critics fixated on false universals in *Catcher*, like the ubiquitous nature of growing up, leading them to neglect the socially specific concerns of the novel. The Ohmanns suggested that "by typing him [Holden] as an adolescent," reviews implied that "a sixteen-year-old's problems have been, are, and will remain the same" (21).

An interpretive essay on the "problems of growing up" in *Catcher*, of course, may well be just as historical (i.e., committed to a radical recontextualization) as a review focusing on the problems of power and wealth. Indeed, part of what I am aiming for myself is a rethinking of *Catcher* in relation to cold war age relations. The Ohmanns were nevertheless quite right to point out that critics and reviewers of *Catcher* almost never considered the class relations depicted in the novel. The Ohmanns explained this omission by suggesting that the prosperity of the early postwar years, which included academics, led to a general neglect of class critique in literary criticism. To this I would add that the reticence of fifties literary critics to discuss class themes was even more strongly tied to a cold war discursive etiquette, that is, to the pressures that anticommunism exerted on their cultural and social (as well as economic) position. American cold war discourse sought to rearticulate a political struggle between the United States and the USSR as an ideological struggle between capitalist democracy and communist dictatorship. Working within this context, literary critics of the fifties rarely read canonical American novels as fictional investigations of class inequality, and they usually demoted those novels that were difficult to read in any other way. Class inequality as a theme not only questioned the substance of American democracy but also threatened to evoke communist critiques of American society. Yet even as the cultural field of the cold war discouraged a critical attention to class difference in *Catcher*, it also enabled nationalist readings based on generational differences. These were not mimetic readings, deriving Holden's alienation from the existing social relations of teenagers and adults. As the Ohmanns rightly observed, *Catcher* was read as a psychological narrative about the developmental process of growing up. What they did not observe is that during the fifties, youth served as far more than a psychological category. As I have already suggested, it was promoted as a characterological metaphor for America itself. Ihab Hassan unequivocally drew the parallel in this way: "the life of the adolescent or youth still in his teens mirrors clearly the ambiguities of rejection and affirmation, revolt and conformity, hope and disenchantment observed in the culture at large. In his life as in our history, the fallacies of innocence and the new slate are exemplified. His predicament reflects the predicament of the self in America" (41). Hassan echoed numerous other liberal critics, particularly R. W. B. Lewis, who proposed an American literary tradition (the "party of Hope") demanding a New World rejection of the Old and a return to the innocence of childhood.[7]

Catcher, then, was not read as mere psychological narrative by cold war literary critics, but as national allegory. Hassan himself praised the novel in these terms, pronouncing in a 1957 essay that "the work of Salinger proves itself to be seriously engaged by . . . the new look of the American Dream, specifically dramatized by the encounter between a vision of innocence and the reality of guilt, between the forms love and power have tended to assume in America. The natural locus of that conflict in the work of Salinger is childhood and adolescence" (58–59). Other liberal critics began joining Hassan that year in writing appreciatively of *Catcher,* not as an incisive social commentary, nor even as an acute psychological study, but rather as a masterful insight into America's presumed youthful personality. Perhaps the first of the influential essays treating *Catcher* as a major accomplishment in American letters was Arthur Heiserman and James Miller's "J.D. Salinger: Some Crazy Cliff." Heiserman and Miller attempted to locate *Catcher* at the intersection of a classically Western Odyssean quest for home and a characteristically American desire to escape from home. The American hero, they argued, is a romantic who flees from the corrupting influences of European civilization in search of New World natural virtue and innocence. *Catcher,* Heiserman and Miller argued, is a novel that depicts this American quest as a tragic impossibility: "In childhood he [Holden Caulfield] had what he is now seeking— non-phoniness, truth, innocence. . . . Still, unlike all of us, Holden refuses to compromise with adulthood and its necessary adulteries: and his heroism drives him berserk" (75–76). The final sentence in this passage is strikingly ambivalent: it sees Holden as refusing adulthood, and in this respect he is "unlike all of us" who presumably reconcile ourselves with maturity. But is this compromise good or bad? Adulthood is slandered as intrinsically corrupt, as merely the state of being adulterous. But does American heroism then reside in refusing maturity's corruptions? So it would seem. And if so, then is this heroism worth the price of insanity?

Heiserman and Miller's essay designated *Catcher* as paradigmatically American by comparing it to, among other novels, *Huckleberry Finn*—Mark Twain's story of an adolescent's escape down river from his "sivilizing" home. Their essay was soon followed by a parade of others that drew blow-by-blow analogies between the two novels, mostly in order to celebrate them as glorious, companion embodiments of the American spirit. In perhaps the bluntest of these, "Holden and Huck: The Odysseys of Youth," Charles Kaplan wrote that "Huck Finn and Holden Caulfield are true blood-brothers" (127). "These two novels thus deal obliquely and poetically with a major theme in American life, past and present—the right of the nonconformist to assert his non-conformity" (132). Kaplan's nationalist argument for *Catcher's* canonization can be crudely expressed by the following chain of equivalences: *The Catcher in the Rye* = *Huckleberry Finn*, *Huckleberry Finn* = great American literature, therefore, *The Catcher in the Rye* = great American literature. But again, the quality Kaplan attributed to the nation is nonconformity, and specifically the right of the young to refuse to conform to the mandates of the adult world. Great American literature therefore lays in depicting the nonconformity of the young.

These striking celebrations of the novel in terms that place youthful rebellion at the very core of Americanness, I argue, have a certain cold war subtext to them that may not be readily apparent. Criticism of Mark Twain's *Huckleberry Finn*, however, the novel that critics repeatedly cited as inspiring Salinger's, brings the cold war much closer to the surface. This is particularly true of two highly influential postwar essays promoting the centrality of *Huck Finn* to American literary self-expression, one by Lionel Trilling and another by Leslie Fiedler. Trilling's essay was first published in 1948, one year after HUAC began its hearings on Hollywood communists, when anticommunist rhetoric had begun to escalate rapidly. It was subsequently reissued in his seminal essay collection, *The Liberal Imagination*. Trilling here affirmed the greatness of *Huck Finn* as "one of the central documents of American culture," which he located in its boyish power of telling the truth: "No one, as he [Twain] well knew, sets a higher value on truth than a boy. Truth is the whole of a boy's conscious demand upon the world of adults. He is likely to believe that the adult world is in a conspiracy to lie to him, and it is this belief, by no means unfounded, that arouses Tom and Huck and all boys to their moral sensitivity, their everlasting concern with justice, what they call fairness" (101). *Catcher* criticism unmistakably echoed Trilling's use of Twain's boy protagonists in praising Holden Caulfield as the embodiment of a moral and truthful America who demands a level of idealism impossible for adults. Trilling's ambivalence regarding such boyishness was also repeated in *Huck Finn* criticism. On the one hand, Trilling admitted that the adult world was a sort of lying conspiracy, and he praised the novel itself for offering the "very voice of unpretentious truth" (113). The character Huck Finn possesses a liberal imagination, a utopic desire for fairness, justice, and democracy that calls on him to refuse any adulterous compromise with an institution like slavery. At the same time, Trilling also suggested that the nov-

el "is a hymn to an older America forever gone" (110), an age of innocence
that was brought to an end by money capitalism.

Indulging here in a sentimental and nostalgic discussion of Huck Finn's
world, Trilling only hinted softly that today such "unpretentious truth" may
no longer be affordable. However, in the introductory essays of *The Liberal
Imagination,* Trilling's sentimentality is nowhere to be found and his tone is
far more blunt: America's liberal character must be tempered, for pure idealism is easily manipulated by political cynics. In his famous attack on Vernon
Parrington, the influential, pre–cold war liberal literary critic of the thirties,
Trilling complained that "ideals are different from ideas; in the liberal criticism
which descends from Parrington ideals consort happily with reality and they
urge us to deal impatiently with ideas—a 'cherished goal' forbids that we stop
to consider how we reach it, or if we may not destroy it in trying to reach it
the wrong way" (19). Trilling then explained this cryptic comment by way of
Theodore Dreiser's affiliation late in his life with the Communist party. Communism, for Trilling, was the "wrong way" to try to achieve one's liberal ideals, and Dreiser's lack of political judgment should prove how mistaken liberals of the thirties like Parrington were to embrace him as "one of the great,
significant expressions of [liberalism's] spirit" (18–19).

Trilling's literary criteria here flatly contradict those he espoused in his
essay on *Huck Finn.* The very qualities that he praised in Twain's work—its
expression of America's democratic desire for human equality and justice,
and most of all its idealism—he denounced Parrington for celebrating in
Theodore Dreiser's novels, because there liberalism can be exploited and
turned against itself by its worst enemy, communism. For a liberal like Trilling, it seems, the cold war forced a fundamental ambivalence toward political idealism. But why does Trilling map his ambivalence so precisely onto
these two authors? Why does Trilling affirm idealism in Twain, but criticize
it in Dreiser? The answer lies in the details. Twain's novel is a boy's novel,
written from the point of view of a boy, and for that matter written at a time
when America was young, before the rise of what Trilling calls the "money-
god" of capitalism (110). Twain therefore locates idealism in youth, where it
belongs. Dreiser's fiction, by contrast, does not put idealism in the mouth of
a boy, nor does it reserve its democratic impulse for America's precapitalist
past. Where Twain's democratic spirit can be safely dealt with in nostalgic,
bygone terms, Dreiser's raises the specter that American democratic idealism,

placed in conflict with capitalism, yields sympathy for twentieth-century communism in a cold war age. Like *Huck Finn, Catcher,* written in the voice of a boy, locates its idealism in youth rather than in the world of adults. In this respect, the novel's "utopic nonconformity" did not need to be criticized by critics who would follow in Trilling's footsteps. Heiserman and Miller could remain silent on the propriety of what they perceived to be Holden's absolute stand against maturity, so long as it was understood that Holden's idealism was a facet of his youth.

Perhaps equal in critical influence to Trilling's interpretation of *Huck Finn* is Leslie Fiedler's "Come Back to the Raft Ag'in, Huck Honey," which also first appeared in 1948. Fiedler discussed *Huckleberry Finn* in less positive terms than Trilling, as a means for critiquing the immaturity of American literature.[8] The central thesis of Fiedler's essay, which would eventually become the premise of his *Love and Death in the American Novel,* is that the great American novels have never told a heterosexual love story, but instead narrate the innocent love of two men, and particularly between a white and a dark man. For Fiedler, this had constituted an (implicitly white male) historic retreat from both racial and sexual responsibility.

Fiedler accused *Huck Finn* of racial irresponsibility because it exhibited white evasion of the nation's moral crimes against blacks. From this perspective, Huck and Jim's love takes on the questionable shape of a liberal guilt fantasy, in which the oppressed does not hold a grudge against his oppressor. Huck and Jim's love is not only racially irresponsible, however, but emblematic of American literature's sexual irresponsibility as well. For Fiedler, the homosocial focus of Twain's adolescent narrative typified an American fear of "mature" romantic love. Thus, Twain's emphasis on Huck and Jim's desexualized, innocent love for one another was childish and unmanly. Fiedler synthesized these two "moral failings" into a unified argument of America's "mythic boyhood," asserting "the regressiveness, in a technical sense, of American life, its implacable nostalgia for the infantile, [is] at once wrong-headed and somehow admirable" (*End* 144).

Fiedler's theory of great American literature strongly anticipated the incorporation of Salinger's novel into the canon. In addition to *Catcher's* adolescent narration, numerous textual elements confirmed its Fiedlerian qualifications for the critics as a classically American boy's book. Most obviously are Holden's various retreats from a heterosexual solution to his alienation, as in his repeated inability to call Jane Gallagher (the girl he really loves), but also in his loss of nerves during an encounter with a prostitute, and in his decision to stop dating the fashionable Sally Hayes. Holden makes clear his preference for innocent over sexual love in his adoration of children, particularly his sister Phoebe.

Catcher even appears to confirm Fiedler's views on the homosocial character of American literature by providing Holden with an adult man, Mr. Antolini, as his only loyal friend. Salinger's novel departs from Fiedler's formula, however, in one important way: late in the novel, Holden wakes up to discover that Mr. Antolini is stroking him and, interpreting this act as sexual, flees. Another liberal critic, Frederic Carpenter, may have had this scene in mind when he wrote that *Catcher* "describes an older boy who confronts the larger problems of sex which *Huck Finn* never faced" (92–93). Published two years after the Kinsey report on male sexuality had documented that fully one-third of all American men had engaged in sex to orgasm with other men, *Catcher*, it seemed, could no longer depend on the sexual innocence of close male relationships. Nevertheless, Holden's wariness of other men's sexual interest only signified to critics that, like preceding American literary characters, Holden too wishes to escape adult sexuality, even if this leaves him with nothing other than the love of innocent children. *Catcher* therefore could be—and clearly was—read as an updating of the Fiedlerian American novel—itself based upon a reading of *Huck Finn*. As Henry Anatole Grunwald asserted in a contribution to his own anthology of Salinger criticism: "Both Huck and Holden are in the same lineage of what Leslie Fiedler calls the Good Bad Boys of American literature. Like Huck, Holden longs to be out of civilization and back in innocent nature. Like Huck, speaking the superbly authentic dialect of his age and his place, Holden is a runaway from respectability, the possessor of a fierce sense of justice, the arbiter of his own morality" (5). Heiserman and Miller's account of the American quest myth as escape from home (and implicitly women) in search of innocence is also clearly indebted to the Fiedlerian theory of American literature. Spawning endless Twain/Salinger comparisons, Fiedler's use of *Huck Finn* effectively dictated the terms for *Catcher*'s canonization as an American masterpiece.

Like Trilling's, Fiedler's reading of *Huck Finn* also responded to the cold war cultural moment. Fiedler wrote ambivalently about the American character, though the key term for his was not idealism, but immaturity. First he condemned American literature for shirking manhood, but then he celebrated its boyish innocence as somehow admirable. Innocence, however, was a very charged term for Fielder that ran through many of his early political essays from the forties and fifties, later republished in a collection titled *The End to Innocence*. Like Trilling, the question for Fielder concerned the fate of liberalism in a cold war era when the Soviet Union had shown its true colors. In these essays, Fiedler repeatedly suggested that, for the sake of some naively utopian vision of bettering humanity, American liberals intentionally kept themselves "innocent" of Stalinism and hence "innocent" of their betrayal of America. This cold war argument is posed in the very first essay of the collection, "Hiss, Chambers, and the Age of Innocence." Like Huck in the literary essays, Hiss, whose guilt Fiedler simply considered beyond question, becomes a paradigmatic character: "Certainly, a generation was on trial with Hiss—on trial not, it must be noticed, for having struggled toward a better world, but for having substituted sentimentality for intelligence in that struggle" (21). By the end of the essay, Fiedler had called for a new liberalism, one that was more toughminded and less sentimental, unwilling to blind itself with its own values but ready to deal realistically with the world. Like Trilling, Fiedler believed that "the age of innocence is dead. The Hiss case marks the death of an era, but it also promises a rebirth if we are willing to learn its lesson. We who would still like to think of ourselves as liberals must be willing to declare that mere liberal principle is not in itself a guarantee against evil" (24).

Fiedler took a similar line in "Afterthoughts on the Rosenbergs." Scoffing at the gullibility of those who believed "two innocents had been falsely condemned for favoring 'roses and the laughter of children,'" Fiedler asked his reader to "look deeper, realize that a code is involved, a substitution of equivalents whose true meaning can be read off immediately by the insider. 'Peace, democracy, and liberty,' like 'roses and the laughter of children,' are only conventional ciphers for the rarely whispered word 'Communism'" (44–45). However inadvertently, Fiedler here provides us with his own "substitution of equivalents," a code that allows us to decipher the cold war political subtext of his earlier essay, "Huck Honey." For the political innocence to which Fiedler objected in these political essays is nothing other than a kind of youthful immaturity—much like that which critics had attributed to Holden. Like the Rosenbergs, Holden's declared love for the "laughter of children" can be read as concealing an unwillingness to face up to responsibility with political maturity. From a different angle, like Holden, Hiss comes to represent an entire generation, one that in the thirties was in fact in its youth, but which must, in the postwar, anticommunist era, grow up and accept, as Fiedler put it, "an end to innocence."

Trilling and Fiedler were far from idiosyncratic in their cold war politics; in their discussions of Huck Finn as exemplary of a problematic American innocence, they articulated positions quite representative of fifties liberal intellectuals. In *American Fiction in the Cold War,* Thomas Schaub has astutely observed a recurring narrative used by liberals in the forties and fifties to explain their postwar shift to the political Right. In this narrative, repeated over and over in intellectual discourse, *liberalism itself* functions as a protagonist who evolves over the course of the story. An old liberalism is posited that was heady, hopeful, and naively sympathetic to communism. Chastened by the disillusioning betrayal of Stalinism, a new liberalism emerges painfully by the end of the story—realistic, responsible, and vigilantly wary of being manipulated by those to its left. Considering a broad range of examples from political, sociological, historical, and literary writing of the forties and fifties, Schaub has characterized the postwar liberal narrative as "a Blakean journey from innocence to experience, from the myopia of the utopian to the twenty-twenty vision of the realist. . . . Their [liberals'] decisions were invariably accompanied by narratives of maturation and realism, of awakening to a more sober and skeptical perception of political reality and human nature" (5–6). The originary position within the narrative (innocent, myopic, utopian) is of course identified with the old liberalism, while the concluding position (experienced, perceptually acute, realistic) characterizes the new liberalism.

Schaub proposes a pair of terms (old vs. new) that are borrowed directly from Richard Chase, a preeminent literary critic of the fifties. However, Chase's terms fail to foreground a second binary, centered around generational conflict. "Old" has two different lexical opposites. "New" evokes a difference between the more distant past and the more recent. Another opposite, of course, is "young," which signifies not simply a lack of age but also a lack of developmental maturity. The latter set of terms more effectively captures the coming-of-age plotting of the liberal narrative. The protagonist begins as a young or adolescent liberalism, wide-eyed, naive, and uncompromising. By the story's end, however, liberalism has matured, evincing its adult willingness to strike a balance between ideals and the practical. The postwar liberal narrative, as Schaub described it, is thus also an *autobiographical* tale of maturation, a story liberals told about their own generational development from a prewar sympathy for communism into the political "adulthood" of cold war anticommunism.

The political motivations for appealing to *Catcher*'s American qualities now become clearer, for *Catcher*, titled after Holden Caulfield's desire to protect innocent children playing on the edge of "some crazy cliff," lends itself strongly to readings framed by the cold war liberal narrative Schaub analyzed. The liberal trope of maturation even appears explicitly in a pivotal scene late in the novel when, arriving exhausted and depressed at the home of Mr. Antolini, Holden asks his former teacher for advice. Antolini warns Holden that he (like the children in his fantasy) is in for a fall, and then quotes the psychoanalyst Wilhelm Stekel: "Here's what he said: 'The mark of the immature man is that he wants to die nobly for a cause, while the mark of the mature man is that he wants to live humbly for one'" (188).

Fingered by Antolini as an immature man, Holden is easily assimilated into the cold war narrative as representative of pre–cold war liberal idealism. If, as Kaplan argues, Holden, like Huck, embodies the American boy as nonconformist, he evokes—to quote Schaub—the "tyrannical idealism and moral crusading" associated with youthful liberalism (15). The same goes for Heiserman and Miller's rather ambivalent characterization of Holden's refusal of adulteries. Even plainer in his appeal to the liberal narrative, John Aldridge described the two novels as parallel studies in "the spiritual picaresque, the journey that for the young is all one way, from holy innocence to such knowledge as the world offers" (126). And explicitly quoting Fiedler, Frederic Carpenter suggested that "the ambivalence of adolescence which runs after experience yet fears it, and admires the mixed up and splendid world while still idealizing innocence, merely reflects the similar ambivalence of American society. And here *Catcher* goes beyond *Huck Finn* . . . in that it describes an America which also has reached 'an end to innocence'" (92–93). Holden's tale is the same as that of the liberal intellectuals, which in turn is the same as the story of America itself. The difference, of course, is that Holden remains a youth and therefore never really does have to "grow up" like everyone else.

Through this mobile narrative, liberal intellectuals were not only rewriting their own past but that of America, defusing the conflictual portrayal of American history, which earlier liberals had insisted on, from the 1890s through as late as the 1940s. The historian John Higham addressed this revision in a maverick review article of 1959 titled "The Cult of the 'American Consensus,'" which attacked the growing conservatism of other postwar liberal historians over the course of the decade. Higham argued that by inventing the category "the American character," historians had homogenized history at the expense of an earlier vision of America, articulated by progressives such as Frederick Jackson Turner, Charles Beard, and Vernon Parrington, "in which democracy, vaguely associated with the West, battled against entrenched economic privilege . . . property rights vs. human rights; Hamiltonianism vs. Jeffersonianism" (93–94). Even for historical moments when these conflicts were undeniable, Higham further noted, historians were "subjectivizing" conflicts so that "divisions, which the previous generation understood as basic opposition between distinct groups, turn into generalized psychological tensions running through the society as a whole" (95).

The postwar liberal narrative identified by Schaub is precisely such a subjectivization; it converts the political conflict between democracy and property into a psychological conflict between an immature self—the naive democrat—and a mature one—the political realist. Higham concluded by cautioning that the new cult of consensus was forcing Americans to "pay a cruel price in dispensing with their [progressive liberals'] deeper values: an appreciation of the crusading spirit, a responsiveness to indignation, a sense of injustice" (100).

Higham's warning notwithstanding, however, these values *are* retained by the postwar liberal narrative—namely in the figure of youth. Though considerably diminished by their association with adolescent indiscretion, progressive liberal politics retained a narrative presence within cold war liberal discourse, as the *Catcher* criticism demonstrates. Literary critics such as Carpenter, for example, who firmly believed that Holden needed to grow up, nevertheless held an appreciation for the idealism of adolescence. We have already seen the tendency of critics to applaud Holden's "nonconformity" or "idealism" and Lionel Trilling's sentimental praise of *Huck Finn*'s boyish truth. If political sentiment were under attack during the cold war, still it could be expressed so long as it was located in the adolescent boy where it belonged. Even Leslie Fiedler, perhaps the most severe critic of America's literary immaturity, evinced a respect for the nobility of youth. However sentimental, nostalgic, or infantile the desire for innocence may be, American boyishness, as Fiedler admitted (again echoing Trilling's ambivalence) is "at once wrong-headed and somehow admirable." This qualification too has a cold war logic to it, for if Fiedler and his peers were to remain liberals, they needed to temper these political values they considered "youthful" rather than abandon them altogether. Maturity, according to the cold war liberal narrative, encouraged a nonabsolutist, realistic politics of compromise, including, of course, a compromise with youthful idealism itself. The boy needed to be incorporated into the man, not abandoned altogether.

This cold war ambivalence toward the uncompromising innocence of youth fit smoothly into the discussion of Salinger's novel. Some critics tended to affirm Mr. Antolini for giving sound adult advice to a naive boy. Others rejected Mr. Antolini for grossly misunderstanding the dignity and value of Holden's nonconformity. *Catcher* allowed for a wide array of political positions, ranging from rather conservative critiques of America's naive democratic tendencies as embodied in Holden to leftist-liberal appreciations for the boy's egalitarian spirit. The novel could accommodate, that is, the entire scope of the imaginary cold war consensus.

LITERATURE AND CAPITALISM: A MASS-MARKET STORY OF DEMOCRACY

Catcher in the Rye's reception was not only structured by the trope of the adolescent as the character in a national allegory. It was also conditioned by the place of youth readers in a changing literary market propelled by consumer capitalism itself. Before World War II, the book market had been dominated by small but prestigious hardcover publishing houses. By the midfifties, innovations in production and distribution had allowed what had once been rather modest softcover reprint houses to overrun the book industry. I am referring, of course, to the development of the mass-market paperback, a book form that constituted the most dramatic breakthrough in the modern history of print capitalism. Kenneth Davis wrote in his *histoire de livre* that "before these inexpensive, widely distributed books came along, only the rarest of books sold more than a hundred thousand copies; a million-seller was a real phenomenon. . . . Overnight, the paperback changed that. Suddenly, a book could reach not hundreds or thousands of readers, but millions, many of whom had never owned a book before" (xii).

As Janice Radway has noted, the paperback and its mass-market predecessors attest not only to commercial efforts at mass-producing books but also
to the production of a mass reading public that could be relied upon to purchase these books (*Reading* 19–45). This presented a critical problem to the
cold war intellectuals and literary critics who were responding to this massification of literature and its audiences. To many critics, Salinger's novel represented a significant test case in the effects of the paperback on literary culture. As I noted earlier, *Catcher* was initially neglected by the literary
establishment, dismissed as an unexceptional, middlebrow book for adults.
In 1953, however, New American Library (NAL), the most prestigious of the
paperback companies, acquired the rights to *Catcher* from its hardcover publisher, Little, Brown. NAL's paperback edition became an enormous success,
selling a quarter million copies every year through 1964, when its rights to
the book expired.

The explosion of critical attention paid to *Catcher* coincides almost exactly
with the novel's enormous success in the literary marketplace, and virtually
every critical essay on Salinger would discuss his following among young
paperback readers. Typical was Robert Gutwillig's pronouncement that
"many an observer of the manners and mores of American youth contends
that a first novel published ten years ago occupies much the same place in
the affection of today's college generation as F. Scott Fitzgerald's *This Side of
Paradise* did for their parents in the Nineteen Twenties. The novel is *The
Catcher in the Rye,* by J.D. Salinger, which since its publication on July 16,
1951, has sold a total of 1,500,000 copies in the United States alone—
1,250,000 of them, significantly enough, in paperbound form" (1). Here adolescence again plays a crucial role in Salinger criticism. Now, however, it does
so not as a figure for America—youth as national metaphor—but through
concern with actual young people who read paperbacks. And in discussing
the recent directions of postpaperback fiction, Leslie Fiedler mounted this
strong and influential argument:

We have been . . . living through a revolution in taste, a radical transformation of the widest American literary audience from one in which wom-
en predominate to one in which adolescents make up the majority. . . . And
the mode demands, in lieu of the teen-age novelists who somehow refuse
to appear, Teen-age Impersonators, among whom one might list, say, Nor-

man Mailer, Jack Kerouac, even William Burroughs—certainly the Salinger who wrote *The Catcher in the Rye* and invented Holden Caulfield, a figure emulated by the young themselves. ("Up" 236)

For Fiedler, *Catcher* signified that literature itself was being cannibalized by America's rapidly growing youth culture. Such an argument, however, makes little empirical sense. Teenagers have never made up an overwhelming majority of book readership. Even paperbacks, after all, come in an enormous variety of genres and styles and appeal to a highly heterogeneous audience. Nevertheless, Fiedler's blurring of the distinction between mass culture and youth culture is commonplace in the culture debates of the fifties, particularly among liberals who feared massification.

Such rhetorical confusions of youth with mass culture usually rested upon questionable assumptions regarding the composition of both audience and text. On the one hand, mass culture was associated with youth because it was increasingly suspected during the fifties that a new peer culture (movies, comic books, rock 'n' roll, and apparently even paperbacks) was coming between adults and their children, socializing the latter in some alternative way that did not guarantee any final move into adulthood.[9] On the other hand, intellectual characterizations of kitsch as a culture of predigested meaning were mobilized as evidence that mass culture infantilized *anyone* who consumed it—including adults. The net effect on the nation, argued Dwight Macdonald in his influential essay "A Theory of Mass Culture," is the production of "Adultized Children" and "Infantile Adults," so that "Peter Pan might be a better symbol of America than Uncle Sam" (66).

Cold war critics dismayed by Salinger's popularity typically applied Macdonald's opinion about mass culture's puerility to the paperback, accusing the new book form of juvenilizing literature.[10] Ironically echoing Holden (as we shall see), George Steiner's bitter polemic of 1957, "The Salinger Industry," insisted on a distinction between genuine literature and commercial literature, arguing, of course, that Salinger leaned heavily toward the latter: "Salinger flatters the very ignorance and moral shallowness of his young readers. He suggests to them that formal ignorance, political apathy and a vague *tristesse* are positive virtues" (64). Salinger was a panderer, complained Steiner, prostituting to his audiences what they wanted to read rather than what was good for them. Harvey Swados and Mary McCarthy penned similar attacks, complaining that, as serious authors, they dreaded being publicly drowned out by the commercial success of an opportunist like Salinger.

Other critics, however, who admired Salinger's work and were satisfied that *Catcher* merited its growing reputation, were offended by the paternalistic dismissal of Salinger's young readership. In the first issue of *New World Writing*, NAL's experimental paperback literary journal of the fifties, Dan Wakefield rebutted Salinger's critics, complaining that "it seems to follow in the eyes of some older observers that if Salinger is indeed a myth and mentor of many young people, interest in his work is restricted to young people and that this is symptomatic of the fact that it is really childish, sentimental, adolescent, and irrelevant" (195). Most critics, siding with Wakefield, accepted Salinger's novel as a contemporary American classic whose mass availability and popularity signaled, if anything, that perhaps young Americans could be wooed into reading great American literature. The well-known cultural critic David Manning White argued that, along with the other mass media, paperback books "hold out the greatest promise to the 'average' man that a cultural richness no previous age could give him is at hand" (19). For critics sharing White's enthusiasm for the paperback, *Catcher* came to symbolize that literary quality and popularity were, in fact, compatible.

Cold war discourse complicated the question of literary interest among juvenile readers. The American literary tradition, as noted earlier, had been characterized as immature in its idealism and rebelliousness by Trilling, Fiedler, and other cold war liberals. There was a certain vulnerability, therefore, to contentions that the paperback distribution of American literature, already understood to be adolescent in character, would assist the masses (let alone the young masses) in a cultural coming of age.

If anything, the American character of *Catcher* seemed more likely to reinject a sense of rebelliousness into the adolescent identity of young Americans. John Skow, for one, believed that "a generation or two of high school and college students . . . see in *Catcher* their hymn, their epic, their Treasury of Humor, and their manifesto against the world" (qtd. in Grunwald, "Invisible Man" 4–5). David Leitch called Salinger's young fans "recruits to the ranks of the disaffiliated, [who] regard society from a safe distance, convinced of one thing at least. For them it has nothing to offer" (76). Though critics hesitantly praised the characteristic idealism of *Catcher* as American literature, they simultaneously feared that the novel might discourage young readers from seeking maturity. Henry Anatole Grunwald worried that "if the young, in particular, have made Salinger their laureate, it must be . . . because he meets their needs. . . . The end of the tragic hero is death; the end of the adolescent hero is the death of youth, which is growing up. The extraordinary thing about Salinger is that he does not really accept this simple fact. [Unlike other writers] to Salinger it [youth] is something to be kept and cherished" (xxxi). Grunwald's comments evince a common anxiety that *Catcher* encouraged youths to value their very immaturity.

Some critics rejected an interpretation that saw Holden forsaking maturity. Yet even a critic in this camp such as Granville Hicks felt compelled to assuage the widespread apprehension regarding the novel's effects on readers. Recalling that he had nearly not bothered to include *Catcher* on his syllabus because he had heard that this was the one novel that "every undergraduate in America has read," Hicks happily reported to his fellow critics that the selection had turned out to be a smashing success: "Holden Caulfield meant more [to students] than Jake Barnes or Jay Gatsby or Augie March or any other character we encountered in the course, and in the discussion of the novel there was a sense of direct involvement such as I felt on no other occasion" (109). The reason for this unique engagement with the novel, Hicks admitted, was that it spoke the language of youths and expressed their rebellion against "meanness, stupidity, and especially phoniness." Lest this make *Catcher* too threatening a form of youth culture, Hicks placed *Catcher* squarely within an affirmative, maturity-bound literary enterprise, which he called the "search for wisdom." Hicks thereby reassured his fellow critics; *The Catcher in the Rye* did not truly encourage the rebellion of youth, or at the least, that whatever rebellion it might incite was worthwhile. Hicks was here in the majority. Regardless of how they read the novel, most critics both acknowledged their common fears for the paperback's mass readership and yet somehow attempted to mitigate them.

In "Mail-Order Culture and Its Critics," Janice Radway pointed out a basic conflict of interest between literary critics and the massification of literature, which indicated how extraordinary these affirmative gestures toward *Catcher* really were. Radway examined the establishment of the Book-of-the-Month Club (BOMC) in the twenties as a significant moment in the massification of literature and analyzed the dispute this occasioned between the BOMC's founder, Harry Scherman, and literary critics. Though couched in aesthetic terms, the struggle, Radway concluded, was ultimately one over cultural authority. The BOMC threatened to break the critics' monopoly as judges of books for the reading public: "The controversy over the Book-of-the-Month Club developed as an instance of an intra-class dispute over who precisely would stake the claim to cultural authority even while denying that was what was being done. At issue was whether cultural selection would continue to be the province of the urban Protestant elite of the Northeastern cities who controlled most of the respected literary journals or the newly arrived immigrant entrepreneurs like Scherman who were beginning to dominate the culture industry" (523). As yet another step in the massification of literature, the paperback presented a similar threat to critics. The stakes for literary critics were if anything even higher with the paperback than they had been with the BOMC, since the mass distribution of paperback books to nonliterary outlets—drugstores, magazine stands, airport gift shops—meant that readers might conceivably not consult anyone at all on what to read but buy their books instead on the strength of their covers or on word of mouth. The most unexpected axis of Salinger criticism, then, is not Steiner's, whose "The Salinger Industry," after all, rightly accused literary critics of caving in to the mass cultural marketplace's usurpation of their literary authority. It is the critics who supported *Catcher* and its mass readership, thereby compromising their own cultural authority, who present a puzzle.

A clue as to why they might have done so emerges in an extensive symposium of 1952 that appeared in the liberal/leftist journal *Partisan Review,* titled "Our Country and Our Culture," meant to commemorate a reconciliation of American intellectuals to their nation. Since World War II, *Partisan Review* argued, intellectuals had come to realize that American democracy required their assistance in the struggle against its communist enemy. Most writers and intellectuals therefore no longer considered themselves rebels. Liberals, once again, claimed to have transcended an adolescent politics of naiveté to a more mature, mainstream politics of responsibility. But *Partisan Review* also complained that this new affirmation could not be complete because the postwar growth of mass culture posed a new obstacle to the successful integration of the intellectual into American life.

The fears that cold war intellectuals expressed regarding mass culture are often assumed to derive from their association of fascism, Stalinism, and even

McCarthyism with mass behavior.[11] In "Our Country and Our Culture," however, *Partisan Review*'s editors reluctantly suggested that mass culture seemed to emerge out of the very democratic American values liberal intellectuals were now defending. Intellectuals' generally cautious approach to mass culture, the editors warned, did not indicate that they did not therefore champion democracy:

> We are certain that these [democratic American] values are necessary conditions for civilization and represent the only immediate alternative as long as Russian totalitarianism threatens world domination. Nevertheless, there are serious cultural consequences: mass culture not only weakens the position of the artist and the intellectual profoundly by separating him from his natural audience, but it also removes the mass of people from the kind of art which might express their human and aesthetic needs. . . . Its increasing power is one of the chief causes of the spiritual and economic insecurity of the intellectual minority. (285)

This passage is enormously revealing, for it suggests that liberal intellectuals recognized full well that the expansion of mass culture jeopardized their own elite status as proprietors of American culture. Nevertheless, it also indicates that they felt compelled to forego a full-scale counterattack on mass culture *because their own cold war politics demanded it.* While the critics of the twenties discussed by Radway had been entirely unforgiving of the BOMC, then by the fifties, I suggest, cold war ideology had muted critics' denunciations of literary massification. Insofar as mass culture took the form of the "cultural consequences of democracy" in America, cold war intellectuals, however reluctantly, refrained from total condemnation. This too was a calculated move, since their cooperation in the ideological struggle with communism seemed necessary for intellectuals to maintain their status. Just as they had equivocated in their judgment of the putatively adolescent, democratic character of America, so liberal intellectuals, their own interests divided, came to an ambivalent position on the paperback's potential to democratize reading. Salinger's novel became representative of this issue; the cultural consequences of democracy became concretized in the critics' discussions about the cultural consequences for *Catcher*'s youthful readers.

FROM MASSIFICATION TO COMMODIFICATION: A PROGRESSIVE
READING OF *CATCHER*

The liberal intellectual dilemma over how to respond to the paperback grew from an unexamined assumption, namely that the rise of mass culture stems from a historical movement toward the *democratization* of culture. This, I believe, was an ideologically motivated mistake; the rise of mass culture, including the paperback, in fact represents a movement toward the *commodification* of culture. Mass culture is not merely a contemporary analogue of folk culture, but a new phenomenon entirely, in which cultural goods are produced, distributed, and consumed on a mass scale for private profit. The rise of mass culture, that is, derives from the expansionary dynamics of capitalism, not democracy. One might say that, as the evolving cultural form of capitalism, mass culture is *antithetical* to democracy. The commodification of culture makes all products formally available to everyone in the marketplace, but in practice it limits access to only those individuals who can actually afford them. Culture and cultural authority thus become yet another form of private property that produce hierarchical distinctions between social classes.

This argument, revived in the cultural analyses of Pierre Bourdieu and Jean Baudrillard, can be found as early as the turn of the century in the work of the progressive American critic Thorstein Veblen, who argued that "conspicuous consumption" serves to maintain "invidious distinctions" between classes. Indeed, as noted previously, until the fifties, the positing of a conflict between democracy and capitalism, or equality and property, had been the organizing principle of the progressive liberal narrative of American history.[12]

As discussed previously, the Ohmanns have already argued that *The Catcher in the Rye* can and should be read as the story of a privileged boy's growing disillusionment with the divisiveness of America's class society, and they criticized cold war critics for failing to do so. Let me suggest that it is no surprise that cold war liberal critics did not read *Catcher* along such lines. The Ohmanns proposed a progressive liberal reading of Salinger's novel, redeploying a political metanarrative that had been explicitly rejected by cold war critics. From our present vantage point, however, *Catcher* can be read quite easily as a progressive critique, not only of class society, but also of the fifties culture industry and capitalist economy within which, paradoxically, it thrived.

Consider, as did the Ohmanns, Holden Caulfield's favorite negative epithet, "phony." According to the Ohmanns, whenever Holden derisively condemns a person or an action as phony, he is objecting to some exercise of class privilege. "Phoniness" thus serves as the novel's master signifier for critique. But why would Holden call class privilege phony as opposed, say, to bourgeois (his old roommate Dick Slagle's term), snobbish, abusive, or even just plain nasty? In what sense is class privilege "phony"?

Holden does not accuse only the bourgeois elite of phoniness, but rather anyone at all who produces himself or herself for exchange: the schoolmaster who sells himself to the parents of the wealthy students, Ernie the black pianist who panders to his college crowd, the Lunts with their self-inflated acting, and the audience members at their performance, who have only come to be seen by one another in the lobby. Holden views these and many other people as phonies, whose self-promotion for the consumption of others is an index of their inauthenticity. What should ideally be a social world built upon acts of communication, hence communion, instead has become one in which people are instrumentalized as objects of one another's exchange.

It is in this sense that "phoniness" mars Holden's encounter with the prostitute, Sunny, with whom he desperately wants to establish genuine—i.e., noncommodified—contact. His failure to do so, and indeed her unwillingness to intercede when her pimp, Maurice, squeezes him for extra money, is what invests the encounter with such frustrating pathos. Phoniness-as-commodification also accounts for Holden's deep disappointment when his former teacher, Mr. Antolini, strokes him while he is sleeping on the couch. Compounding his fear of "flits" is Holden's sudden anxiety that Antolini's generosity and advice were not genuine after all but calculated as an exchange for sexual favors.

In invoking commodification, I obviously do not refer strictly to production for money. Financial gain may be at issue, as in the case of Sunny the prostitute, Mr. Haas the headmaster, and Mr. Ossenburger the pious undertaker, a "big phony bastard" whom Holden imagines "shifting into first gear and asking Jesus to send him a few more stiffs" (16–17). Just as often, however, phoniness correlates with what Jean Baudrillard has termed "sign exchange value" and Pierre Bourdieu has referred to as "cultural capital," that other form of "wealth" which circulates in the bourgeois cultural economy of prestige rather than the financial economy of money. A good illustration of this form of exchange value is Holden's distinction between genuine charity work, as performed by the plainly garbed nuns, and self-commodifying charity work, as Holden imagines Sally Hayes's stylish mother might do it: "The only way *she* could go around with a basket collecting dough would be if everybody kissed her ass for her when they made a contribution. If they just dropped their dough in her basket, then walked away without saying anything to her, ignoring her and all, she'd quit in about an hour. She'd get bored. She'd hand in her basket and then go someplace swanky for lunch" (114).

This reading invests a different meaning into the generational differences of Salinger's novel. The children Holden adores—Phoebe, the little boy who whistles "If a Body Catch a Body," the kids at the museum of natural history and the park, and of course the children whom Holden imagines protecting as a catcher in the rye—share an innocence of commodification, whether financial, symbolic, or sexual. Immaturity represents a precorrupted willingness to interact with people honestly, and for reasons other than market imperatives.[13]

The paradox of this neo-progressive interpretation lies in the history of the extensive commodification of *Catcher* itself and, more generally, in its place as part of the growing commodification of youth culture during the fifties. Salinger occupied the approximate literary space that his novel condemns—a successful, commercial writer much like those Holden despises for writing those "dumb stories in a magazine" (52). Holden attacks the very organization that propelled *Catcher* to its initial successes, the Book-of-the-Month Club. And finally, there is the mass-market phenomenon of the paperback itself, for which, as I have shown, *Catcher* became representative. The type of literary "prostitution" that Holden condemns for making "lots of dough," ironically, bears a powerful resemblance to the career of the book in which he appeared (1–2).

A progressive reading of *Catcher* is therefore a viable interpretive strategy. Holden's labeling of commercial culture as phony can be effectively linked with issues of status and privilege or, more precisely, with the undemocratic creation of unequal patterns of consumption. In the cold war climate of the fifties, however, such progressive readings were conspicuously absent. If Holden, in his objection to commercial culture, is a democrat who abhors the capitalist organization of his social world by economies of unequal status and wealth, then Salinger's novel converges with the *pre*–cold war liberal narrative of a Vernon Parrington or a Charles Beard. As a progressive hero, Holden could well have represented the Jeffersonian, human rights–focused, democratic America of the West in its struggle against the Hamiltonian, property rights–oriented, capitalist America of the East. From the perspective of John Dos Passos's cry of the thirties, "All right we are two nations," Holden could easily have been read as the champion of American democracy in its historical conflict with American capitalism. Just as *The Catcher in the Rye* was readily assimilated to the cold war liberal narrative, it could also have been adapted to the preceding progressive liberal narrative of the thirties. The absence of such a reading is a significant event in the political history of literary criticism.

What can be learned from the political unviability in the fifties of a progressive reading of *The Catcher in the Rye?* The Ohmanns argued that reviewers and critics of the fifties missed the novel's condemnation of American class society because of their universalizing framework. I would offer a slightly different perspective: cold war liberals could not offer a reading of *Catcher* that emphasized class or commodification because to address either issue was to question the most fundamental of all cold war beliefs—the essential compatibility of capitalism and democracy. Anxieties arising within a framework that assumes their compatibility—the fear, for example, that capitalism might, through the conformist power of mass culture, achieve a dubious democracy of sameness or even puerility—were acceptable propositions for intellectuals of the fifties. But a fear that capitalism's commodification of everything might actually *create* class distinctions, reproducing a hierarchy that would not be compatible with democracy at all—this possibility remained beyond the accepted boundaries of cold war discourse.

Perhaps equally important was the class positional reason for intellectuals' silence about *Catcher's* treatment of commodification. Holden's concern with cultural, as opposed to strictly financial, exchange may have struck a little too close to home. Insofar as Holden's contempt for Hollywood and magazine literature can be read as a refusal of kitsch and conformity, intellectuals might have embraced Holden as a fictional ally in their own half-hearted struggle against mass culture. Their reluctance to seize this opportunity, however, is quite understandable: while the rapid postwar growth of mass culture threatened the cultural status of intellectuals, it was the logic of commodification that granted that status in the first place. As critics of culture, intellectuals are conspicuous accumulators of cultural capital and important beneficiaries of economies of prestige. Or to put it in progressivist terms, within the political economy of culture, intellectuals operate as capitalists rather than as democrats. This remained the case in the fifties even if, in Veblen's terms, the conspicuous consumption of art and literature was losing some market share to the new products of the culture industries.

Holden's complaint, if associated with commodification, therefore still presented a profound challenge to intellectuals, particularly because his examples of phoniness extend *across* cultural categories, not only in the lowbrow realm of the movies and in the middlebrow arenas of Pencey Prep School or commercial theater, but even among intellectuals like Mr. Antolini or Holden's snobby acquaintance, Luce, who refuses to talk to Holden on a personal level because "he wants to run the show, like all intellectuals" (147).

As embattled arbiters of taste in cold war America, liberal intellectuals had strong motivations to avoid taking Holden's reproach directly in progressive directions that could undercut both cold war politics and their own intellectual class interests. Nevertheless, it is vital to note that the critics did not so much *repress* the conflict between democracy and capitalism as *transform* it by mapping the progressive metanarrative onto the respective generational categories of adolescence and adulthood. In *Catcher* criticism, the forces of Jeffersonian democracy became embodied in an overly idealistic boy, while property and capital were represented by adults who made the moral compromises demanded by social necessity. Recasting the relationship of democracy and capitalism in this way, as a developmental movement from innocence to responsibility, critics could safely play out their political ambivalences and disagreements. As a text that allowed them to express their loyalties to *both* sides of the progressive conflict—their nostalgic respect for Holden's democratic ethos, on the one hand, and their commitments to a capitalistic adult society, on the other, *Catcher* allowed them to articulate the very instability of cold war ideology.

RECONSIDERING THE CANONIZATION OF
THE CATCHER IN THE RYE

As a mass-market paperback, *The Catcher in the Rye* can be analyzed as part of the culture industry's expanding production of youth culture in the fifties. The question remains, however, why cold war literary critics chose to canonize a novel whose effects on readers they suspected might threaten America's supposed consensus, not to mention their own authority as cultural leaders. There is in fact no single answer to this question, because the critics did not necessarily share a common political position. Some, like Trilling and Fiedler, were committed liberal anticommunists. Others, like Granville Hicks, might have remained more positively predisposed toward thirties radicalism. Still others would become advocates of radical writing in the sixties, like Maxwell Geismar, who promoted the work of Eldridge Cleaver. Yet there is a certain formal similarity to all of their writing, in that all the critics attempted to maintain democracy, alongside capitalism, as intrinsically American. This they accomplished by locating democracy in the transitory moment of youth: in America's past, in their own "youthful indiscretions of the thirties," or in the recapitulation of both moments in an idealistic teenage character like Holden Caulfield. Given that cold war critics had already drawn an equation between American youth and American democracy, however, it seemed only fitting to them that young Americans had chosen to read it. *Catcher's* popularity even seemed to confirm that postwar American capitalism's mass cultural forms, such as the paperback, could fulfill (for better or worse) America's cultural democratic potential by delivering the nation's youthful character to the next generation of citizens.

For those critics who wished to play down democracy, this turn of events was dangerous, a potential revival of immature feeling in an America that should have outgrown it. And *Catcher* itself could be interpreted either as encouraging such folly or as critical and aware of the need for maturity. By contrast, for other critics who appreciated the persistence of what they considered a democratic ethos, the novel showed that the "search for wisdom" in America had perhaps not been abandoned after all. Regardless of which particular reading of the novel they promoted, however, all the critics shared a hermeneutic horizon of expectations—an imaginary liberal consensus—within which *The Catcher in the Rye* served as a privileged expression of the vicissitudes of the democratic American character. As a result, even those critics who feared the vulnerability of America's youthful idealism (like the liberalism of the thirties) to the temptations of communism, or who feared their own loss of influence to mass culture, tended to celebrate *The Catcher in the Rye.*

If, as some would argue, *The Catcher in the Rye* signaled an "emergent six-ties," then the novel's critical reception as a youthfully democratic American novel must simultaneously be considered a sign of the "residual thirties." The imagined consensus of the cold war, far from representing a static political moment sandwiched between two tumultuous and conflictual decades, may be best understood as a complex and fractured cultural formation through which the class radicalism of the Old Left was reconstructed via the cold war figura-tion of youth into the generational radicalism of the New Left. By construct-ing a past American ideal of democracy in relation to a present-day capitalist America, the cold war hegemony of the fifties undermined itself, granting cultural influence to oppositional youth. *Catcher* was read by teenagers, but it was patronized by the most culturally influential of adults. The "emergence" of the sixties therefore found sustenance not only at the periphery of the fif-ties, outside the "consensus," as most conventional histories would have it, but squarely at its shaky imaginary center. As the reception of *The Catcher in the Rye* reveals, cold war intellectual culture authorized dissent in youth culture by proclaiming—whether for better or worse—the quintessentially American character of idealistic, adolescent rebellion and the fundamentally democratic character of its commercial, mass-mediated forms.

NOTES

My friends and colleagues gave me invaluable assistance and advice on the writing of this essay. I would especially like to thank the generosity of Shay Brawn, Joel Foreman, Regenia Gagnier, Kim Gillespie, Lisa Hogeland, Miranda Joseph, Marcia Klotz, Rob Latham, Ben Robinson, David Schmid, and Eric Schocket.

1   In addition to Cook and Bloom, see also Jezer. Even J. Ronald Oakley, in his modestly revisionist *God's Country*, still considers the fifties to be a "qualified yes" as a "golden age" (434). Occasionally, these histories of the fifties are com-plicated by a subplot exploring seeds of an "emergent sixties" at the margins of the cold war consensus: maverick political criticism by C. Wright Mills, for-ward-looking civil rights struggles such as the Montgomery Bus Boycott, un-derground sexual and lifestyle experimentations by the Beats, and the devel-opment of an antagonistic youth culture typified by rock 'n' roll. Despite these notable instances of budding dissent at their periphery, however, the predom-

inant institutions and discourses of the fifties are assumed to have been politically stable and ideologically coherent.

2   For similar critiques see Pells, Boyer, and Lary May.

3   Feminist historians and critics have made similar arguments vis-à-vis the obscuring of highly volatile gender relations in the fifties. See Elaine Tyler May and Byars.

4   With the theoretical texts that inspire this conception which Laclau and Mouffe, Zizek, Anderson, and Pease, especially his notion of the "field-imaginary."

5   For one of the best studies see Gilbert.

6   This argument will be more fully fleshed out in my forthcoming book on fifties youth culture. In addition, the rebellious figure of youth that received so much attention during the cold war was a decisively masculine one. While I do not enter into the substantive gender and sexual issues of youth and the cold war in this particular essay, they do represent a principal subject of the larger study from which it is drawn.

7   Lewis claims two other American traditions, the party of Memory and the party of Irony. However, as Russell Reising has noted, Lewis writes almost exclusively about the first. The party of Memory serves as an analytically constructed "other" for that of Hope, and the party of Irony as some similarly nonexistent synthesis of the first two that Lewis finds the most intellectually viable party line. Donald Pease has argued in *Visionary Compacts* that this cold war liberal approach to American literature constructed a tradition based on the idealization of "negative freedom," opposition to totalitarian forces. In some sense, what I am about to argue is that "youth" became the primary figure in whom literary critics would embody this principle of rebellion.

8   The critique of American immaturity would continue to occupy Fiedler for nearly two more decades, well through *Love and Death in the American Novel* and until *The Return of the Vanishing American*.

9   See Gilbert for how this belief operated in discussions of juvenile delinquency.

10   Of course to condemn the Salinger phenomena also required denouncing the majority of critics who had praised the novel. Steiner therefore railed not only against *Catcher* and its childish readership but also against the intellectual establishment's inexcusable canonization of Salinger through outlandish comparisons of *Catcher* with American masterpieces.

11   See Ross for the best analysis of cold war intellectuals' frustration with mass culture from this point of view.

12   This argument has reappeared in leftist American social theory. For a neo-progressive discussion of democracy and capitalism as the two rival revolutions of our time, see Bowles and Gintis.

13   It is worth noting that even interpretations of *Catcher* as critical of a commodified society need not be progressive, for the political implications of Holden's attack on commodification are indeterminate. Holden's contempt for the commodified could also be taken to express a nostalgia for precapitalism, a spiritual distaste for the crass commercialism of a secular age. His anticapitalism, that is, might be religious rather than radical in its orientation. Indeed, the mystical solutions of Salinger's later fiction, such as that which Franny espouses in *Franny and Zooey,* would encourage such nonradical interpretations.

WORKS CONSULTED

Aldridge, John W. "The Society of Three Novels." *In Search of Heresy: American Literature in an Age of Conformity.* New York: McGraw-Hill, 1956. 126–48.

Anderson, Benedict. *Imagined Communities: Reflections on the Origin and Spread of Nationalism.* New York: Verso Press, 1990.

Baudrillard, Jean. *For a Critique of the Political Economy of the Sign.* St. Louis: Telos Press, 1991.

Bloom, Allan. *The Closing of the American Mind.* New York: Simon and Schuster, 1987.

Bourdieu, Pierre. *Distinction: A Social Critique of the Judgement of Taste.* Cambridge, Mass.: Harvard University Press, 1984.

Bowles, Samuel, and Herbert Gintis. *Capitalism and Democracy: Property, Community, and the Contradictions of Modern Social Thought.* New York: Basic Books, 1987.

Boyer, Paul. *By the Bomb's Early Light: American Thought and Culture at the Dawn of the Atomic Age.* New York: Pantheon Books, 1985.

Byars, Jackie. *All That Hollywood Allows: Re-Reading Gender in 1950s Melodrama.* Chapel Hill: University of North Carolina Press, 1991.

Carpenter, Frederic. "The Adolescent in American Fiction." In *Salinger's "Catcher in the Rye": Clamor vs. Criticism.* Ed. Harold P. Simonson and Philip E. Hager. Boston: D. C. Heath, 1963. 92–93.

Cook, Fred J. *The Nightmare Decade: The Life and Times of Senator Joe McCarthy.* New York: Random House, 1971.

Davis, Kenneth C. *Two-Bit Culture: The Paperbacking of America.* Boston: Houghton Mifflin, 1984.

Fiedler, Leslie. *An End to Innocence.* New York: Stein and Day, 1971.

———. *Love and Death in the American Novel.* New York: Stein and Day, 1966.

————. *The Return of the Vanishing American*. New York: Stein and Day, 1969.

————. "Up from Adolescence." In *Salinger: A Critical and Personal Portrait*. Ed. Henry Anatole Grunwald. New York: Giant Cardinal, 1963. 62–68.

Gilbert, James. *A Cycle of Outrage: America's Reaction to the Juvenile Delinquent in the 1950s*. New York: Oxford University Press, 1986.

Grunwald, Henry Anatole. Introduction. *Salinger: A Critical and Personal Portrait*. Ed. Henry Anatole Grunwald. New York: Giant Cardinal, 1963. ix–xxxiii.

————. "The Invisible Man: A Biographical Collage." In *Salinger: A Critical and Personal Portrait*. Ed. Henry Anatole Grunwald. New York: Giant Cardinal, 1963. 1–23.

Gutwillig, Robert. "Everybody's Caught *The Catcher in the Rye*." In *Studies in J. D. Salinger: Reviews, Essays, and Critiques of the Catcher in the Rye and Other Fiction*. Ed. Marvin Laser and Norman Fruman. New York: Odyssey Press, 1963. 1–5.

Hassan, Ihab. "J.D. Salinger: Rare Quixotic Gesture." In *Salinger: A Critical and Personal Portrait*. Ed. Henry Anatole Grunwald. New York: Giant Cardinal, 1963. 150–79.

————. *Radical Innocence: The Contemporary American Novel*. Princeton: Princeton University Press, 1961.

Heiserman, Arthur, and James E. Miller Jr. "J.D. Salinger: Some Crazy Cliff." In *Salinger's "Catcher in the Rye": Clamor vs. Criticism*. Ed. Harold P. Simonson and Philip E. Hager. Boston: D. C. Heath, 1963. 74–80.

Hicks, Granville. "J.D. Salinger: Search for Wisdom." In *Salinger's "Catcher in the Rye": Clamor vs. Criticism*. Ed. Harold P. Simonson and Philip E. Hager. Boston: D. C. Heath, 1963. 109.

Higham, John. "The Cult of the 'American Consensus': Homogenizing Our History." *Commentary* 27.2 (Feb. 1959): 93–100.

Jezer, Marty. *The Dark Ages: Life in the United States, 1945–1960*. Boston: South End Press, 1982.

Kaplan, Charles. "Holden and Huck: The Odysseys of Youth." In *If You Really Want to Know: A Catcher Casebook*. Ed. Malcolm S. Marsden. Chicago: Scott, Foresman, 1963. 127–32.

Laclau, Ernest, and Chantal Mouffe. *Hegemony and Socialist Strategy: Towards a Radical Democratic Politics*. New York: Verso Press, 1989.

Lears, Jackson. "A Matter of Taste: Corporate Cultural Hegemony in a Mass-Consumption Society." In *Recasting America: Culture and Politics in the Age of Cold War*. Ed. Lary May. Chicago: University of Chicago Press, 1989. 38–57.

Leitch, David. "The Salinger Myth." *Twentieth Century* 168 (Nov. 1960): 428–35.

Lewis, R. W. B. *The American Adam: Innocence, Tragedy, and Tradition in the Nine-teenth Century*. Chicago: University of Chicago Press, 1955.

Macdonald, Dwight. "A Theory of Mass Culture." In *Mass Culture: The Popular Arts in America*. Ed. Bernard Rosenberg and David Manning White. New York: Free Press, 1957. 59–73.

May, Elaine Tyler. *Homeward Bound: American Families in the Cold War Era*. New York: Basic Books, 1987.

May, Lary. Introduction. *Recasting America: Culture and Politics in the Age of Cold War*. Ed. Lary May. Chicago: University of Chicago Press, 1989. 1–13.

Nadel, Alan. "Rhetoric, Sanity, and the Cold War: The Significance of Holden Caulfield's Testimony." *Centennial Review* 32.4 (Fall 1988): 351–71.

Oakley, Ronald J. *God's Country: America in the Fifties*. New York: Dembner Books, 1990.

Ohmann, Carol, and Richard Ohmann. "Reviewers, Critics, and *The Catcher in the Rye*." *Critical Inquiry* 3.1 (Fall 1976): 15–37.

"Our Country and Our Culture: A Symposium." Part 1. *Partisan Review* 19.3 (May–June 1952): 282–326.

Pease, Donald. "New Americanists: Revisionist Interventions into the Canon." *Boundary 2*, no. 17 (1990): 1–37.

———. *Visionary Compacts: American Renaissance Writings in Cultural Context*. Madison: University of Wisconsin Press, 1987.

Pells, Richard H. *The Liberal Mind in a Conservative Age: American Intellectuals in the 1940s and 1950s*. New York: Harper and Row, 1985.

Radway, Janice. "Mail-Order Culture and Its Critics: The Book-of-the-Month Club, Commodification and Consumption, and the Problem of Cultural Authority." In *Cultural Studies*. Ed. Lawrence Grossberg, Cary Nelson, and Paula Treichler. New York: Routledge, 1992. 512–30.

———. *Reading the Romance: Women, Patriarchy, and Popular Literature*. 2d ed. Chapel Hill: University of North Carolina Press, 1991.

Reising, Russell. *The Unusable Past: Theory and the Study of American Literature*. New York: Methuen, 1986.

Rosenberg, Bernard. "Mass Culture in America." In *Mass Culture: The Popular Arts in America*. Ed. Bernard Rosenberg and David Manning White. New York: Free Press, 1957. 3–12.

Ross, Andrew. "Containing Culture in the Cold War." *No Respect: Intellectuals and Popular Culture*. New York: Routledge, 1989. 42–64.

Salinger, J. D. *The Catcher in the Rye*. New York: Bantam Books, 1964.

Schaub, Thomas Hill. *American Fiction in the Cold War*. Madison: University of Wisconsin Press, 1991.

Steiner, George. "The Salinger Industry." In *If You Really Want to Know: A Catcher Casebook*. Ed. Malcolm S. Marsden. Chicago: Scott, Foresman, 1963. 62–66

Swados, Harvey. "Must Writers Be Characters?" In *Salinger's "Catcher in the Rye": Clamor vs. Criticism*. Ed. Harold P. Simonson and Philip E. Hager. Boston: D. C. Heath, 1963. 464–65.

Trilling, Lionel. *The Liberal Imagination: Essays on Literature and Society*. Garden City, N.Y.: Doubleday-Anchor, 1953.

Veblen, Thorstein. *The Theory of the Leisure Class*. New York: Mentor, 1953.

Wakefield, Dan. "Salinger and the Search for Love." In *If You Really Want to Know: A Catcher Casebook*. Ed. Malcolm S. Marsden. Chicago: Scott, Foresman, 1963. 193–210.

White, David Manning. "Mass Culture in America: Another Point of View." In *Mass Culture: The Popular Arts in America*. Ed. Bernard Rosenberg and David Manning White. New York: Free Press, 1957. 13–21.

Zizek, Slavoj. *The Sublime Object of Ideology*. New York: Verso Press, 1989.

Stacey Olster ▬

Eleven

SOMETHING OLD, SOMETHING NEW, SOMETHING BORROWED, SOMETHING (RED, WHITE, AND) BLUE
Ayn Rand's *Atlas Shrugged* and
Objectivist Ideology

I can't explain what it feels like, I can't catch hold of it— and that's part of the terror," says Cherryl Brooks in *Atlas Shrugged* when trying to describe to her sister-in-law the fear that makes her feel she has "no place to run." Searching desperately for words adequate to her needs, she continues: "It's as if the whole world were suddenly destroyed, but not by an explosion—an explosion is something hard and solid—but destroyed by . . . by some horrible kind of softening . . . and that would be the end of the world, not fire and brim-

Ayn Rand, 1948.
(Used by permission)

stone, but goo" (826). Neither a pretty prospect nor one portrayed with especial eloquence, the threat finally drives its speaker to run into a river to drown herself. Yet articulating its horrors before her death turns an otherwise minor character, a dime store salesgirl among industrialist gods and goddesses, into a spokesperson for the underlying sense of anomie that inspired Ayn Rand's 1957 novel. And describing those horrors in terms almost identical to those employed by more memorable figures of the decade turns Rand herself into more than an idiosyncratic *Isolato* upsetting celebrations of consensus with a solitary jeremiad on the country's ills. Renouncing a world that might end with a whimper instead of a bang hardly liberates Cherryl in the way that recognizing "that spiral business" as "that progress goo" does for the invisible man when he rejects both communist historicism and Christian millennialism in Ralph Ellison's novel (509). The "No" that serves as her final shriek does not reverberate nearly as thunderously as Leslie Fiedler's own battle cry for the decade. But portraying cultural anomie as a consequence of ideological stalemate does align Rand with authors at all points on America's political spectrum as commentators on the same cultural phenomenon.

According to Rand, who defined culture as "a complex battlefield of different ideas and influences," America in the fifties simply had no culture, just a "grotesque spectacle of such attributes as militant uncertainty, crusading cynicism, dogmatic agnosticism, boastful self-abasement and self-righteous depravity" (*Philosophy* 251, 72). In particular, America in the fifties had no political ideas capable of constituting a culture, what with conservatism and liberalism so indistinguishable their terms "could be stretched to mean all things to all men" (*Capitalism* 178). And believing that a "majority without an ideology is a helpless mob, to be taken over by anyone" (*Capitalism* 138), Rand saw America of this period in a position of extreme peril, rapidly succumbing to collectivism and primed for all those political corollaries she grouped under the heading of statism.

With the Objectivist movement she championed, Rand sought to fill that ideological void. "We are *radicals for capitalism*," she wrote in a piece entitled, appropriately enough, "Call Your Issues" (1). Yet feeling that capitalism "never had a philosophical base" and presuming that "America has never had an *original* culture" with which to portray the country's "profound difference from all other countries in history," she set out to provide those missing foundations in her novels (*Capitalism* 30; *Philosophy* 256). In *Atlas Shrugged*, the work intended as the culmination of a lifetime's efforts, she defined that uniqueness concretely: "To the glory of mankind, there was, for the first and only time in history, a *country of money*. . . . For the first time, . . . there appeared the real maker of wealth, the greatest worker, the highest type of human being—the self-made man—the American industrialist" (391).

As Richard Pells has pointed out, such searches for the source of America's uniqueness and the uniqueness of the national character formed very much a part of fifties discourse, particularly after the failure of leftist politics abroad kept intellectuals scrambling to differentiate between the United States and Europe, thereby "'proving' that the history of America had always been a conspicuous exception to the Marxist prophecy" (181). Unfortunately for Rand, representing those distinguishing traits in fiction exposed the fault line of an ideological alternative that, in theory, was meant to supply America with "the only social system based on the recognition of individual rights and, therefore, the only system that bans force from social relationships" (*Capitalism* 38). Nowhere is the fissure in that fault line more clearly illustrated than in the treatment of sexual relationships that permeates *Atlas Shrugged*. Evidenced by scenes in which conquest of superior women by superior men is presented as a form of commodities acquisition and in which feminine submission is predicated upon sexual submissiveness, Rand's depiction of sexuality reveals the laissez-faire capitalism she championed to be grounded in the same use of brute force she abhorred. When viewed with respect to the productive work she posited as the basis of her ideal society, the contrast between Rand's economic theories and her gender politics reveals that the productive work she prescribed for each individual was limited to certain individual types. When extrapolated beyond the personal, it shows the industrial American society she hailed as providing deliverance to be all too similar to those European dictatorships she despised for having ended in enslavement. "Who is John Galt?" goes the novel's most famous refrain. Just your average industrialist *Übermensch*.

AMERICA'S MORAL CRISIS: THE TOPICALITY OF *ATLAS SHRUGGED*

Rand was not the only one in the fifties who discerned extreme anxiety underlying the era that Henry Luce saw ushering in the American Century. Just how widespread the sentiments she attributed to her shopgirl were can be seen when looking at the remarks of those intellectuals who comprised the very different audience that responded to *Partisan Review*'s 1952 symposium "Our Country and Our Culture." United in finding "little direct criticism of society in current writing, but no enthusiasm either," as one writer stated (578), respondents refuted, almost to a person, the patriotic contentions about a shift from alienation to celebration that formed the editors' opening statement. Equally united in seeing intellectuals "adjusting themselves to circumstances [rather] than really affirming any point of view" (439), respondents also agreed that even that adjustment should be construed as "largely a product of the will, a forced march of intellect" (579). If many did cite the demise of the communist ideal and subsequent threat of the Soviet Union as the particular political circumstances from which much of that reconciliation stemmed, they embraced the alternative America seemed to offer only to the degree that any lesser evil could be advocated ("Between the inadequate democracy of the capitalist world and the total repression of the Stalinist world there is the difference between life, however afflicted, and death" [577], "What has happened is not that American culture has become better in that time, but the world much worse" [291]). And if any indicated what political belief had been substituted for the one renounced, they identified the affiliation, more often than not, by negation ("anticommunist," "anti-Stalinist"), recognizing full well the limited degree of support that any stance so defined could command. William Phillips thus understood that making anti-Stalinism "the sole content of one's thinking, that is, an end in itself," was "simply another way of losing one's identity, for even alliances on the grounds of expediency cannot be substituted for one's own ideas or feelings" (589). Philip Rahv went even further in condemning those ex-Marxists who returned to the fold as "trying to turn anti-Stalinism into something which it can never be: a total outlook on life, no less, or even a philosophy of history" (307).

In conceiving of ideology as an all-encompassing philosophical system that embraced more than just political and social structures, Rahv's remarks suggest the limitations of designating this period in America, as Daniel Bell did, a mere "end of ideology," for the "exhaustion of political ideas in the fifties" that the subtitle of Bell's 1960 book cites is inadequate to describe "the desperate makeshift of our time," as Mark Schorer put it (317), that those living through the period experienced. It was not until Delmore Schwartz's response appeared in the third issue devoted to the symposium that the degree of desperation underlying so many of the earlier remarks became fully exposed. "It is in the light of this darkness that the will to conformism, which is now the chief prevailing fashion among intellectuals, reveals its true nature," Schwartz wrote in a concluding entry that could not have been more effectively placed had it been the work of a major dramatist. "It is a flight from the flux, chaos and uncertainty of the present, a forced and false affirmation of stability in the face of immense and continually mounting instability" (594). Having thus pierced through the mood of emotional impasse that characterized "Our Country and Our Culture" earlier, he transformed the fifties from a decade of complacency into a period of reconceptualization: "The more we reflect upon the changes of past and present, the clearer it becomes that the present, whatever else it may be, is essentially an intermediate period, a period of both *after* and *before,* a time of waiting in darkness before what may be a new beginning and morning, or a catastrophic degradation of civilization" (594).

Such a period of intermediacy, in fact, constitutes the entire temporal setting of Rand's novel in which the men (mainly) and women of ability withdraw themselves from the world of everyday affairs to a Rocky Mountain Shangri-la, there to await the destruction of the United States that its current practices make inevitable. John Galt, the charismatic leader who spirits them away from businesses on the brink of failure, opts for such removal long before the action of the novel commences, when he refuses to surrender control of a motor he has invented to his employer and literally quits the Twentieth Century, as the factory for which he has worked is named. The drama to which the majority of the novel is devoted is the growing realization of its other heroic industrialists (oil oligarch Ellis Wyatt, copper king Francisco d'Anconia, metal magnate Hank Rearden, and, most of all, railroad vice president Dagny Taggart) that a society driven by altruistic need and a country run by middle managers and influence peddlers cannot be redeemed by individual effort but only rejected, that, in short, a country veering toward financial bankruptcy is also veering toward moral bankruptcy. Dagny, the one woman in the group and the character conceived by Rand as herself "with any possible flaws eliminated" (B. Branden 225), arrives at this conclusion through romances with the three most impressive industrialist men.

In choosing withdrawal rather than engagement as their response, Rand's characters select a path that was hardly unique in the postwar period. In withholding the products of their minds from society and adhering to a

"moratorium on brains" (531), they virtually duplicate the stance of "nega-
tivism" that Dwight Macdonald proposed when commending those British
and American scientists who refused to work on the atom bomb for fear of
the destructive purposes to which generals and politicians might put the
product of their efforts (*Memoirs* 179). Likewise, in opting for physical removal as a means of ensuring their nonparticipation, they chose a mode of
action quite popular among protagonists struggling to define an ideological
stance for themselves during the postwar period: Saul Bellow's dangling man
retires to a room (1944), Norman Mailer's Barbary Shore occupants retreat to
a boarding house (1951), Ralph Ellison's invisible man jumps down a man-
hole (1952), and Joseph Heller's Yossarian tries to circumvent catch-22 by
rowing to Sweden, a country socialist in a way that the Soviet Union is not
(1961).

The distinctiveness of the choice made by Rand's characters, however,
stems from the circumstances that inspire the withdrawal they undertake.
Unlike those coeval characters created by former leftists, whose flights orig-
inate in reaction against political violations of human rights (as exemplified
by a hypnotist's act at a party of comrades for Bellow, the Nazi-Soviet Pact
for Mailer, the Brotherhood for Ellison, and the U.S. military for Heller),
Rand's refugees flee political infringements of economic rights. Only when
their businesses are about to fall under government control do Rand's industrialists vanish, thus avoiding that final surrendering that is prefigured in the
book by a steady stream of regulatory legislation (Anti-dog-eat-dog Rule,
Equalization of Opportunity Bill, Preservation of Livelihood Law, Fair Share
Law, Public Stability Law) meant to limit ownership of the means of production, abolish private trademarks, and regularize both the output of all competitors and the purchasing of all consumers.

In fact, for all the book's mention of foreign nations becoming socialized
People's States one by one—first Mexico, then Norway, France, England,
Portugal, and Turkey, finally Argentina and Chile—rarely does Rand depict
the abrogation of civil liberties she repeatedly emphasized in her public ha-
rangues against statism. ("Try to imagine what it is like if you are in constant
terror from morning till night and at night you are waiting for the doorbell
to ring, where you are afraid of anything and everybody, living in a country
where human life is nothing, less than nothing, and you know it," she charged
the House Un-American Activities Committee in 1947 ["Testimony" 90].)

Rather, changes of political systems gain significance only to the extent that changes in governing structures affect industrial structures (as occurs with the nationalization of the railroads and public ownership of the mines in Mexico). It is not until the very end of the novel that the human consequences in which such economic practices can end are fully realized. Even then, the realization is portrayed only indirectly, personified in the figure of Cuffy Meigs, the Washington representative in charge of standardizing the country's cardiovascular system of railroads, who, in military tunic and leather leggings, goosesteps his way to a coup d'état capital (imaginatively dubbed "Meigsville"), an appropriation of property he justifies by patting the gun slung at his hip.

THE AMERICAN POLITICAL TRADITION: MONEY IS THE ROOT OF ALL GOODNESS

When it came to pointing the finger of blame for such deplorable conditions, Rand was careful to distance herself from all political movements of her time, not just the fascism, socialism, and communism she considered different from each other only in degree (the difference between communism and socialism being, in her view, the difference between murder and suicide). Having defined democracy with respect to "unlimited majority rule," she included democracy as another form of collectivism that denied individual rights (*Lexicon* 121). Similarly, despite the friendly testimony she provided the House Un-American Activities Committee and her outrage that later defamation of the term "McCarthyism" prevented further investigations into communist penetration from being undertaken (*Capitalism* 176), she declared herself not to be an admirer of the Wisconsin senator, found most of the committee members "intellectually out of their depth, and motivated by a desire for headlines," and finally granted the hearings on the movie industry at which she appeared to have been a "very dubious undertaking" (B. Branden 201, 202).

Her strongest condemnation she reserved for those conservatives with whom she had grown steadily disaffected since her campaigning for Wendell Willkie in 1940 and whose name in print she typically surrounded with quotation marks. Lambasting them in particular for failing to admit that "the *American* way of life" they championed *was* capitalism, offended by the infringement of individual rights she saw their favoring censorship and military conscription illustrating, she condemned them as "futile, impotent, and, culturally, dead," as the title of her piece "Conservatism: An Obituary" indicates (*Capitalism* 194). As imaginative compensation, she offered the figure of John Galt, whose resuscitating promises of economic renewal she portrayed as offering nothing less than national regeneration. "We will open the gates of our city to those who deserve to enter," proclaims the messianic leader when describing the society that those who emerge from self-imposed exile will eventually initiate. "With the sign of the dollar as our symbol—the sign of free trade and free minds—we will move to reclaim the country once more from the impotent savages who never discovered its nature, its meaning, its splendor" (991–92).

Likened, in alphabetical order, to Atlas, Moses, and Prometheus specifically and resembling all Greek gods generically, alternately rumored to have discovered both Atlantis and the fountain of youth, Galt is perhaps the most overdetermined character in history. He also is the American Adam par excellence, "self-made in every sense, out of nowhere, penniless, parentless, tie-less" (731), so overendowed with Americanist resonance as to cross gender lines when depicted carrying his laborer's lantern like the Statue of Liberty (893). Fittingly, the reclamation he heralds is presented as a supreme act of patriotism—with all echoes to persons living or dead fully intended. "A country's political system is based on its code of morality. We will rebuild America's system on the moral premise which had been its foundation, . . . the premise that man is an end in himself, not the means to the ends of others, that man's life, his freedom, his happiness are *his* by inalienable right" (985). The questions that remain to be considered, though, are just how "inalienable" those individual rights attributed to America's political system were and just what practical consequences derived from presuming the country's moral supremacy to rest upon their foundation. For that it is necessary to turn to Rand's rereading of America's origins as justifying the country's supremacy among nations.

Rand had few doubts about the supremacy of the American system she chose to have Galt rebuild, a certainty that, at least in part, is attributable to the fact that the lives of Objectivism's two chief proponents of the fifties presented almost stereotypical scenarios of American success: the Russian Alice Rosenbaum arrives in New York's harbor with a typewriter and a new name and lives to do the lecture circuit wearing a gold brooch in the shape of a dollar sign as her emblem; the Canadian Nathan Blumenthal rechristens himself Nathaniel Branden (much like an earlier Nathan [Weinstein] who emerged as Nathanael West), founds an institute to bear his name, and within seven years is offering lecture courses in over eighty cities, not to mention one on board a Polaris submarine in the mid-Atlantic. Nor did Rand have any doubts about just what role in the reconstruction of the country's political system she should assign herself. Viewing the political philosophy of the country as "buried under decades of statist misrepresentations on one side and empty lip-service on the other," she deemed it her mission to rescue America's political tradition from "the shameful barnacles now hiding it" and returned to the revolutionary period to facilitate her task of salvage (*Lexicon* 172).

Yet far from being alone in her return to the past to rediscover America's virtues, Rand typified the approach of many during the fifties who, as evidenced by scholars such as Daniel Boorstin, Perry Miller, and David Potter, returned to the past to chart a history of ongoing tradition and harmony in place of that history of conflict and division that was bequeathed to them by immediate predecessors such as Turner and Beard (Pells 148–49). Equally representative was Rand in emphasizing uniqueness as well as continuity when returning to the revolutionary period to revive the nation's inceptive principles ("the United States of America is the greatest, the noblest and, in its original founding principles, the *only* moral country in the history of the world" [*Philosophy* 12], "the only country in history born, not of chance and blind tribal warfare, but as a rational product of man's mind" [717]), particularly as the principles of its founders distinguished the country from older nations in Europe. As indicated by the list of works published in the fifties that Richard Pells includes in his own work (Henry Nash Smith's *The Virgin Land* [1950], Perry Miller's second volume of *The New England Mind* [1954], R. W. B. Lewis's *The American Adam* [1955], John William Ward's *Andrew Jackson: Symbol for an Age* [1955], Marvin Meyer's *The Jacksonian Persuasion* [1957]), investigations into the qualities that defined the nation's character were quite prominent during this time, especially among those in the growing American Studies movement (149–50).

To the well-known adages concerning the origins of life, liberty, and the pursuit of happiness in the eighteenth-century period she favored for her investigative return, however, Rand added a few contributions of her own. "If you ask me to name the proudest distinction of Americans, I would choose—because it contains all the others—the fact that they were the people who created the phrase 'to *make* money'" (391), says *Atlas Shrugged's* copper king, Francisco Domingo Carlos Andres Sebastián d'Anconia, in the book's famous "Money Is the Root of All Evil" speech. Rand later elaborates on the point after one of the employees that Dagny Taggart has lost to Galt's withdrawal explains to her the origin of the dollar sign in the initials of the United States. "It was the only country in history where wealth was not acquired by looting, but by production, not by force, but by trade," Owen Kellogg informs the vice president of Taggart Transcontinental. "The only country whose money was the symbol of man's right to his own mind, to his work, to his life, to his happiness, to himself" (637). Having thus employed a rhetoric of distinction to establish the country's greatness, Kellogg invokes a similar mode of discourse to define its present ignominy: "The United States is the only country in history that has ever used its own monogram as a symbol of depravity" (637).

Speaking in strict historical terms, Rand's assumption was wrong—the American dollar sign was taken from the Spanish milled dollar. Speaking in sociological terms, however, her presumption very accurately reflected her own time in that its "recharg[ing] tradition for its own uses," to quote W. T. Lhamon Jr., typified the kind of "collective kinking" of cultural forms that defined the "oppositional culture" Lhamon has found prevailing during the decade (29, 28). Indeed, viewed within the Americanist context in which so many during the fifties were working, the seemingly hair-brained monologues about money even *gain* a certain validity, especially when the word "money" is replaced by its eighteenth-century analogue "property," for it was the preservation of property that lay at the heart of the political theory adopted (and adapted) by the country's founders.

Rand admitted the development of that political theory to have been a long struggle that preceded the actual formation of the United States, "stretching from Aristotle to John Locke to the Founding Fathers" (*Capitalism* 138), Locke's contribution in particular being a view of property ownership that defined property with respect to labor instead of land. Consistent with such a preference for manufacture over nature, none of the heroic industrialists who parades through *Atlas Shrugged* has much appreciation for unblemished landscapes—the rolling curves of Wisconsin's hills make Hank Rearden wish for a billboard (266). All, in fact, make their names by vanquishing nature, extracting raw materials from the environment in order to found their industrial empires: oil in the case of Ellis Wyatt, ore for Francisco d'Anconia and Hank Rearden, and, most astoundingly, static energy from the atmosphere to be converted into kinetic power by John Galt. The one exception, Dagny's grandfather Nat Taggart, immortalized in a statue in the terminal that bears his name and exemplifying for Rand the industrialist at his nineteenth-century pinnacle, does not make his fortune from the ground but gains it by razing the earth in order to build a transcontinental railroad.

According to Louis Hartz, whose *Liberal Tradition in America* provided "An Interpretation of American Political Thought since the Revolution," as the subtitle of his 1955 work makes clear, Locke's domination of American political thought "as no thinker anywhere dominates the political thought of a nation" constituted "a massive national cliché" (140); because such a narrow intellectual "tyranny" proved especially ineffectual in the fifties when exported to compete with the challenge of communism abroad, what was needed, in Hartz's view, was "nothing less than a new level of consciousness, a transcending of irrational Lockianism, in which an understanding of self and an understanding of others go hand in hand" (8, 308). Rand, in contrast, only expanded Locke's purview and redefined each industrialist's right to accrue wealth as a natural right of every man: "Just as man can't exist without his body, so no rights can exist without the right to translate one's right into reality . . . which means: the right to property" (986).

Nowhere is the latitude Rand gave that redefined right more apparent than in her invocation of the Declaration of Independence's right to pursue happiness (the word Jefferson substituted for Locke's "property") as a sanction for rampant individualism. In *The Fountainhead*'s climactic courtroom scene, for instance, Howard Roark specifically targets "man's right to the pursuit of happiness" as *the* basis upon which America was founded when defending his demolition of a public housing project—both for the Keynesian welfare state it symbolized and the taint that conforming to its structural dictates would have left on his architectural talents (684). In *Atlas Shrugged*, the characters justify both personal and professional aggrandizement upon the same basis, as befits that work intended to be a more "social" novel than its predecessor, in which, as Rand's preparatory notes indicate, "the personal is necessary only to the extent needed to make the [social] relationships clear" (ii).

Hank Rearden thus recognizes "happiness" as "the greatest agent of purification" early in the book (38); he just cannot use it to sanction his extramarital affair with Dagny Taggart ("I hid my happiness as a shameful secret" [529]). Only after he hears Dagny announce (over the radio no less) having been his mistress with the simple statement, "I wanted him, I had him, I was happy" (792), can he accept, in personal terms, his pursuit of happiness with her as an inalienable right. Moreover, justifying personal dealings with Dagny as a pursuit of happiness enables Rearden to justify professional dealings with her with respect to the same sanction. Like Dagny's earlier relationship with Francisco d'Anconia, which her own mother considers "an international industrial cartel" instead of a romance (101), the affair with Rearden is more merger than marriage: it is his new metal that enables her to build the tracks for the John Galt Line that saves her railroad from bankruptcy at the beginning of the book; the forced closing of the line later impels his wife to rush to Dagny and gloat over "what was, in effect, the funeral of your child by my husband" (495).

With the justification of the personal relationship as a pursuit of happiness reverberating doubly in this manner, it takes little imagination to see Rand's rationale eventuating in the code of self-interest that those industrialists who secede from the world take as their creed: "I swear by my life and my love of it that I will never live for the sake of another man, nor ask another man to live for mine" (680). Even less does it take to figure out the very limited form of government that those who subscribe to such a code and seek to protect the products of their labor would find tolerable. Locke confined its legislative powers to "never hav[ing] a Power to take to themselves the whole or any part of the Subjects *Property,* without their own consent" (407). Rand went even further and restricted its function to one legitimate purpose: "to protect man's rights, which means: to protect him from physical violence" (987).

ROMANTIC REALISM: PROPERTY, POWER, AND (SEXUAL) POSSESSION

In theory, of course, any person was entitled to such protection, just as, in theory, any person was entitled to pursue wealth. In fact, however, the operative word for Rand was "man's," a possessive that, in *Atlas Shrugged,* signals all sorts of subjects for possession in addition to Locke's property. To the extent that "man's rights" reflects Rand's belief that the "essence of femininity" was "hero-worship—the desire to look up to man," not for any special virtue any singular man may possess, but for the *metaphysical* concept of masculinity" that, no doubt, came attached to a Y chromosome (*Lexicon* 166), the phrase signifies more than a convention of grammar used to delineate that which belongs to humankind in general. It indicates quite clearly the unequal power dynamic that Rand ascribed to relations between men and women. Yet to the extent that Rand's adherence to the tenets of "Romantic Realism," as she termed her aesthetics, subordinated individualized characterization to "*concretized abstraction[s]*" of moral ideals (*Romantic* 142), the unequal power dynamic that constituted Rand's delineation of appropriate gender roles also provides a revealing look at Rand's true feelings about power itself. The result in *Atlas Shrugged* is a sanctioning of physical violence that shifts according to the gender of the doer and the nature of the deed being performed.

The most revealing evidence of that selective sanctioning is provided by Rand's portraits of sexual possession, all of which are presented as acts of physical combat between men and women, with women forced into positions of subservience and loving every minute of it. D'Anconia slaps Dagny, and she feels pleasure from both the pain in her cheek and the taste of blood in the corner of her mouth (100); d'Anconia grabs Dagny, and she knows "that he left nothing possible to her except the thing she wanted most—to submit" (107). Rearden jerks her head back and plants his lips on hers "as if he were inflicting a wound," throws her inside his room to let her know "he needed no sign of consent or resistance" (as indeed he does not, since Dagny realizes she is "only a tool for the satisfaction of his desire"), and leaves her bruised "after hours of a violence which they could not name" in which "she had been ready to accept anything he had wished to do" (240, 241). By the time it comes for her to submit to Galt, the man for whom all Dagny's earlier encounters have been practice runs and who, true to Randian form, throws her onto a pile of burlap sandbags in order to have his way, it is no wonder that Dagny feels herself reduced to "not a person any longer, only a sensation" (888). After all the previous Olympic trials through which Rand has put her, what new words of self-abnegation can possibly remain?

As anyone acquainted with *The Fountainhead* will recognize, the violence of physical passion is familiar Rand territory—sex with Howard Roark entails pinned wrists, purple bruises, and clenched teeth for Dominique Francon, which this self-described "utterly frigid woman" accepts in order to experience "the kind of rapture she had wanted" (181, 218). (To those who protested the act as rape, Rand's rejoinder was to call it rape by engraved invitation. To those who read Ferdinand Lundberg and Marynia Farnham's treatise *Modern Woman: The Lost Sex* in the fifties, it would have confirmed the authors' "psychosocial rule" that "the more educated a woman is, the greater chance there is of sexual disorder, more or less severe" [qtd. in Halberstam 590].) And certainly, Dagny's being put in her proverbial place enables Rand to extricate herself from the violations of gender roles with which a fifties heroine endowed with much too angular a physique and too many professional skills (running a railroad, flying a plane) leaves her. It is, after all, not just the villains in the book who see Dagny as "a symptom of the illness of our century . . . a woman who runs a railroad, instead of practicing the beautiful craft of the handloom and bearing children" (135). Eddie Willers, her right-hand man, cannot think of her as a woman or even imagine anyone else having the audacity to do so (609), and Dagny reinforces such a view by introducing herself as the man in the Taggart family to her new sister-in-law (374).

Because of the analogical rhetoric adopted throughout *Atlas Shrugged*, however, the violence of sexuality has ramifications that extend beyond issues of appropriate social roles. "A man's sexual choice is the result and the sum of his fundamental convictions," d'Anconia tells Rearden. "Tell me what a man finds sexually attractive and I will tell you his entire philosophy of life" (460). In Rearden's case, this kind of deduction proves extremely easy to ascertain. What Rearden finds attractive, specifically, is a "railroad executive who was a woman he owned," whom he looks at "with the glance of a property appraisal" (266), and who, in turn, conceives of their sexual coupling as giving him a "safer hold" on her "than on any other property you own" and grants him permission to "dispose of me as you please" (244).

Dagny, moreover, is not just any piece of property, but a luxury item. "I'd give up anything I've ever had in my life, except my being a . . . luxury object of your amusement," she tells Rearden, who has just draped over her shoulders a blue fox cape (352). To Galt, quite simply, she is a "symbol of luxury" (724). And luxury items were precisely what characterized the American feeding frenzy of the fifties that Walt Rostow called the stage of "high mass consumption" (Chafe 112), in which purchasing power was portrayed as a question of mind over matter (or, more to the point, money). Poverty, according to Henry Luce, was simply the "habit of thinking poorly";

businessmen were told to convince the buyer that "'the hedonistic approach to his life is a moral, not an immoral one'"; and Ben Franklin was resurrected by advertisers who quoted him as having endorsed spending as each citizen's contribution to the health of the nation's economy: "'Is not the hope of being one day able to purchase and enjoy luxuries a great spur to labor and industry?'" (qtd. in Miller and Nowak 118, 119).

In Rand's view, luxury spending was the logical consequence of living in a country distinguished from other nations by its commitment to making money. In the 1947 testimony about the movie industry that she provided Congress, for example, outrage at *Song of Russia*'s portrait of a Russia without human terror is matched by outrage at its portrait of a Russia saturated with consumer goods and oozing affluence: "big, prosperous-looking, clean buildings" and "clean and prosperous-looking" streets; satin skirts, crystal chandeliers, privately owned radios, and long-distance telephones; a restaurant "with a menu such as never existed in Russia at all" and a "luxurious dance" in a ballroom that is "an exaggeration even for this country" ("Testimony" 83–84, 85–86). In *Atlas Shrugged*, significantly, the moment Galt views Dagny as a "symbol of luxury" is the same moment he wants to immortalize her "short hair and the imperious profile of an American woman" in a statue dedicated to "the meaning of an American railroad" (724).

Yet Rand never recognized the human consequences that portraying physical want as commodities acquisition in literature could come to signify. When Dagny gets her wish and is disposed of as nearly every heroic male in the book pleases, she functions—much like the gold standard—as a medium of exchange among them, each of whom, with exemplary grace, cedes her to the other in a paradigm of free trade practices. "Take it," d'Anconia says to Galt when toasting the union of his friend and his former lover. "You've earned it" (753). But if her initial possession and subsequent maintenance are achieved through acts of violence, and if property rights and human rights were viewed by Rand as inextricable, then we are dealing with more than Rand's abstract theories of femininity being a function of male hero-worship and more than fifties questions of whether women should stay in the house or go to work. We are dealing with the abridgement of those human rights that Rand found distinguishing America's founding principles.

Dagny is not just reduced to being a suburban housewife, checking shirts for missing buttons and getting food on the table in time for dinner, when she stays in Galt's house while recuperating from injuries sustained in flying her plane into his Rocky Mountains retreat uninvited. She is turned into his servant—willingly opting to address him as "sir" and lowering her eyes at the appropriate moment when receiving a five-dollar advance on her wages (707). With Rearden, who tosses jewels at her instead of coins, she simply becomes a slave, as is illustrated after Rearden's private possession of Dagny gives him the license to make public claim of his property. He tells her to wear the particular piece of jewelry that gives a woman "the most feminine of all aspects: the look of being chained" (133), a bracelet made from Rearden Metal that even his indolent wife perceives as "the chain by which he holds us all in bondage" (48). Dagny, in turn, accepts her new agent of subjugation accordingly: "In the moment when the clasp clicked shut under his fingers, she bent her head down to them and kissed his hand" (266).

For individualized characters to turn physical want into commodities acquisition is bad enough—much the same occurs in *The Fountainhead* to Dominique Francon, who literally is exchanged by one of her (three) husbands for an architectural building contract. But when enacted by characters conceived as exemplary moral abstractions, in a novel intended to demonstrate the superiority of America's principles over those of Europe's statist nations, severe contradictions result. When the policies of Rand's American redeemers end in practices indistinguishable from those totalitarian ones she had been excoriating for years, the distinction between the one country whose economic and political system allegedly did not involve coercion or conquest and all those statist countries whose did is proven to be completely bogus. When the redemption of the world is at stake, even Dagny, who "would have hesitated to fire at an animal," has no difficulty pumping a bullet into the heart of a guard who denies her access to the room in which Galt is being held prisoner (1066).

Recognizing that the "aristocracy of talents" that Rand proposed just masked her desire for a dictatorship in the making, Whittaker Chambers entitled his review of her book "Big Sister Is Watching You" and ended with a chilling summation: "From almost any page of *Atlas Shrugged,* a voice can be heard, from painful necessity, commanding: 'To a gas chamber—go!'" (596). What he failed to recognize was how much Rand's yearnings reflected nativist rather than foreign influences, specifically, how much her desire for some kind of empowered elite aligned her with those eighteenth-century

Founding Fathers she loved to invoke, all of whom believed in some form of governing aristocracy as a stabilizing force in society, one that would prevent it from being torn apart by the fractious mob. As *The Fountainhead*'s references to "the mob" and "the crowd," "the taste of the people" and "the will of the majority" indicate (409, 414, 533), Rand had nothing but contempt for the multitude that constituted the general public. Her marketing genius in *Atlas Shrugged* was to pitch an aristocracy of money and a billboard coat of arms to those who were most on the rise at the same time that their contributions to the phenomenon of mass culture were consistently being derided by intellectuals. If Dwight Macdonald deemed the middle class a "collective monstrosity" of "passive consumers" held together by a "flaccid Middlebrow Culture that threatens to engulf everything in its spreading ooze" ("Theory" 70, 60, 63–64), Rand, in contrast, hailed the middle class as "a nation's productive—and moral, and intellectual top" (*Lexicon* 297). If Clement Greenberg mourned a shrinking avant-garde as boding ill for "the survival in the near future of culture in general," Rand reversed the emphasis and declared, "The upper classes are merely a nation's past; the middle class is its future" (*Lexicon* 297).

The catch, of course, was that word *intellectual*. Just as accolades about available affluence hid the fact that the richest 1 percent of the population held one-third of the nation's wealth by the end of the fifties and 45 percent of the country's families had less than two hundred dollars in liquid assets, that the richest 0.5 percent of the upper classes actually increased its holdings over the course of the decade from 19.3 percent in 1949 to 25 percent in 1956 (Chafe 143–44), not for a minute did Rand feel that all men (and all women) were created equal in those cognitive skills capable of propelling them to the top of Galt's "intellectual ladder" from which they could trade brains for dollars (989). As she later would admit when describing "The Age of Envy," "nature does not endow all men with equal beauty or equal intelligence," and anyone who advocated an egalitarian social structure was only proposing the establishment of "an inverted social pyramid, with a new aristocracy on top—*the aristocracy of non-value*" (*New Left* 165).

Ultimately, the aristocracy of intellect Rand proposed allowed for only one aristocrat, herself, who required absolute fealty of her followers. Rand justified such total dedication on the basis of what she gave in return—not just an ideology but a complete philosophy that provided "a comprehensive view of life" and, even more, "the realization that a comprehensive view of existence is to be reached by man's *mind*" (*New Left* 107, 108). The testimony of those who stayed with her as long as they did—despite the purges that fractured the Objectivist movement bit by bit and finally ended with the Great Schism between Rand and Nathaniel Branden in 1968—suggests that the people to whom she preached concurred with her own estimation. "She was a philosophical system-builder—during a century when system-builders were out of fashion and almost impossible to find," said Branden when recalling the moral quagmire in which those coming of age in the fifties felt they were sinking. "And today, reflecting back on those years, it is clear to me that what matters is not whether her vision was correct in all respects—I know now that it wasn't—but that she *had* a vision, a highly developed one, that promised comprehensiveness, intelligibility, and clarity" (244). One cannot help being more impressed, though, by the memory of another Objectivist that Branden cites immediately before his own mellifluous elegy, a recollection that suggests just how disadvantageous—indeed, dangerous—the intellectual rate of exchange that Rand offered her readers really was. "Look how much she had to offer! Look at how much I was learning!" the anonymous former disciple is quoted as having said. "If she got a little berserk now and again, *so what?*" (244). So what, indeed.

WORKS CONSULTED

Bell, Daniel. *The End of Ideology: On the Exhaustion of Political Ideas in the Fifties.* Glencoe, Ill.: Free Press, 1960.

Bellow, Saul. *Dangling Man.* 1944. New York: Bard-Avon, 1975.

Branden, Barbara. *The Passion of Ayn Rand.* New York: Doubleday, 1986.

Branden, Nathaniel. *Judgment Day: My Years with Ayn Rand.* Boston: Houghton Mifflin, 1989.

Chafe, William H. *The Unfinished Journey: America since World War II.* 1986. New York: Oxford University Press, 1991.

Chambers, Whittaker. "Big Sister Is Watching You." *National Review,* Dec. 28, 1957, 594–96.

Ellison, Ralph. *Invisible Man.* 1952. New York: Vintage-Random, 1990.

Fiedler, Leslie A. *No! in Thunder: Essays on Myth and Literature.* Boston: Beacon, 1960.

Greenberg, Clement. "Avant-Garde and Kitsch." 1939. Rpt. in *Mass Culture: The Popular Arts in America.* Ed. Bernard Rosenberg and David Manning White. New York: Free Press, 1957. 98–107.

Halberstam, David. *The Fifties.* New York: Villard, 1993.

Hartz, Louis. *The Liberal Tradition in America: An Interpretation of American Political Thought since the Revolution.* New York: Harcourt, 1955.

Heller, Joseph. *Catch-22.* 1961. New York: Dell, 1974.

Lhamon, W. T., Jr. *Deliberate Speed: The Origins of a Cultural Style in the American 1950s.* Washington, D.C.: Smithsonian Institution Press, 1990.

Locke, John. *Two Treatises of Government.* 1690. Ed. Peter Laslett. 1960. New York: New American Library, 1965.

Lundberg, Ferdinand, and Marynia F. Farnham. *Modern Woman: The Lost Sex.* New York: Grosset and Dunlap, 1947.

Macdonald, Dwight. *Memoirs of a Revolutionist.* 1957. Rpt. as *Politics Past: Essays in Political Criticism.* New York: Compass-Viking, 1970.

———. "A Theory of Mass Culture." 1953. Rpt. in *Mass Culture: The Popular Arts in America.* Ed. Bernard Rosenberg and David Manning White. New York: Free Press, 1957. 59–73.

Mailer, Norman. *Barbary Shore.* New York: Signet–New American Library, 1951.

Miller, Douglas T., and Marion Nowak. *The Fifties: The Way We Really Were.* New York: Doubleday, 1977.

"Our Country and Our Culture." *Partisan Review* 19.3–5 (1952): 282–326, 420–50, 562–97.

Pells, Richard H. *The Liberal Mind in a Conservative Age: American Intellectuals in the 1940s and 1950s.* New York: Harper and Row, 1985.

Rand, Ayn. *Atlas Shrugged.* New York: Signet–New American Library, 1957.

———. *The Ayn Rand Lexicon.* Ed. Harry Binswanger. New York: New American Library, 1986.

———. "Call Your Issues." *Objectivist Newsletter,* Jan. 1962, 1.

———. *Capitalism: The Unknown Ideal.* 1966. New York: Signet–New American Library, 1967.

———. *The Fountainhead.* 1943. New York: Signet–New American Library, 1952.

———. *The New Left: The Anti-Industrial Revolution.* 1971. New York: Signet–New American Library, 1975.

———. *Philosophy: Who Needs It?* New York: Bobbs-Merrill, 1982.

———. *The Romantic Manifesto.* New York: World, 1969.

———. "Testimony of Miss Ayn Rand." United States. Cong. House Committee on Communism in Motion Picture Industry. *Hearings.* 80th Cong. Senate Library, vol. 1169. Washington: GPO, 1947. 82–90.

Stephen J. Whitfield ━━

Twelve

THE ROAD TO RAPPROCHEMENT
Khrushchev's 1959 Visit to America

Soviet Premier Nikita Krushchev, 1959.
(Ollie Atkins Photographic Collection, Special Collections and Archives, George Mason University Libraries, Fairfax, Va.)

T HE principal instrument" of the United States, Alexis de Tocqueville had asserted in 1835, is "freedom," in contrast with the "servitude" of Russia. While "the Anglo-American relies upon personal interest to accomplish his ends and gives free scope to the unguided strength and common sense of the citizens, the Russian centers all the authority of society in a single arm." Tocqueville acknowledged that "their starting-point is different, and their courses are not the same." Yet he predicted that "each of them seems marked out by the will of Heaven to sway the destinies of half the globe" (1:452). This bipolar prophecy seemed especially apt in September 1959, when a Soviet ruler first set foot in America, when the cold war aggravated those cultural and political differences, and when the nuclear peril encouraged some sort of wary trust. The visit of Nikita Sergeyevich Khrushchev forced much of the populace to reconcile its instinctive antipathy to communism with its native hospitality. The event was not quite transformative. But it signaled a mellowing of the geopolitical rivalry that put everyone at risk and should be interpreted as a catalysis of the 1950s into the 1960s.

The impetus was not cultural but diplomatic: a crisis over West Berlin made this dramatic visit almost necessary, and the death of a secretary of state made it possible. John Foster Dulles succumbed to cancer in May 1959, believing so tenaciously in the "balance of terror" that his last intelligible words on earth were chillingly confident. "If the United States is willing to go to war over Berlin," he told an aide, "there won't be a war over Berlin," where ten thousand Western troops were then stationed within an enclave of East Germany, whose government none of the Western nations recognized (qtd. in Mosley 448; LaFeber 212–13). The death of the brinksman lifted the burden of implacable hostility, enabling President Eisenhower to try to decelerate an arms race that seemed to threaten ever more massive destruction. By inviting to the United States the personification of the system that had been defined for over a decade as prepotent evil, Ike gave citizens the opportunity to confront what was no longer a distant abstraction, but a robust and earthy visitor whose volatile curiosity about "the American way of life" forced its proponents to hold up a mirror to themselves. These were not quite thirteen days that shook the world. But a thaw was discernible; the world's thermostat was raised. By rendering the USSR and its leader a bit less demonic, the event evoked the promise of a substitute for victory, a finessing of the Manicheanism that animated the cold war.

It happened inadvertently, however. Ike had agreed to a bilateral summit that was not supposed to happen while Khrushchev threatened a deadline to convert Berlin into a "free city." The West had officially sought free elections within a unified Germany; the Soviets by contrast feared a unified Germany bristling with nuclear weapons. For a decade an isolated West Berlin had also encouraged about three million East Germans to take refuge from communism there, thereby creating a "brain drain" that the regime of Walter Ulbricht was determined to stanch. In the summer of 1959, the foreign ministers' meeting in Geneva could not reconcile these conflicting policies. Khrushchev happened to tell some American governors who were touring in Moscow of his interest in coming to America. The Department of State explored the possibility but misunderstood the president's instruction that an invitation should be tied to lifting the Soviet ultimatum that required the West to sign a peace treaty with East Germany. The premier instead received—and accepted—an unconditional offer to see the United States. On August 3 the president was obliged to confirm an exchange of visits between the two superpower leaders. Khrushchev would come in September, despite the ultimatum; and Ike would reciprocate with a later visit to the USSR, as though the question of Berlin had already been evaded. Eisenhower, according to Undersecretary of State Robert Murphy, "agreed very reluctantly" (Murphy 438; Eisenhower 405–8; Divine 132; Parmet 547; Beschloss 177–78).

The announcement was made during Captive Nations Week—the flamboyant congressional designation that Khrushchev told Richard M. Nixon, visiting Moscow that summer, "stinks like fresh horse shit." Eisenhower had informed his vice president of the premier's coming shortly before Nixon's departure for the Soviet Union on July 22 and later explicitly absolved him of any responsibility for arranging Khrushchev's tour (Nixon, *Six Crises* 242–43 and *RN* 207; Parmet 548). Some choleric conservatives nevertheless blamed the vice president, whom Senator Barry M. Goldwater (R-Ariz.) defended against their wrath, claiming that Nixon was "shocked and surprised the invitation was made" without prior diplomatic success at Geneva. The president also pricked Nixon's authority at an August 12 press conference. Asked what the Soviet premier should see on his travels, Eisenhower cited Abilene, Kansas, because the townsfolk could tell Khrushchev "the story of how hard I worked until I was twenty-one." Ike reminded reporters that three weeks earlier Khrushchev had berated Nixon during their kitchen debate in Sokolniki Park: "What do you know about work? You never worked." But, said the president, "I can show him the evidence that *I* did, and I would like him to see it." (This rationale for the itinerary impugned Nixon's childhood and youth, which had been as soaked in toil as Eisenhower's, even though the vice president failed to rebut Khrushchev's charge.) Another major purpose, Ike added, was to fly by helicopter from Washington to Camp David, preferably during rush hour, so that the spectacle of all the cars and houses below might disabuse the Soviet ruler of his Marxism and enable him to see the fruits of the work ethic under capitalism (Ambrose, *Eisenhower* 536 and *Nixon* 528–29; Eisenhower 433n).

Conservatives were fearful however, especially with Dulles no longer alive to correct the president's naiveté. The continuation of *any* diplomatic relations with Moscow troubled pugnacious Senator William Knowland (R-Calif.), one critic of the visit (Parmet 545–46; Hoopes 292–93, 295; Roberts 161). Red dye should be poured in the Hudson River, journalist William F. Buckley Jr. suggested, so that Khrushchev's entrance at the harbor of New York would be awash on a "river of blood" (qtd. in Ambrose, *Nixon* 528). Still, the damage was already done—less by Khrushchev than by Americans to themselves. Though only a fifth of them opposed the visit and nine in ten told Gallup that they favored courteous treatment (3:1628), the presence of the mephitic premier "profanes the nation," Buckley asserted (qtd. in Ross 33; Stone 291). A special problem was posed as well for many other Catholics, who identified intimately with the fate of the Captive Nations. Prelates were especially troubled. When John Francis Cardinal O'Hara of Philadelphia heard the news of the exchange of visits, he not only offered an immediate mass for Eisenhower's welfare but also cabled him that "today's announcement leaves a deep wound." Though the president assured Francis Cardinal Spellman by telephone that the talks with the Soviet premier would entail neither "surrender" nor any alteration of the tough posture on Berlin, Spellman so feared the ideological contamination of the tour that he ordered the daily addition of three Hail Marys to the liturgy of parochial schools. Archbishop Patrick O'Boyle advised Washington's Catholics to avoid any contact with Khrushchev. Because Boston was omitted from the itinerary, Richard Cardinal Cushing asked citizens simply to "pray in the street, pray any place" during the visit (Eisenhower 432n; Parmet 546; Stone 284; Frankland 162).

The chairman of the Council of Ministers and first party secretary left Moscow on September 14, accompanied by his wife Nina Petrovna Khrushcheva, their daughter and son-in-law, plus many other officials and scientists. At noon the following day, their gleaming white TU-114 turbojet, the biggest passenger plane ever built, landed in Maryland at Andrews Air Force Base (because the runway at National Airport was too short). Never before had a Russian leader come "face to face with America," a land "which I'd read about in Ilf and Petrov and Gorky—now I'd be able to see it with my own eyes, to touch it with my own fingers" (Beschloss 187; Khrushchev, *The Last Testament* 375). Three days earlier his government had launched an 855-

pound missile and lobbed it onto the moon, miscalculating its landing by only eighty-four seconds. Khrushchev had barely disembarked to the sound of a twenty-one-gun salute before handing a model of the Lunik II to a rather grim president, who "stood waiting outside for Khrushchev's plane door to open," journalist Murray Kempton observed, "as though he were waiting for some White House attendant to come in with a package that ticked" (217). Eisenhower had not only contracted a cold and a sore throat while golfing in Scotland but also, out of respect for the shade of Dulles, intended to grin only a little. (The hopes of the citizenry must not be inflated.) The shadow of Lunik II offered little pleasure in any event. "We have no doubt that the splendid scientists, engineers and workers of the United States . . . will likewise deliver their emblem to the moon," the premier gloated. "The Soviet emblem, as an old resident . . . will welcome your emblem." Ike winced (Solberg 410; Beschloss 186; Lyon 799–800; *Khrushchev in America* 15).

Though Khrushchev got—quite literally—the red carpet treatment and later professed to be "terribly impressed" by the dazzling arrangements, his welcome was not warm (Khrushchev, *The Last Testament* 376). "Whenever important foreign visitors arrived in Washington," one historian generalized, "their national flag was festooned from the Capitol to the White House. But this time no one dared droop the Hammer and Sickle the length of Pennsylvania Avenue" (Perrett 437). The crowds were sparse and, according to one journalist, "confused and inhibited" (Stone 284). While riflemen checked the route and police helicopters buzzed overhead, a skywriter tried some exorcism by making a huge white cross (Kempton 216, 217). Even as the guest fitfully waved his homburg, signs like "Go Home Tyrant" greeted him; and police had to disperse hawkers of black skull-and-crossbones stickers ("K Confronts the Republic" 40; Beschloss 189). The nervousness was depicted in Herblock's cartoon of the two leaders in a limousine, smiling at the crowd with arms upraised—and fingers crossed (Block 124).

At a meeting held in the west wing of the White House that afternoon, Khrushchev taunted his host yet again by gleefully handing him some replicas of the pennants and spheres that Lunik had deposited on the moon. Eisenhower tried to suggest the centrality and urgency of better relations. Both agreed on the value of achieving mutual trust, which Khrushchev asserted had not been helped by a recent speech that Nixon had given. The president tried to distance himself from the vice president's remarks by promising to read the speech itself, but Nixon himself then reminded their guest of some strong salvos of his own prior to the vice president's visit to the Soviet Union. "*You* read the speeches. *You* be the judge," the premier told the president, who was thus asked to adjudicate this dispute over a suitably hospitable atmosphere. Nor did Khrushchev, who had just come from a capital where even the telephone directory was classified, think much of the First Amendment: "Of course, the American government gets printed what it wants printed and is able to suppress what it does not want printed." Eisenhower challenged him to test the independence of American journalists by offering to have him meet alone with any of them. A different understanding of freedom of information indeed marked the two societies, though the differences were hardly absolute. Late in November 1960, after NBC analyzed the U-2 incident of May 1960, Eisenhower protested so angrily that RCA's David Sarnoff vowed "to correct any unpleasantness or embarrassment" and ordered NBC News to pay tribute to Ike upon his leaving office the following January (Eisenhower 435, 436–37; Beschloss 190, 191–92, 342).

After their initial chat Eisenhower invited Khrushchev to see Washington by vaunted helicopter, which the premier feared might be exploded or might eject him. He accepted only after the president promised to join him, showing him the panorama of the private homes, the government monuments, above all the rush hour traffic. Khrushchev—still apparently a Marxist—told a reporter right afterwards: "We're never going to have automobiles like you have in this country, jamming up the highways. Absolutely uneconomic." Later, back in Moscow, at least one consumer exercised sovereignty by demanding an even better helicopter than Ike's (Kempton 217; Eisenhower 438–39; Murphy 439). That night the White House sponsored a state dinner in which the men in the Soviet entourage disdained the required white tie and tails; the guest of honor showed up in the same kind of suit he had worn earlier that day. At the reception Khrushchev met the director of the Central Intelligence Agency, and with some ice-breaking humor speculated to Allen Dulles: "I believe we get the same reports—and probably from the same people." Dulles playfully recommended an economy move: "Maybe we should pool our efforts." Nixon introduced the obdurate J. Edgar Hoover, who was escorting Perle Mesta ("the hostess with the mostest"), to Khrushchev as well. The musical entertainment, which fully reflected the Eisenhowers' banal taste, was provided by Fred Waring and his Pennsylvanians, who closed with "The

Battle Hymn of the Republic" (qtd. in Solberg 410; Beschloss 193–94; Kempton 217).

At a Washington luncheon the next day, the premier delivered a televised speech before the National Press Club and then answered the journalists' questions. Asked about the notorious prediction that he uttered at a Kremlin reception in November 1956 ("We will bury you"), he explained: "The expression I used was distorted, and on purpose, because what was meant was not the physical burial of any people but the question of the historical forces of development. . . . We believe . . . the social system of socialism would take the place of capitalism" (*New York Times,* Sept. 17, 1959, 18, and Sept. 12, 1971, 79). Even this clarification may not have relieved national anxieties that the representative of a more dynamic political economy had arrived while the phlegmatic Eisenhower was playing on the fairways. (Soviet steel production, for example, had been 17 percent of American production at the end of World War II. Fifteen years later it was already 72 percent of the American figure.) The superiority of socialism fortified Khrushchev's ebullience and confidence, even though his doctrinal exposition did not awe a reporter like Kempton, who reflected that, under the Smith Act, "Elizabeth Gurley Flynn was sent to jail in America for three years for presenting these ideas more intelligently and coherently than Khrushchev did, and Khrushchev was permitted all major networks, but then I am aware that in America we have one standard for those who own real estate and another for the poor" (Kempton 219; Khrushchev, *Khrushchev Speaks* 318–19).

Then, meeting with the Senate Foreign Relations Committee, he complained about CIA "subversion of other countries[, which] is hardly conducive to peaceful coexistence." All innocence, Richard Russell (D-Ga.) denied knowledge of any "appropriations anywhere for any subversive work in Russia—and I have been a member of the Appropriations Committee for twenty-five years" (Beschloss 195–96). Though the junior senator from Massachusetts arrived late, Khrushchev recalled being "impressed with Kennedy. I remember liking his face, which was sometimes stern but which often broke into a good-natured smile" (Khrushchev, *Khrushchev Remembers* 458). In less than two years, they would meet again—in Vienna. Another young American with an engaging smile, pianist Van Cliburn, was among the guests at a Soviet embassy reception on the evening of September 16. Perhaps as a gesture to Soviet-American friendship, the forbidding portraits of Lenin and

Stalin were taken down. "The ice of the Cold War has not only cracked," their successor in the Kremlin announced, "but has indeed begun to crumble" ("Speech" in *Khrushchev in America* 45). It was beginning to happen.

The next morning he and approximately a hundred comrades boarded a silver Pennsylvania Railroad train (with its windows suddenly washed) to begin their tour of the rest of America. Their host was not the official whom protocol might have demanded, because the vice president's previous friction with Khrushchev convinced Eisenhower of their persistence in rubbing one another the wrong way (Eisenhower 433). No wonder: Khrushchev's memoirs dismiss "that son-of-a-bitch Richard Nixon" as an "unprincipled" McCarthyite (*Khrushchev Remembers* 458). The honor went instead to Henry Cabot Lodge Jr., the patrician whom Kennedy had beaten for the Senate in 1952. Lodge had thereupon become the first UN ambassador to achieve Cabinet status as well. While fueling speculation that an alternative to Nixon was being groomed for the GOP ticket in 1960, Ike hoped that Lodge would serve as a one-man "truth squad," blunting the prejudices that flowed from Khrushchev's Marxist determinism. But an Eisenhower speech writer doubted the effectiveness of the escort, who "initially offered, on all public occasions permitting such oratory, the accompaniment of little homilies on . . . capitalism. These were intended to sound assertive but succeeded only in sounding apologetic, and Khrushchev soon discouraged the rhetoric by puncturing it with such steely, anti-capitalist thrusts as, 'Only the grave can correct a hunchback!'" (Hughes 291).

New York City denied the guest of honor a ticker tape parade, or even a raucous welcome; and from a closed limousine Khrushchev saw what he later called a "huge noisy city" with "vast quantities of exhaust fumes that were choking people" (Khrushchev, *The Last Testament* 381). After an intimate lunch with Mayor Robert Wagner and a thousand others at the Commodore Hotel, he visited W. Averell Harriman, the ex-governor of New York and ex-ambassador to the Soviet Union. The heir to the fortune of his father's Union Pacific Railroad scarcely embodied the work ethic that the president had initially told the press was to have been a key revelation of the visit. "Averell looks terrific," someone told Mrs. Harriman two years later, when Averell was seventy. "You'd look terrific too," she replied, "if you did nothing but play polo until you were forty years old" (qtd. in Halberstam 191). A living symbol of Soviet-American cooperation, he had invited for the occasion over two dozen guests whom Khrushchev might have guessed were the nation's un-elected powers—not front-men who held public office, but members of the ruling class, the counterparts of his own *nomenklatura*. Commanders of as-sets of at least $100 million—the entry level for eligibility that the host had set—included John D. Rockefeller III; Dean Rusk, who was then president of the Rockefeller Foundation and would soon become secretary of state; attorney John J. McCloy, the chairman of the Chase Manhattan Bank; W. Alton Jones of Cities Service; George Woods of the First Boston Corporation; President Grayson Kirk of Columbia University; and former senator Herbert Lehman, who had headed the wartime United Nations Relief and Rehabili-tation Administration. Khrushchev had run its Ukrainian branch—making Lehman "my boss" (Galbraith 257–59, 261; Beschloss 197; Abramson 574–75). RCA's Sarnoff, born in Minsk, made a memorable impression on the guest. Speaking excellent Russian, this "obese . . . Jew by nationality" brusquely asked him what proved to be a prophetically apt question: "Why should we trade with you? What do you have to sell us?" (Khrushchev, *The Last Testa-ment* 382).

Sitting beneath a Picasso in the library of the East 81st Street apartment, Khrushchev fielded questions that resembled declamations. The first to speak was, fittingly, McCloy, whom one astute journalist fingered as the grand pa-sha of the Establishment. McCloy assured Khrushchev that Wall Street lacked influence in Washington, where big bankers' support of legislation would be enough to discredit and kill it. Nor did Wall Street wish to continue the arms race for pecuniary motives. "No one among the American people is try-ing to preserve international tension for profits," Harriman recalled McCloy declaring. "No one in this room knows of any such person" (Harriman 38–39; Bird 485–87)—an odd claim, given the inclusion of Frank Pace Jr., former secretary of the army and the current chairman of General Dynamics, which derived much of its income from Pentagon contracts. He and RCA's Sarnoff, whose stockholders also heavily ploughed their shares into swords, did not directly challenge Khrushchev's stubborn insistence that weaponry was profitable for business, at least some businesses, though Pace's claim that he would be pleased to relinquish the armaments division of his company might have shocked his shareholders. Harriman had also invited a friend, John Kenneth Galbraith, a financially ineligible professor who explained how Keynesianism was keeping the economy out of a state of crisis. The fervor with which hugely successful men felt obliged to disavow any communist sympathies amused the Harvard economist; and the enthusiasm with which they professed unquenchable faith in the system of free enterprise revealed a defensiveness that typified the timidity of discourse in the fifties. The Establishment was so inept at *mano á mano* ideological combat that an attorney, who was also exceptional in falling well under the $100 million threshold, asked Galbraith afterwards: "Do you have any doubt as to who was the smartest man in there tonight?" (Rovere 11; Galbraith 263–67; Khrushchev, *The Last Testament* 382–83).

In his honor the Economic Club of New York held a banquet that evening at the Waldorf-Astoria Hotel on Park Avenue, where picketers demanded "Freedom for Hungary" and denounced "Khrushchev the Butcher of the Ukraine." Lodge persisted in giving what the reporters labeled "civics lectures," including the claim that, because laws against monopoly were so "strict" and because high taxes supported welfare, the Soviet leader ought to cease referring to the system as "monopoly capitalism." Lodge suggested "economic humanism," a phrase so inspiring that the economic humanists themselves spontaneously rose to sing the national anthem (Hearst, Coniff, and Considine 248–49; Galbraith 260). The next day, September 18, Khrushchev addressed the General Assembly of the United Nations, proposing a four-year plan for "total disarmament" that, needless to say, stirred very little response among the delegates (Parmet 549–50). Before leaving New York the next day, the representative of the proletariat interrupted his meetings with the U.S. "ruling circles" to get a tour of Harlem. "Well, this isn't bad. We have a lot of areas just like this in the Soviet Union," he told Lodge, who assured him of imminent slum clearance: "These buildings are all coming down very soon" (Lodge 162). The premier then ascended to the top of the Empire State Building and met with Governor Nelson A. Rockefeller—yet another exception to Ike's faith in the virtues of childhood toil (Hearst, Coniff, and Considine 250–52; Beschloss 198).

An Air Force Boeing 707 next took the premier to Hollywood, which he cleverly called "a special republic within the larger republic of the U. S. A." On Saturday, September 19, Twentieth Century-Fox threw a luncheon in his honor in its commissary, for which the elite of the film community scrambled for seats. Such eagerness to fete the "Butcher of Budapest" was paradoxical, if not hypocritical, since the studios were still blacklisting and stigmatizing his alleged acolytes in Hollywood itself with such vigor that some became expatriates. (In choosing the high road of boycotting the affair, which was televised live, Ronald Reagan and the Hungarian Eva Gabor were exceptional.) Marilyn Monroe was instructed to wear her "tightest, sexiest dress" and to leave her husband, a playwright of disturbingly liberal opinions, at home. In the commissary Khrushchev flattered such glitterati as "not only intellectuals, but toilers of the most refined, I might say the most delicate, of arts" (*The Last Testament* 386; Barnouw 131; Beschloss 199; "Speech . . . at Twentieth Century-Fox Studios" in Khrushchev, *Khrushchev Speaks* 326).

From the dais the guest of honor also thundered with a complaint, however. Disneyland was off-limits, ostensibly for reasons of security. Eisenhower later claimed that Soviet personnel had themselves blocked the visit, but Khrushchev was infuriated that the Anaheim constabulary could not guarantee his safety in the Magic Kingdom. "Is it by any chance because you now have rocket-launching pads there?" he asked. "Or has Disneyland been seized by bandits who might destroy me? . . . I should like to go to Disneyland . . . and see how Americans spend their leisure," but he was stymied (Eisenhower 441; Lodge 163–64; "Speech . . . at Twentieth Century-Fox Studios" in Khrushchev, *Khrushchev Speaks* 329). Perhaps, in his disappointment, the premier was the first postmodernist, anticipating the *aperçu* of the sociologist Jean Baudrillard that Disneyland "is there to conceal the fact that it is the 'real' country, all of 'real' America, which *is* Disneyland. . . . Disneyland is presented as imaginary in order to make us believe that the rest is real" (25). Madame Khrushcheva also told the actor David Niven of her own regret that the Magic Kingdom would be terra incognita. "Screw the cops!" Frank Sinatra told Niven. "Tell the old broad you and I'll take 'em down there this afternoon"—a pledge that could not be honored (qtd. in *Washington Post,* 8 Aug. 1983; Niven 262–64).

The commissary luncheon included a couple of unscheduled speeches that reeked of pride and prejudice. Spyros P. Skouras, the president of Twentieth Century-Fox, spontaneously decided to vindicate America in autobiographical terms, using the dizzying upward mobility that he had experienced as an impoverished Greek immigrant to epitomize equality of opportunity. This was bait that Khrushchev, whose grandfather had been a serf, could not resist. "I began working when I learned to walk," he replied. "I tended calves, then sheep, and then the landlord's cows." He had worked in coal pits and factories, and "now I am Prime Minister of the great Soviet State" ("Speech . . . at Twentieth Century-Fox Studios" in Khrushchev, *Khrushchev Speaks* 322). Such a resumé might have been expected to trump Skouras's; the depths were lower, the top higher. But "this being Hollywood," with clout confined to the biggest studios, a reporter noted that Skouras reacted "as though the guest of honor had boasted that he was head of Monogram Pictures" (Kempton 225–26). (In the cross fire of these dueling success stories, Ambassador Lodge, the grandson of a U.S. senator, was silent.) Of course neither speaker could acknowledge the price the system exacted, such as Khrushchev's service to a bloodthirsty tyranny, which to be sure far overshadowed Hollywood's corruption of cultural standards. Nor could either speaker have foreseen how the images of a better life that American movies projected helped scuttle the ideological defenses of Soviet rule itself.

Though Skouras's instincts were sound in locating the moral justification for American society, he had pushed too far the doctrine of "American exceptionalism." Had he missed reading the famous special issue of *Life* magazine (March 29, 1943) that lauded the Russians as "one hell of a people . . . [who] to a remarkable degree . . . look like Americans, dress like Americans and think like Americans"? (qtd. in Gaddis 38). What of Dale Carnegie's *Biographical Roundup* (1946), a set of "inspirational profiles providing examples of 'getting ahead' for the rising businessman"? Among those whom Carnegie included was Comrade Stalin, who was quoted as an authority on sound management style: "The main thing is to have the courage to admit one's errors and to have the strength to correct them in the shortest possible time!" (qtd. in Siegel 24). But the effect of the 1959 exchange in Hollywood, drawing on a pitifully small statistical sample, was to undermine the claim that the sociologist Lloyd Warner had advanced, as recently as 1949, that "our social positions are not fixed artificially, as they are in the so-called 'classless' society of Russia. . . . Though all are not equal in ability, the [American] Dream is still true" (qtd. in "Sociologist Looks" 118). The lure of upward mobility was not so distinctive a facet of American society as many of its members wanted to believe.

After lunch the Khrushchevs were given their only opportunity to confront the vitality of American culture. It was the set of *Can-Can,* a phony version of *fin-de-siècle* Paris, "an especially dishonest bit of goods," Kempton complained, "of the type that sneaks past the Breen [censorship] office, since it offers smut without precisely delivering it" (226–27). The movie featured Shirley MacLaine, Maurice Chevalier, Louis Jourdan, and Sinatra, who serenaded the visitors with his version of "peaceful coexistence" ("Live and Let Live"). "It's a marvelous idea," he told the Soviets (Beschloss 199). The crooner then shook hands with Khrushchev, who posed with the dancing "girls" and later astonished his entourage by turning his back, bending over, lifting up his coat and doing a can-can imitation. "This is what you call freedom," he sneered, "freedom for the girls to show their backsides. To us, it's pornography. . . . It's capitalism that makes the girls that way." The spectacle that he had just witnessed was "the culture of surfeited and depraved people" (Khrushchev, *The Last Testament* 386; "Summary of Meeting" and "Meeting with U. S. Trade Union Leaders" in Khrushchev, *Khrushchev Speaks,* 342–43, 355).

Khrushchev's sojourn in Los Angeles deteriorated further. No local newspaper had bothered to print his itinerary, forcing him to ride down virtually deserted streets that weekend. He nevertheless managed to spot a woman, dressed in mourning, who held up a sign: "Death to Khrushchev, Butcher of Hungary." He exploded in fury, assuming that such hostility had been orchestrated by the federal government. (The dialectic of history makes few allowances for contingency.) Mayor Norris Poulson had already greeted him with a speech that could scarcely have been icier in its brevity: "Welcome to Los Angeles, the City of the Angels, the city where the impossible always happens." These had been the entire words of welcome. Lodge had also warned Poulson not to tweak their guest for having warned of national interment, during the banquet that was scheduled for the Ambassador Hotel (ex-McCarthyite G. David Schine, president). The mayor nevertheless ignored not only this advice but also Khrushchev's recent clarification at the National Press Club, which had alluded to the historical inevitability of socialist economic victory (Lodge 165, 166–67; Perrett 437; Beschloss 200).

Instead Poulson played good southern California politics and did an imitation of Patrick Henry: "Now, Mr. Chairman, I want to make this statement in the most friendly fashion. We do not agree with your widely quoted phrase 'We shall bury you.' You shall not bury us and we shall not bury you. We are happy with our way of life. We recognize its shortcomings and are always trying to improve it. But if challenged, we shall fight to death to preserve it. . . . I tell you these things not to boast or to threaten, but to give you a picture of what the people of Southern California feel in their hearts. . . . We are planning no funerals, yours *or* our own. There will never be a funeral for the free spirit that lives in every man." The object of these remarks reached the podium in a rage: "I come here with serious intentions, and you try to reduce the matter to a simple joke. It is a question of the life and death of the people. . . . One should not play on words. We hold positions of too much responsibility and the consequences of a play on words can be too sad for our people." He even threatened to fly on to Vladivostok: "I can go, and I don't know when—*if ever*—another Soviet premier will visit your country" (qtd. in Goldman 331–32). The scene was awful, Kempton reported. "We had permitted . . . Khrushchev to make us look like bums" (227–28). True enough; but as another journalist, I. F. Stone, noted, the premier stressed "what a plain-spoken and undiplomatic man he is. But when people speak to him plainly, he flies off the handle. . . . Khrushchev is creating the impression that he likes to dish it out, but he can't take it" (286).

Afterwards, in his suite, the guest still could not contain his wrath, screaming at the shabby treatment that he ascribed to Washington. But occasionally his diatribes were punctuated with his finger pointing to the ceiling, expecting that bugging devices would pick up his cue for more gracious hospitality. Khrushchev also instructed Foreign Minister Andrei Gromyko to repeat his complaints to Lodge. In any event the message was received. It was apparent that the Los Angeles phase had proven such a fiasco that the White House immediately urged citizens to show greater politeness to the man Ike later called "our energetic and unpredictable visitor," who calmed down when briefed on federalism and mayoral independence: "Now I begin to understand some of the problems of President Eisenhower." When Khrushchev left the railroad station for a Southern Pacific ride up the California coast, no city official showed up to see him off, nor was he offered a microphone to say *dosvedanya* to the Angelenos (S. Khrushchev 357–58; Khrushchev, *The Last Testament* 388–89; Lodge 167–68, 171; Eisenhower 441, 445).

But the White House appeal may have worked, because the trip north to San Francisco stirred more gracious sentiments. Fastening hammer-and-sickle pins on greeters in Santa Barbara, kissing babies in San Luis Obispo, Khrushchev managed to earn favorable notices on his whistle-stop tour. More enthusiastic crowds responded to his directness and his impulsiveness—what Lodge called "his personal magnetism." Inspecting an IBM plant in San Jose, the premier seemed to fathom the significance of what may have eluded his host, Thomas J. Watson Jr.—a vision of classless labor. The blurred lines between "white collar" and "blue collar" in the factory suggested an unintended fulfillment of the Marxist ideal of toilers whom their bosses no longer exploited as a separate class. Thanks in part to cooperative mayor George W. Christopher, San Francisco was a delight. Mobbed outside of his hotel, Khrushchev was driven through the hills at sunset and was "quite bewitched," he told Lodge, later conceding that capitalistic accomplishments there made him "slightly envious" (*New York Times,* June 3, 1990, 12; Lodge 159, 173, 177; Salisbury 483–84; Khrushchev, *The Last Testament* 390–91).

But friction developed quickly with the representatives of the proletariat—seven AFL-CIO vice presidents—whom he met in a closed session on September 20. One notable absentee was the president of the labor federation, George Meany, whose speeches, the premier complained, "sound like Dulles." Khrushchev was especially nettled by the president of the United Auto Workers, Walter P. Reuther, who had worked in a Ford factory in Gorki in 1933–35, for settling for an "extra nickel or dime" rather than pursuing the "victory of the working class." When Reuther challenged his right to speak for that class, Khrushchev impugned *his* right "to poke your nose into East Germany," where Reuther had charged the workers were victimized. When the UAW leader pointed out the absence of an independent trade union movement in the Soviet Union, the premier asked him: "Why poke your nose into our business?" Reuther's reply was devastating: "Freedom is everybody's business—you are always expressing a concern for the workers of Asia—there is a thing called international labor solidarity." This exchange provoked more heated words. "You are like a nightingale," Khrushchev told him. "It closes its eyes when it sings, and sees nothing and hears nobody but itself." The capitalists had bought Reuther off, the visitor concluded, unlike Harry Bridges, the militant head of the West Coast longshoremen whom he met at their union hall the following day. This "true progressive" was praised for his support of the Soviet Union, which was not exactly the bear hug that Bridges needed—given the remorseless efforts to deport him ("Summary of Meeting" and "Meeting with U. S. Trade Union Leaders" in Khrushchev, *Khrushchev Speaks* 336–37, 340–41, 346, 353; Khrushchev, *The Last Testament* 393–96; Hearst, Coniff, and Considine 265–66; Kutler 118–51). The labor leaders had given their guest an even cooler reception than had East Coast businessmen, ideological bumblers who at least weighed the prospect of commerce with the Soviet Union. Nonplussed by his more abrasive encounter with the working-class spokesmen ("capitalist lackeys"), especially the articulate and well-informed Reuther, Khrushchev headed on September 22 for the heartland (*New York Times,* June 3, 1990, 12; "Summary of Meeting" in Khrushchev, *Khrushchev Speaks* 341; Stone 288; Hughes 291).

"We Butcher Hogs, Not People" read a sign in Des Moines; but otherwise his welcome in Iowa was effusive. At the Des Moines Packing Company, he put on a butcher's hat and devoured his first hot dog but, as usual, couldn't pay a compliment without also needling his hosts: "We have beaten you to the moon but you have beaten us in sausage-making" (*New York Times,* Sept. 12, 1971, 79, and June 3, 1990, 12; Khrushchev, *The Last Testament,* 403n). In Coon Rapids the premier visited the farm of Roswell (Bob) Garst, a millionaire hybrid corn breeder who traded with the Soviet Union and had already met the premier on the Black Sea. "He may have been a capitalist" and therefore a class enemy, Khrushchev later recalled, but "he knew agriculture backwards and forwards" (Khrushchev, *The Last Testament* 398–99, 400). While munching on fried chicken and barbecued ribs, Khrushchev talked arms control and trade with Adlai E. Stevenson, whom he assured would "not be investigated by the Bureau of Un-American Affairs." The gentleman farmer from Libertyville, Illinois, remarked that Khrushchev seemed changed from their Moscow meeting a year earlier and quite "serious" about disarmament (Martin 459)—though, according to Gallup, 59 percent of Americans polled considered Khrushchev insincere on this issue (3:1631). He was jovial, whether spotting two healthy-looking blondes and announcing, "I want to meet these slaves of capitalism," or patting the stomach of a 240–pound farmer, whom he called "a good advertisement for America." He turned out to be Jack Christensen, a gate-crasher who easily penetrated the tight security. Misidentified as one of Garth's sons, then posing as a policemen, Christensen gleefully joined the premier's inner circle for part of his visit to Iowa (Lodge 175–76; "K Confronts the Republic" 36; Hughes 291; Kempton 232; *New York Times,* June 3, 1990, 12; Christensen 38–39).

In Pittsburgh a strike confined the tour to a nonunion factory that the in-laws of Perle Mesta owned. Khrushchev called it "a good plant." A Mesta Machine Company vice president was gracious: "I'm sure that you have better ones in your country." The premier replied: "Don't be so sure. We have better ones; we have the same kind; we even have worse. I don't say that all you have is bad and all we have is good. We can learn from you" (qtd. in Kempton 234). He later conceded: "You have good cadres of engineers and skilled workers. You can make use of all that science can give you" ("Education of Mr. K" 21). The compulsion to make invidious comparisons was fading.

Then Khrushchev went to Maryland for nearly three days of discussions with Eisenhower in Camp David. This first bilateral summit conference fulfilled Kipling's poem about "two strong men stand[ing] face to face, though they come from the ends of the earth." They represented the radically divergent traditions that Tocqueville had earlier classified. Eisenhower was the amiable heir of that democratic consensus that Jefferson had expressed in his first inaugural address: "We are all Republicans, we are all Federalists" (292). But when Party cadres were "fighting against imperialism," Khrushchev had vowed a century and a half later, "we are all Stalinists" (qtd. in Crankshaw 243). By taking meals together, walking along the gravel pathways of the Catoctin Mountain, the two leaders nevertheless seized the opportunity to talk and to size each other up. They even shared grievances about how hard-liners were pushing up the costs of defense (Goldman 330; Eisenhower 444; Khrushchev, *Khrushchev Remembers* 519–20; Khrushchev, *The Last Testament* 411–12; Ambrose 543). What they did not do together, however, was worship, which was Billy Graham's all-purpose remedy. He wanted the president to invite the premier to attend church: "Khrushchev is his house-guest, and if he should refuse to go, it will put Khrushchev on the spot" (qtd. in Frady 420). On Sunday morning Ike indeed attended the Presbyterian church in Gettysburg; but the invitation to join him was declined, because prayer would come as a "shock" to the Soviet people (Khrushchev, *The Last Testament* 408). But meeting the president's grandchildren on the farm and inspecting the Black Angus cattle raised there, Ike recalled, helped turn the premier into "a benign and entertaining guest" (Beschloss 209; Eisenhower 444).

The major diplomatic problem remained the status of the victors in Berlin and the Soviet yearning for Western recognition of the German Democratic Republic, which would ensure a divided Germany. The president had refused to attend a summit conference so long as the Soviet government threatened to relinquish its authority over East Berlin to the Ulbricht regime. At Camp David Khrushchev yielded. He lifted his time limit, with the expectation that negotiations would not be prolonged indefinitely, and promised to maintain

Western rights in Berlin. Such signs of flexibility averted a crisis (of his own making) and encouraged the prospect of détente. Nine months earlier General Nathan Twining, who chaired the Joint Chiefs of Staff, had assured the White House of his readiness "to fight a general nuclear war," an assurance that would not suddenly have to be tested (qtd. in Divine 134). A showdown had been postponed. The return to the status quo ante would not be announced, however, until after Khrushchev's return to Moscow, which hinted at the power of his own hawks.

With the element of compulsion lifted, Eisenhower conceded that the Berlin arrangements were "abnormal" and agreed to attend a Big Four summit. This became the Paris conference of May 1960, which was wrecked when Eisenhower accepted responsibility for the U-2 surveillance of Soviet territory. The CIA planes had been flying over Soviet territory since 1956. But Khrushchev did not protest the violations at Camp David in September 1959—perhaps because previous diplomatic protests had not stopped them, perhaps because the genial rapport that had been achieved with Ike was too precious to be disrupted, perhaps because the failure of Soviet air defenses would be made obvious—and Khrushchev did not wish to negotiate from weakness. Had he vigorously objected to the violations, Undersecretary of State C. Douglas Dillon later speculated, Ike might have stopped the CIA missions—and the rapprochement might have deepened. But when nothing was mentioned at Camp David, the CIA revved up its proposals for more penetration of Soviet airspace. (Eisenhower had ordered the suspension of overflights for September 15–28, to avoid the risk of the unexpected [Alexander 250–51; Beschloss 215, 233, 238, 371, 380]. Since the U-2's purpose was to catch a surprise attack, the least likely moment for the Soviets to strike would be when their leader was near ground zero.)

What a GOP speech writer called "a transcontinental display of political showmanship" culminated on September 27 with a revelation. "I have come here to see how the slaves of capitalism are living," Khrushchev admitted in Washington. "I see that the way they live is not bad at all." (Such a discovery came cheap. The visit had cost the federal government only about $100,000—or the equivalent of one army tank.) Speaking for an hour on NBC television, Khrushchev praised "your beautiful cities and wonderful roads, but most of all, your amiable and kindhearted people." He concluded in his newly minted English: "Goodbye, good luck, friends!" and, waving farewell at Andrews Air Force Base, added: "Thank you all from the bottom of my heart for your hospitality and, as we say in Russia, for your bread and salt" (Hughes 290–91; *New York Times,* Sept. 28, 1959, 17, 19, and June 3, 1990, 12; "Great Encounter" 23; "K. Goes Home" 19). Khrushchev returned to Moscow encouraged by the authenticity of his host's quest for peace. The "I Like Ike" button that the premier virtually pinned to his lapel was probably not the sort of memento to endear him to the hard-liners in the Kremlin; and though Khrushchev spoke often of "the spirit of Camp David," Eisenhower himself neither used nor liked the term (Khrushchev, *The Last Testament* 410, 411; Beschloss 7, 213–15; Eisenhower 432, 448).

Chalmers Roberts, who covered the White House for the *Washington Post,* listed Khrushchev's trip as "undoubtedly the most fascinating story" that he had handled in four decades. "It had everything: a fabulous personality, conflict, human interest, the unexpected" (160). A combustible personality made Khrushchev, in Harrison Salisbury's phrase, "a reporter's dream" (495); but the impression that lingered was also how formidable the visitor was. "Born in a hut of mud and reeds . . . and a youth barely literate until his mid-twenties, Khrushchev showed himself a volatile but sophisticated merchant of Marxist doctrine spiced with wit and drollery," Emmet John Hughes noted (291). "We now know that he is no buffoon reeling drunkenly through the Kremlin," *Newsweek* opined, "but a shrewd, tough and able adversary" ("Great Encounter" 19) whom Ike called "a remarkable . . . [and] very difficult man" (qtd. in Brendon 379). "He is shrewd, he is tough, he is vigorous, well informed, and confident," Senator Kennedy commented a week after the visit. Skilled at ideological thrusts, "the Khrushchev with whom I met, in his session with the Senate Foreign Relations Committee, was a tough-minded, articulate, hard-reasoning spokesman for a system in which he was thoroughly versed and in which he thoroughly believed. He was not the prisoner of any ancient dogma or limited vision," Kennedy said. "He was not engaging in any idle boasts when he talked of the inevitable triumph of the Communist system, of their eventual superiority in production, education, scientific achievement, and world influence. . . . It is well that the American people saw and heard this kind of man and this kind of talk. . . . It is important that we realize what we are up against. And . . . also that Mr. Khrushchev recognize what he is up against" (34).

This prepossessing figure nevertheless dangled the prospect of "the normalization of relations," a glimpse of human warmth that predecessors like Georgy Malenkov or certainly Stalin could hardly have offered had they even tried to win the hearts of foreigners. Eisenhower's future successor reflected some of this ambivalence. The gusto and resoluteness that Khrushchev exuded, Senator Kennedy asserted, obliged the United States to redouble its efforts in the cold war. Negotiations were nevertheless desirable: "It is far better that we meet at the summit than at the brink." He advocated "a new approach to the Russians—one that is just as hard-headed . . . as Mr. Khrushchev's," he argued, "but one that might well end the current phase—the frozen, belligerent, brink-of-war phase—of the long Cold War." Five points of common interest could be tabulated: reduction of the arms race; a guarantee of no nuclear war; no nuclear proliferation; no radioactive air; and closer economic, scientific, and cultural exchanges. "Mr. Khrushchev had reason to be confident on his visit here," Kennedy conceded. "His country was the first into outer space and the first to the moon. Its growth in productivity, resource development, and education has been phenomenal. Its successes in penetrating non-Communist areas politically and economically have been unprecedented. But now that we know what we are up against . . . we, too, can be confident. We, too, can be just as tough, just as realistic, just as hard bargainers as Mr. Khrushchev" (35, 36–37, 39).

The yearning for a thaw made the visit politically feasible, but hardly inevitable; and perhaps only Ike's extraordinary popularity cushioned the shock of the Antichrist's presence in the Oval Office and blunted the ferocity of right-wing resentment. Had Eisenhower's predecessor dared to invite Stalin to the White House, Senator Stuart Symington (D-Mo.) conjectured, Harry Truman might have been impeached. But Eisenhower's credibility and prestige sanctioned a less suspicious atmosphere, which the visit itself reinforced. When Khrushchev reached New York City, the president was asked at his press conference if his guest's skills as a propagandist did not create a risk. What if citizens concluded that Khrushchev was not such a hobgoblin after all? Eisenhower's attempt to allay the fear of political seduction merited an eight-column headline on the front page of the *Washington Post* (*New York Times,* Sept. 28, 1959, 19; Galbraith 259). The reduction in fear that the visit accelerated also merits the attention of historians; the concerns of the right-wing proved to be warranted.

For "the atmosphere miraculously has been changed," I. F. Stone exulted immediately after Khrushchev's departure; cold war relations shifted from "rigidly hostile" to "rigidly friendly" (290–91). The softening of primitive anti-Soviet sentiments was indeed an effect of the visit, which is why J. Edgar Hoover managed to restrain his own enthusiasm for it. Compulsively operating on "red alert," the FBI director offered a paranoic spin the following January, warning the Senate internal security subcommittee that Khrushchev's tour had "done much to create an atmosphere favorable to communism among Americans," a mood that the dormant Communist party might somehow contrive to exploit. Its cadres "see the possibility of gaining still more influence in American society" (*New York Times*, Jan. 17, 1960, 44). But Roy Medvedev's historical assessment was obviously sounder. Despite Khrushchev's visit, the Soviet Marxist wrote, "neither the membership nor the influence of the Communist Party of the U. S. A. increased," though "his popularity soared" throughout the world, except among the Chinese comrades (147). Though the two leaders had sensed a shared desire to reduce the arms race and to control military spending, Khrushchev realized that his counterpart was subject to countervailing power: "The plain people of America like me. It's just those bastards around Eisenhower that don't" (Lodge 169–70; Khrushchev, *The Last Testament* 392–93). The popular success of the visit was worrisome for those who, as Galbraith noted, made the cold war "a contest . . . that was very closely scored" (259).

One sign of mellowness was the response of the most mordant and apocalyptic of witnesses to the dangers of subversion. Having resigned from *Time* magazine in the wake of the Hiss case in 1948, Whittaker Chambers had signed on with the right-wing *National Review* nine years later. "The almost continuous press coverage of Khrushchev is technically superb; intellectually (most of it) [is] for retarded children," he complained to Buckley on September 20. "So the TV press has presented Khrushchev in terms of not being the scarecrow they had hitherto presented (and really imagined he was). But the tone is one of literal intense resentment that he should not be. Result: we know from these worthies no more about Khrush than we knew before." Chambers acknowledged that "those pig eyes, that shark's face—they are not my dish. But this does not make me suppose that this is not a fateful man, and that I had better be at better business than dreaming up animal terms to describe him. He is no monster either, in the sense that Stalin *was* a monster; and it does much disservice to say he is. It blurs when we need clear windowpanes. His speech to [the] UN was also a de-Stalinization speech. That bears brooding on, too." Chambers resigned from the magazine's editorial board later that year, in part due to its opposition to the Khrushchev visit. If discussions were ruled out, Chambers asserted, the alternative logic would lead to war (244, 260–61, 265). Switching from a faith in a dichotomy of God or nothing, he told Buckley that the United States had nothing to sell but affluence and freedom. No more concise formulation could have been devised to explain "the American way of life" to the Marxist visitor.

Khrushchev himself was very proud of the trip and felt that it had strengthened his own status within the Kremlin. He recalled it as "a colossal moral victory. I still remember how delighted I was the first time my interpreter told me that Eisenhower had called me, in English, 'my friend'" (*New York Times*, June 3, 1990, 12). A Khrushchev biographer called the visit "a turning point politically and personally." According to William Taubman, "being invited to the United States, being wined and dined by Eisenhower and by American businessmen represented acceptance for Khrushchev and his country. He took the invitation as recognition of the full political equality of the Soviet Union"—hence the "touchy pride" that caused him to "fly off the handle at perceived insults" (S. Khrushchev 356, 357; Crankshaw 274). By 1959 even "the United States, which had conducted reactionary policies against the Soviet Union as far back as the Civil War," he crowed in his memoirs, "had at last been forced to invite our representatives to its capital and to receive us with honor!" (Khrushchev, *The Last Testament* 414–15). An ideological war would begin to lose its intensity. The road to rapprochement was open.

The openness of that road was not immediately obvious, and the expectation of better relations would be dashed only seven months later. The aborted summit conference and the cancellation of the president's visit to the Soviet Union momentarily halted rapprochement, nor could Khrushchev hide his contempt for Eisenhower's failure to put the most ardent cold warriors on a leash: "When he stops being President, the best job we could give him in our country would be as director of a kindergarten. He would not harm children. But as head of a mighty state he is more dangerous. . . . I say so because I know him" (*New York Times*, June 4, 1960, 1, 7). The summit failure left Ike in despair, feeling that his remaining months in office would be marred by emptiness and waste, even as Khrushchev himself became more of an "adventurist." He recklessly reheated the Berlin crisis in 1961 and then tried installing ground-to-ground missiles in Cuba the following year. Weaker

at home than Ike had suspected in 1959, Khrushchev was dramatically removed from office in 1964, placed under house arrest, and then exiled. When
he died in 1971, the obituary notice in *Pravda* consisted of one sentence. The
declaration of his son Sergei, standing in front of the open coffin in a Moscow cemetery, was too resounding to be quoted: "There are people who love
him and people who hate him, but no one can pass by without turning to
look" (Lyon, *Eisenhower* 801–2; Beschloss 386–87).

The pungency of his personality, the audacity of his geopolitical strategy would fix for the American public the image of the adversary, giving communism a face—a human face. He was a promise and a menace, offering peaceful coexistence as well as a relentless challenge to Western hegemony. So
volatile and cunning a statesman was an inescapable, if not dominant, presence for almost a decade; and so irrepressible a figure helped, in a paradoxical way, to shift the focus of American politics. The fifties had begun when
a hand that proved to be quicker than the eye held up a list of 205 communists in the State Department, though the number changed to 57, 81, 116, 121,
106, and then, ultimately, none. The following decade began when the Democratic party's candidate for the presidency decried a "missile gap" that he
later discovered did not exist. The Air Force claimed that Khrushchev could
brandish at least 600 ICBM's, the CIA claimed 450, the U.S. Navy claimed 200,
and Britain's Institute of Strategic Studies claimed 35. Between these mysterious flurries of numbers, public fears had shifted from a domestic peril to a
foreign one, from phantoms within to an identifiable foe without—even as
Khrushchev himself had come, however slightly, to repudiate the schematic
either/or of Marxist dogma. The affluence and dynamism he had observed
up close would not easily be defeated. But the terms of the conflict might at
least be altered, and the competition need not be lethal. Thirteen days in
September cannot alone account for a shift that was, admittedly, less than
seismic. But the visit did reinforce the possibility of peaceful coexistence and
helped make the cold war a little less dismal.

There would be a historical coda to such an interpretation of Khrushchev's
visit. Slightly over two decades later, his son Sergei joined a barnstorming
delegation of 290 Soviet citizens visiting Kansas. They were honored at a
football game and entertained in about 150 homes, and the local *Lawrence
Daily Journal-World* thoughtfully provided a daily column of news from Tass.
On that occasion Sergei graciously acknowledged the invalidity of his father's

famous prediction, for history had falsified the bumper sticker simplicity of "we will bury you": "He proved to be wrong in the sense that socialism would triumph over capitalism." At the opening meeting on October 15, 1990, the *New York Times* reported, "it was announced that the Soviet President, Mikhail S. Gorbachev, had won the Nobel Peace Prize. The audience reacted at first with stunned silence, then a round of applause from both the Kansans and the guests who once counted each other as enemies" (*New York Times,* Oct. 21, 1990, E7). They had joined one another only 127 miles from the town that Eisenhower did not get the chance to show his guest, the Abilene that Nikita S. Khrushchev never saw.

WORKS CONSULTED

Abramson, Rudy. *Spanning the Century: The Life of W. Averell Harriman, 1891–1986.* New York: Morrow, 1992.

Alexander, Charles C. *Holding the Line: The Eisenhower Era, 1952–1961.* Bloomington: Indiana University Press, 1975.

Ambrose, Stephen E. *Eisenhower: The President.* New York: Simon and Schuster, 1984.

———. *Nixon: The Education of a Politician, 1913–1962.* New York: Simon and Schuster, 1987.

Barnouw, Erik. *The Image Empire: A History of Broadcasting in the United States.* New York: Oxford University Press, 1970.

Baudrillard, Jean. *Simulations.* Trans. Paul Foss, Paul Patton, and Philip Beitchman. New York: Semiotexte, 1983.

Beschloss, Michael R. *Mayday: Eisenhower, Khrushchev, and the U-2 Affair.* New York: Harper and Row, 1986.

Bird, Kai. *The Chairman: John J. McCloy, the Making of the American Establishment.* New York: Simon and Schuster, 1992.

Block, Herbert. *Straight Herblock.* New York: Simon and Schuster, 1963.

Brendon, Piers. *Ike: His Life and Times.* New York: Harper and Row, 1986.

Chambers, Whittaker. *Odyssey of a Friend: Letters to William F. Buckley, 1954–1961.* New York: Putnam's, 1969.

Christensen, Jack. "Brash Gate-Crasher's Busy Round with Mr. K." *Life,* Oct. 5, 1959, 38–39.

Crankshaw, Edward. *Khrushchev: A Career.* New York: Viking, 1966.

Divine, Robert A. *Eisenhower and the Cold War.* New York: Oxford University Press, 1981.

"The Education of Mr. K." *Time,* Oct. 5, 1959, 19–21.

Eisenhower, Dwight D. *The White House Years: Waging Peace, 1956–1961*. Garden City, N.Y.: Doubleday, 1965.

Frady, Marshall. *Billy Graham: A Parable of American Righteousness*. Boston: Little, Brown, 1979.

Frankland, Mark. *Khrushchev*. New York: Stein and Day, 1967

Gaddis, John Lewis. *The United States and the Origins of the Cold War, 1941–1947*. New York: Columbia University Press, 1972.

Galbraith, John Kenneth. *A Contemporary Guide to Economics, Peace, and Laughter*. Boston: Houghton Mifflin, 1971.

Gallup, George H., ed. *The Gallup Poll: Public Opinion, 1935–1971*. 3 vols. New York: Random House, 1972.

Goldman, Eric F. *The Crucial Decade—and After: America, 1945–1960*. New York: Vintage, 1960.

"Great Encounter." *Newsweek*, Oct. 5, 1959, 19–24.

Halberstam, David. *The Best and the Brightest*. New York: Random House, 1972.

Harriman, Averell. "Exclusive Report: Mr. K. Meets U. S. 'Ruling Class.'" *Life*, Sept. 28, 1959, 38–39.

Hearst, William Randolph, Jr., Frank Coniff, and Bob Considine. *Ask Me Anything: Our Adventures with Khrushchev*. New York: McGraw-Hill, 1960.

Hoopes, Townsend. *The Devil and John Foster Dulles*. Boston: Little, Brown, 1973.

Hughes, Emmet John. *The Ordeal of Power: A Political Memoir of the Eisenhower Years*. New York: Atheneum, 1963.

Jefferson, Thomas. *The Portable Thomas Jefferson*. Ed. Merrill D. Peterson. New York: Viking, 1975.

"K Confronts the Republic." *Life*, Sept. 28, 1959, 28–45.

Kempton, Murray. *America Comes of Middle Age: Columns, 1950–1962*. Boston: Little, Brown, 1963.

Kennedy, John F. *The Strategy of Peace*. Ed. Allan Nevins. New York: Popular Library, 1961.

"K. Goes Home." *Time*, Oct. 5, 1959, 19–21.

Khrushchev, Nikita S. *Khrushchev Remembers*. Trans. and ed. Strobe Talbott. Boston: Little, Brown, 1970.

———. *Khrushchev Remembers: The Last Testament*. Trans. and ed. Strobe Talbott. Boston: Little, Brown, 1974.

———. *Khrushchev Speaks: Selected Speeches, Articles, and Press Conferences, 1949–1961*. Ed. Thomas P. Whitney. Ann Arbor: University of Michigan Press, 1963.

Khrushchev, Sergei. *Khrushchev on Khrushchev: An Inside Account of the Man and His Era*. Trans and ed. William Taubman. Boston: Little, Brown, 1990.

Khrushchev in America. New York: Crosscurrents, 1960.

Kutler, Stanley I. *The American Inquisition: Justice and Injustice in the Cold War.* New York: Hill and Wang, 1982.

LaFeber, Walter. *America, Russia, and the Cold War, 1945–1992.* 7th ed. New York: John Wiley, 1993.

Lodge, Henry Cabot. *The Storm Has Many Eyes: A Personal Narrative.* New York: Norton, 1973.

Lyon, Peter. *Eisenhower: Portrait of the Hero.* Boston: Little, Brown, 1974.

Martin, John Bartlow. *Adlai Stevenson and the World: The Life of Adlai E. Stevenson.* Garden City, N.Y.: Doubleday, 1977.

Medvedev, Roy. *Khrushchev.* Trans. Brian Pearce. Garden City, N.Y.: Doubleday, 1983.

Mosley, Leonard. *Dulles: A Biography of Eleanor, Allen, and John Foster Dulles and Their Family Network.* New York: Dial/James Wade, 1978.

Murphy, Robert. *Diplomat among Warriors.* Garden City, N.Y.: Doubleday, 1964.

Niven, David. *Bring On the Empty Horses.* New York: Putnam's, 1975.

Nixon, Richard M. *RN: The Memoirs of Richard Nixon.* New York: Grosset and Dunlap, 1978.

———. *Six Crises.* Garden City, N.Y.: Doubleday, 1962.

Parmet, Herbert S. *Eisenhower and the American Crusades.* New York: Macmillan, 1972.

Perrett, Geoffrey. *A Dream of Greatness: The American People, 1945–1963.* New York: Coward, McCann, and Geoghegan, 1979.

Roberts, Chalmers M. *First Rough Draft: A Journalist's Journal of Our Times.* New York: Praeger, 1973.

Ross, Mitchell S. *The Literary Politicians.* Garden City, N.Y.: Doubleday, 1978.

Rovere, Richard H. *The American Establishment and Other Reports, Opinions, and Speculations.* New York: Harcourt, Brace, and World, 1962.

Salisbury, Harrison E. *Journey for Our Times: A Memoir.* New York: Harper and Row, 1983.

Siegel, Frederick F. *Troubled Journey: From Pearl Harbor to Ronald Reagan.* New York: Hill and Wang, 1984.

"A Sociologist Looks at an American Community." *Life,* Sept. 12, 1949, 108–19.

Solberg, Carl. *Riding High: America in the Cold War.* New York: Mason and Lipscomb, 1973.

Stone, I. F. *The Haunted Fifties, 1953–1963.* Boston: Little, Brown, 1969.

Tocqueville, Alexis de. *Democracy in America.* Ed. Phillips Bradley. Trans. Henry Reeve. 2 vols. New York: Knopf, 1945.

CONTRIBUTORS ━━

JAMES L. BAUGHMAN is a professor of journalism and mass communication at the University of Wisconsin at Madison. His most recent book is *Republic of Mass Culture: Journalism, Filmmaking, and Broadcasting in America since 1941.*

WINI BREINES is a professor of sociology and women's studies at Northeastern University in Boston. Her most recent books are *Takin' It to the Streets: A Sixties Reader,* coedited with Alexander Bloom, and *Young, White, and Miserable: Growing Up Female in the Fifties.* Her latest project is a study of the sexual/racial tensions in the civil rights and black power movements that led to separate women's movements and identity politics.

JACKIE BYARS is an associate professor of radio, television, and film in the Department of Communciation at Wayne State University. The author of *All That Hollywood Allows: Rereading Gender in 1950s Melodrama,* Byars is currently working with Eileen R. Meehan on a book on Lifetime, the only cable television network that specifically targets a female audience.

JOEL FOREMAN is an associate professor at George Mason University where he has joint appointments in the English department and the Program on Social and Organizational Learning. He has published articles on cultural studies, theory, computer-generated imagery, and the postmodern organization. He has created a number of television documentaries on such figures as Rita Mae Brown, Carlos Fuentes, and William Styron.

CYNTHIA J. FUCHS is an associate professor in English and film and media studies at George Mason University. Her recent work includes articles on Michael Jackson, the artist formerly known as Prince, and cyborg movies.

333

LEEROM MEDOVOI is an adjunct assistant professor of English at the University of Utah. He has published on popular culture, global politics, and cultural studies in such journals as *Socialist Review* and *Cultural Critique*. He is currently completing a book on American youth culture, consumer capitalism, and the cold war.

HORACE NEWCOMB is the F. J. Heyne Centennial Professor in Communication in the Department of Radio-Television-Film at the University of Texas at Austin. He recently served as curator of the Museum of Broadcast Communications in Chicago, where his principle duty was to edit the *Encyclopedia of Television*, a major reference that surveys the history of television in the United States, the United Kingdom, Canada, and Australia. He has recently published articles on the implications of the North American Free Trade Agreement for media and culture industries and on the Western in 1960s television. He is the editor of *Television: The Critical View*.

STACEY OLSTER is an associate professor of English at the State University of New York at Stony Brook. She is the author of *Reminiscence and Re-Creation in Contemporary American Fiction* and has published articles on such contemporary American authors as Thomas Pynchon, John Updike, Ann Beattie, and Norman Mailer. At the present time she is working on "The Trash Phenomenon," which explores the intersection of contemporary American fiction and popular culture.

DAVID R. SHUMWAY is an associate professor of literary and cultural studies in the English department of Carnegie Mellon University. He is the author of *Michel Foucault* and *Creating American Civilization: A Genealogy of American Literature as an Academic*. He is currently at work on "Modern Love: Discourses of Romance in America."

DAVID VAN LEER is a professor of English and American literature at the University of California at Davis. A regular contributor to the *New Republic*, he is the author of *Emerson's Epistemology* and *The Queening of America* and editor of *Looking Over: New Queer Film*.

DONALD WEBER is a professor of English and American studies at Mount Holyoke College. He is the author of *Rhetoric and History in Revolutionary New England* as well as articles on Jonathan Edwards, Nathaniel Hawthorne,

Perry Miller, American intellectual history, Henry James, and Abraham Cahan. He is currently at work on a study of ethnic expression in America between 1880 and 1960.

STEPHEN J. WHITFIELD holds the Max Richter Chair in American Civilization at Brandeis University, where he has taught since 1972. Among his books are *A Death in the Delta: The Story of Emmett Till* and *The Culture of the Cold War.*

INDEX

337